D0520359

# Effective Supply Management Performance

DARIN L. MATTHEWS, CPPO, C.P.M.
LINDA L. STANLEY, PH.D.

This publication is designed to provide accurate and authoritative information in regard to the subject matter covered. It is sold with the understanding that the publisher is not engaged in rendering legal, accounting or other professional service. If legal advice or other expert assistance is required, the services of a competent professional person should be sought.

Published by: Institute for Supply Management, Inc.™
Paul Novak, CPSM, C.P.M., A.P.P., Chief Executive Officer

©2008 Institute for Supply Management, Inc.
P.O. Box 22160, Tempe, AZ 85285 USA
www.ism.ws

ISBN: 978-0-9815770-1-2

# Introduction

Institute for Supply Management™ became the name for our association on January 1, 2001. The name was changed in recognition of the shifting role that you play in your profession. That role is not just about purchasing any more and has not been for many years.

The knowledge required to be a successful supply management professional has broadened more quickly than any of us might have predicted. Many factors caused this change, but none were more important than your willingness and ability to take on an expanded role.

ISM's new qualification, which will be launched in 2008, recognizes the expanded body of knowledge that you are expected to master. The Certified Professional in Supply Management (CPSM) is a qualification through which you demonstrate your mastery of the body of knowledge and commitment to the profession.

This three-book series represents a compendium of the broad knowledge of our profession. While these books don't represent all there is to know about our profession, they serve to open the door to the complete body of knowledge.

ISM is committed to the development and communication of this body of knowledge. These books, along with the resources that membership in ISM offers, will help you expand your knowledge and skills throughout your career.

*Paul Novak,* CPSM, C.P.M., A.P.P.
CEO
Institute for Supply Management™

# ISM — Your Source for Supply Management Resources

Institute for Supply Management, Inc.™ (ISM) has served the supply management profession since 1915. As the first and largest supply management institute in the world, ISM works with affiliated associations to continually keep its members well informed and trained on the latest trends and developments in the field. ISM's membership base includes more than 40,000 individual supply management professionals. A not-for-profit institute, ISM provides opportunities for the promotion of the profession and the expansion of professional skills and knowledge.

The information available from ISM is extensive. One of the greatest resources is the ISM Web site, www.ism.ws. In addition to general information, this expansive site features a vast database of supply management information, including a list of general supply management references as well as an extensive article database, listings of available products and seminars, periodicals, contact information for ISM affiliate organizations worldwide and links to other related Web sites. The *members only* online Career Center is a valuable resource for both individuals seeking jobs and organizations recruiting prospective employees.

The monthly Manufacturing and Non-Manufacturing *Report On Business*®, including the PMI for the manufacturing survey and the NMI for the non-manufacturing survey, continues to be one of the key economic indicators available today. ISM members receive this valuable report in the pages of *Inside Supply Management*® magazine. *Inside Supply Management*®, a monthly magazine (available to members only), is the authoritative resource for supply management executives, focusing on leadership strategies and trends.

The A.T. Kearney Center for Strategic Supply Leadership at ISM (CSSL) is an exclusive organization where today's and tomorrow's forward-thinking senior supply executives convene for thought leadership and a view into solutions and opportunities for the next two to four years.

Founded in 2004, the Center emerged because of a gap identified by today's senior leaders. The Center is committed to exploring the future two-year to four-year supply management horizon and translating it into robust, strategic development programs designed for executives.

The Center serves as a catalyst for new thought in the field of supply management. It is dedicated to closing the gap between the growing expectations of CEOs and the results delivered by their organizations' supply partners.

ISM also publishes the *Journal of Supply Chain Management,* a one-of-a-kind publication for supply management scholars. Authored exclusively by highly recognized scholars in supply-chain management, this quarterly subscription publication offers up-to-date research and thought-provoking studies.

Members also enjoy discounts on a wide variety of educational products and services, along with reduced enrollment fees for educational seminars and conferences.

For supply management professionals interested in a professional qualification, ISM administers the Certified Professional in Supply Management (CPSM) program. ISM members receive discounts on test preparation materials, study books and materials and examination fees.

To provide a forum for educational enhancement and networking, ISM sponsors the Annual International Supply Management Conference. The annual conference, which attracts more than 2,000 participants worldwide, provides a unique opportunity for members and nonmembers alike to learn from each other and share success strategies.

To learn more about ISM and the many ways it can help you advance your career or to join online, visit ISM at www.ism.ws. To apply for membership by telephone, call ISM customer service at 800/888-6276 (United States and Canada only) or +1 480/752-6276, extension 401.

## Foundation of Supply Management
Joseph R. Carter, DBA, CPSM, C.P.M.
Thomas Y. Choi, Ph.D.

## Effective Supply Management Performance
Darin L. Matthews, CPPO, C.P.M.
Linda L. Stanley, Ph.D.

## Leadership in Supply Management
Anna E. Flynn, Ph.D.

# Series Overview

In recent years, the supply management profession has begun to mature. No longer looked at as just "purchasing" or "procurement," supply management is viewed today as an integrative process that spans many disciplines and activities, providing both internal and external linkages across the supply chain. Today, ISM defines supply management as:

> *The identification, acquisition, access, positioning and management of resources and related capabilities that an organization needs or potentially needs in the attainment of its strategic objectives.*

> *Supply management includes the following components: disposition/ investment recovery, distribution, inventory control, logistics, manufacturing supervision, materials management, packaging, product/service development, strategic sourcing, procurement/purchasing, quality, receiving, transportation/traffic/shipping and warehousing.*

This definition cuts across industry sectors, global economies, private and public organizations and types of purchases. It covers both the day-to-day issues faced by supply management professionals and the strategic issues that shape supply management's structure and its influence in the organization.

In keeping with the spirit of the new, broader definition of supply management, Institute for Supply Management™ has broadened the scope of its new qualification to fit the latest demands on supply management professionals. This three-book series was designed to specifically address the issues of concern to supply management professionals today. These books help professionals better understand the potential scope and concerns within supply management. These books also are designed to support the new Certified Professional in Supply Management (CPSM) examination and professional credentials.

The three books are organized around the three examinations of the CPSM as follows:

1. *Foundation of Supply Management*

2. *Effective Supply Management Performance*

3. *Leadership in Supply Management*

These three books all support the strategic supply management process across various industries, cultures and types of purchases. The strategic supply management process is illustrated in the following Figure I-1:

**Figure I-1    Strategic Supply Management Process**

On the far left of the figure is the vertical box, "Supply Management Strategy and Philosophy." This is the way that supply management is viewed by the organization and the way that supply management views itself. It embodies the culture of the supply management organization as it works to support the objectives of the larger organization.

At the top of the figure, the small vertical box "Overarching Concerns" deals with five major issues that supply management professionals face today: Risk Management, Social Responsibility, Strategic Outsourcing, Globalization Issues and Supplier Relationship Management. Supply management professionals must consider all five major issues in their strategic decision-making. While supplier relationship management has long been recognized as important by most progressive organizations, the other four issues have taken on a new importance in recent years. Because of their overarching nature, these issues are touched on in each of the three books in a variety of ways. More specifically, supply management professionals must ask the following questions:

1.  What risks might we face and how can we plan for these risks?

2.  How does the decision we are making fit with the organization's social responsibility objectives?

3.  Is outsourcing an option for this particular decision? How would this affect the answers to these other questions?

4.  Are there global solutions available, and how does the source of supply fit with the market in which we are selling? This may be particularly relevant for purchased services.

5.  What type of relationship do we want to have with our supplier(s) for this item and why?

Within supply management, some basic "Process Steps" must occur, as illustrated in the middle of the figure. Virtually all organizations have a model for the execution of the supply management process that includes all these activities, although they may be divided into a different number of steps. The process begins with a thorough analysis of internal and external data to better understand the threats and opportunities in the internal and external environment. Next, specific strategies are developed for the particular purchase category and tactics for developing those strategies are identified. Closely related to this, the organization engages in a cost analysis of the item, looking for ways to better manage and reduce costs. It then narrows down the choice of suppliers through data analysis and bidding, negotiates and develops the contract. Finally, ongoing supplier measurement and management occurs, and may include supplier development efforts to improve supplier performance.

To support these activities, a supply management professional must work closely with other supply management professionals responsible for operations and logistics, as well as have an excellent system in place for managing and developing the organization's most valuable resource, its people. These are the "Supporting Structures" for supply management.

Volume 1, *Foundation of Supply Management,* deals with several of the more traditional areas of concern for supply management, yet looks at these issues from a leading-edge perspective. This volume covers data analysis, budgeting, cost management, including cost-price analysis and total cost of ownership analysis, and leasing arrangements. This book also provides an in-depth view of sourcing, negotiating and contracting with suppliers. Taken as a whole, these chapters provide an excellent perspective on the process steps associated with strategic sourcing. The final third of the book focuses on three of the overarching concerns of supply management: supplier relationship management, social and legal responsibility and international issues, including global sourcing, logistics and exchange rate and countertrade issues. This book is a critical read for those who might be relatively new to supply management, those who have not had a formal education in supply management and anyone who wants to stay abreast of the latest practices in supply management.

Volume 2, *Effective Supply Management Performance,* focuses on many of the operational issues that are part of a successful supply management performance. The latest surveys show that supply management professionals are responsible for a majority of the components of supply management; many of these are detailed in the definition of supply management provided previously. These are new areas of interaction for many supply management professionals. Volume 2 provides coverage of many operational issues such as project management, new product and service development, forecasting, warehousing, materials handling, logistics and international transportation, asset and inventory management and quality. These all provide supporting structures for supply management. The book closes with an in-depth discussion of supplier performance management and metrics and information systems as key ways to integrate knowledge within and across organizations. This book is a must-read for anyone newly assigned to operations-oriented issues or who supervises or manages transportation, logistics or inventory management personnel as part of his or her supply management responsibilities.

Volume 3, *Leadership in Supply Management,* focuses on many of the human resources issues that supply management professionals face. The first half of the book, "Creating a Shared Vision," explores management issues within the supply organization, such as managing and leading, developing shared values and setting direction, creating alignment and creating commitment for the supply organization's shared vision. These chapters deal with issues such as various leadership styles, developing strategies, aligning with internal and external stakeholders, team building and managing conflict. These are critical supporting structures for supply management. The second half of the book, "Managing Complexity," focuses on risk management and mitigation, developing business plans and linking these to the strategic sourcing process, including outsourcing, developing and staffing the supply management organization, providing rewards and professional development for supply management and executing the strategic sourcing process. This section includes a look at issues related to the overarching concerns of supply management, the process steps of supply management and the supporting structures. Taken as a whole, it deals with human resources and strategic issues of management that all supply management functions face. This book should be read by anyone who manages the supply management function or who is involved in the supply management strategy setting and planning process.

It has been a privilege to be involved in this important project, supporting the continued growth and recognition of the supply management profession. It has been challenging for all of those involved to capture the vast amount of material represented in these three volumes. The extensive practical and theoretical knowledge and expertise of the excellent group of authors will provide the reader with both a broad and deep perspective of the topics covered here. I hope you find these books both interesting and valuable as you study for the new CPSM examination or simply work on enhancing your own knowledge of supply management.

Lisa Ellram, Ph.D.
C.P.M., A.P.P., CMA
Series Editor


Lisa M. Ellram, Ph.D., C.P.M., is chair of the department of management at Colorado State University's College of Business. Ellram joined the CSU College of Business as Allen Professor of Business in 2006. Prior to that, she was the John and Barbara Bebbling Professor of Business at Arizona State University's W.P. Carey School of Business. Dr. Ellram earned her undergraduate degree and her MBA from the University of Minnesota. She earned her master's and doctorate from The Ohio State University. She is a certified management accountant.

Dr. Ellram is an award-winning educator and prolific publisher, and has spoken to audiences throughout the world. She has garnered sizeable grants for research in areas including strategic cost management, outsourcing, total cost modeling and supply chain sustainability. Dr. Ellram is a member of the Institute for Supply Management™ (ISM) and a member of the editorial review board for *Inside Supply Management*®. She is currently Editor-in-Chief of the *Journal of Supply Chain Management*.

# Preface

The role and importance of supply management probably has changed more in the past 15 years than in its entire history. This is due in great part to the desire of most organizations to become and remain competitive on a global scale. To attain that global competitiveness, the best organizations work to create a world-class supply management process that develops mutually beneficial relationships with suppliers, effectively manages inventories and logistics and sets up a solid information and communication system that provides transparency among supply-chain members. Quality management programs are commonly in place to continuously improve purchasing practices and supplier quality, and best-in-class measurement systems are tied to an organization's strategy.

Globalization also has resulted in organizations placing more emphasis on outsourcing for the best quality, lowest cost materials and services that can be efficiently delivered — a tall order! Organizations today are also working to lower the *total cost of ownership*. In other words, all the costs associated with making the sourcing decision, the purchase itself and post-transaction expenses are being considered in supply management decisions. Lastly, many see the supply function as a means to remain competitive because its performance affects overall corporate performance. Together, these factors make the role of suppliers and the sourcing process itself very important to organizations and, as a result, senior executives are viewing supply management more strategically. Supply management initiatives are being factored into the organizational strategy and, thus, organizations need a more effective supply management group.

Supply management professionals are developing multiple initiatives to deal with the different types of challenges that take place. One trend has been to reduce or optimize the supply base to manage the remaining suppliers more easily and create closer relationships. A related phenomenon has been an increase in single or dual sourcing with suppliers. Organizations also are bringing supply management professionals and suppliers into the new product design and development process as team members. Recent developments in information technology have enabled supply professionals to integrate their knowledge internally and, with suppliers, streamline the supply management process and make transactional processes such as the requisition/purchase order process more seamless and transparent. Thus, today they are able to perform their job more effectively and efficiently.

The primary purpose of this book is to provide a framework for achieving strong supply management performance through the supporting structures of the strategic supply management process (see Figure P-1). Specifically, this book should help organizations become more operationally competitive. Figure P-2 identifies those chapters that cover the key tasks a supply management professional should fully

Figure P-1   Strategic Supply Management Process

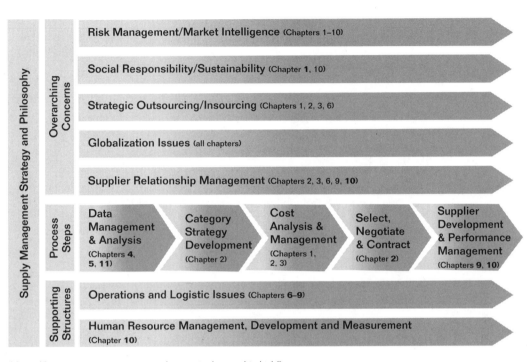

(Note: Heavy topic coverage in a chapter is denoted in bold)

understand to successfully pass the Certified Professional in Supply Management (CPSM) examinations.

## About the Authors

**Darin Matthews** has nearly twenty years of purchasing and supply management experience in state and local government, as well as private industry. He is currently the chief procurement officer for Metro, the regional government of Portland, Oregon. Mr. Matthews has served on the National Institute of Governmental Purchasing's (NIGP) Board of Directors since 2001, and was recently appointed to the Governing Board of the Universal Public Purchasing Certification Council (UPPCC). He also served as a Board Member for the Public Procurement Research Center at Florida Atlantic University.

Mr. Matthews speaks throughout North America on a variety of procurement topics, and his writings have been featured in *Government Procurement*, *The Public Manager* and *The Journal of Public Procurement*. He has authored book chapters for NIGP's

## Figure P-2. Chapter Coverage by Task Description

| CHAPTER | TASK DESCRIPTION | |
|---|---|---|
| Chapter 2 | Implement a continuous improvement process within the supply chain in accordance with organizational objectives. | Perform project management activities representing the supply management organization. |
| Chapter 3 | Participate in product/service development or specification/requirement changes that support organizational merchandising and marketing efforts to meet customer needs. | Manage ramp-up strategy and implementation to full-scale production for new product introductions. |
| Chapters 4, 5 | Develop supply forecasts in light of economic, competitive, technology, market and currency trends and conditions that affect procurement. | Perform analysis and provide data on current and future and global/domestic market conditions, benchmarks and industry trends to management and/or user departments. |
| Chapter 6 | Develop/implement a material and/or service standardization program. | Coordinate and/or monitor the movement of equipment and assets within the organization. |
| Chapter 7 | Design/modify logistics facility layouts and equipment designs to support the business model, increase productivity and lower operating costs. | Manage international transportation, invoicing and documentation functions to ensure corporate compliance with all governmental import, export, hazmat and air freight regulations. |
| Chapters 8 | Develop/implement a warehouse and inventory management system. | Develop, oversee and execute multi-channel disposition plan for excess inventory and finished goods. |
| Chapter 9 | Develop measurements for continuous quality improvement and target setting. | Develop, measure and evaluate quality requirements to continuously improve supplier performance. |
| Chapter 10 | Develop tools and processes to measure, report and improve compliance with supply management policies. | Monitor work against business plans and take action to resolve variances or adjust plans as appropriate. |
| Chapter 11 | Implement or utilize requirements planning (xRP — e.g., ERP, MRP, MRP II, DRP, DRP II, WMS) to align supply management and operations activities to support organizational strategy. | |

| | | |
|---|---|---|
| | | |
| Manage forecast data with suppliers. | | |
| Develop, implement, maintain and monitor the forecasting, operations planning, scheduling and inventory control functions to ensure optimum use of capacity and resources. | Manage forecasted data with suppliers. | |
| Develop/implement a warehouse and inventory management system. | | |
| Manage the resolution of delivery/receiving problems, including freight loss and damage claims. | Direct traffic/distribution policies and procedures to ensure optimum flow of material and consolidation of freight. | Develop/implement a warehouse and inventory management system. |
| Develop, implement, maintain and monitor the forecasting, operations planning, scheduling and inventory control functions to ensure optimum use of capacity and resources. | Design/modify logistics facility layouts and equipment designs to support the business model, increase productivity and lower operating costs. | Coordinate and/or monitor the movement of equipment and assets within the organization. |
| Develop/administer a supplier certification program. | Develop a continuous improvement process within the supply chain in accordance with organizational objectives. | |
| Analyze and resolve issues raised in supply management audit reports. | Develop performance criteria and evaluate supply management staff performance. | |
| | | |

*Logistics and Transportation* and *Warehousing and Inventory Control,* as well as the *Encyclopedia of Public Administration and Public Policy*. Mr. Matthews has served as a panelist for the ISM's satellite seminar series, and has been a featured speaker for many ISM affiliates.

He is a Certified Public Purchasing Officer (CPPO) and a Certified Purchasing Manager (C.P.M.). Mr. Matthews holds a bachelor's degree in Business/Political Science and a Master's Certificate in Acquisition Management. Mr. Mathews is an adjunct instructor for Florida Atlantic University, and has lectured at the University of Victoria, Rose State College, and Cleveland State University.

**Linda L. Stanley** is a faculty associate in the W.P. Carey School of Business at Arizona State University. Previously she was a visiting professor at Arizona State University West and associate professor and chair of the Management Department at Our Lady of the Lake University. She earned her Ph.D. in business administration with a concentration in purchasing and logistics management at Arizona State University. Dr. Stanley's expertise is in supplier relations and negotiation, project management, operations management, and supply management performance.

Dr. Stanley has published articles in several journals, including *Journal of Operations Management, Journal of Supply Chain Management,* and *Journal of Business Logistics.* She also is a member of the editorial review board for the *International Journal of Integrated Supply Chain Management* and reviews articles regularly for the *Journal of Operations Management.* Dr. Stanley has co-authored two books, *Transportation and Logistics Management* and *Process Management: Creating Value Across the Supply Chain.* She is an active member of the Institute for Supply Management™.

# Contents

## Chapter 1: Supply Management Defined

## Chapter 2: Project Management

## Chapter 3: Product and Service Development

## Chapter 4: Foundations of Forecasting Practices

## Chapter 5: Forecasting Models and Methods

## Chapter 6: Warehouse Management and Materials Handling

## Chapter 7: Logistics Management and International Transportation

## Chapter 8: Asset and Inventory Management

## Chapter 9: Quality in Supply Management

## Chapter 10: Performance Evaluation

## Chapter 11: Knowledge Integration

1

# Supply Management Defined

This chapter provides the foundation for the remainder of the book, beginning with some supply management definitions and a discussion of the historical foundation of supply management. Next, the importance of supply management is discussed. Leading-edge process improvement methods that are being used today and supply management's role are then described. Lastly, the measurement of process performance, which is key to continuous improvement and attaining organizational objectives, is discussed.

## CHAPTER OBJECTIVES

• Define the field of supply management.

• Provide a historical background of supply management.

• Describe the benefits of a high-performing supply management organization.

• Explain the value of risk analysis.

• Describe the importance of a process view.

## Definitions

Although the field of supply management has evolved significantly, no universally accepted or used descriptor exists. Rather, organizations vary in their use of titles to describe the supply management field, including purchasing, procurement, materials management and materiel. However, some distinctions are apparent and in reality these other terms are really subcomponents of supply management. The following definitions from the *ISM Glossary of Key Supply Management Terms* should help the reader delineate among the terms.

*Purchasing* is "a major function of an organization that is responsible for acquisition of required materials, services and equipment," while *procurement* is broader — an "organizational function that includes specifications development, value analysis, supplier market research, negotiation, buying activities, contract administration, inventory control, traffic, receiving and stores." *Materials management* is broader still because it extends beyond the actual purchase and is defined as "a managerial and organizational approach used to integrate the supply management functions in an organization. It involves the planning, acquisition, flow and distribution of production materials from the raw material state to the finished product state. Activities include procurement, inventory management, receiving, stores and warehousing, in-plant materials handling, production planning and control, traffic, and surplus and salvage." *Materiel* is a military and government term that generally includes the same activities as materials management. More on materials management can be found in Chapter 6.

Historically, the use of the word *supply* in North America referred to the storing or warehousing of materials and supplies for internal usage. Others including government agencies, the United Kingdom and Europe, however, have interpreted the use of the word *supply* in a broader context to encompass purchasing, storing and receiving materials and supplies. In 2002, the National Association of Purchasing Management changed its name to the Institute for Supply Management™ (ISM) to incorporate that broader meaning and has defined *supply management* as "the identification, acquisition, access, positioning and management of resources and related capabilities the organization needs or potentially needs in the attainment of its strategic objectives." The components of supply management are:

- Disposition/investment recovery
- Distribution
- Inventory control
- Logistics
- Materials management
- Packaging
- Product/service development
- Procurement/purchasing
- Quality
- Receiving
- Strategic sourcing

- Transportation/traffic/shipping

- Warehousing

- Production management/manufacturing supervision

This text covers these multiple components of supply management. For example, the subject of product/service development is discussed in Chapter 3; materials management is covered in Chapter 6; transportation/traffic/shipping, receiving, warehousing, distribution, inventory control and asset recovery in Chapters 7 and 8; and quality in Chapter 9. To identify sources of supply, supply management professionals also must be involved in some forms of forecasting. Thus, the importance and role of forecasting to supply professionals is found in Chapters 4 and 5. In addition, supply management professionals act in a boundary-spanning position, meeting the needs of internal users and end customers through their interactions with external suppliers. Thus, knowledge integration through information technology is important and further discussion can be found in Chapter 11.

Lastly, supply-chain management is defined as "the design and management of seamless, value-added processes across organizational boundaries to meet the real needs of the end customer. The development and integration of people and technological resources are critical to successful supply chain integration." (*ISM Glossary,* 2006) Supply-chain management involves the multiple stakeholders, including supply management, that are involved in planning and executing the delivery of an organization's products and services to the end customer.

## Historical Background

The interest in supply management really developed in the latter part of the 20th century, although the U.S. railroads realized the importance of the function as early as the mid-1800s. A railroad executive actually authored the first handbook on purchasing — *The Handling of Railway Supplies: Their Purchase and Distribution* — in 1887. By 1915, several other books and articles on purchasing were written. However, purchasing was still viewed primarily as a tactical activity. During World War I and World War II, the status of purchasing actually increased because effectively buying the materials and services needed to run the factories was essential to organizational success. Following World War II, and into the 1960s, the processes to make purchases continued to be refined and more people were hired and trained. Thus, the decision-making process improved. More organizations improved the status of purchasing and a chief purchasing officer could hold the title of vice president of purchasing or purchasing director, among others.

In the early 1970s, organizations were facing a global shortage of most basic raw materials required for operations, with accompanying price and interest rate increases beyond what had been experienced after World War II. OPEC's oil embargo in 1973 resulted in additional shortages and price increases. At the same time, countries were working to ease trade restrictions, which opened up world trade but also increased competition. Organizations began outsourcing materials and parts from countries with lower cost structures to gain a competitive advantage. Thus, throughout the 1970s and 1980s, the focus again was on purchasing, which could spell the difference between successful organization performance or dismal failure.

Beginning in the 1980s, the purchase of services was increasingly taken over by supply management. In the past, buying services was often left to other functions to handle but changed in part because of the impact of downsizing and the willingness of other functions to give up noncore activities. Purchasing was also found to be best positioned within an organization to take over the responsibility based on its expertise in cost reduction.

Early in the 1990s, purchasing also became more integrated into corporate strategy as organizations faced greater domestic and global competition. Senior executives realized that cost control, improved quality and supplier services could be attained through a stronger purchasing group. Some organizations have since changed the functional name to purchasing and supply management or simply supply management to reflect a more process-oriented, strategic focus.

Gordon Cole, manager of corporate purchasing at pharmaceutical giant Allergan, Inc., in Irvine, California, says that since 1992, Allergan has dramatically changed the nature and function of its corporate purchasing department and has updated the job functions and skill sets of the purchasing staff along with it. "I've watched the department's role grow from a strictly local, MRO-oriented function to our present role of global responsibility," says Cole. "In my department, half of the 'buying team' doesn't even place orders: They locate and develop new sources and/or develop and administer contracts. They're also involved in marketing plans, research and development efforts, supplier qualification, technology transfer, logistics and distribution, and are heading closer and closer to actual involvement with the end customer."[1]

In the 21st century, supply management is increasingly becoming more integrated with its network of suppliers through the advances in information technology. Organizations are using commodity teams, category management and cross-functional teams to make purchases and supply management professionals are incorporating e-commerce options and networking solutions into their daily operations. Global purchasing is more commonplace and supply management professionals have moved away from simply a reactive approach to buying to an increasingly integrative strategy as they gain experience in the complexities of sourcing from foreign suppliers. A 2004 A.T. Kearney study of senior executives found that the traditional role of supply management is moving from strictly cost reduction to one of "capturing value from the supply market."[2] Thus, supply management has been integrated to a greater extent into an organization's strategic planning process.

As a 2006 CAPS Research study points out, however, organizations still are working on several issues, including:

- How to make information available worldwide,

- Finding enough qualified people with the necessary worldwide knowledge and skills,

- Gaining the knowledge needed on suppliers that are available worldwide,

- Finding the time to develop worldwide strategies,

- Using cross-functional teams for global purchases and

- Finding suppliers with worldwide capabilities.[3]

The use of e-commerce solutions to support supply management's operations also has become more prevalent. According to a 2006 *Supply Chain Management Review* article, supply management software was "one of the fastest growing segments of the enterprise software market" in 2005, spurred by the need to "quickly capture the potential of strategic relationships."[4] However, transactional systems are also important and increasing in use. Patricia Hanson, C.P.M. and vice president and director of purchasing operations for JC Penney Company, Inc., in Plano, Texas, says that "Seven years ago, before it was fashionable, we created an in-house order processing system. It is now Web-based and used by 1,200 stores and business units throughout the country. The billing process is automated, orders are transmitted via EDI [electronic data interchange] and it interfaces with all of our other legacy systems. Early on, we realized there was a more efficient way to process approvals and paperwork, so our e-commerce direction stemmed out of that."[5] More on knowledge integration can be found in Chapter 11.

## The Importance of Supply Management

A number of quantifiable benefits are attributed to high-performing supply management organizations, including lower operating costs, improved return on investment (ROI) and return on assets (ROA), and a direct positive impact to the bottom line. However, there are also other less tangible benefits. Some of these tangible and intangible benefits are discussed further in the following sections.

## Return on Investment

A *return on investment* is defined as "the ratio of annual operating income to the total capital invested in the business" (*ISM Glossary*, 2006) and has been applied specifically to supply management. A 2005 in-depth study of purchasing practices conducted by the Hackett Group found that world-class supply management operations were able to produce a 133 percent bigger return on investment within their supply organizations than the average organization was in its peer group. World-class organizations also were spending 20 percent less on supply management operations than the average organizations and had a comparative advantage in staffing levels and supply base optimization.[6]

## Profit Impact and Return on Assets

*Return on assets* is defined by the *ISM Glossary* (2006) as "a profitability ratio used to measure how hard the assets of an organization are working. ROA is calculated by dividing the net income by total assets." Reducing purchasing costs, for example, by 5 percent, improves profitability by 2.5 percent and increases ROA by 5.225 percent. The following example provides an example, illustrating the benefit of lowering purchasing costs.

The calculation of return on assets requires three steps:

1. Calculate investment turnover by dividing sales by total assets. In this example, investment turnover improves if inventory can be reduced by 5 percent.

| | 2005 | Investment Turns | Less 5% | 2006 | Investment Turns |
|---|---|---|---|---|---|
| Sales | $1,300,000 | | | $1,300,000 | |
| Inventory | $ 200,000 | | $10,000 | $ 190,000 | |
| Total Assets | $ 650,000 | 2.0* | $10,000 | $ 640,000 | 2.03 |

*$1,300,000/$650,000 = 2.0

2. Calculate the profit margin by dividing profit by sales. Because purchasing costs were reduced by 5 percent, profit margin in 2006 improved by 2.5 percent.

| | 2005 | Profit Margin | 2006 | Profit Margin |
|---|---|---|---|---|
| Sales | $1,300,000 | | $1,300,000 | |
| Total Costs | $1,235,000* | | $1,202,500*** | |
| Profit | $ 65,000** | 5% | $ 97,500 | 7.5% |

*Total costs include purchasing costs, which account for 50 percent of sales or $650,000.
**$65,000/$1,300,000 = .05 × 100 = 5%
***Total costs = $1,235,000 − ($650,000 × 5%) = $1,202,500

3. The return on assets then is calculated using the investment turnover and profit margin calculations. In 2006, the ROA improved by more than 5 percent.

|  | 2005 | 2006 |
|---|---|---|
| Investment Turnover | 2.0 | 2.03 |
| Profit Margin | 5% | 7.5% |
| ROA | $2.0 \times 5\% = 10\%$ | $2.03 \times 7.5\% = 15.225\%$ |

## A Source of Information

Supply management provides valuable information to others within an organization because of its heavy contact with market information sources such as suppliers, external research reports and trade shows. The availability of goods and services, new sources of supply, replacement parts and emerging technologies are important to those in production and operations, marketing and new product design, among others.

## Meeting Strategic Objectives

The supply management department's performance is a key element to the success of an organization in terms of its contribution to the strategic objectives. Because a significant percentage of sales revenue is spent with suppliers — generally ranging anywhere from 30 percent to 70 percent — any improvement in supply management's effectiveness in terms of reducing the cost of materials, ensuring suppliers meet delivery and quality specifications for incoming products and services or improving the internal operating efficiency of the supply management function can translate to improved organizational performance.

## Creating Goodwill

Any actions taken by supply management personnel with suppliers reflect on the public image of an organization. Thus, conducting business in a professional and socially responsible manner with suppliers should generate a positive reputation and an ability to attract new and better suppliers. Carla Lallatin, C.P.M. and president of Lallatin & Associates of Rego Park, New York, states that "We have seen the impact unethical conduct has not only on profitability, but in some cases, on the ability of a company merely to survive."[7] ISM has published the principles of social responsibility that covers seven areas including a code of ethics (see Figure 1-1 for a synopsis).[8] Supply management organizations, for instance, can make a positive impact by (1) supporting and adding value to their communities and those members in their supply chains, (2) encouraging others within their supply chains to add value in their communities and (3) actively promoting the development and buying from socially

**Figure 1-1    ISM Principles of Social Responsibility**

**Community**
1. Provide support and add value to your communities and those of your supply chain.
2. Encourage members of your supply chain to add value in their communities.

**Diversity**
1. Proactively promote purchasing from, and the development of, socially diverse suppliers.
2. Encourage diversity within your own organization.
3. Proactively promote diverse employment practices throughout the supply chain.

**Environment**
1. Encourage your own organization and others to be proactive in examining the opportunities to be environmentally responsible within their supply chains either "upstream" or "downstream."
2. Encourage the environmental responsibility of your suppliers.
3. Encourage the development and diffusion of environmentally friendly practices and products throughout your organization.

**Ethics**
1. Be aware of ISM's *Principles and Standards of Ethical Supply Management Conduct.*
2. Abide by your organization's code of conduct.

**Financial Responsibility**
1. Become knowledgeable of, and follow, applicable financial standards and requirements.
2. Apply sound financial practices and ensure transparency in financial dealings.
3. Actively promote and practice responsible financial behavior throughout the supply chain.

**Human Rights**
1. Treat people with dignity and respect.
2. Support and respect the protection of international human rights within the organization's sphere of influence.
3. Encourage your organization and its supply chains to avoid complicity in human or employment rights abuses.

**Safety**
1. Promote a safe environment for each employee in your organization and supply chain. (Each organization is responsible for defining "safe" within its organization.)
2. Support the continuous development and diffusion of safety practices throughout your organization and the supply chain.

*Source:* Julie S. Roberts, "Responsible Business = Good Business," *Inside Supply Management*® (May 2004), 2–3.

diverse suppliers. Some of the most serious forms of unethical behavior to avoid include revealing information to one supplier about another supplier's quote, accepting gifts, overstating the seriousness of the situation to obtain concessions in a negotiation situation and giving preference to some suppliers over others because of pressure from top management.[9]

# Making Supply Management Decisions

As evidenced by the previous discussion, supply management is multifaceted and faces many complex decisions in its daily operations. One of the most common questions that must be addressed is whether an item or service should be made in-house or outsourced — the classic *make-or-buy* or *insource/outsource* decision. If the item or service will be outsourced, suppliers must be evaluated and selected. Furthermore, another decision is whether to source from one, two or multiple suppliers (if there is a choice). The means to negotiate prices, whether short-term or long-term contracts will be decided and other issues related to the purchase of those goods and services will require additional decision-making as well. For example, supply professionals might use reverse auctions to purchase commodity parts and carry on lengthy negotiations to buy more strategic services such as healthcare coverage for employees. They also must select transportation modes and carriers, determine when deliveries of materials should be taken and where inventory will be stored (with the supplier, a public warehouse or company-owned warehouses). The process of making these decisions is known as *risk analysis,* which is "the process of identifying elements or factors, and their probability of occurrence that could lead to injury, damage, loss or failure" according to the *ISM Glossary* (2006). Two forms of risk analysis include *decision tree analysis* and the *two-by-two portfolio matrix.* Both are discussed in more detail in the next section.

## Decision Tree Analysis

The *decision tree* is one means to help supply professionals make interdependent decisions under uncertain conditions. A *decision tree* is "a decision-making tool that maps alternative courses of action and their consequences. Its components include decision forks, outcome forks, outcome probabilities, outcome rewards and expected values." (*ISM Glossary,* 2006) Decision trees are useful because they give some structure to decision-making and provide a more objective way of analyzing the alternatives. Computer software packages are available, which make the process relatively easy.

The diagram is read from left to right but to make the evaluation, the diagram values are calculated beginning on the right side. The alternative with the highest value then is selected. For example, a decision tree as shown in Figure 1-2 might be used to make the choice between two different suppliers.

Figure 1-2    Decision Tree Analysis

The new product design team at the Jones Company has developed a new product requiring a new part not used in other existing products. The supply professional does some research and has narrowed the selection of a supplier for a new part down to the top two. She uses decision tree analysis to help her chose between the two suppliers based on expected cost, beginning with an estimation of the possible demand for the part and the expected price/unit (based on demand).

| ALTERNATIVE | DEMAND | PRICE/UNIT | TOTAL COST |
|---|---|---|---|
| Supplier 1 | | | |
| Strong demand | 150,000 | $50 | $7,500,000 |
| Medium demand | 100,000 | $60 | $6,000,000 |
| Modest demand | 50,000 | $75 | $3,750,000 |
| Supplier 2 | | | |
| Strong demand | 150,000 | $45 | $6,750,000 |
| Medium demand | 100,000 | $55 | $5,500,000 |
| Modest demand | 50,000 | $80 | $4,000,000 |

The owner then creates a decision tree. The value shown under each decision is the dollar amount the Jones Company should expect to spend, using probability analysis. The calculations are shown in the following table:

| ALTERNATIVE | CALCULATION | RESULT |
|---|---|---|
| Supplier 1 | $7,500,000 x 0.20 + $6,000,000 x 0.45 + $3,750,000 x .035 | $5,512,500 |
| Supplier 2 | $6,750,000 x 0.20 + $5,500,000 x 0.45 + $4,000,000 x 0.35 | $5,225,000 |

## Two-by-Two Portfolio Matrix

While supply management has become more strategic, all purchases cannot simply be lumped into one category; thus, strategies must be tailored to the type of buy. Peter Kraljic, senior director for the McKinsey Advisory Council, developed a two-by-two portfolio matrix to help supply management personnel develop an appropriate sourcing strategy for items purchased, based on profit impact (low to high) and supply risk (low to high).[10] As shown in Figure 1-3, items under review are classified in one of four risk categories: (1) *noncritical items,* (2) *leveraged items,* (3) *bottleneck items* or

**Figure 1-2     continued**

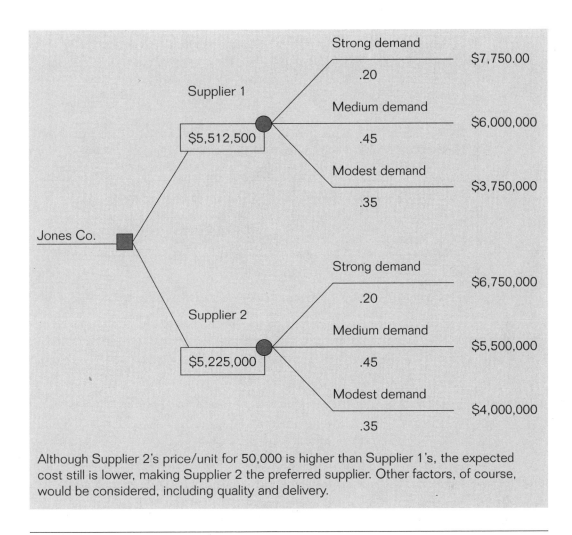

Although Supplier 2's price/unit for 50,000 is higher than Supplier 1's, the expected cost still is lower, making Supplier 2 the preferred supplier. Other factors, of course, would be considered, including quality and delivery.

(4) *strategic items.* Noncritical items are considered low-value commodity-like because they can be easily standardized, are highly substitutable and are purchased using simple contracts or p–cards, which are multipurpose bank cards with predetermined company-set policies and procedures that eliminate the traditional requisition/purchase order process. German airline carrier Lufthansa, with a purchasing group of 250, has created commodity specialists. The organization also participates in cooperatives with other organizations to negotiate the lowest prices. According to Gerald Carl, e-purchasing manager, "Today we cooperate with other large German companies

Figure 1-3    Kraljic's Two-by-Two Matrix

| | |
|---|---|
| **Leverage Items**<br>Large volume purchases<br>Unit cost important<br>Can find substitutes<br>Many suppliers available | **Strategic Items**<br>Continuous usage<br>Unique specifications<br>Supplier technology critical<br>Few suppliers available<br>Difficult to substitute |
| **Noncritcal Items**<br>Commodities<br>Easy to find substitute products<br>Many suppliers available | **Bottleneck items**<br>Unique requirements<br>Supplier's technology critical<br>Scarce sources of supply<br>Difficult to substitute<br>Difficult to forecast usage |

PROFIT IMPACT (High → Low)

SUPPLY RISK (Low → High)

*Source:* Adapted from Peter Kraljic, "Purchasing Must Become Supply Management," *Harvard Business Review* 61(5), 109–117.

to increase our purchasing clout for certain types of [noncritical commodity] products — this is another way to get level with suppliers."[11]

According to a 2000 *NAPM InfoEdge* article, a leveraged item is one where there are "a large number of suppliers who are all capable of supplying the same product, and the dollars spent are significant. [Some] examples of leveraged commodities are injection moldings, metals, stampings, resins, insurance benefits, travel, telephones, car fleets and temporary employment organizations." Relationships with suppliers of leveraged goods and services will, in most cases, be arm's-length, unless the supply management professional has created a short-term preferred relationship. Because of the large amount of expenditure in this area, a supply management professional could realize substantial savings through continually lowering costs. Supply management professionals may make a site visit to such a supplier, "focusing on cost and continuous improvement." The payback potential for a site visit "is high as these items are normally purchased in high volumes."[12] Substitution is possible, however, because the marketplace is competitive with multiple sources of supply.

Bottleneck items, on the other hand, are unique high-risk products with customized specifications and technologies. Items in this category generally are purchased in larger quantities and inventory levels are monitored more closely to avoid interruptions to supply. The relationship with the supplier is important to the buying organization, but supply management professionals will search for alternative suppliers to avoid the risk of supply interruptions. Skanska, a Swedish construction organization, is working to broaden its supply base for its bottleneck items while at the same time working more closely with current suppliers to help them improve their design and production processes.[13]

Lastly, strategic items are extremely important to production or service delivery because of their unique characteristics. Only a few suppliers — perhaps only one — have the technical capability and capacity to meet the buying organization's needs so it is difficult to switch suppliers. Expenditures for strategic items also generally are high. Thus, these items generally are managed through closer, win–win, partnership-type relationships.

Another important decision area is how to improve supply management processes by taking a process view. The following section discusses this topic in more detail.

## A Process View

First, organizations must think in terms of processes instead of functions. An organization has literally hundreds of processes operating simultaneously. The goal is to add value for customers through these processes. Some examples of processes include order fulfillment, supplier selection and contract management. Managers need to define, understand and improve those processes that are most essential to their strategies and customer value proposition, support the mission and contribute to improving the bottom line. Process mapping is a good place to start in terms of defining and understanding an organization's processes.

There has been a growing trend among larger organizations to map processes as a part of continuous improvement efforts. Process mapping, which involves creating a visual depiction of a process, is the starting point to help understand each process and identify the sequencing of each process. Process mapping also helps spell out the boundaries and ownership of each process.

Generally, a team of people familiar with the process will be assigned to map it; they may come from many parts of the organization. Cross-functional teams usually begin by taking a "high-level" view of the major core processes and then breaking those core processes into the subprocesses and subsubprocesses. High-level process mapping is frequently used first to identify an organization's core and supporting processes. Organizations typically have five to eight core processes with five to seven supporting processes for each core process, although this is not always true. For example, Bronson Methodist Hospital, a 2005 recipient of the Malcolm Baldrige National Quality Award, identified only one key core process, Healthcare Service Delivery, with six supporting processes: (1) Materials Management, (2) Environmental and Safety Management, (3) Financial Management, (4) Human Resources Management, (5) Information Management and (6) Guest Services Management. A partial process map is illustrated in Figure 1-4.[14]

More detailed maps then are used to identify the inputs, each step of the process as it currently exists and the outputs associated with each step. For example, Figure 1-5 is a process map for a generic order fulfillment process. Note that the process crosses over functional boundaries, including customer service, logistics, transportation and supply management. The map then can be used to identify and minimize non-value-adding activities, streamline the process or convert the process from a manual to an automated one.

A common method used to identify process steps is to use Post-it® Notes to create the process map on a wall. As more of the process is revealed, the team can easily move or rearrange the Post-it® Notes. Software, such as iGrafx® FlowCharter™ and SmartDraw, also is available to create process maps. Citibank, for example, sets up

**Figure 1-4    Core Processes for Bronson Methodist Hospital**

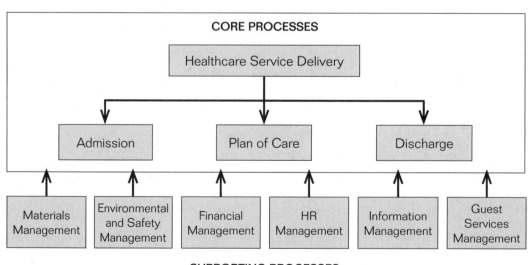

*Source:* Adapted from Bronson Methodist Hospital Malcolm Baldrige National Quality Award Summary, 2005, available from www.quality.nist.gov/PDF_files/Bronson_Methodist_Hospital_Application_Summary.pdf.

**Figure 1-5    Order Fulfillment Process**

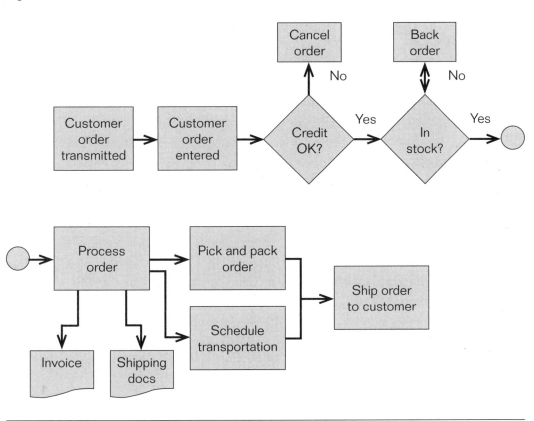

process mapping teams comprised of 30 to 50 people from every unit that make a contribution to the process. The teams are empowered to make any process changes that will reduce cycle time and make customers happier.[15]

The difficulty for many organizations lies in identifying those core processes and then working to excel at the ones that will support the organization's strategy and customer value proposition. A good approach to identifying an organization's core and supporting processes is to document all information and material flows that occur throughout the organization and with suppliers and customers. Part of the mapping process will initially involve collecting supporting data, including organization documents such as process descriptions, strategy documents, past presentations or training documents. These documents then can be used to create the process maps.

These internal work processes, however, do not take place in isolation. Organizations must possess a good understanding of how their internal processes interact with each other and with the processes of other external organizations, including customers, suppliers, distributors and competitors. These interactions usually are clarified as mapping is performed. Then, with a firm understanding, organizations can begin to integrate their processes internally and with customers and suppliers.

Moreover, an organization must analyze these processes and identify those key value-added activities. These include strategic activities that are critical to achieving existing organizational strategies and significantly impact customer satisfaction and product quality. Also, those business activities that usually support high value-added strategic activities and are critical to attaining general business operations are important. Lastly, organizations need to focus on those process improvements that extend from the suppliers' suppliers to the customers' customers, or the supply chain. This is only possible when a disciplined, structured approach is in place that applies quality management principles.

Once identified, each process should be named, along with a definition of its unique purpose and any links to other processes. Measures of effectiveness can be created for each process and the maps can be used as a basis for training and discussion. *Process flow costing,* which tracks those process costs across functions for each process using activity-based costing, also can be used. Costs are typically separated into value-added and non-value-added categories.[16] Organizations then look for ways to minimize or eliminate those non-value-added costs by performing an appraisal of each process. Organizations also have adopted several broad-based initiatives to improve processes; these are discussed in the next section.

# Process Improvement Methods

Organizations have adopted a number of assessment and improvement initiatives within the past 15 years; the two most commonly found in the popular press include Six Sigma and lean operations. The *Six Sigma methodology,* a quality improvement initiative originally developed by Motorola, has experienced widespread adoption by manufacturers worldwide while having a more limited implementation by service industries.[17] *Lean operation* is an operations philosophy that stresses creating customer value through the elimination of waste. If a supplier is running out of capacity, if its total lead time is too long or if the quality of its products and services does not consistently meet buyer specifications, Six Sigma and lean operations can help uncover the solutions to these problems and requires the involvement of supply management.

## Six Sigma

Six Sigma is a data-driven framework designed by Motorola to make breakthrough, rather than incremental, quality improvements in an organization's value-adding processes while simultaneously saving money or increasing revenues (see a fuller discussion on Six Sigma in Chapter 9). This represents the goal of having a defect occur in a process only 0.00034 percent of the time, or 3.4 times out of every million measurement opportunities — a goal beyond the reach of the typical organization today. Six Sigma is also meant to embody a philosophy or culture in which everyone from CEO to frontline service employee is involved in improving quality and uses a project management approach.

Many world-class organizations have implemented Six Sigma programs to come as close to Six Sigma as possible in their processes, including Honeywell International, Inc., Bank of America, the Vanguard Group, General Electric Co., the Dow Chemical Co. and others. Mount Carmel Health System, located in Columbus, Ohio, was facing rising healthcare costs of 4 percent to 6 percent annually with no increase in reimbursements. As a result, it had to lay off 200 workers in 2000, which was affecting patient care. Realizing that something had to change, the leadership team initially attended a Six Sigma training seminar, followed by individual executive training on fact-based problem-solving. Vice presidents then were trained in Six Sigma processes and methodologies. The training continued to cascade down through the ranks. Although Mount Carmel spent $650,000 to roll out the program, it saved approximately $7.5 million from Six Sigma projects in the first two years.[18]

## Lean Operations

*Lean operations* is a phrase coined in the United States but is based on the Toyota Production System (TPS) and a philosophy of continuous improvement. The TPS follows a philosophy of continuous learning and keeping things simple. An organization should make the best use of its time, people and physical assets to optimize productivity. Organizations also work to connect each value-added step in a process, in the best sequence and most effective way possible without interruption, at a point in time when another entity places an order somewhere downstream. That entity might be the customer or another point in the production system. Thus, lean principles can be applied to both services and manufacturing, with the ultimate goal to make lean thinking pervasive throughout the supply chain.

The British Broadcasting Corporation (BBC), for example, has deployed a multiyear project to increase efficiency and improve work practices within its supply management organization. In the past, the BBC had 36 financial systems that contained information on suppliers and each business unit developed its own list of suppliers and supply processes. During the first three years of the project, a centralized supply management organization was developed that began to look for inefficiencies in the supply process. As a result, the supply base was reduced from 141,000 to 8,000 and an online system was created for low-cost items that were frequently purchased. These changes resulted in a significant cost savings.[19]

To develop lean operations, organizations first must understand the various forms of waste that can occur, as shown in Figure 1-6. Organizations then use lean tools such as just-in-time production or service delivery, small lot sizes, short setup times and the *5S system* (sort, straighten, shine, standardize and sustain) to improve productivity.

*Lean supply management* involves optimizing the size of the supply base and then working collaboratively with key suppliers on product or service development, developing a systems approach by focusing on the total cost of ownership and total supply lead time responsiveness beginning with the raw material supplier and an attitude of continuous improvement with a customer focus. (More on product and service development can be found in Chapter 3.) This is achieved by using *value stream mapping,* a technique in which the transformation of materials is traced from beginning to end to determine if there is waste in the process either in the form of a step where no value is added or a point of "wait time" when material is being stored to await further value-adding transformation. This concept also may be applied to services. (*ISM Glossary,* 2006) It provides a blueprint for implementing any improvements, helping those involved visualize all the flows in a process.

---

**Figure 1-6    Areas of Interorganizational Waste**

| FORMS OF INTERCOMPANY WASTE | |
| --- | --- |
| Misquotations | Waiting customers |
| Incomplete purchase orders | Misplaced paperwork |
| Receiving errors | Paperwork errors |
| Inspection errors | Reporting errors |
| Misplaced inventory | Rejects |
| Inventory counting errors | Rework |
| Picking or kitting order errors | Miscommunications |
| Expediting orders | Damage during transport |
| Inventory shortages | Delivery errors |

*Source:* Adapted from S.R. Gordon, "Applying Lean Thinking to Your Company and Your Supply Chain," a presentation made at the 85th Annual International Purchasing Conference and Educational Exhibit, New Orleans, Louisiana, May, 2000.

---

Some organizations are also taking a *lean supply chain* approach by applying lean principles cooperatively throughout the supply chain. Together, supply-chain members identify product/service value and target costs for each product or product family. They then work to find and eliminate waste within the supply chain to meet joint target cost and return-on-investment goals. As they meet their target costs, they continue to search for new forms of waste and then set new target costs. Supply-chain members also strive to align their key processes and inventory policies with a goal to deliver an uninterrupted flow of goods and services. Lastly, because transparency of all activities in the supply chain is very important, information support is key.

As an organization strives to improve its processes, it needs an effective system to measure and assess its current state, create goals and move toward a world-class organization. The following section provides a description of this process.

## Process Improvement Metrics

Supply management uses measures and measurement systems to help develop strategies, evaluate process performance and reward personnel. Measures have been extensively revised as supply management has become more visible and strategically important to organizations. Thus, it is imperative that valid and reliable measurement results, tied to strategic goals, are communicated regularly to senior management. It is also important that these measures and goals are jointly determined by the chief supply management officer and senior management.

The measurement process begins once a corporate strategy has been set. Supply management then works closely with the strategic business units (SBUs) and other functional areas, such as operations, new product development and accounting, to develop measures and goals that will determine organizational priorities, motivate personnel and effectively track each process. Good measures help focus personnel on the most important process activities and outcomes. More on performance evaluation can be found in Chapter 10.

## Summary

This is an exciting yet challenging time for those in the supply management field. According to the same A. T. Kearney study cited at the beginning of this chapter, supply management professionals in leading organizations were found to spend about half their time in strategic planning activities and half related to tactical issues in 2002, while in 2004, that number had increased to two-thirds strategic and one-third tactical. According to the same study, "Supply management organizations are driving companywide adoption of common policies, approaches and practices."[20] Thus, supply management professionals today must be more prepared than ever to meet an organization's demands for higher levels of performance.

Expect to see an increasing presence of supply management at the executive table in the areas of planning, forecasting and new product/service development. In addition, better integration and performance in the supporting operational areas of inventory management, materials management, warehousing, logistics and transportation through knowledge integration will be expected of the supply management organization in the 21st century. Initiatives to increase that involvement, create value and improve operations will require a project orientation and thus we will see supply management professionals as contributing members to project teams. To make measurable improvements, however, effective performance measurement systems, covering both supply management and supplier performance, will be required. This book covers these topical areas as a basis to increase the supply management professional's knowledge and as a foundation for organizational improvement.

## Key Points

1. A number of terms are used interchangeably to describe the subcomponents within supply management, including *purchasing, procurement, materials management* and *materiel,* but each has a slightly different meaning. The terms *supply management* and *supply-chain management* sometimes are used interchangeably.

2. *Supply management* is "the identification, acquisition, access, positioning and management of resources and related capabilities the organization needs or potentially needs in the attainment of its strategic objectives." (*ISM Glossary,* 2006)

3. *Supply chain management* is "the design and management of seamless, value-added processes across organizational boundaries to meet the real needs of the end customer." (*ISM Glossary,* 2006)

4. The interest in supply management really developed in the latter part of the 20th century, although the U.S. railroads realized the importance of the function as early as the mid–1800s.

5. Beginning in the 1980s, purchasing began to assume greater responsibility for the purchase of services, in part because of the impact of downsizing and the willingness of other functions to give up noncore activities, while in the 1990s purchasing became more integrated into corporate strategy as organizations faced greater domestic and global competition.

6. A number of quantifiable benefits are attributed to high-performing supply management organizations, including lower operating costs, improved return on investment (ROI) and return on assets (ROA) and a direct positive impact on the bottom line.

7. Some of the intangible benefits associated with supply management include: (1) serves as a good source of information; (2) assists in meeting an organization's strategic objectives and (3) helps create goodwill.

8. One of the most common questions that organizations must address is whether an item or service should be made or created in-house or outsourced — the classic make-or-buy decision.

9. Two common forms of risk analysis include decision tree analysis and the two-by-two portfolio matrix.

10. Organizations have adopted a number of assessment and improvement initiatives within the past 15 years. The two most commonly adopted include Six Sigma and lean operations. Some organizations also are taking a *lean supply chain* approach by applying lean principles cooperatively throughout the supply chain.

11. It is imperative that valid and reliable measurement results, tied to strategic goals, are communicated regularly to senior management. It is also important that measures and goals are jointly determined by the chief supply management officer and senior management.

# 2

# Project Management

**T**oday, more than ever, supply management professionals are active participants on projects, particularly with the advent of outsourcing. They may be involved in enterprisewide projects, projects with other functions including engineering, operations, marketing and sales or their own internal projects. Most often they are concerned with the acquisition, purchase and value to the organization of those goods and services that will be needed to deploy any organization-related project plans. Some supply management professionals work in a project environment on a full-time basis while others are brought into a project as needed. Examples of projects where supply management lends expertise and will most likely be involved include:

- Creating a supplier certification program,
- Developing and implementing an online auction program,
- Selecting and recommending materials or developing a statement of work for a new product or service,
- Contract preparation and negotiation and
- Developing a key supplier.

Thus, it is important to understand the discipline of project management and its application to the strategic supply management process framework, particularly the overarching concerns of risk management and supplier relationship management and measurement, and the fourth process step, negotiate and contract (see Figure I-1). This chapter will begin by looking at the role of supply management professionals in a project environment, introducing some definitions and taking a look at the life cycle of a project. The next section will examine the types of organizational structures that exist to support projects. The remainder of this chapter will discuss five project processes and supply management's role within each process.

**CHAPTER OBJECTIVES**

• Define the field of project management.

• Describe the role of supply management during a project's life cycle.

• Discuss the tools available to assess projects.

# Defining Projects

The Project Management Institute (PMI), a nonprofit organization devoted to the education and certification of project management professionals, has defined a *project* as "a temporary endeavor undertaken to create a unique product or service,"[1] while the *ISM Glossary* (2006) defines a project as "a special piece of work outside the normal flow of daily activities that has a specific objective and a time and budget limit." Note the key characteristics of a project common to both definitions. First, each project has a beginning and an end, although the length of time may vary from a few days to several weeks, months or even years. Second, each project is distinctive in some respects from other projects. For many supply management professionals, project management is a way of life, as most of their time is spent developing new suppliers, negotiating contracts or supporting new products. Each contract, for example, has its own unique terms and conditions: quantities purchased, pricing, delivery dates and performance requirements, among others.

Projects are typically created to meet at least one of five objectives: (1) create a change in an organization, (2) exploit new opportunities, (3) implement the strategic plan, (4) fulfill a contractual agreement or (5) solve some problem. Thus, for projects to be successful, projects take more planning as a rule of thumb than the typical day-to-day routines found in most organizations.

Because organizations run so many projects, *project management* has evolved into a specialized field. Project management has been defined in the *ISM Glossary* (2006) as "the process of coordinating the organization, planning, scheduling, controlling, monitoring and evaluating of activities so that the objectives of a project are met." Project managers set specific targets and allocate resources such as time, money, people, energy and space over the course of a project.

# Project Life Cycle

As shown in Figure 2-1, each project typically will go through a sequence of activities throughout its life to accomplish specific goals and objectives; this is known collectively as the *project life cycle*. A project's life cycle activities are usually divided into several phases or stages for better control, beginning with an initial planning phase, progressing

**Figure 2-1    Project Life Cycle — New Product Development**

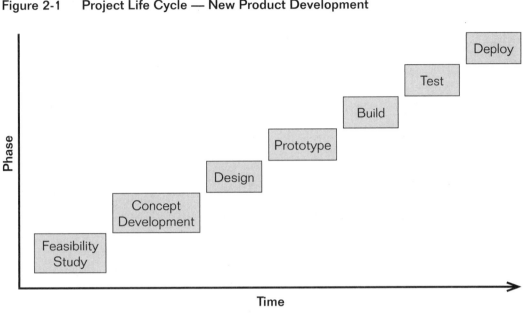

through at least one intermediary phase where the plans are executed and ending in a final phase that terminates the project. When a phase contains many complex activities, it may be broken down into smaller subphases for better monitoring and control. During each phase the project management team will be faced with prioritizing tasks, minimizing sources of conflict such as schedules or cost and identifying those critical factors that will make the project successful. The end of each phase is usually defined by the completion and acceptance of one or more *deliverables* (a measurable, verifiable work product). If a deliverable is not acceptable, additional work still may be needed, delaying the move onto the next phase. For example, during the initial phase, *stakeholders* (parties with a vested interest in the project) should review the description of the project's scope (a deliverable) to be sure it meets the acceptance criteria.

Not all projects will complete their life cycles. Some projects will fail before they are completed, perhaps because of budget overruns, a change in organizational direction or personnel issues. Other projects may skip the project's initial planning stage and move immediately into the project execution with no prototyping or testing and little monitoring or control. Still other projects may go through project planning, execution and testing several times before termination.

Projects also can be thought of as sets of interlinking processes. PMI breaks down projects into five *process groups,* each with a set of interrelated project activities "normally . . . repeated for each phase or subproject."[2] It is not mandatory, however, that each process group of activities is repeated at each phase of a project — a project should be tailored to meet its necessary objectives. For example, the initiating process may take place only at the onset of a project. The five process groups are further described in Figure 2-2.

Figure 2-2    Project Process Groups

| PROCESS GROUP | DESCRIPTION | ACTIVITIES | DELIVERABLES/OUTPUTS |
|---|---|---|---|
| Initiating | Processes for formalizing authorization to begin new project or project phase | Evaluate alternatives<br><br>Clarify objectives<br><br>Develop project scope<br><br>Develop project charter<br><br>ID available resources | Project charter<br><br>Preliminary project scope statement |
| Planning | Planning and managing a successful project | Gather information<br><br>Finalize scope<br><br>Develop cost budget<br><br>Develop schedule<br><br>Identify risks<br><br>Establish quality requirements<br><br>Plan purchases | Project management plan<br><br>Scope management plan<br><br>Staffing plan<br><br>Budget<br><br>Quality control plan<br><br>Supply management plan<br><br>Contract statement of work |
| Executing | Processes to complete the work and meet project requirements | Coordinate people and resources<br><br>Perform project activities<br><br>Obtain information, bids, quotes, proposals from suppliers<br><br>Select suppliers<br><br>Implement any approved changes | Updated plans<br><br>Implemented changes<br><br>Team performance assessments<br><br>Project-specific deliverables<br><br>Supplier proposals<br><br>Contract<br><br>Contract management plan |

| PROCESS GROUP | DESCRIPTION | ACTIVITIES | DELIVERABLES/OUTPUTS |
|---|---|---|---|
| **Monitoring and Control** | Processes to examine project execution, identify problems and take corrective action | Observe/monitor<br><br>Review supplier performance<br><br>Measure against project plans and performance baselines<br><br>Implement corrective actions<br><br>Establish preventive measures | Performance reports<br><br>Updated supply management plan<br><br>Updated contract management plan |
| **Closing** | Formal termination of a project or project phase; handing off a project; canceling a project | Finalize all process group activities<br><br>Close out contracts<br><br>Resolve contract issues | Closed contract<br><br>Final product, service, result |

*Source:* Adapted from *A Guide to the Project Management Body of Knowledge,* 3rd. ed. *(PMBOK® Guide)* (Newtown Square, PA: Project Management Institute, 2004).

PMI's *PMBOK® Guide* also describes nine knowledge areas of project management as shown in Figure 2-3. The knowledge area of project procurement management includes a discussion of:

- Plan purchases and acquisitions,
- Plan contracting,
- Request seller responses,
- Select sellers,
- Contract administration and
- Contract closure.

A supply management professional may be involved at one time or another in one or more of the other knowledge areas shown in Figure 2-3. He or she may need to work on critical issues in cost management, quality management or risk

Figure 2-3    PMI Knowledge Areas

| KNOWLEDGE AREA | DESCRIPTION | EXAMPLES |
|---|---|---|
| **Integration Management** | Processes and activities that integrate project management elements | Develop project charter<br><br>Develop preliminary project scope statement<br><br>Monitor/control project work |
| **Scope Management** | Processes used to make sure project work matches project scope | Planning and defining scope<br><br>Verifying scope<br><br>Controlling scope |
| **Time Management** | Processes that ensure project is completed in a timely manner | Defining project activities<br><br>Sequencing activities; estimating resource requirements<br><br>Estimating activity duration |
| **Cost Management** | Processes that ensure project is completed within the planned budget | Planning and estimating costs<br><br>Budgeting<br><br>Controlling costs |
| **Quality Management** | Processes that ensure project will meet quality objectives | Quality planning<br><br>Quality assurance<br><br>Quality control |
| **Human Resources Management** | Processes to organize and manage the project team | HR planning<br><br>Select and develop project team<br><br>Manage the project team |
| **Communications Management** | Processes for the collection, dissemination and disposal of project information | Communication planning<br><br>Distributing information<br><br>Reporting performance<br><br>Manage communication to stakeholders |
| **Risk Management** | Processes to oversee risk management | Risk management planning<br><br>Identifying risks |

| KNOWLEDGE AREA | DESCRIPTION | EXAMPLES |
|---|---|---|
| **Risk Management** (continued) | | Qualitative and quantitative risk analysis<br><br>Risk responsive planning<br><br>Risk monitoring and control |
| **Procurement Management** | Processes to acquire materials and services to support the project and manage contracts | Purchase and acquisition planning<br><br>Contract planning<br><br>Requesting supplier responses<br><br>Selecting suppliers<br><br>Administering contracts; closing out contracts |

*Source:* Adapted from *A Guide to the Project Management Body of Knowledge,* 3rd. ed. *(PMBOK® Guide) (*Newtown Square. PA: Project Management Institute, 2004).

management, for example. This discussion will focus on the procurement management knowledge area for purposes of illustration. Further discussion of the six knowledge areas for procurement management can be found in the sections on project planning, execution and closeout.

# The Project Organization

Projects are most often configured within the constraints of the overall organizational structure. Figure 2-4 identifies three generic approaches to organizing projects.

## Functional Structure

Organizations less familiar with the discipline of project management usually begin by creating task forces or committees within each function to tackle problems, known as a *functional structure.* The majority of organizations operate with functional areas such as marketing, accounting, operations, supply management and so on. The advantage of a functional structure is that the employees generally are more dedicated to the project because they see the potential results will directly affect them. A disadvantage with these types of structures is that the organization's goals often are subordinated

**Figure 2-4    Project Organizational Structures**

|  | FUNCTIONAL | MATRIX | PROJECTIZED |
|---|---|---|---|
| Project Manager's Authority | Little or none | Limited to high | High to almost total |
| Percent of Performing Organization's Personnel Assigned Full-time to Project Work | Virtually none | 0–95% | 85–100% |
| Project Manager's Role | Part-time | Part-time to Full-time | Full-time |
| Common Titles for Project Manager's Role | Project Coordinator/ Project Leader | Project Coordinator Project Manager Project Officer Program Manager | Project Manager Program Manager |
| Project Management Administrative Staff | Part-time | Part-time to Full-time | Full-time |
| Level of Commitment | Inside group: high Outside group: low | Varies | Highest |
| Communication | More difficult | More difficult | Least difficult More structured |
| Priority | Inside group: high Outside group: low | Varies | Highest |
| Potential Conflicts | Low | High | Low |

*Source:* Adapted from *A Guide to the Project Management Body of Knowledge,* 3rd. ed. *(PMBOK® Guide)* (Newtown Square, PA: Project Management Institute, 2004).

to the needs of the functional area. A second disadvantage is that those outside the functional area, such as supply management personnel, also may be requested by the functional department at times when their skills are needed and they may not always be available when needed, impeding the success of the project.

## Projectized Structure

Organizations also may adopt a *projectized structure* to implement projects. In this type of structure, full-time project managers recruit people from the various functional areas who are then relieved of their regular duties and assigned to the project. Large accounting firms and construction organizations are just two examples of organizations that operate in this type of environment. These project managers often report directly to a senior executive and, as a result, the approved projects are more cohesive in nature, are aimed at common organizational goals and have a higher success factor. In this type of environment, supply management personnel, for instance, are assigned directly to the project manager.

While the projectized form of project management has its advantages, there are some disadvantages. First, there probably will be some overlap in human resource needs for individuals will be assigned to each project on a full-time basis and pulled away from day-to-day activities. Secondly, there may be duplication of equipment and facilities among the many projects. Both duplication of people and equipment will result in higher costs during a time when organizations are trying to trim costs. Lastly, there is always the issue of what to do with personnel once the project is completed. If another project is not available, an employee may be temporarily without work or at worst case permanently without a job.

## Matrix Organization

To overcome some of the disadvantages of functional and projectized structures, a third option is the *matrix organization*. Personnel are not assigned to a project full-time but rather are shared with the functional department. A project manager is assigned to a project, either full-time or part-time, depending on the size of the project, and then must negotiate for the services of individual team members with each appropriate functional manager. For example, the project manager might talk to the supply management director about using a specific commodities specialist on his or her project. The two managers must work out the details of the arrangement, such as project time requirements.

There are some significant advantages to the matrix organization. First, the project manager's control of any resources allocated to the project increases his or her accountability for completing the project. The project manager also has some flexibility in how the project funds are used. Moreover, because the functional manager has been included in the process, he or she tends to be more supportive of the project. Lastly, if a person has been assigned to the project full-time, the functional manager should be holding the person's job for him when he or she completes the required project activities. However, when personnel are assigned to a project on a part-time basis, there is a greater chance for conflict if the functional manager feels the project is using too much of the assigned person's time. The matrix organization also requires more personnel, thus increasing the costs.

In an effort to improve project performance, the Los Angeles Bureau of Engineering moved from a functional organization to a matrix structure. As a result, a program manager was given responsibility for all projects that fell under one of four areas: wastewater, street, stormwater and municipal facilities. Project managers were assigned to individual projects with responsibility for a project's scope, budget and schedule. Each functional manager negotiated the scope, budget and schedule for the technical tasks that were needed to complete his or her portion of the project. Functional managers also supervised the staff assigned to a project and participated in project information meetings. As a result, project costs did not change significantly and projects were completed within the budget cycle more consistently.[3]

Because projects come in all shapes and sizes, most organizations will adapt by incorporating more than one of the structures described previously. This adaptation is known as an *organic structure,* which responds to the needs of the organization by using a combination of functional, matrix and projectized structures. For example, some supply management professionals may be assigned some projects on an ad hoc basis, while others are involved in contract negotiation full-time.

The organizational and project structures set the stage for how tasks will be performed, what will be required to complete the tasks and how the organization will meet the project's objectives. It is also directly related to the planning and execution of a project. Thus, the following sections describe the stages of a project from a process point of view, beginning with the initiation of a project.

## Project Initiation

Projects, as stated at the beginning of the chapter, often are created because a problem has arisen or a new process or procedure needs to be developed — there is a specific organizational need or internal requirements or some law has changed. For example, a supply management team may be experiencing performance problems with one of its suppliers. In other instances, an organization might face a change in an environmental law, which requires it to alter the disposal process for certain chemicals. Baxter International, Inc., an Illinois-based global healthcare organization, implemented a project in 2000 because it needed to integrate environmental criteria into its supply management process.[4] In these instances, a team generally is assigned to identify and then solve problems.

## Define the Problem

Usually someone — an individual, a department, senior management or the CEO — realizes that a complex issue is affecting the organization. In these situations, it is a good idea to clarify that complex issue in writing. For example, a U.S. hospital created the following problem statement: "Ten percent of the InVision [healthcare information software] system updates last month had to be backed up, resulting in an 18 percent increase in service issues."[5] The statement is concise and gets to the root of the problem.

While it may sound simple, projects often fail because a complex issue has incorrectly been identified. A project team may be assigned to solving a problem that does not really exist or is insignificant compared to other more important problems. In other instances, a manager clearly "sees the problem" but is unable to make it clear to the rest of the team. Because the manager is the manager, the team often follows along without argument even through they might disagree, something known as the *Abilene Paradox*.[6] As a result, the scope of the project does not address the manager's real concerns and fails.

To make the best use of a team's time and address problems that will improve an organization's competitiveness, a manager should work together with the team to uncover and define an actual problem and its underlying or root causes using some form of data collection and analysis. This also may be the time to bring in outside "experts" in the form of consultants or contractors, who can provide an outsider's perspective. The process often starts with a *SWOT analysis* as described in the following section. (*Leadership in Supply Management,* Volume 3 of the ISM Professional Series, also includes a discussion of SWOT analysis.)

**SWOT Analysis.** SWOT analysis is a macrolevel evaluation of an organization's internal and external forces — its strengths, weaknesses, opportunities and threats — to help senior management evaluate the organization's current environment that triggered the need for this particular project. A relatively simple form of risk assessment, a SWOT analysis provides direction and serves as a basis to create a *project business case,* which is a written justification for the project's deployment. The analysis also can be used to help the project team accomplish its objectives or overcome some obstacle.

Both internal and external characteristics of an organization's business environment are in flux. For example, internally an organization's vision, strategy or objectives change over time. An organization experiences problems with its current processes or technologies. Externally, new technologies become available, creating an opportunity to improve competitiveness. Other external changes also may be occurring in the legislative or environmental arena. Still other external pressures may come from the competition, shifts in consumer preferences or changing economic cycles.

Strengths and weaknesses are the internal things an organization currently can and cannot do, respectively. A strength is something the organization does well, from both the customer's as well as the organization's viewpoint. A weakness can be something the organization is doing poorly or something that can be improved. In evaluating those strengths and weaknesses, it is important to be realistic — in other words, not overly critical but modest in the assessment.

On the other hand, opportunities and threats are the potentially favorable and unfavorable conditions in the external environment. Thus, every organization should make an evaluation. Figure 2-5 illustrates a SWOT analysis created by Tesco PLC, a grocery food chain based in the United Kingdom.[7] Tesco identified opportunities that were a good fit to its strengths but also would help overcome internal organizational weaknesses. Organizations should use their strengths to reduce vulnerability to any external threats. At the same time, they should create a defensive plan to prevent weaknesses from making them highly susceptible to external threats. Once the SWOT analysis has been completed, the team should have a better understanding of the environment that created the problem(s) and be able to identify projects that will minimize or eliminate these problems and as a result improve their competitiveness.

At this point, the team may decide that one particular problem stands out but is multifaceted and just too large to tackle in one project or that multiple unrelated problems exist. The team then should resort to *brainstorming* with a group of stakeholders, which may include the process users, managers, customers and suppliers, to further understand the problem. Based on its analysis, the team should determine which problems should be tackled or what areas of a much larger problem should be addressed. During the brainstorming session, any ideas should be written down without prejudice. Three important issues should be addressed for each problem under consideration for a project:

1. How frequently does the problem or complex issue occur?

2. How important is the problem or complex issue?

3. How likely is it that we can resolve the problem or complex issue (feasibility)?

The frequency of the problem can be estimated by collecting some data, while the importance and feasibility can be evaluated using a Likert-type scale. The results then can be rank-ordered using a *prioritization matrix*. Figure 2-6 provides an example.

## Kepner-Tregoe Rational Process Analysis

*Kepner-Tregoe Rational Process Analysis,* developed by Charles Kepner and Benjamin Tregoe in *The New Rational Manager* (1981), is a set of systematic procedures to apply

## Figure 2-5   SWOT Analysis Matrix at Tesco PLC

| STRENGTHS | WEAKNESSES |
|---|---|
| Powerful retail brand | Inefficiencies in bureaucracy because of size |
| Substantial financial power | |
| Well-established customer base | Large amount of debt |
| Loyal, trusting customers | Highly dependent on UK market |
| Reputation, value for money | Lack of integration between online and offline resources |
| Great store locations | Too much product diversity |
| Superb warehousing and logistics capabilities | Large capital expenditures on new stores and infrastructure, resulting in less cash to innovate |
| Club card scheme enhances customer loyalty | New areas (personal finance) lack experience and expertise |
| Quickly expanding | |
| Different store types match customer demand | |
| Economies of scale | |

| OPPORTUNITIES | THREATS |
|---|---|
| Improve customer relations | A tax increase on alcoholic beverages |
| Increase sales through better integration of Internet resources | Possible takeovers |
| | Tax on food and books |
| Integrate offline and online data to better serve customers | Expansion of low-cost supermarkets |
| | A weakening economy |
| Form strategic alliances with other organizations to improve experience and expertise | An increase in unemployment |
| | Bigger supermarkets (Wal-Mart) taking them on |
| Add new locations (Eastern Europe, southeastern United Kingdom) | Customer worry over the end of local shops; Tesco becomes brunt of blame |
| | Monopolies and mergers commission finds Tesco is too powerful and splits up the organization |

*Source:* Adapted from Paul Evans, *An Analysis of Tesco PLC: Structure, Hierarchy and Organisation,* December 2006, available from www.321books.co.uk/catalog/tesco-structure.htm.

**Figure 2-6    Prioritization Matrix**

| Problem Description | (1) Frequency of Occurrence | (2) Importance | (3) Feasibility of Resolution | (4) Total Score |
|---|---|---|---|---|
| Delivery Problems with Supplier X | 3 | 3 | 2 | 18 |
| | | | | |
| | | | | |
| | | | | |
| | | | | |

Ranking:
1 = Low
2 = Medium
3 = High

To obtain score, calculate the product of columns 1, 2 and 3. For example, in the instance of delivery problems, the total score is calculated as $3 \times 3 \times 2 = 18$.

critical thinking to information, data and experience for the purpose of solving problems, making decisions, anticipating future problems and appraising situations. (*ISM Glossary,* 2006) Kepner and Tregoe identify four patterns of thinking that managers use everyday and can be applied to specific problems that require a project:

1. The project team needs to assess what is going on. In other words, what is the current environment? Answering this question helps managers regain order when there has been uncertainty or confusion, establish priorities and determine the project parameters that will have good results.

2. The team needs to be able to determine the causes of the problem. Why did this happen?

3. The team will determine what course of action should be taken to help them meet their project goals.

4. The team should determine what lies ahead. What kinds of decisions will the team have to make in the future?

The first question requires a *situation appraisal* — looking at the actual situation at hand and identifying any problems that need to be solved. The second question requires a *problem analysis.* As shown in Figure 2-7, by focusing on a specific issue, the team begins by identifying a problem and then describing it, which is otherwise known as a *deviation statement.* This stage is important because the problem description will be the basis for the scope of the project. With the deviation statement in hand, the team then can describe the identity, location, timing and magnitude of the problem. It is important to develop a good understanding of both what the problem *is* and *is not,* by asking how often it is happening, where the problem is occurring, when it is happening, what the extent or degree of the problem and its occurrence is and who is involved in the situation/problem. This process helps the team narrow down the possible causes of the problem and the team then can develop a project to address the third question.

**Figure 2-7    Kepner-Tregoe Problem Analysis**

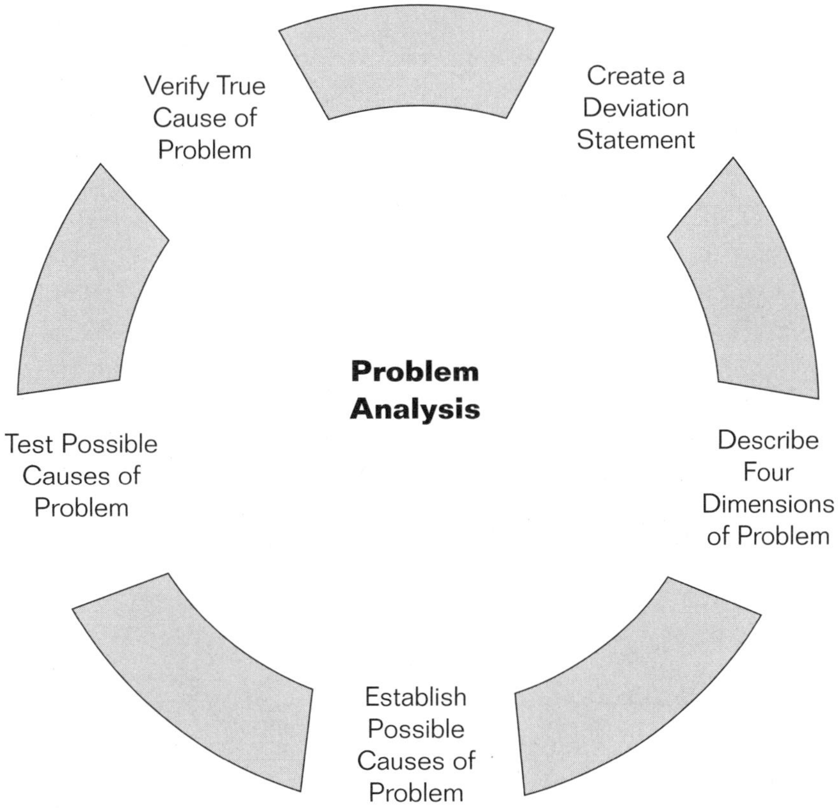

*Source:* Adapted from Charles H. Kepner and Benjamin B. Tregoe, *The New Rational Manager* (Princeton, NJ: Princeton Research Press, 1981).

Kepner and Tregoe refer to this as *decision analysis.* The last question helps organizations anticipate the future and requires a *potential problem (opportunity) analysis.*[8]

Richmond, Virginia–based Interbake Foods LLC, for example, maker of baked goods such as Girl Scout cookies, ice-cream cones and crackers, had acquired two other organizations, resulting in an attempt to mesh three different ways of doing business, three different cultures, disparate sales forces, an inefficient distribution system and less-than-ideal manufacturing locations. The new organization used project management along with Kepner-Tregoe's Rational Process Analysis to successfully complete the integration process. Teams were assembled from the three different cultures, including members from different functions and management levels to address all the issues. As a result, costs in distribution and manufacturing dropped significantly and revenues increased by 30 percent within two years of the acquisitions.[9]

Two other tools that can help a project team uncover and pinpoint the reasons a problem is occurring are cause-and-effect analysis and Pareto analysis.

## Cause-and-Effect Analysis

A *cause-and-effect diagram,* also known as a fishbone diagram, is a chart that captures all the possible causes of a problem in a format designed to show their relationships to the problem (the effect) and to each other. The diagram resembles the skeleton of a fish. (*ISM Glossary,* 2006) For example, a commodity manager might receive continuing quality problem reports from manufacturing with regard to a particular part he or she purchases from a supplier. The cause-and-effect diagram can be an effective tool for some initial brainstorming. Its use, however, also can result in an oversimplification of the problem or too much detail for a realistic analysis. Figure 2-8 provides an example of a cause-and-effect diagram. To create the diagram, a team identifies key problem

**Figure 2-8    Cause-and-Effect Diagram**

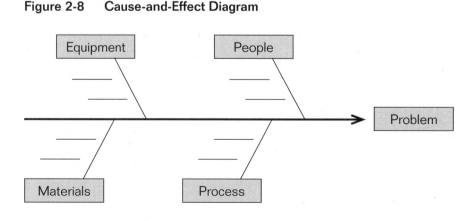

categories. Causes usually are categorized by machine, manpower, management and materials, but other categories may be identified. For each category, the team then would brainstorm a list of possible causes of this problem category. The team could be even more specific and list the causes of a cause.

## Pareto Analysis

*Pareto analysis* is a process of determining the small minority of a population that accounts for the majority of a given effect. For example, in inventory management, 20 percent of the inventoried items account for 80 percent of the total dollars. (*ISM Glossary,* 2006) A Pareto analysis typically is performed once a cause-and-effect diagram has been created. Data are collected to determine the frequency of each possible cause of the problem. The collected data then can be plotted to create a *Pareto chart.* A Pareto chart is a combination bar chart and cumulative percentage chart, showing the frequency with which events occur, arranged in order of descending frequency. It is used to rank-order the issues so that resources can be applied first to those with the largest potential return. (*ISM Glossary,* 2006) The Pareto chart should help the team determine the biggest issues facing it and where it should place its greatest efforts. An example of a Pareto chart is provided in Figure 2-9.

**Figure 2-9    Pareto Chart Example**

Adams Automotive Parts sells automotive supplies to retailers. In the past three months, the owner has noticed the number of customer complaints has increased. He assigns a team to investigate the problem. The team collects the customer complaint data and creates a Pareto diagram. The bars indicate the number of complaints attributed to each problem and the line indicates the cumulative percentage of complaints. The team concludes that 62 percent of the complaints can be attributed to damaged or late deliveries.

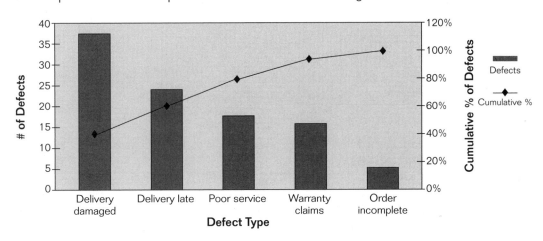

## Option Assessment

Once the problem or opportunity under consideration for the project has been identi-fied, the possible solutions, in the form of project proposals, with their related benefits, costs, risks and feasibility, should be listed. The benefits and costs may be financial and qualitative, with some examples provided in Figure 2-10 and Figure 2-11.

Risks generally are associated with the project itself, such as the risk that the project will not be completed on time or that the funding needed to complete the project is not available. The team should assess the probability that the risk will occur, the potential effect of the risk and any countermeasures the team would need to take in the event a risk occurs. An example of a survey form used in risk analysis is provided in Figure 2-12. Additional risk assessment should be performed during the planning stage and is covered later in this chapter.

Based on each solution's benefits, costs and risks, a *feasibility study* will help limit the number of solutions under consideration by determining the chance that each

**Figure 2-10    Examples of Project Benefits to the Business**

| BENEFIT | DESCRIPTION |
|---|---|
| Financial | $ of new revenue generated<br>$ cost savings<br>% increase in profit margin |
| Market | % gain in market share<br>Estimated increase in competitiveness<br>% increase in customer awareness |
| Customer | % increase in customer satisfaction<br>% increase in customer retention<br>Increase in customer loyalty |
| Supply Management | % increase in efficiency<br>% improvement in supplier quality<br>% improvement in supplier delivery |

*Source:* Adapted from Jason Westland, *Project Management Life Cycle* (London: Kogan Page, Ltd., 2006), 19.

**Figure 2-11    Examples of Project Costs**

| COST | DESCRIPTION |
| --- | --- |
| Project Participants | Project staff salaries |
| | Training costs for employees |
| | Purchasing costs of contractors or consultants |
| Internal Organization | Downtime during testing |
| | Losses in productivity during transition |
| | Resistance to change |
| | New manuals |
| Physical Assets | Equipment and materials |
| | Computers, phones, printers |
| | Office space dedicated to project |
| External Suppliers | Training costs |
| | Temporary losses in productivity or service delivery |
| | Resistance to change |
| | Search costs for new supplier(s) |

*Source:* Adapted from Jason Westland, *Project Management Life Cycle* (London: Kogan Page, Ltd., 2006), 19.

solution actually will solve the problem at hand or take advantage of an opportunity. Several aspects of each solution should be considered, and some method should be used to assess the feasibility of each aspect. Figure 2-13 provides an example of a feasibility study for one alternative solution.

Managers also may incorporate *net present value* (NPV) and *internal rate of return* (IRR) analyses into their feasibility study, which generally are used for capital improvement projects. Net present value is the difference between the present value of all cash inflows and the present value of all cash outflows during the life cycle of the improvement. Cash outflows generally include the cost of the project itself and other expenditures that result from implementation of the project. Cash inflows occur after the project has been completed and could be either additional revenues or cost savings.

**Figure 2-12    Project Risk Analysis Survey**

**PROJECT NAME: SUPPLIER DEVELOPMENT**

1.  Description of risk: Funds will be not be available in the budget for the project.

    Rate the following based on a scale of: High = 2; Medium = 1; Low = 0

2.  a)  Risk probability score: _____

    b)  Impact of risk score: _____

                         Total:        _____

3.  a)  Difficulty in avoiding risk: _____

    b)  Probability of avoiding risk: _____

                         Total:        _____

4.  a)  Difficulty in mitigating risk: _____

    b)  Probability of mitigating risk: _____

                         Total:        _____

5.  If steps are taken to avoid the risk, what will be the impact on project costs?

    _____ Remain the same  _____ Increase 1% to 5%  _____ Increase 6% to 10%

    _____ Increase more than 10%

6.  If steps are taken to mitigate the risk, what will be the impact on project schedule?

    _____ Remain the same  _____ Increase 1% to 5%  _____ Increase 6% to 10%

    _____ Increase by more than 10%

7.  Recommendation:

    _____ Take no action  _____ Avoid the risk  _____ Mitigate the risk

    _____ Do further analysis

Figure 2-13    Feasibility Study for Solution "A"

| CATEGORY | RATING | METHODOLOGY USED |
|---|---|---|
| Additional people needed to complete project. | 7 | Survey of available employees take to identify skill sets. |
| New processes will have to be adopted. | 4 | Processes at other organizations were benchmarked. |
| New capital equipment will have to be purchased. | 8 | Current capital equipment was inspected. |
| New technology will be needed to complete the project. | 8 | A team created a technology prototype. |

Feasibility Rating:
1 = extremely low feasibility
10 = extremely high feasibility

If the NPV is positive, this indicates that a project should be approved because cash flows will be positive. The formula for net present value is:

$$NPV = \sum_{t=1}^{T} \frac{C_t}{(1+r)^t}$$

where:

$C_t$ = net cash flow for Year t

$r$ = expected rate of return

$t$ = year

$T$ = number of years under analysis

For example, imagine a supply management team is reviewing a project proposal to investigate substituting a less expensive component part in an existing product. Marketing has informed the team that the product will be on the market for another four years. The project is expected to take one year. The proposal contains a net present value analysis based on expected 8 percent return each year as shown in Figure 2-14. Because the sum of the net present values is a negative number, the project would likely be rejected.

Figure 2-14    Net Present Value

| YEAR | COST SAVINGS | EXPENSES | NET CASH FLOW | NET PRESENT VALUE |
|------|--------------|----------|---------------|-------------------|
| 0 | $ 0 | $150,000 | −$150,000 | −$150,000 |
| 1 | 50,000 | 5,000 | 45,000 | 41,666 |
| 2 | 50,000 | 5,000 | 45,000 | 38,580 |
| 3 | 50,000 | 5,000 | 45,000 | 35,722 |
| 4 | 50,000 | 5,000 | 45,000 | 33,076 |
| | | | Sum of NPVs = | −956 |

The internal rate of return (IRR) is the rate of return that would make the present value of future cash flows plus the final market value of an investment or business opportunity equal the current market price of the investment or opportunity. In other words, the IRR answers the question: At what rate of return will the project break even? Basically, the IRR is the return that an organization would receive in the event it invested in itself rather than elsewhere. The IRR is calculated similarly to NPV, but the NPV is set to zero; then solve for the IRR. Using Figure 2-14, solve for the IRR as follows:

$$0 = -\$150,000 + \$45,000/[(1 + r)/100]^1 + \$45,000/[(1+r)/100]^2 + \$45,000/[(1+r)/100]^3 + \$45,000[(1+r)/100]^4$$
$$IRR = 7.71\%$$

Because of the complexity of solving for the IRR by hand, electronic spreadsheets with built-in formulas, such as Microsoft Excel, can simplify the process. Experts do not recommend that the IRR be used to compare different projects unless the discount rate is the same, cash flows are predictable, the projects share an equal amount of risk and the project length is relatively similar. They argue that discount rates vary over time and the IRR assumes only one discount rate. Thus, it would be difficult to judge a one-year project against a five-year project. On the other hand, the NPV can be used to compare various projects and a different interest rate can be used each year or for only certain years.

## Stakeholder Analysis

A stakeholder analysis also assists a project team in assessing the project environment by identifying each stakeholder and his or her role as well as that person's level of interest and influence in the project. Moreover, this analysis should help the team determine the level of risk and variability that could occur in the project, ultimately affecting the chance of project success.

A project typically will have *primary stakeholders* (those ultimately affected by the project's deliverables) and *secondary stakeholders* (intermediaries that aid in the project delivery process). For example, if a supply management team is conducting a project to create a supplier development program, the primary stakeholders would be the supply management department, the affected suppliers and possibly the internal stakeholders. Some secondary stakeholders would include the project manager and the project team.

A stakeholder analysis can help the team identify any potential conflicts among the stakeholders, which could negatively affect the project's success. These types of conflicts must be resolved early in the project. Conversely, if there are already some strong positive relationships that exist between stakeholders, the team can build on those relationships to strengthen project sponsorship and cooperation. Lastly, the analysis can be used to help a team assess the appropriate level of participation of the various stakeholders during successive stages of the project life cycle. Some questions to consider during the analysis include:

- What are each stakeholder's expectations with regard to the project?

- What are the likely benefits each stakeholder will accrue from the project?

- What resources will the stakeholder want to commit (or avoid committing) to the project?

- What other interests does the stakeholder have that could conflict with the project?

- How does the stakeholder feel about other stakeholders involved in the project?

## Project Approval

Once the problem has been defined and studied, project proposals are submitted for approval. If a project is relatively small and will be assigned to a single person, approval is fairly simple. Contract renegotiations also may be an automatic process and may not require preapproval. However, larger projects typically require a more formal presentation either to a project sponsor, senior management or the client. For midsize projects that require some funding, organizations may have a project management group in place that does nothing but review project proposals and decide which projects will move forward.

In the larger more complex projects such as road construction or building a new facility, senior management often will develop a *project business case* mentioned previously, which is presented to the client and incorporates the process described so far into one document. The project business case essentially justifies the deployment of a project. According to Jason Westland, author of *Project Management Life Cycle,* a business case should include the following:

- A description of the problem under consideration,

- The options available to solve the problem,

- The benefits, costs, risks and feasibility for each available option and

- The recommended solution.[10]

### Project Charter

Once a project is approved, a *project charter* often is developed. A project charter defines the project but also establishes the authority of the project sponsor to the project manager and is used to announce the project to relevant stakeholders. Generally reserved for larger projects, it is a good referral document and begins the "paper trail." Team members also can use the project charter as a guide when in doubt as to the project scope.

Usually, the charter is created by the project manager and project sponsor although others may be involved. While there is no set format, a general template may be followed (see Figure 2-15). The project charter may be in the form of a memo, an e-mail or a more formal document, any of which should be kept with the project documentation. However, some important areas should be addressed. For example, the project's scope and any constraints, the project's important *milestones* (important deliverables or events that signify noteworthy progress on the project), the assigned project manager and team members and a risk analysis should be included. The charter also should be signed and dated by the project sponsor or other responsible party as a formal indication of project approval.

# Project Planning

Planning provides the roadmap for a project once it has been approved. Projects should have a formal project plan that provides each project team member with the project details. Certain essential planning steps will increase the chances that a project will be successful.

Figure 2-15    Project Charter Template

| Project Title | |
|---|---|
| Project Manager: | Project Team Members: |
| Problem Statement: | Goal Statement: |
| Project Scope Statement:<br><br>Constraints: | Stakeholders: |
| Project Risks:<br>1)<br><br>2)<br><br>3) | Risk Strategy: |

| Project Milestones:<br>1)<br><br>2)<br><br>3)<br><br>4) | Deliverables: | Target Completion Date: | Actual Completion Date: |
|---|---|---|---|

| Sponsor Signature: | Date: |
|---|---|

Project planning generally begins with the project team writing a description of the project along with a clear statement of the project objectives. The team then creates a *work breakdown structure* (WBS) with a corresponding project *organization and functional responsibility chart*. The WBS provides an illustration of the project's scope and all tasks become the basis for monitoring the project's progress. The organization and functional responsibility chart identifies the project team and shows the responsibilities assigned to the team members for the various tasks. A project schedule also will be prepared and resource requirements will be planned, also known as *resource loading*. Resource loading involves scheduling the necessary resources (people and equipment, for example) for given project activities at given times.

The results of these planning efforts then should be compiled into a document known as the *project plan*. A project plan should be *written,* even if only one person is involved, so the project member(s) can track the progress of the project. In other words, at any point during the project the plan provides the stakeholders information on what tasks need to be completed at what time, when should they be completed and by what person or team, and what other resources have been assigned to the task at hand. The project plan goes through a review and approval process, which will be individual to each organization. Small functional projects may simply need the approval of the functional manager. For larger projects, the project manager and/or project sponsor may be responsible for approving the project. In the public sector, project plans often go through a formal review process. Once the review and approval of the project is complete, however, the project now is ready to be executed.

In 2001, Sears and Michelin executives initiated discussions to improve inter-company collaboration and visibility across their supply chain and to cut supply-chain costs by reducing inventory levels. They concluded that collaborative planning, forecasting and replenishment (CPFR) could be a viable solution and a joint Sears/Michelin team developed a business case to gain management support and obtain the resources needed to complete the project. (See Chapter 5 for an additional discussion of CPFR.) Once approval was received, the Sears/Michelin project team developed a list of activities that would need to be performed before CPFR could be implemented. This list became the basis for the project plan and the team assigned task responsibilities to cross-company teams and timelines for each activity with target completion dates. The project plan was the blueprint for the teams and central to the timely completion and success of the project.

The nine essential elements of a project plan include:

1. *Overview.* Short project description, deliverables; major milestones.

2. *Objectives.* Details of project deliverables.

3. *Technical and managerial approaches.* Special practices beyond normal procedures.

4. *Contractual agreements.* Detailed description of agreements with client and suppliers.

5. *Project schedule.* Timeline of all project-related activities and major deliverables, milestones.

6. *Project budget.* Capital and operating expenses.

7. *Risk management.* Develop solutions to eliminate or mitigate potential problems.

8. *Resource requirements.* Project team and skill requirements.

9. *Evaluation methods.* Evaluation standards and procedures; monitoring requirements.[11]

The following sections provide a more detailed discussion on the project schedule, project budget, resource requirements and risk analysis.

## The Project Schedule

A project consists of many interdependent tasks involving multiple functions including supply management. Thus, supply management professionals should be involved in the development of the project schedule as it relates to those supply management activities required in the project. The project manager and team members should identify all required tasks to complete the project, estimate the duration of each task and compile them into a schedule that is logical and meets delivery requirements. Once the schedule is complete, the project manager, with supply management and other team members, should use the schedule to monitor and control the project tasks to assure they stay on schedule and complete the project on time.

Project teams generally start with a *work breakdown structure* (WBS) as a basis for the project schedule, as mentioned earlier, which is a collection of all project activities grouped in some logical fashion under major categories. Figure 2-16 provides an example of a WBS.

The WBS then becomes one input to the schedule. Other inputs are the expected task times and any time or resource constraints to the schedule. For example, the supply management professional assigned to the project may be available only for a certain number of hours each day, which would extend the expected time to complete the assigned tasks. Ideally, task time estimates should be determined based on historical data and estimates from the people who will actually be performing the tasks. In reality, these estimates often are based on the project due date (and often the reason for many late projects).

**Figure 2-16    Work Breakdown Structure (WBS)**

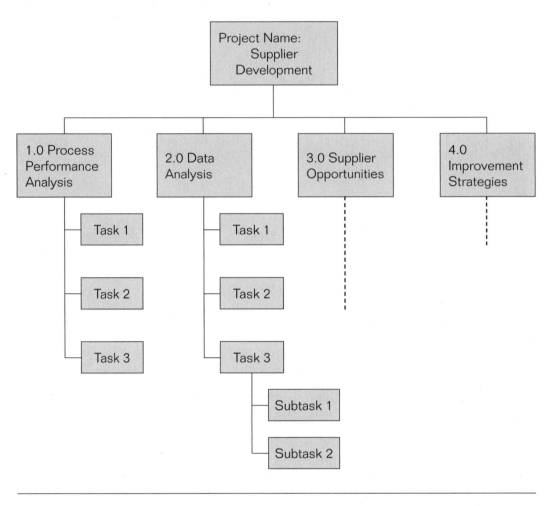

Based on this information, the schedule is created, which shows each project activity along with start and end times. Many organizations use *Gantt charts* because they are relatively easy to create and read. The Gantt chart is a horizontal bar chart used in project management that is commonly used to plot the planned and actual progress of project activities (*ISM Glossary,* 2006). These forms may include any standard contract templates, descriptions of the items or services that will be purchased, all nondisclosure agreements, and evaluation criteria for the proposals.

The disadvantages of these charts lies in the difficulty of interpreting them when there are several activities that begin and end at the same time, and visually determining the *critical path*. The critical path is the set of those tasks that cannot be delayed without delaying the entire project.

The *Critical Path Method* (CPM) and *Program Evaluation and Review Technique* (PERT) are two similar forms of network diagrams that graphically portray the sequential relationships and interdependencies between the project tasks. The CPM involves analyzing all the steps in a complex project to identify the shortest path in which any segment delay would cause delay in the final completion of the entire project. The shortest route is called the "critical path." (*ISM Glossary,* 2006) The PERT is a network planning technique used for controlling the activities in a project. Each activity is assigned a pessimistic, probable and optimistic estimate of duration. The critical path and project duration are determined and progress monitored using this data. (*ISM Glossary,* 2006) The diagrams look much the same with precedent and subsequent tasks clearly identified in the network and the time duration and function of each task included. The networks also are used to identify the critical path.

However, the method used to calculate the estimated start and end times for each task differs between the CPM and the PERT. The CPM uses concrete time estimates while the PERT uses probabilistic time estimates. The advantage of the CPM is time savings in the calculations, while the PERT should offer more realistic time estimates. The PERT also allows for what-if analyses by changing the probabilities. Today, Gantt charts and CPM and PERT diagrams usually are created using Excel spreadsheets for simpler projects and project scheduling software such as Microsoft Project™ or Primavera™ for complex projects. The benefits of using a project management software tool include:

- Increased ability to effectively manage and understand project schedules,

- Improved ability to become productive quickly,

- Increased capability to build effective charts, graphs and diagrams,

- Better communication within the project team,

- Improved understanding of change impacts,

- Increased control over finances and the resources allocated to the project and

- More effective tracking according to the project teams needs.[12]

## Project Budget

The *budget,* a plan to allocate resources to the project, must be developed to gain approval for the project plan. Once developed, the budget is used by senior management to monitor and control the project. To make the budget meaningful and relevant, data on expenditures need to be collected and then reported in a timely fashion. Otherwise, current or impending financial difficulties with the project will be missed, possibly shutting down the project when these problems eventually are uncovered. Thus, the budgeting system must be carefully designed so that the numbers are accurately reported at specific needed times for decision-making.

While traditional budgets are organized by activity such as phone, electricity and salaries, project budgets are more relevant and easier to understand by the project team and senior management if they are organized by project task and the expected timing of the expense associated with that task. Project expenses then can be separated from those of regular operations. Figure 2-17 provides an example of a project budget. Supply management's role in the budgeting process is to provide information on contracted prices for materials and services and estimates for related human resources expenses to solicit, negotiate and manage any contracts.

**Figure 2-17    Project Budget**

| Task | Cost Estimate | MONTHLY BUDGET | | | | | |
|---|---|---|---|---|---|---|---|
| | | 1 | 2 | 3 | 4 | 5 | 6 |
| 1 | $8,000 | 4,500 | 3,500 | | | | |
| 2 | 10,500 | | 5,500 | 5,000 | | | |
| 3 | 12,000 | | 6,700 | 3,000 | 2,300 | | |
| 4 | 7,000 | | 1,000 | 3,300 | 2,700 | | |
| 5 | 14,000 | | | 5,400 | 5,400 | 3,200 | |
| 6 | 1,500 | | | | 1,500 | | |
| 7 | 8,000 | | | 4,000 | | 4,000 | |
| 8 | 3,500 | | | | 3,500 | | |
| 9 | 9,000 | | | | 6,200 | 2,800 | |
| 10 | 7,500 | | | | | 5,000 | 2,500 |
| Totals | $81,000 | $4,500 | $16,700 | $20,700 | $21,600 | $15,000 | $2,500 |

There are many examples of projects that run over budget. No matter how much time and effort is spent on the process, the budget is still a forecast and, as a result, subject to error. Thus, it is important to look at some of the project issues and address ways to overcome them during the planning process. One of the most common reasons for budget overruns is that unexpected expenses are incurred during the project in the form of machinery, equipment or personnel. To avoid underbudgeting, either an additional percentage is sometimes added to the budgeted amounts or the project manager identifies the items that have the most significant impact on the budget and then estimates a price change rate for each one.

There are also other reasons budgets are inaccurate. Waste, in the form of rework and defects, often is overlooked and should be factored into the budget. Also, as the project progresses, additional workers may be hired to meet deadlines; these workers then must be trained. As is often the case, existing workers are expected to train the new workers, which takes time out of their schedule and lengthens the project time. Lastly, estimators may be overly optimistic at the beginning of the project or there may be pressure from upper management to keep costs down, resulting in eventual budget overruns. Past experience, common sense and procedures can help overcome these problems.

## Risk Management

*Risk management* in general is the process of identifying elements or factors, and their probability of occurrence, that could lead to injury, damage, loss or failure. (*ISM Glossary,* 2006) When applied to project management, risk management is the identification, analysis and planned response to potential project risks. (An additional discussion of risk is covered in *Leadership in Supply Management,* Volume 3 of the ISM Professional Series.) As mentioned previously in this chapter, some initial risk analysis should be undertaken to assess the possible chance that a project will not be successful. A more detailed risk analysis then should be performed and documented during the project planning stage. Possible risks may be associated with the project team itself, the customer, senior management, the budget, quality issues or acts of nature, to name a few. There also may be risks that are interrelated and those connections need to be addressed. For example, the risk of a shortfall in the budget may be related to project quality. Supply management's assessment of risk is an important part of the analysis, because there is the chance for supply interruptions or delays, or the threat of rising prices for goods or services, among other risks, particularly for longer projects.

To identify the possible project risks, meeting with the stakeholders, either through a brainstorming session or individual interviews, is important. The project manager may incorporate *scenario analysis* into the interviews and meetings, where possible sequences of events are generated. An analysis of the schedule by reviewing the network diagram or Gantt chart also may turn up possible risks. Lastly, reviews of similar past projects may help the team identify potential risks for the current project. With collected data in hand, the project team can develop a risk profile that contains a list of the possible risks and the possible magnitude of the risks. Figure 2-18 provides an example of a risk assessment document that may be used to track associated project risks. The most important risks should be kept at the top of the document and at least one person should be assigned the responsibility for monitoring and managing that risk. This record also should be updated regularly. A *risk matrix* (see Figure 2-19) also may be helpful in visually assessing the various project risks in terms of the probability of each risk occurring and the consequences of that risk.

## Resource Requirements Plan

The project manager will need to select the project management team(s) and each project team member will have certain roles and responsibilities throughout the life of the project based on his or her expertise. A *responsibility matrix* is a referral tool that will help the project manager, particularly in complex projects. Shown in Figure 2-20, it identifies the responsibilities for each person or group for the major project activities. It also should show the interactions that will take place across the various departments and organizations involved in the project. Sometimes coding of responsibilities for each task is helpful for the project team. Coding activities might include (1) direct responsibility, (2) needs notification, (3) issues approval or (4) support. The project manager must determine or forecast any necessary resources to complete the project, which become the basis for the budget discussed previously.

**Figure 2-18    Risk Analysis**

| Risk # | Description of Risk | Related Risk(s) | Probability of Risk Occurring | Consequences of Risk | Rank | Actions to Manage/ Mitigate Risk |
|---|---|---|---|---|---|---|
|  |  |  |  |  |  |  |
|  |  |  |  |  |  |  |
|  |  |  |  |  |  |  |
|  |  |  |  |  |  |  |

**Figure 2-19    Risk Matrix**

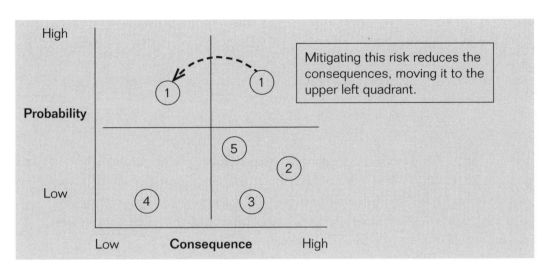

**Figure 2-20    Responsibility Assignment Matrix**

| Project Phase | Task | Project Manager | Supply Mgt. — Contracts Team | Technical Team | Operations Improvement Team | |
|---|---|---|---|---|---|---|
| | | | **PROJECT TEAM** | | | |
| Analyze Need | A1 | ○ | ● | ● | ● | |
| | A2 | ● | ○ | ○ | ◆ | |
| | A3 | ◆ | ● | ● | ■ | |
| Solicit Quotes | B2 | ○ | ◆ | ● | | |
| | B2 | ■ | ○ | ● | | |
| Write RFP | C1 | | ■ | ◆ | ○ | |
| | C2 | ◆ | ◆ | ■ | ○ | |
| | . . . . | | | | | |

**Coding:**   ○ Approval   ● Responsible   ◆ Notification   ■ Support

# Supply Management's Role in Project Planning

During the planning stage, the project manager should involve the relevant stakeholders, including supply management, to decide what should be outsourced. While the project team may develop the specifications and/or drawings for all contracted work, supply management should be included in these meetings to offer its expertise. For example, supply management professionals provide needed input on the contractual aspects of the project plan and their expertise on product or service specifications.

Generally, purchase and acquisition planning starts because the project team has performed an insourcing/outsourcing analysis and determined that at least some portions of the project will be outsourced to a third party. Outsourcing usually occurs when an organization does not have the internal expertise, time or all the resources required to complete the project on its own. In this event, the team can use the resource requirement estimates performed during this stage to solicit and review incoming proposals from potential suppliers.

The insourcing/outsourcing analysis is performed by estimating the resources, skills, equipment and services that will be required as well as any time constraints placed on the project. For example, the World Bank Group, with a mission "to fight poverty and improve the living standards of people in the developing world," lends about $20 billion each year. The Washington, D.C.–based bank "contracts with thousands of service providers and contractors every year to provide technical and managerial services for projects in more than 80 countries." A project was developed to move from a highly manual process that was used to select consulting services to a "robust Web-based e-procurement solution" that required supply management's expertise. One of the first steps was to perform what the bank termed *discovery and assessment.* The project team "conducted stakeholder interviews, user interviews and focus group meetings on specific topics." This phase allowed the team to identify any strengths and weaknesses in the current process and provide recommendations for process improvements.[13]

At this stage, supply management personnel may draw up a *Procurement Management Plan.* This plan details how supply management will oversee the procurement process. According to the *PMBOK®,*[14] the plan may include:

- The types of contracts that will be used,

- The person(s) assigned to any required estimates,

- The responsibilities of the project team related to procurement,

- Documentation that will be used,

- Coordination between supply management, scheduling and performance reporting,

- Management of lead times,

- Management of risk,

- Format for statements of work,

- Process to identify qualified suppliers and

- Performance metrics that will be used to manage the contracts and evaluate suppliers.

Supply management professionals prepare any documentation needed to define the scope of work, request responses from suppliers and select the suppliers that will be contracted for the project, develop the project schedule for supply management-related activities and create the budget. Some examples of these documents are discussed in the next section.

## Scope of Work Documentation

The assigned supply management professional or team typically develops a description of the work that will be required of each supplier/contractor, otherwise known as the *scope of work*. This supply management person or team also will have to determine the terms of the contract and how the supplier/contractor will be evaluated. All requirements will be developed into a document that could be a *request for proposal* (RFP), a *request for quotation* (RFQ) or an *invitation for bid* (IFB). According to the *ISM Glossary* (2006), an RFQ is "a solicitation document used to obtain price quotes for a specified product or service. These are often a follow-up to an earlier Request for Information (RFI). The law may or may not treat a quotation as a binding offer." RFQs often are used in the event supply management is buying commodities or services that can be priced on an hourly basis. If the project team already knows the scope of work required, such as in the case of a road construction project, an IFB is appropriate. An IFB is "the request made to potential suppliers for a bid on goods or services to be purchased" or for government purchasing, "the solicitation document used in sealed bidding and in the second step of two-step bidding." (*ISM Glossary,* 2006) The RFP, defined by ISM as "a solicitation document used to obtain offers of price and proposed method of execution of a project," often is used when the complete scope of work has not yet been determined and the project team needs the supplier's technical expertise in this area (although this is not always the case). RFPs often are used for information technology or research projects.

Metro Health, an acute care osteopathic teaching hospital headquartered in Grand Rapids, Michigan, decided to build a $150 million facility that would house its information technology infrastructure and data center. Part of the project entailed selecting a strategic partner as Metro Health's hardware provider. All potential suppliers went through a "full RFI/RFP, bidding and contract negotiation process." The teaching hospital also hired an independent consultant to provide expertise in IT procurement and lease negotiations.[15]

The *statement of work* (SOW) becomes an attachment to a request for proposal and is described in more detail in the following section.

## Statement of Work (SOW)

The SOW is "a statement outlining the specific services a contractor is expected to perform, generally indicating the type, level and quality of service, as well as the time schedule required," according to the *ISM Glossary* (2006). There are actually four types of SOWs. The first type, a *design SOW,* provides precise design specifications and how the work will be performed; the second type, *level-of-effort SOW,* defines the number of personnel in each labor category (project managers, design engineers and account managers, for instance) and hours required to perform the work and is used for service contracts; a third type is the *performance SOW* that states what will be needed — the technical standards — but does not include a description of how the work will be accomplished; and the fourth type is the *functional SOW,* which does not include performance or technical standards but simply states the purpose of the purchased product. With a functional SOW, the responsibility falls on the supplier to develop the performance standards that will meet the project needs. To prepare the SOW, the supply professional typically works with the project manager to determine his or her perception of the marketplace and glean any past experiences with acquisitions of this nature. It is important to remember that the SOW is subject to contract law. Thus, it needs to be understandable to the reader and not ambiguous.

The SOW will help potential suppliers to cost or price their proposal as accurately as possible. It also can be used as a benchmark to help supply management evaluate the contractor's performance during its administration. A well-written SOW will minimize the need for change orders and reduce the number of contract claims and disputes that may arise. Once the RFPs have been reviewed and a bidder has been selected, the SOW is incorporated into the contract along with other parts of the bidder's proposal and any changes or conditions.

# Project Execution

Once the project plan has been approved, the team moves into the next phase, the actual deployment of the project. If the project was initiated for organizational process improvements or supplier process improvements, for example, a specific timeline (developed during the project planning phase) is followed for the process improvement implementation. When the project results require the procuring of a good or service from a new or existing supplier, supply management professionals, with plans in hand, begin the actual solicitation of suppliers and negotiation of contracts to support the project, one of the core steps in the Strategic Supply Management Process framework found in the "Series Overview" of this book.

## Requesting Sellers' Responses

The supply management team member, with any specifications provided by the project manager, develops a list of suppliers who should be qualified to meet the project's sourcing needs. The department should have on hand a list of suppliers it has dealt with previously along with their performance ratings. If the project need is new, the supply professional may have to find and qualify new suppliers. The supply management professional can use a number of sources to locate new suppliers, including trade journals, supplier catalogs, trade shows, trade registers and Internet searches. He or she also might talk to supply management professionals at other organizations or to salespeople within his or her own organization to obtain leads. Once a pool of possible suppliers is assembled, the supply management professional(s) and project manager analyze each supplier to assess whether its actual technical and manufacturing capabilities, and financial stability, will meet the project need. There is generally a direct correlation between the complexity and the expected cost to meet a project's need, and the time spent on this assessment.

Supply management personnel will develop a *qualified sellers list,* which contains those suppliers who will be asked to submit a proposal or quote. The requests for proposals or quotes will be sent to those on the qualified sellers list and those interested suppliers will prepare and submit their written proposals. The project team also may request an oral presentation if a potential supplier is new to the organization. Once the analysis is complete, supply management should have a list of desirable suppliers from which to select.

Before the proposals have been prepared and sent to potential bidders, there also should be a time period for suppliers to ask questions regarding the customer's requirements. The project team or the supply management team in charge of the contract may set up a meeting for the potential bidders, also known as a *bidder's conference,* to entertain questions. Alternatively, potential bidders may simply present questions in writing. The questions raised during this time period can be used to clarify the supply management documents in an addendum. For example, suppliers may need clarification on the statement of work requirements, the deliverables or special terms and conditions. Suppliers will be especially interested in how they will be evaluated in the selection process and in particular how prices will be scored.

Once these activities are concluded, supply management now is ready for the next stage of the process, proposal solicitation.

**Proposal Solicitation.** There are actually three steps to proposal solicitation: (1) origination, (2) qualification and (3) negotiation.

ORIGINATION. At this point, supply management has determined the type of contract that will be used during the planning stage. In the case of standardized items or commodities, a purchase order will most likely be used with no negotiation involved. In other situations with relatively low-value items, the project manager may provide a set of needs to the supply management team member. It is then up to that person to determine the materials, supplies or services that will meet the project needs and request quotes from different suppliers on a given contract. The supply management professional will review the credentials of available suppliers, select the ones that seem most capable of fulfilling the project manager's needs and send the request for quotes.

QUALIFICATION. Once the quotes are received, they are reviewed and one is selected. In certain instances, there may be large monetary gaps between the quotes, requiring the supply management professional to do some negotiating to resolve issues and settle on a price.

When the materials or services are relatively complex, the supply management professional will make a request for proposal as described previously. RFPs may have already been prepared during the planning stages to help with the budgeting process.

NEGOTIATION. If the project need is relatively simple, one person may be assigned to negotiate the terms of the contract with the supplier. However, for more complex, high-dollar value needs, a team often is assigned to the negotiation. A contracts specialist generally is assigned to lead the negotiation, but the team also should include the project manager who most closely understands the project requirements. Additional team members may represent various departments, including engineering, marketing, legal and cost accounting, depending on the specific project. Face-to-face negotiation is a complex process requiring a great deal of upfront preparation and training, beyond the scope of this chapter (additional information can be found in the *Foundation of Supply Management,* Volume 1 of the ISM Professional Series). The objective of the negotiation, from the project manager's standpoint, is to secure a fair, reasonable price while at the same time feeling confident that the supplier will meet the contract requirements within the time and performance constraints. The supply management department wants to be sure that the contract allows it control over the execution of the contract terms while still maintaining good relations with the supplier. Cooperation is important during those times when contentious issues arise during the project. Supply management also is looking at the possibility of future dealings with the supplier beyond the current project.

## Supplier Selection

Once the bids are in, one supplier is selected based on interviews, presentations, negotiation or some combination of the three. For larger contracts, a team generally is involved in the selection process and may include the project manager, a supply or contracts manager and technical specialists. In the event a bidding process is used, the lowest bidder usually is selected if it is capable of meeting the terms of the contract.

An important process step in the Strategic Supply Management Process framework is developing the written contract. It is important that contract clauses expressly limit the liability exposure to the purchasing organization. Once the contract is prepared, it will be sent to the supplier for signature. If the contract is signed, supply management then will administer the contract. Should the supplier refuse to sign the contract for some reason, the negotiation process begins again. A supplier may also *conditionally* accept the contract. At this point, the team has the option of accepting these conditions, refusing them or entering into additional negotiations. Any details specific to the contract(s) are included in the project plan and the contract is administered, a subject covered later under "Project Administration and Control" in this chapter. (A discussion of contract administration can also be found in *Foundation of Supply Management,* Volume 1 of the ISM Professional Series.)

## Team Management

As the previous sections suggest, a great deal of teamwork is required to successfully qualify suppliers and negotiate contracts for a project. However, large projects with cross-functional teams are normally comprised of a mix of people with different backgrounds, skills and attitudes, which must be managed effectively if the project is to be a success. The team members' working relationships will affect individual and project productivity, as well as impact the project customer and other stakeholders. Thus, the project manager should initially perform appropriate team-building exercises. Often a project kickoff meeting is used to generate excitement for the project and create a team environment. During the project, the project manager needs to quickly identify potential and actual conflicts and rectify them before they deteriorate too far, jeopardizing the project. During project execution, the project manager must not only be task-oriented — working on completing the project on time within cost and quality constraints — but also people-oriented — keeping the team members satisfied and motivated to stay on task.

There is also the matter of working with the suppliers who provide supporting materials and services. Outside suppliers are, in one sense, part of the project team. They are part of the project management process and the decision-making process. They become internal stakeholders because they have a vested interest in the project outcome and are providing valuable inputs to the project. As such, it is important that the avenues of communication remain open and suppliers are treated honestly and with respect to increase mutual trust. As a result, suppliers should recognize the reciprocal benefits of being involved in the project.

On the other hand, suppliers are independent contractors, there to fulfill their contractual obligations. Their commitment to the project may not be to the same degree as other internal stakeholders and they may, rightly so, be concerned about their own organizations' welfare and needs. In most cases, however, suppliers will recognize the benefits of a good working relationship because satisfying the project manager's needs increases the chances for additional business. Thus, the project manager must manage and motivate the suppliers similarly as the other team members, recognizing the differences mentioned.

## Change Management

Changes are inevitable with projects, mostly because the occurrence of some events will not always be anticipated. Change requests are more likely to occur as the complexity of a project increases or the project extends over a number of years, as in many construction and technology improvement projects. If the project becomes larger as a result of change or there are changes occurring outside the control of the project team, the phenomenon known as *scope creep* has occurred. Completely eliminating scope creep is impossible, but a good planning and control process is important to avoid excessive scope creep. Change requests are also the biggest reason for increases in project budget overruns. It is important, then, to establish who will have the authority to initiate change requests, what will be the procedures for processing and funding any changes and who will have the final authority to approve changes. It will be up to the project manager to control the change process.

Project changes also can affect the contracting process. Thus, the terms of the contract are very important because they can be written in such a way that is too restrictive. Contracts for complex multiple-year projects often are written on a cost-plus basis rather than with a fixed price to increase project flexibility. For example, a *cost-plus-percentage-of-cost* contract means that the supplier will be reimbursed for allowable costs based on contract performance plus an agreed-on additional percentage of the estimated cost, or profit. A *cost-plus-fixed-fee* is similar to the cost-plus-percentage-of-cost contract but the supplier receives a fixed fee, which remains the same unless the scope of work changes. In both instances, the buyer assumes a great deal of risk because the supplier has no incentive to contain its costs and the buyer will need to pay special attention to charges for materials and labor during the contracted period. A more favorable contract is the *cost-plus-incentive fee.* In this instance, the supplier receives a bonus if a cost savings is realized to the buyer based on a prenegotiated formula. Perhaps even more favorable to the buyer but more complex is the *fixed-price-with-incentive fee* contract. In this instance, a target cost, target profit, target price, ceiling price and share ratio are negotiated. The purchasing organization agrees to pay no more than a specified ceiling price. However, if the supplier's costs are less than the target cost, any savings will be shared based on the negotiated formula. The following example illustrates how this works:

Organization X and Supplier A have negotiated a fixed-price-plus-incentive fee contract. The two parties agree to the following:

Ceiling price:   $220,000
Target price:    $210,000
Target cost:     $200,000
Target profit:   $ 10,000
Share ratio: 65/35

In this instance, if Supplier A's costs exceed the ceiling price of $220,000, it will make no profit. If Supplier A's target costs are $190,000, it will make the $10,000 profit, plus it will split the cost savings of $10,000 ($200,000 − $190,000) with the buyer 65/35. Thus, it will make an additional $3,500 ($10,000 × 35%).

The terms for making changes to the contract also should be clearly specified within the agreement, including those parties allowed to initiate and authorize changes.

## Project Administration and Control

Once the project tasks are under way and any contracted work has begun, the project must be administered. This phase includes monitoring the project by collecting, reporting and documenting any project information that is important to the project manager and other stakeholders. The project manager then uses that information to control the project by making sure actual performance meets the plan. In other words, the project manager should make sure that the project meets cost, time and performance constraints. If the project is not meeting these constraints, it is up to the project manager to take whatever action is necessary to bring the project back on track. Part of the administration and control process is overseeing any contracts. The project manager, in conjunction with supply management, is typically responsible for administering the contract(s).

## Contract Administration

The project manager typically will supervise any work that is performed under the terms of the contract and by others on the project team who often interact with the suppliers as part of their project tasks. Contract administration responsibilities will include approving invoices from suppliers as the work is completed, preparation and processing of change orders and any interpretation of contract terms that might be required, among others.

To administer the contract, the supply management professional and project manager should create and then follow a set of control procedures to assure compliance with current contracting and compensation policies. All work should be properly authorized and certainly no work should begin without a signed contract. The supply professional should set up a contract file that contains the contract, budget, any constraints, work authorizations and scope change authorizations.

The supply professional and the project manager also should perform periodic inspections to ensure the terms of the contract have been met. The required quality specifications should have been written into the contract and provide a basis for the inspections. There also should be remediation and warranty clauses within the contract, in the event the supplier's work does not meet set quality standards. In projects, time is of the essence so setting time constraints for warranty work is important.

Additionally, a system should be set in place to deal with change orders because, as mentioned previously, they can make a difference in the total cost of the project. A complete review of each proposed change should be conducted either by the project manager or in a team meeting. Any concerns should be addressed, as well as the impact of the change on the project schedule, performance and cost. An information system that tracks cost variances — the difference between budgeted cost and actual cost based on the proposed change — can be useful. Each change should be documented and authorized along with any associated price changes and then be incorporated into the project plan. The following section provides a further discussion of creating a *change control system*.

## Change Control

Changes, as mentioned previously, generally come about because a stakeholder, usually the client or user, wants to improve the outcome of the project. As the project progresses, for example, the stakeholder may become aware of a new material or technology he or she would like to use. The team also may face changes in organization protocols or external requirements that affect the project's scope. As a result, changes may be requested that affect the project's plan, its processes, the budget or schedule or one or more deliverables.

Thus, the project plan should include a *change control system* that will handle the processing and consideration of all change requests. The change control process begins with a written *change order,* which provides a description of the changes along with proposed changes to the plan, process, budget, schedule or deliverables. To maintain control of the change process, all change approvals should be in writing and signed off by those affected by the change, such as the client and a senior manager. Although the project manager's approval is not required, he or she should be included in the discussion on any proposed change before it is formally sent for approval. If the change is approved, any portions of the project plan affected by the change need to be revised.

## Project Performance Evaluation

The project manager and other stakeholders have a vested interest in how the project is progressing. In other words, they want to know the status of the project in terms of meeting delivery, performance and cost objectives. *Earned value* is a measure used to ascertain project progress in terms of these three constraints. Earned value is computed by multiplying the budgeted cost of each task by the estimated percentage completed of that task. The values for each task then are summed together. Earned value is calculated periodically through the life of the project. A graph can be created to provide a visual representation of the project's actual progress, known as the *actual cost of work performed* (ACWP) against the cost-schedule plan (*budgeted cost of work scheduled* or BCWS) and the *budgeted cost of work performed* (BCWP) as shown in Figure 2-21. The cost variance is the difference between the BCWP and ACWP while the schedule variance is the difference between the BCWS and BCWP.

There are two difficulties in calculating earned value, first in estimating the percentage completion of a task (it is, at best, an educated guess) and the cost (money is often spent in "clumps" and is not a good indicator of project progress). Thus, project managers may calculate efficiency indicators or variances that reflect cost and schedule performance. A *cost performance index* (CPI) — BCWP/ACWP — also can be calculated to determine cost overruns or underruns, while a *schedule performance index* (SPI) — BCWP/BCWS — helps organizations estimate the project's scheduling efficiency. Any value less than 1.0 is considered unfavorable.

For example, suppose that the expected cost to perform a cost analysis, one of the project tasks, is $2,500 (BCWS) and the supply management professional assigned to the task was scheduled to finish the analysis today. In actuality, $2,250 (ACWP) has

**Figure 2-21    Earned Value Graph**

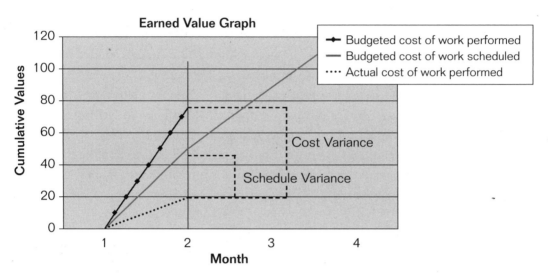

Note: The graph indicates that project is over budget (actual cost of work performed is greater than budgeted cost of work performed) and behind schedule (budgeted cost of work performed is less than budgeted cost of work scheduled).

been spent and the task is about three-quarters completed (BCWP = $2,500 × ¾). The project manager performs the following calculations:

Cost variance = BCWP − ACWP = ($2,500 × ¾) − $2,250 = $1,875 − $2,250 = −$375

Schedule variance = BCWP − BCWS = ($2,500 × ¾) − $2,500 = $1,875 − $2,500 = −$625

CPI = ($2,500 × ¾)/$2,250 = 0.83

SPI = ($2,500 × ¾)/$2,500 = 0.75

From the calculations we can conclude that more was spent on the cost analysis than what was originally planned and the supply professional is not making as much progress on the task as was expected.

These calculations also can be used to estimate the *estimated (remaining cost) to completion* (ETC) and the *projected (total cost) estimated at completion* (EAC) in the event nothing is done to rectify the situation. If we assume that the *budget at completion of the project task* (BAC) is $2,500 and the BCWP is $1,875 ($2,500 × ¾):

ETC = (BAC − BCWP)/CPI = ($2,500 − $1,875)/0.83 = $753

The total cost to finish this task will be:

EAC = ETC + ACWP = $753 + $2,250 = $3,003

Thus, the additional cost to finish this task is projected to be $753. When this cost is added to the money spent to date of $2,250, the total cost to complete the task is now $3,003 rather than the original cost estimate of $2,500.

Other performance measurement tools include trend projections and the *critical ratio*. A trend projection is a visual progress report in graphical format where actual values are plotted against the budget or schedule. The critical ratio is the product of the schedule performance index and cost performance index for a particular task, process or the entire project and is calculated as follows:

Critical ratio = SPI × CPI

James Lewis, author of *Project Planning, Scheduling and Control,* suggests an interpretation of the results:

0.9 – 1.2 — task, process or project is okay.
0.8 – 0.9 or 1.2 – 1.3 — review progress and make corrections.
Less than 0.8 — red-flag the task, process or project.
Less than 0.6 — inform management of serious project problems.[16]

However, it is important to look at both the numerator and denominator. For instance, a project task may be behind schedule but running below cost, suggesting that the project could be okay if that task is not on the critical path.

Using the previous example, the critical ratio can be calculated:

Critical ratio = 0.83 × 0.75 = 0.63

Because the critical ratio is close to 0.6, this indicates that the project task is in trouble and needs attention. If this were the critical ratio for the entire project, it is highly likely that the project manager would report the problem to management. However, because this is a single task, the project management team should be able to resolve the issues.

## Project Performance Reporting

Part of the challenge of working on a project can be all the reporting that must be completed. However, for complex projects, project managers need to maintain a good reporting system to ensure that project requirements are being met. An important factor to consider is what performance data should be collected and what process should be used to collect that data. For example, should special forms be created to collect the data? At what points in the project should the data be collected?

Once the data has been collected, it must be analyzed and then organized into a reporting format. The most common formats are project status reports, variance reports, time/cost reports and updates. The level of detail and reporting frequency should be appropriate for the target audience. For example, data often is aggregated for senior management but provided in more detail for the project team. All stakeholders should be included in the reporting system but not necessarily to the same degree. The client and supply professional may be more interested in cost and scheduling performance, while the supply professional and engineering also may want to know if suppliers are meeting technical specifications.

Supply professionals should keep track of their suppliers' costs, delivery and cost performance throughout the life of the contract. A file for each supplier and subsupplier helps the project manager monitor the contracts and provides the necessary information for a final evaluation.

## Milestone Reviews

The project schedule, as discussed previously, should identify the major milestones or points in the project where an important deliverable should be completed or a decision should be made whether to continue the project or not. An important part of project administration and control is to track the project's milestones, evaluate project progress, make any needed inspections and maintain a file of the milestone reviews. A specific person should be assigned this task, and milestone reviews should be kept with the other project documentation.

# Project Closure

The last step in the project life cycle is closing out the project. At this point, all personnel involved in the project will be transferred back to their functional areas or reassigned to a new project. The completed project also is transferred to the client or user department. An important step at this stage is closing out the contract.

## Contract Closure Process

The contract will be closed out at this stage of the project. Supply management, the client or user and other experts generally make the final inspections to ensure the work has been completed to their satisfaction and met the terms of the contract. Any deficiencies are noted and corrected by the supplier. Any corrections to the work should be performed before final payment is made.

The supplier typically submits a request for final payment along with a release of liens and certification that all bills have been paid. Any work guarantees for materials and workmanship also should be supplied at this time. Other documentation may be required per the project plan or contract and also must be submitted before payment is made. Assuming the supplier has met the contract requirements and submitted the correct documentation, final payment then is processed and delivered. At this point, supply management also should dispose of any inventory or other resources not used in the contract. Once the contract is closed, supply management should evaluate the performance of each contractor/supplier.

### Performance Evaluation

Supply management professionals also should evaluate their suppliers' performance to determine the extent to which they met the terms of the contract. The supply management professional can use the performance file established for each supplier as a basis for a final evaluation. This evaluation then can be used to determine the likelihood that a particular supplier will be considered for future contracts as well as a feedback tool to determine the lessons learned and anything that will improve current practices to manage future contracts.

These evaluations become a part of the *postproject audit*. Essentially, the post-project audit is a constructive review of all aspects of the project — management, methodologies used, procedures, budgets, expenses, record-keeping and progress. In summary, it compares what actually happened to what was supposed to happen. To measure the project's success, the project team may refer back to the schedule, milestone reviews, resource usage reports, change order documentation and progress reports. If systems were not in place or documentation is incomplete or missing, these are clear indicators of things that need to be addressed in future projects. The results of the audit should be formalized into a written document, placed in the project plan file and distributed to the project team and appropriate stakeholders.

Unfortunately, the postproject audit is probably the most neglected element of the project life cycle simply because project members already have been reassigned to other projects or moved back to their functional area. A postproject audit, however, gives the project manager and the organization an excellent opportunity to improve the process, retain those best practices and further develop the project areas that were lacking.

## Summary

Project management is an exciting field and supply management professionals play an important role in the success of complex projects. This chapter provided a discussion of the key phases that most projects follow, along with supply management's contribution at each stage of the process. Probably the key factor that will determine a project's ultimate success or failure is the degree of planning. Supply management personnel provide the expertise in contract planning for any materials or services that will be outsourced.

However, monitoring and controlling a project through the execution stage is also important. Supply management should be an integral part of the project as it administers any contracts. Lastly, a postproject audit will help an organization identify best practices that can be applied to future projects. Supply management professionals can use this opportunity to constructively review the contracting process and suppliers involved in the project.

## Key Points

1. Projects are typically created to (1) create a change in the organization, (2) implement the strategic plan, (3) fulfill a contractual agreement or (4) solve some problem or critical issue facing the organization.

2. Projects go through phases, which consist of several interrelated activities.

3. Each project has a life cycle.

4. Organizations generally align supply management's organizational structure with their project structures.

5. A project business case should be created to justify the approval of a project.

6. Supply management is involved in projects at the planning stage through source solicitation planning and selection.

7. Supply management continues the selection of suppliers and awards contracts during the project execution stage.

8. The monitoring and control of project contracts is the responsibility of supply management and the project manager during project administration and control.

9. The project closeout requires supply management to complete any inspections, ensure the terms of the contract have been met and make final payment to the supplier.

10. A postproject audit allows supply management to constructively review the project and make adjustments for future project contracts.

# 3

# Product and Service Development

$S$uccessful new products and services not only serve some purpose and meet specific quality, design and service performance requirements, but also should introduce some unexpected innovative feature that drives customers to buy them. Today, the consumer appears to have an insatiable need for new products and services, which is evidenced by the shelves at Wal-Mart and other "big box" stores. Organizations need more than one product or service to remain financially successful and competitive. Thus, organizations require some type of framework to help them meet the demands for both innovation and product and service development speed.

According to Steven Wheelwright and Kim Clark, authors of *Leading Product Development,* "By the time a product reaches market, it will have passed through every function, to one degree or another, in the business."[1] The traditional way to manage the process was for each affected function to work independently and then pass its assigned portion on to the next function, or what's known as the "over the wall" approach. However, this process proved to be slow and cumbersome. Operating with cross-functional teams has proven to be more efficient and is being used more than ever to manage the product and service development process. A number of benefits have been attributed to the use of these teams as cited by Michiel Leenders and colleagues, authors of *Purchasing and Supply Management,* including shorter development times, resulting in lower costs, and an improvement in quality.[2]

Supply management professionals have become key members on product development teams across many industries. Rockwell Collins, Inc., for example, includes supply professionals on its commodity teams who add value by identifying preferred sources of supply and recommending product components and technologies.[3] This increasingly important role in product and service development today has come about for two main reasons: (1) organizations have increased their focus on new product and service development as a means to compete and (2) organizations have moved further away from vertical integration in which several steps to produce and deliver a product or service are controlled by one organization. Today, 50 percent of a product's costs, on average, are outsourced to outside suppliers. As a result, the role of suppliers has increased and organizations are moving more toward involving them early in the planning process. Because of these factors, supply management takes a central role in collaborating and managing those key suppliers.

Thus, the subject of product and service development is important to supply management and will be covered more fully in this chapter. The first part of the chapter will include a general discussion of the product and service development process. The next sections will describe many of the inputs that go into the process. Finally, the chapter concludes with a discussion of the role of supply professionals in the process.

## CHAPTER OBJECTIVES

• Describe the product and service development process.

• Define the inputs to the product and service development process.

• Explain the role of supply management in the product and service development process.

# Product and Service Development Process

The product and service development process is a series of overlapping, interdependent steps or phases beginning with the generation of new or revamped product or service ideas as shown in Figure 3-1. Although sometimes it is difficult to distinguish between the steps, there are usually checkpoints between each phase where it is determined whether the project should move forward or not. Any outstanding issues are resolved at these checkpoints, if possible, before the project moves on to the next step. While some may argue about the actual number of steps, this text identifies and describes five in more detail in the following section.

## Step 1. Generate and Screen New Product and Service Ideas

New product ideas fall into four general categories[4]:

1. *Breakthrough ideas.* Breakthrough ideas usually redefine a family of products or services. If successful, these products or services result in an organization making significant strides in passing its competition and improving profitability. This was the case in the 1980s when Ford created the Taurus and Kodak introduced the disposable camera.

Figure 3-1    New Product or Service Development Process

| Generate and Screen Ideas | Preliminary Market, Financial and Technical Assessment | Develop Product/ Service Concept | Test Market | Launch, Commercialize |
|---|---|---|---|---|
| Market research | Business plan | Preliminary production plan | Marketing plan | Market response data |
| Forecast | Staffing requirements | Preliminary staffing plan | Formal production plan | Revised marketing plan |
| Product design | Logistics capabilities | Preliminary distribution plan | Formal staffing plan | Revised distribution plan |
| Service specifications | Supplier capabilities | Supply contracts | Formal distribution plan | Revised staffing plan |
| | Production capabilities | | | |

**INFORMATION INPUTS**

2. *Incremental ideas.* Incremental ideas are process changes that improve the delivery or quality of an existing product and service, while reducing costs result from incremental ideas. For example, digitization — the replacement of human effort with computers and networking — has resulted in a shift to online banking, increasing customer convenience at a significant cost savings for financial institutions. An online transaction costs a bank about 2 cents while a teller-initiated transaction costs an average of $1.24 and an ATM transaction costs approximately 24 cents.[5]

3. *Derivative ideas.* These ideas result in add-on features that extend, improve or modify existing products, services or processes. For example, many airlines provide ATM-style kiosks at their ticket counters that allow customers to check in without the help of a gate agent. In Japan, cell phones now also function as credit cards, train commuter passes, cameras and e-mail terminals.[6]

4. *Customized ideas.* Organizations also develop ideas that result in products and services that are uniquely created to meet the specific demands of one customer.

These ideas may also result in customized add-on features to new or existing products. For example, Apple Professional Services, with headquarters in California, will help an organization assess its current legacy system and then tailor software applications to meet its technological needs, providing a turnkey service.[7]

To generate new ideas, marketing and design teams begin by evaluating the need for the product, service or process. Organizations may have their own research and development in-house or they may contract for design services or new product ideas. For example, an entrepreneur may need some help creating the interior design for a new restaurant concept. IDEO, a global organization headquartered in California, helps organizations innovate by providing leading-edge ideas and designs for products, services, spaces, media and software. If an organization requires design services, supply management will be involved in the process, searching for potential suppliers, developing requests for proposals and negotiating the final agreement.[8]

An organization also will often use customer input for ideas. Many organizations offer a toll-free number that consumers may call to register complaints or make suggestions to improve an existing product or service. Most organizations also collect data through customer surveys, focus groups and interviews. The development of "green" mutual funds such as the Spectra Green Fund[9] or the Renewable Energy for Development Fund offered by the Netherlands' Triodos Bank,[10] for example, was driven by individuals who wanted to invest their funds in a socially responsible manner. In some instances, business customers may make a direct request for a specific product, using an RFP with specifications attached. They usually are looking to their suppliers for new product or process technologies that would support the team's development efforts. However, suppliers also may develop product or process ideas internally in anticipation of an expected customer need. Michigan-based Cooper-Standard Automotive, Inc., for example, developed a window frame module that replaced 15 separate parts used previously in car designs. Rather than wait to hear from the automakers, the supplier approached the customers' designers directly to convince them to use the new module in future cars. As a result, the window frame is used on the 2007 Cadillac Escalade.[11]

Additionally, organizations may use design tools such as *quality function deployment* (QFD) to develop the technical specifications necessary to meet customer requirements. As defined in the *ISM Glossary* (2006), quality function deployment is "a structured method for translating user requirements into detailed design specifications using a continual stream of 'what-how' matrices. QFD links the needs of the customer (or end user) with design, development, engineering, manufacturing and service functions. It helps organizations seek out both spoken and unspoken needs, translate these into actions and designs and focus various business functions toward achieving this common goal." HMSHost Corp., a food-and-beverage service subsidiary of Italian-owned Autogrill S.p.A. with more than 200 U.S. stores including Burger King, Pizza Hut and KFC, started using QFD in 1995. In a pilot test at Sky Harbor International Airport in Phoenix, Arizona, consumers were surveyed regarding their preferences for one of its menu items, bagel and cream cheese, and a *house of quality* (a "what-how" matrix as shown in Figure 3-2) then was developed. Different display cases, new heating equipment and changes in sourcing strategy were incorporated into the process flows to determine if key customer, process and product reliability, functional and financial performance requirements could be met. As a result of the changes, sales doubled within 30 days and remained stable over the next six months, and HMSHost expanded its efforts to other products and markets.[12]

A "what-how" matrix is known as a house of quality because it resembles a house. Notice that the house of quality takes the voice of the customer and translates those needs and wants into technical specifications. The "roof" of the house displays the correlations, or trade-offs between the product's technical characteristics. The

**Figure 3-2  House of Quality for Product or Service Planning**

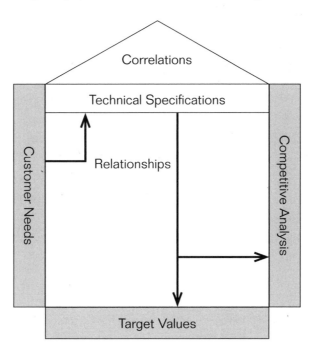

center of the house shows the relationships between the customer needs and technical characteristics, the technical characteristics and target values (specifications) and an analysis of competitors' similar product offerings.

The design team may use some other tools to help it screen new product ideas. Some of these tools will be discussed later in the chapter.

## Step 2. Obtain Concept Approval

Once the product or service idea is more fully developed, the design team presents its proposal for approval to fully develop and commercialize the product or service (see Steps 3 through 5). The best-performing organizations take a systems approach, creating a portfolio process to choose projects based on the organization's strategic objectives.[13] The advantage of product portfolio management is that it incorporates some discipline and rigor to the selection of projects and helps guide an organization in the allocation of resources. Using this approach, product ideas generally are broken down into the four categories discussed in Step 1. Screening and evaluation then are tailored to the specific product category. For example, financial measures such as payback or expected profitability might be applied to derivative and incremental ideas, while a more comprehensive set of qualitative and strategic criteria could be used to evaluate innovative and customized ideas.

To increase the chances for project acceptance, the design team should develop a *business case,* which outlines the justification for marketing the product or service based on a *needs analysis,* technical requirements, cost analysis, any environmental constraints, market size and potential, projected revenues and expected profit. A needs analysis identifies the target audience, the *customer benefit package* (the tangible and intangible product or service features desired by the customer), sales projections and the product's or service's expected fit with the organizational mission, vision and strategy. The business case also should include the customers' reaction to the proposed product characteristics and to pricing.

An organizational team or the owner (if the organization is relatively small) will assess the feasibility of the product or service design. For innovative ideas, the more completely a design team develops the business case, the better chance the product or service concept has for getting approved. When senior management is involved, it may use a scorecard to evaluate the project as shown in Figure 3-3. The criteria used in the scorecard should be easily found in the business case.

## Step 3. Develop Product/Service Concept

If the proposal is approved, the product or service concept is fully designed and the specifications are firmed up. A prototype is built in the case of a manufactured

---

**Figure 3-3    Sample Scorecard Criteria for Product and Service Selection**

| **Criteria 1: Fit With Mission and Strategy** | **Criteria 4: Core Competencies** |
|---|---|
| Alignment with mission | Potential for leveraging core competencies and strengths in |
| Importance to strategy | Technology |
| Fit with strategy | Operations |
| Effect on business strategy | Distribution |
| Effect on mission | Sales Force |
| | Marketing |
| **Criteria 2: Competitive Advantage** | **Criteria 5: Technical Capabilities** |
| Degree of unique customer/user benefits | Current capabilities |
| Degree of value to customer (value proposition) | Gaps |
| | Barriers |
| Degree of differentiation from other products/services in the market | Past track record |
| Customer feedback | Technical results, to date |
| **Criteria 3: Market Evaluation** | **Criteria 6: Financial Impact** |
| Current size of market | Return on investment (NPV, IRR, etc.) |
| Potential for market growth | Soundness of financial estimates |
| Degree of competition | Potential financial impact |
| Profit margins (if similar products sold by competitors) | Level of risk |
| | Ability to mitigate risks |

**Scoring:**
0 – poor or low
10 – excellent or very high

*Source:* Adapted from R.G. Cooper and S.J. Edgett, "Ten Ways to Make Better Portfolio and Project Selection Decisions," *Visions* (June), available from www.pdma.org/visions.

---

product or with services, the delivery system is created, which includes both the tangible and intangible elements. Marketing also may do some preliminary testing to determine a price point for the new product or service.

Fast-casual restaurant chain Captain D's, for example, was experiencing a shrinking core market and not attracting younger people. In response, the organization introduced a new store prototype in 2006 that included a name change from Captain D's Seafood to Captain D's Seafood Kitchen, a new logo, a new store design and an updated menu. As a result, "Guest counts are up significantly" and "customer feedback has been positive."[14] REpower Systems AG of Hamburg, Germany, approved the idea of a larger wind turbine to produce electricity that could be positioned on offshore wind farms. A prototype was first tested in 2003 at the organization's onshore test site in Brunsbüttel, Schleswig-Holstein, for maintainability and ease of service. Subsequently, the product was successfully introduced into the market in 2006 with its first installation in Scotland.[15]

In the event a supplier is developing a major component or module, the product development team will need to see a prototype to evaluate its performance. With the aid of *computer-aided design* (CAD) and *computer-aided manufacturing* (CAM) software, prototyping has become an easier process. The supplier submits its plans and design specifications for its portion electronically to the design team, which then is "preassembled" and evaluated against the organization's own design. In the late 1980s, Boeing used CAD/CAM software to design the Boeing 777 airplane. Its suppliers submitted their designs, which were viewed as three-dimensional images. The software simulated the assembly of those parts on-screen and corrections were automatically made regarding fit, interference or other problems.[16]

## Step 4. Test Products and Services

Once the concept is fully developed into a product or service, it should be tested in the marketplace. For instance, in 2005, Canadian-based Dairy Fresh Farms, Inc., partnered with Lucerne dairy and Safeway Stores, Inc., to test a unique patented dairy process that combines skim milk with canola oil to create a new 2 percent milk equivalent product. The product was tested in 205 Safeway stores in Canada by offering demonstrations, samples and educational materials to 300,000 consumers.[17]

There are several ways to improve product testing. First, an organization should create a standardized system for product and service testing. In other words, each product or service should be tested using the same survey questions, sampling plans and analytical methods. As an organization continues to test, over time some normative data will develop, which will help it to interpret any test scores. An important issue to address is how good the product or service is against the norm for other like products or services developed in the past. The product or service also should be tested in a "real" environment because the results are usually more accurate than the results from lab tests. Tire organizations, for example, road test their tires on streets and freeways; cleansers or detergents are tested in the home; new menu items usually are tested in restaurants.[18]

### Step 5. Commercialize Product

If the response to the product/service is positive, production is ramped up and distrib-uted in Step 5. Experience shows that organizations generally should start small and then change production and delivery as evidenced by demand patterns. New services may be initiated in selected markets and if they are successful, they may be expanded throughout the enterprise.

To increase the success rate of the development process, organizations should optimize the analysis process and evaluation of its current capabilities. The next sec-tion describes some of the inputs to the product or service development process.

## Inputs to the Product and Service Development Process

As shown in Figure 3-4, the product and service development process relies on a number of inputs for success. The product or service design should be in line with

**Figure 3-4    Inputs to New Product or Service Development Process**

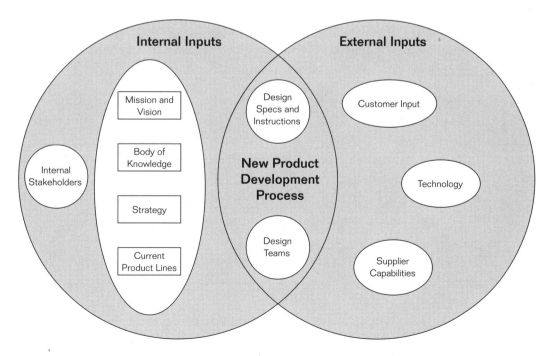

the organization's mission, vision and strategy. (See *Leadership in Supply Management,* Volume 3 of the ISM Professional Series, for additional discussion on these topics.) Any new product or service ideas also should be developed in consideration of the current product line or services being offered; generally, it is most successful when it is an extension of, or complementary to, the existing product or service. Customer needs and desires should certainly be a major factor in developing new product and service ideas. However, product and service development will be constrained by either an organization's own internal capabilities or those that can be attained from outside suppliers. For example, an organization will have a given body of knowledge and technology that will serve as a boundary, which can be extended through an external supplier's expertise.

Thus, an organization should evaluate a number of areas to help it develop products and services that will be commercially successful. This includes an analysis of the marketplace, whether international or domestic, as well as the current capabilities of its functions such as operations, staff, supply management and logistics. These areas will be discussed in more detail in the following sections.

## Market Analysis

First, an organization should perform a market analysis. Three popular methods employed to understand the marketplace more fully are the SWOT analysis, Porter's Five Forces analysis and benchmarking. The *SWOT analysis,* an analysis of an organization's strengths, weaknesses, opportunities and threats, is frequently used and was discussed more fully in Chapter 2. Porter's Five Forces analysis and benchmarking are other tools, which will be described further in the following section.

**Porter's Five Forces Analysis.** Michael Porter, a Harvard Business School professor and pre-eminent scholar in the field of management, developed the five forces model to help organizations develop a competitive strategy by examining their environment.[19] At the center of the model is the specific industry and level of competition or rivalry among the organizations. Other environmental forces that affect the level of intensity among the competition are the existing rivalry among competitors, the potential for new entrants into the marketplace, the threat of substitute products or services, the relative bargaining power of buyers and the relative bargaining strength of suppliers. Porter's Five Forces analysis model, depicted in Figure 3-5, suggests the importance of the role of supply management early on in Step 1 of the product development process.

Rivalry happens when one or more existing competitors realize an opportunity to improve their position or when they are responding to the pressure from other

**Figure 3-5    Porter's Five Forces Analysis**

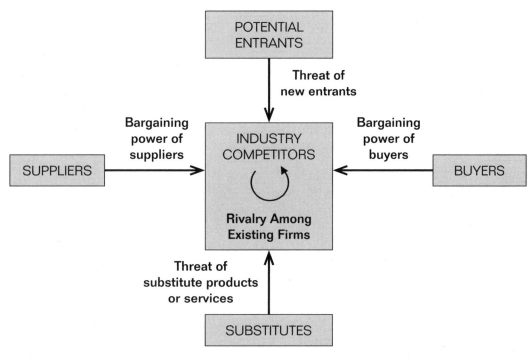

competitors. Pressures may come in the form of new product and service introductions, mergers or acquisitions or price cuts. Much of the rivalry and jockeying for position depends on the size of the industry (number of competitors), the pace of industry growth (slow to fast) and the extent of product differentiation (low to high), to name a few factors. For example, in the running shoe industry, there are two major competitors — Adidas and Nike — and many smaller ones. Industry growth is relatively flat while product differentiation is generally based on branding strategies. German-owned Adidas acquired Reebok International, Ltd., in 2006 to gain market share, increasing pressure on U.S.-owned Nike and other rivals. Adidas also has been aggressive in developing new technologies to increase sales. In 2005, it introduced a shoe into the U.S. market, for instance, with an insole computer that adjusts the amount of cushioning in real time.[20]

New entrants in an industry look to gain a share of the market but also bring in added capacity. They may introduce products by undercutting current prices, thus reducing profitability for the industry. However, the extent of new competition depends on existing barriers to entry, which include restricted or closed distribution channels; economies of scale; existing customer loyalties; the need for large financial investment; the cost for the customer to switch to another product or service; other cost issues such as proprietary technologies, favorable access to materials or locations or government subsidies; and government policies. Another related issue is the response from existing competitors. For example, Reno Air, a new entrant in the U.S. airline industry, was perceived as a threat to American Airlines in 1998. In response, American matched or undercut Reno Air's fares, recapturing its market share. Next, it purchased Reno Air to eliminate the competition.[21]

Suppliers can exert power by threatening to reduce the quality of their products and services or raise prices. When the supplier is powerful relative to the industry, such as the only supplier or one of a handful of suppliers, its threat is all that much greater. If the industry is not that important to the supplier's business, the supplier provides a product or service important to the buyer's survival, there is a lack of substitute products, switching costs for the buyer are high or the supplier has the potential to integrate forward into the buyer's business, the supplier becomes all that more powerful. For example, De Beers, a family of diamond exploration, mining and trading organizations with headquarters in Johannesburg, South Africa, has a great deal of influence in the diamond industry because it controls the most productive diamond mines. The privately held organization produces approximately 40 percent of the supply of rough-cut diamonds.[22]

Supply management organizations also can exert influence over their suppliers for a number of reasons. According to Michael Porter, the buyer is more powerful when the volume of purchases is larger compared to the supplier's sales, the cost of purchases is significant, the product purchased is considered a commodity, switching costs are low, profit margins are low (increasing pressure to negotiate lower prices) and there is a threat of the buyer integrating backward toward the supplier.

Lastly, substitute products essentially limit the extent of price increases to the customer. The price of aluminum cans, for example, is constrained because there are several substitutes including glass, plastic and steel. The price of televisions continues to come down as competition increases between organizations that produce plasma and rear-projection formats.

**Benchmarking.** According to the *ISM Glossary* (2006), a *benchmark* is "a standard or point of reference used in measuring or judging an organization's performance according to selected criteria." A benchmark also is considered the standard of excellence for a particular business process. Any benchmarking should always be conducted with the customers' expectations in mind, which can be gathered through surveys or interviews.

The results of the benchmarking process help organizations measure their own performance by examining other processes within their own organizations or against other outside organizations considered "the best" at what they do. In other words, benchmarking is "a process by which selected practices and results of one organization are compared to those of one or more other organizations to establish targets for improvement. Benchmarking can be performed by identifying world-class organizations and visiting them for information-gathering and comparison or by responding to surveys from third-party independent research organizations that collect, aggregate and disseminate benchmark data." (*ISM Glossary,* 2006)

## Production and Staff Capabilities

When new products or services are being added to an organization's product line, this will potentially impact production and staffing requirements if capacity is being fully utilized. Thus, it is important to go through a structured planning process to estimate human resources, production or new equipment needs based on the addition of new products or services. These plans essentially translate an organization's *business plan* into an *operational plan,* often referred to as production and staffing plans. A business plan includes the organization's projections for income, expenses and profit, which are supported by budgets, a projected cash-flow statement and a pro forma balance sheet. The plan should provide information on any new product introductions, expected market share gains and capital investments.

A number of inputs go into the staffing and production plans, as shown in Figure 3-6. An important component to successful planning is feedback from the product development team, including new product introductions and any planned changes to product or service designs. Distribution and marketing also provide important information, including demand forecasts and firm orders. This type of feedback and more will be collected to start the planning process. In general, a team will review the demand requirements, period by period, over the planning horizon. The length of the period will depend on the organization and could be a week, a month or a quarter.

The team then will identify the constraints and costs of the plan, as well as possible alternatives that might improve the plan. Constraints include the current operational capacity and capabilities of any equipment and the workforce based on the existing line of products or services. Operations should have the data on the use of current capacity (80 percent, for instance) and desired *capacity cushion.* The capacity cushion is "the amount of reserve capacity that a firm maintains to handle sudden increases in demand or temporary losses of production capacity" and will vary from

**Figure 3-6    Inputs to Production/Service Delivery and Staffing Plans**

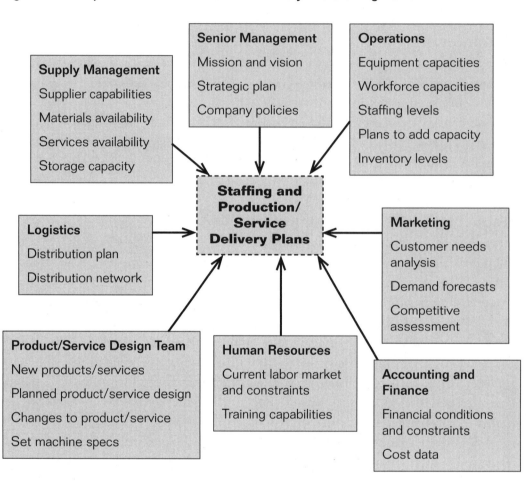

industry to industry.[23] U.S. manufacturers, in general, keep an average cushion of 18 percent; electric utilities prefer a cushion of 15 percent to 20 percent to avoid loss of service; hotels experience customer service problems if the capacity cushion drops below 20 percent.[24] In conjunction with capacity cushion estimates, an organization needs to know how much flexibility operations has in its ability to respond to change. For example, does operations have a trained temporary workforce available in the event demand for a new product or service is higher than initially anticipated? How quickly can new workers be trained or temporary workers be brought on board to fill the gap? If capacity is limited, an organization might decide to outsource the design and production of certain parts, components or even the entire product to avoid additional capital investments if the supplier can provide equal or higher levels of quality at a lower cost. A service provider may decide to expand its hours or hire additional workers to increase capacity, take reservations or make appointments to control demand or simply let customers wait.

Based on organizational needs and constraints, the plan then is prepared, usually through a series of revisions, until it is found to be acceptable. Once the plan is approved, the plan may be changed or updated as circumstances change.

## Logistics and Distribution Capabilities

The capabilities of both inbound logistics and distribution also are important when evaluating a new product's or service's potential for successful market introduction. If the product or service cannot reach the marketplace because of distribution problems, certainly customers cannot buy it. Borders Group, Inc., for example, transferred its online bookstore business to Amazon in 2001 after experiencing distribution problems. (In 2007, it discontinued its agreement with Amazon and relaunched its own Web site.[25]) Leapfrog Enterprises, Inc., a small U.S. toy manufacturer, ran into distribution problems introducing its 15 new toy products for the 2004 Christmas season. As a result, fourth quarter sales dropped 23 percent from the previous year as Mattel drained off market share with competing products.[26] In another example, Japanese-owned technology solutions provider Hitachi, Ltd., redesigned its global logistics operation in 2003 after experiencing excessively long lead times of 70 days to produce and deliver new products to its European markets.[27]

The best organizations integrate logistical decisions with all other aspects of new product development. For example, IBM introduces new product platforms approximately every 12 to 18 months, with small upgrades in between. When a new product is planned for production in one of its global factories, IBM must determine if there will be enough transportation capacity for inbound shipment of parts and then enough outbound transportation to ship product to its international markets.[28] In 2007, AT&T started laying 40,000 miles of fiber-optic cable to support an all-Internet network that will offer a series of new video programming services. The services will be provided through distribution agreements with cable channels in the United States.[29]

Some important factors, however, must be considered. For example, what will be the distribution channel(s) for the new product? Banks offer new products, such as certificates of deposit and other investments, through brick-and-mortar facilities as well as online. The Coca-Cola Company distributes its line of soft-drink and water products through several channels, including vending machines, grocery stores, gas stations and restaurants. Each channel has different transportation and storage requirements. Two other important issues are whether a new channel must be created and if the current system has the capability to add the new product. Sunny Delight Beverages Co., a beverage organization, uses a third-party logistics provider (3PL) to distribute its line of refrigerated drinks. In 2005, the organization launched a new shelf-stable drink. Sunny Delight owned no dry van carriers and projected demand for the new drink was highly uncertain, so it faced difficulties in developing contracts with new carriers. As a result, the organization went back to its 3PL and asked it to develop a carrier base for the new product based on some very rough demand estimates.[30]

Logistics also needs to have a good understanding of the organization's manufacturing (or service) strategy for the product. This is why it is important to have cross-functional design teams. If an organization plans to use a just-in-time or lean strategy for manufacturing, for example, logistics' inbound approach will vary from using a more traditional strategy. On the outbound side, if the organization plans a mass customization strategy, logistics requirements will differ from traditional manufacturing approaches. Because Hewlett-Packard (HP) sells computers and peripherals (printers, for example), it uses a mass customization strategy. Thus, power cords and instruction manuals are packed right before shipment.[31]

U.S.-based printing solutions provider Lexmark International, Inc., developed cross-functional teams to improve the new product development process, with several goals in mind: (1) increase design flexibility to allow for more product differentiation at the point of distribution; (2) significantly reduce the number of times a product is touched during final assembly and distribution; (3) incorporate an early review of size and weight requirements to reduce shipping costs; and (4) improve pallet configuration at the factory so handling at the distribution center could be streamlined. As a result, the team came up with a two-pronged approach to supply-chain management. The organization's high-end printers, with many features, are produced using a mass customization strategy, postponing final assembly until an order is received. Inexpensive inkjet printers, with fairly predictable demand, are mass-produced and shipped directly to retail outlets.[32]

Logistics also needs to be involved in product design when it comes to packaging. Packaging not only is a tool to help sell a product, but it also provides protection during shipment. Proper packaging can help reduce transportation costs as well. Packaging should be designed to fit on pallets and maximize the use of shipping space within a container, truck, train, ship or plane.

To minimize waste, organizations should perform packaging optimization, which can eliminate the use of unnecessary packaging by balancing the use of packaging materials against the protection each material will provide. The goal is to use the least amount of packaging that will provide an adequate level of protection within the shipping environment. The benefits of optimizing the packaging include a reduction in waste and cost savings in packaging materials and shipping costs. To improve delivery and restocking speed, UK healthcare retailer Boots decided to modernize its shelf-filling processes. The organization developed "fit-to-shelf" store delivery where products arrive in reusable plastic trays that can be stacked directly onto the shelves. The new process eliminated the need for outer packaging such as cardboard trays and shrink-wrap, resulting in less waste and a significant cost savings.[33]

The packaging optimization process begins by understanding the product, such as its value; its physical characteristics such as length, height, width and weight; and its fragility. It is also important to have information on the packaging materials that are available and the properties of each packaging material, along with the recommended application. Third, an organization should be familiar with the acceptable level of damage to the package, the modes of transportation that will be used and whether the package will be reused, for instance, as a container. With all this in mind, the final decision will depend on the packaging budget.

Several important questions to consider during this process include: Does the existing or proposed packaging material just meet or exceed requirements? Will less protection still adequately protect the product? Is any cushioning material required, such as Bubble Wrap? If so, will less cushioning still protect the product from damage during shipment?

The packaging material and the product will normally be tested to evaluate the potential for damage during shipment. Typically, the packaging material will be continually refined until just the right amount is found to protect the product at the lowest cost. If a package must meet certain national or international standards, some outside professional help may be required. The American Society for Testing and Materials (ASTM) and the International Safe Transit Association (ISTA) have developed testing standards to assess the various transport packaging materials available today. Testing labs also are available that have been certified by the ISTA. These labs perform drop and vibration testing through ISTA's Transit Tested program. The ISTA also offers certification programs for packaged products and packaging professionals.

Lastly, logistics will need to plan for the expected lead times and initial inventory levels required to meet product launch requirements and storage locations. These decisions naturally tie in with the location of target markets, transportation requirements, product launch strategy and product availability. In some instances, current warehouse facilities may be adequate if the organization plans a slow ramp-up in production. If, on the other hand, the organization plans to "flood" the market, logistics may have to contract for additional warehouse space. HP, for example, uses contract manufacturers located in countries such as China, Malaysia, Thailand and Singapore. Because it ships via ocean carriers in bulk, HP ships early to build up inventory levels in anticipation of its new product launches with resellers. Often, the product software is not in its final release so HP provides downloadable updates at its Web site.[34] In another example, Finnish mobile phone giant Nokia considers logistics one of its core competencies, coordinating the delivery of 275 million components daily to nine handset factories located in Europe, Asia and the Americas using a sophisticated software system. Finished handsets are produced and then delivered to resellers such as Sprint Nextel, MobileOne and Verizon based on an assemble-to-order system.[35]

## Supplier Capability and Capacity Analysis

One of supply management's responsibilities is to be knowledgeable about current supplier capabilities and to develop new suppliers. To make this happen, the supply management professional must understand the makeup and incorporation of any materials or resources that will be used to manufacture the product or support the service delivery process. Thus, specialists will be involved in assessing the capabilities and capacity of suppliers during the evaluation and selection process. Some questions that generally arise include: Which suppliers should be involved in the product or service development process? Will the supplier be able to meet our requirements? Does the supplier's technology "roadmap" align with ours? To what level should the supplier be part of the project, given the complexity of the product or service?

This analysis begins with *supply forecasts* to determine whether an adequate supply of the materials, parts or resources will be available to the buying organization in sufficient quantities to meet production or service delivery requirements, at the right quality and in the required timeframe. Any forecasting should be balanced by economic conditions and trends that might affect supply such as:

- Fluctuating lead times because of demand increases, supply constraints or a supplier's poor financial condition,

- Uncertain labor conditions, because of strikes or threats of strikes,

- Restraint on capital, affecting the supplier's ability to meet production or service provision commitments,

- Political events, such as new environmental laws, changes in political appointments or inflation,

- Natural disasters, new discoveries or depletion of a commodity and

- Changing trade rules or regulations.[36]

This information then can be used to develop a supply management strategy, including the insource/outsource decision. Once a strategy is set, a supply management team creates plans and options that are unique to each commodity. The forecasts, market conditions and proposed strategy then are presented to the design team and management.

If the supply professional determines it would be better to outsource, he or she begins the process of identifying, evaluating and selecting specific suppliers. Some suppliers may already have a working relationship with the supply management organization. Thus, those suppliers' past history and prior experience with the organization, as well as their industry reputations, would be evaluated. The supply professional also may have to seek and develop new or alternate sources of supply for materials and equipment.

If an identified supplier has not been prequalified, supply management does so at this time, essentially performing a risk assessment. Under consideration would be issues such as whether the supplier has the capability to meet the necessary requirements to integrate into the product or service development process. For example, does it have the technical capabilities, such as the necessary tooling? Does the supplier meet quality requirements? Does it have adequately trained personnel? Does it have the capability to meet the product development schedule? Can the supplier meet the lead time requirements for production and delivery? Will it meet the cost constraints?[37] This type of analysis may require a visit to the supplier's facilities. The supply professional also might confer with colleagues at other organizations who have had a relationship with the supplier to estimate the supplier's capabilities.

More frequently today we find that suppliers are involved in product development from the ground up, as mentioned at the beginning of this chapter and described in the Boeing example cited earlier. *Early supplier involvement* (ESI), according to the *ISM Glossary* (2006), is "a practice that brings together one or more selected suppliers with a buyer's product or service design team early in the product development process. The objective is to use the supplier's expertise and experience in developing a product specification or process that is designed for effective and efficient product or service roll-out." Suppliers may offer substitute products, processes or technologies of equal quality.

# Supply Management's Role in Product and Service Design

As mentioned throughout this chapter, supply professionals can make a number of significant contributions to new product or service development. They can help in the insource/outsource decision, estimate supply-chain requirements and recommend the best suppliers for a given project. Additionally, supply professionals can help the product or service development team select a design based on the available alternatives, which will help reduce the amount of resources used, inventory holding costs and transportation and production costs; improve quality; and reduce time to market. Lastly, supply professionals can contribute in planning for the expected obsolescence of component parts or resources as necessary or the discontinuance of a specific service provision. This is especially important for organizations that create products and services with long expected life cycles but short component or resource life cycles such as in the electronics industry. Some alternatives that organizations may use to mitigate the risk of obsolescence and the supply management's role include:

1. The organization decides to self-fund a lifetime buy of the component or resource. The supply management professional develops an agreement with the supplier to ensure that a component or resource will be available until the product or service is redesigned or discontinued.

2. An organization negotiates a commitment from the customer to financially support the future availability of a component or resource. The supply management professional negotiates with the supplier for a lifetime supply of the component or resource.

3. The organization does no preplanning for obsolescence. In the event a component or resource no longer is available, the supply management professional attempts to source for an alternate component or resource solution that will be an equivalent in form, fit and function.

4. The organization decides to redesign the product or service. At this point, the supply management professional sources the new components or resources.

5. The organization chooses to sunset the product or service because the component parts or resources are obsolete.[38]

As evidenced in this chapter, the supply management professional's role really extends across the entire product and service development process. However, organizations involve this area in varying degrees based on the type of product or service, the amount of required outsourcing and their attitude toward early involvement and cross-functional teaming. Figure 3-7 illustrates a number of ways supply management may be integrated into the process.[39] On some projects, supply management professionals are needed full-time and are fully integrated into the development project, teaming with engineers on the design of many specific parts that require a particular

## Figure 3-7  Supply Management's Involvement in Product or Service Development

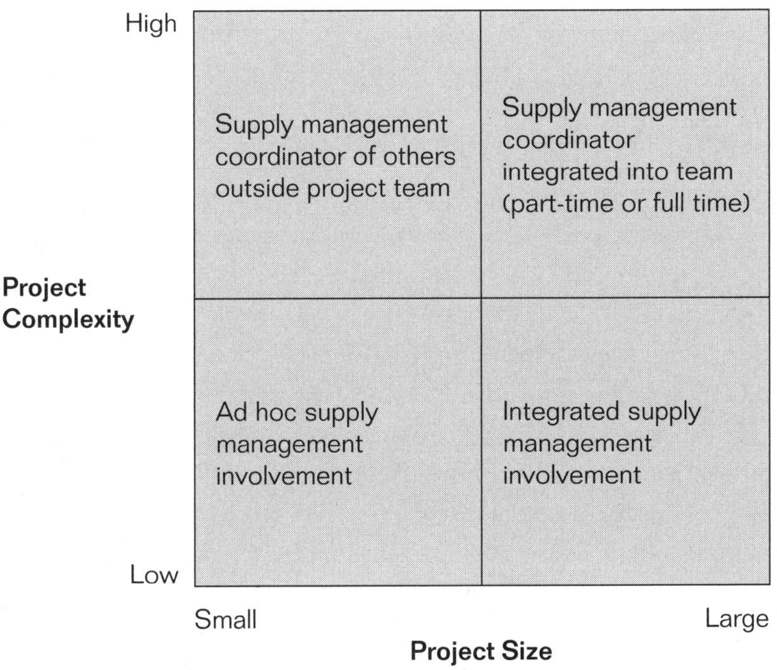

*Source:* Adapted from Nicolette Lakemond, Ferrie van Echtelt and Finn Wynstra, "A Configuration Typology for Involving Purchasing Specialists in Product Development," *The Journal of Supply Chain Management* (Fall 2001), 11–20.

technology. In the event the number of parts required is fewer, a supply management professional still may work closely with engineering but on a part-time basis. Supply also may team with internal customers on the development of statements of work (SOW) or service level agreements (SLAs). When supply management expertise is needed infrequently, someone may be called into the project on an ad hoc basis. While these first three scenarios involve a greater degree of supply management dedication, there are other instances where the supply management professional plays the role of coordinator. A supply management coordinator is on the project development team, managing a supply specialist external to the team; or a supply coordinator, along with his or her team, are product or service development team members on a part-time or full-time basis.

There has been a trend toward *early purchasing involvement* (EPI), which is "a practice that involves purchasing professionals in the new product or service development process from its inception." (*ISM Glossary,* 2006) Some attributes of EPI include:

- Participating in new product or service cross-functional teams,

- Helping evaluate and select suppliers,

- Working with key suppliers on new product or service provision projects,

- Using target costing to improve competitiveness and

- Using a quality management system to improve performance.[40]

At Cisco Systems, Inc., headquartered in San Jose, California, supply management works closely with engineers to establish the technology needs for its future networking products such as integrated circuits and microprocessors. It also helps decide which suppliers will be involved in the new product development process and then carefully oversees the suppliers' technology roadmaps to make sure they are investing in technologies based on Cisco's future needs.[41] In a CAPS Research study, M.A. McGinnis and R.M. Vallopra found that if suppliers are involved in the new product development process, success will be more likely if supply management also "has a significant new product development role."[42]

Supply management also may create a *qualified products list* (QPL), which will help it speed up the supplier selection decision. A QPL is a listing of products, product families, supplies and equipment that are known to meet the needs of the organization. Prequalified products or product families have been evaluated to verify that they meet all applicable specification requirements. These products usually have been tested in advance of purchase because they take some time to test and evaluate.

In whatever capacity, supply management might participate in a number of activities. These activities are discussed in more detail in the following sections.

## Research and Development

**Benchmarking.** Benchmarking, described in greater detail in Chapter 2 and earlier in this chapter, is a common approach for setting performance standards, objectives, measurements and processes. One form of benchmarking is to disassemble a competitor's product to uncover any clues regarding its superiority. If any organization is building a similar product, this may help supply management in the buying process.

To uncover information about competitors' products or services, supply management also may refer to trade journals, the Internet or other industry-related publications to gain information on top-notch organizations. Suppliers are also a good direct source of information. They can provide the names of organizations they find to be "the best" in a particular functional area or business practice. Lastly, supply management might benchmark by searching published industry databases.

**Request for Information.** Supply management also may gather information about available products, processes or technology by sending out a *request for information* to at least one supplier. According to the *ISM Glossary* (2006), a request for information is "a solicitation document used to obtain general information about products, services or suppliers. It is an information request, not binding on either the supplier or the purchaser, and is often used prior to specific requisitions for items."

**Supplier Research.** The purpose of supplier research is to learn more about current as well as potential suppliers in terms of the way they operate and their market positions. This knowledge helps supply management to develop and select a base of suitable alternative sources of supply, as well as prepare for the negotiation process.

Sources of information may include literature provided by the supplier, government reports, the *Thomas Register,* past supply management files on suppliers or database searches via the Internet. Supply management also may discuss the situation with customers or users, economic development forums, foreign embassies and other colleagues in the supply management field.

## Target Costing

*Target costing* is "a structured approach to determine the life cycle costs at which a proposed product with a specified functionality and quality must be produced to generate the desired level of profitability over its life cycle when sold at its anticipated selling price." (*ISM Glossary,* 2006) Supply management professionals use this approach to identify and communicate the allowable price for a supplier's product or service and create performance guidelines. Target costing has the promise to improve both the cost and functionality of a new product. According to a *Purchasing Today®* article, "Target costing is useful to supply management specifically in understanding supplier costs, taking full advantage of supplier expertise, understanding cost drivers and increasing the expertise of the supply function in understanding and contributing to a more competitive cost structure for the organization's products and services."[43]

As shown in Figure 3-8, when a product is developed, the new product development team has to keep pricing in mind and consider not only whether the customer will buy this product but at what price. Thus, a sales price will have to be set. The profit margin is the difference between the sales price and the costs to produce the product. Typically, organizations will start with a sales price — what the market will bear — and the desired profit.

The target cost is calculated as:

Target cost = expected sales price − desired profit

**Figure 3-8    Target Costing Process Map**

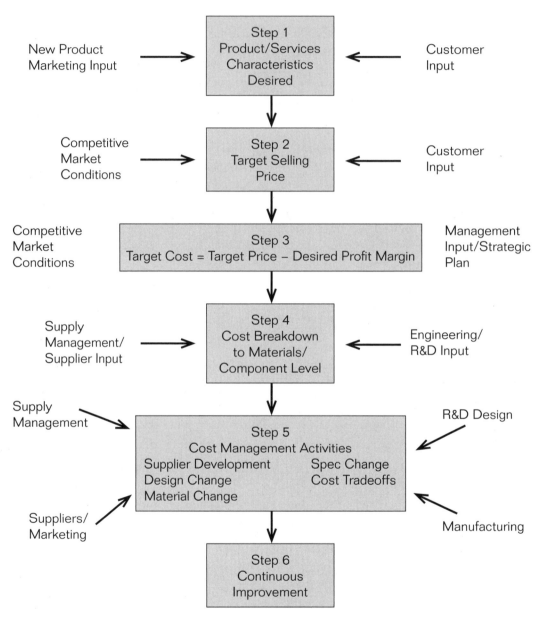

*Source:* Lisa Ellram, *The Role of Supply Management in Target Costing* (Tempe, AZ: CAPS Research, 1999).

The amount remaining is the total allowable cost to make that product or to perform that service, including materials. This cost then is allocated among all related purchases and internal costs, resulting in a target cost for each item.

Meeting the target cost, however, probably will require some cost management activities. Some changes may have to be made either to the original design, specifications or materials. This will mean performing a cost trade-off analysis. Internally, negotiations may take place between design, engineering, marketing and others to compromise to reach the target cost. Supply professionals also most likely will have to work with suppliers to be sure their prices come in at or below the target cost. Often further analysis and negotiation is needed in an effort to remove costs from both the organization's and supplier's operations to reduce the price to an acceptable target level. The purchasing organization may have to take a critical look at its own internal processes and make improvements. This process also may require some additional supplier development to help the suppliers find ways to cut their own internal costs. The following example shows how a hypothetical manufacturer performed target cost analysis.

ABC, a Silicon Valley manufacturer, negotiated a contract to produce 15,000 units of one of its products for $98/unit. ABC's normal profit margin is 25 percent. Thus, the target cost was calculated as follows:

Target cost = target price − expected profit margin
= 15,000($98) − .25(15,000 × $98)
= $1,470,000 − $367,500
= $1,102,500

The target cost/unit is:

$1,102,500/15,000 = $73.50

The product development team estimated the cost for materials and production at $80. Thus, there was a gap of:

$80 − $73.50 = $6.50/unit

or a total cost of:

$6.50 × 15,000 units = $97,500

The team first analyzed material scrap and made recommendations to improve performance by 35 percent, which will reduce the unit cost by $4. Some improvements in material handling also were made to reduce the distance materials traveled and supply management negotiated with its suppliers in an effort to reduce their costs. These two efforts further reduced costs by $1.50 a unit. The overall result was a cost savings of $82,500. Management applauded the team's efforts and approved the contract, although the target costs were higher than expected. Later, management went to the marketing department to review the pricing structure for the product and some adjustments were made upward.

## Green Product Evaluation

While keeping costs down is certainly a priority, supply management professionals should keep in mind ISM's *Principles of Social Responsibility*. Specifically, they should work to reduce the amount of packaging materials used, challenge suppliers to commit to and implement waste-reduction goals, participate in the design of products that can be disassembled, recycled or reused and assess the environmental responsibility of suppliers as one of their selection criteria. It is also important that they assess and approve their active suppliers' environmental plans.[44] In many instances, governments worldwide are putting common environmental practices into law, such as the use of recycled materials, the disposal of waste materials and compliance with local, regional and national regulations.

Supply management can influence the creation of "greener" products at a number of points in the product or service development process. However, involving supply management at the inception of all product development on the design team will make the biggest impact on the environment. For instance, in the product design stage, supply management may research and make recommendations regarding changing out product materials that contain less ozone-depleting substances or hazardous waste. It also may be possible to reduce the amount of materials used without reducing functionality. Life cycle analysis also can be performed, which is the evaluation of all the inflows and outflows of materials on the bill of materials, as well as any by-products of the production process. Supply management professionals can determine the potential to recycle or reuse the product once it reaches the end of its life cycle. As mentioned earlier in this chapter, quality function deployment also may be used to produce more environmentally friendly products.

Additionally, supply management professionals and senior management must work with suppliers to ensure they meet organization standards. Suppliers should be implementing similar process improvement initiatives to reduce waste and emissions. They also need a formal environmental plan in place that supply management can review and evaluate and make recommendations for improvement. Lastly, the organization should send the message that environmental responsibility is a priority and will be part of the suppliers' evaluations in determining future business dealings.[45]

# Summary

Supply management professionals have played an increasingly important role in the product and service development process. This chapter provides a discussion of the role of supply management in the development process. A general overview of product or service development was provided. The need for assessing the market and internal capabilities also was discussed at length. Lastly, supply management activities that can make a positive impact on the process were described.

## Key Points

1. The product and service development process is a series of overlapping, inter-dependent steps or phases beginning with the generation of new or revamped product or service ideas.

2. Organizations that perform best in product and service development take a systems approach, creating a systematic portfolio process to choose projects based on the organization's strategic objectives.

3. To increase the chances for project acceptance, the design team should develop a *business case,* which outlines the justification for marketing the product/service based on a *needs analysis,* technical requirements, cost analysis, any environmental constraints, market size and potential, projected revenues and expected profit.

4. When new products or services are being introduced, an organization should go through a planning process to estimate human resources, production and other resource needs based on an organization's business plan. The team also should identify the constraints and costs of the plan, as well as possible alternatives that might work better.

5. An organization's logistical capabilities should be assessed. Factors that affect logistical capability include the availability of distribution channels, the effect of the manufacturing or service strategy on logistics and packaging issues.

6. Supplier capabilities also should be determined. Some questions supply management professionals need to consider that affect supplier capabilities include: (1) Which suppliers should be involved in the product or service development process? (2) Will the supplier be able to meet our requirements? (3) Does the supplier's technology "roadmap" align with ours? (4) To what level should the supplier be part of the project, given the complexity of the product?

7. Supply forecasts are used to determine whether an adequate supply of the materials and supporting services will be sufficiently available to the buying organization to support production of the new product or delivery of the new service.

8. Suppliers today are involved in product or service development from the ground up, known as early supplier involvement (ESI), with the goal to use the supplier's expertise and experience in developing a product or service specification that is designed for effective and efficient roll-out.

9. Supply professionals can contribute to the development process by establishing supply-chain requirements, benchmarking, helping assess designs, supplier research and target costing.

# 4

# Foundations of Forecasting Practices

In today's world, organizations are operating in a dynamic environment with constantly changing conditions. Customers change their minds resulting in quickly needed adjustments to production, delivery and service provision schedules. Disruptions in supply also may occur because of any number of factors, including weather, political upheavals, terrorism or new restrictive government regulations, among others. Businesses go through acquisitions, mergers or changes in leadership. New opportunities for growth also may arise through new product lines, strategic alliances or expansion. Thus, organizations are faced with making decisions based on this continual change. Typically, decisions are based on a *forecast* — a prediction of the future or, as defined in the *ISM Glossary* (2006), a prediction based on quantitative (numeric) or qualitative (non-numeric) data. Forecasters attempt to predict future activities, such as demand, with sufficient accuracy to use as the basis for planning. The overall purpose of the forecast is to minimize uncertainty in the decision-making process. Inherent in this definition is the idea that forecasters are involved in first recognizing and then evaluating the various forms of risk, identified as one of the top concerns in the Strategic Supply Management Process framework. (See the "Series Overview" at the beginning of this book.)

Forecasting is necessary to planning and operating any business, helping leaders take the proper course of action. Thus, it is important to make sure the forecasting process is effective. Poor forecasting can lead to customer service problems, understocking or overstocking of materials, underproduction or overproduction, too few or too many employees, among other issues, with negative financial implications. Large organizations usually have special forecasting units; however, whether large or small, organizations need some type of forecasting system that will support the decision-making process. Although forecasting will never be perfect, organizations should strive to come up with the best, unbiased view of the future.

Supply management professionals are actively involved in the forecasting process for two main reasons, beginning with the need to assure a sufficient supply of goods and services is available to run the organization. This means selecting and working with the most qualified suppliers so they are prepared to deliver the needed quantities of materials or services at the proper point in time. To better prepare the supplier, the best organizations share forecast data and jointly make adjustments as actual demand varies from that forecast. Second, supply management professionals must make sure that goods and services are available at an acceptable price and quality level. This is important because the price of intermediary inputs will have an impact on finished product and service prices, which may have an effect on demand.

Because of the importance of forecasting, two chapters are devoted to this subject. Chapter 4 begins with several basic economic issues and a discussion of business cycles. Next, a review of the evolution of the global marketplace is provided, followed by a discussion of the value of leading, lagging and coincident economic indicators, with some examples of each. Lastly, some sources of data used to develop forecasts then are presented. Chapter 5 provides a discussion of the models and mechanics used to prepare demand forecasts.

## CHAPTER OBJECTIVES
• Describe the economic factors that affect a forecast.

• Explain the impact of globalization on forecasting.

• Discuss the role of economic indicators in the forecasting process.

• Describe some commonly used publications and data sources used in the forecasting process.

# General Issues in Economics
The world operates with a combination of economic markets, and it is difficult to find a standardization of terms. However, this section will briefly describe three common types of economies.

## A Market Economy
A *pure market* or *free market economy* exists when the production and distribution of goods and services takes place through the mechanism of free markets guided by a free pricing system. In other words, businesses have the freedom to determine what materials and services they will purchase and what products and services they will produce and sell based on current prices, available supply and demand. Likewise,

consumers can freely buy what they want based on price, supply and demand. All labor, goods, services and capital are free from any government restriction or trade barriers so they can move freely across national borders.

In reality, no country operates with a pure market economy. The United States has restrictions to prevent monopolies from forming, although monopolies do exist. For instance, the U.S. Post Office controls the majority of letter mail delivery (FedEx and UPS provide premium express mail services), and cable service providers operate as a monopoly. Since the 1980s, Australia has shifted to an "open, internationally competitive, export-oriented economy." Although it still does not have a pure market economy, the Australian government has worked to cut tariffs and other trade barriers, deregulated the financial service industry and privatized many of the previously government-owned monopolies.[1]

In general, economists believe that the government plays a legitimate role in a market economy, because it defines and enforces the basic rules of the market. However, there is some argument regarding the level of protectionist tariffs (a discriminatory tax imposed on imported goods by customs authorities) (*ISM Glossary,* 2006), the amount of federal control over interest rates and the level of industry subsidies that should be imposed.

### Closed Economies and Mixed Economies

Two other types of economies that exist in the world today are the *closed economy* and the *mixed economy*. A closed economy is one in which a country severely limits the amount of trade with the outside world and relies on its own resources to support production and trade. While there are no completely closed economies in the world today, North Korea and Cuba exhibit many of the traits of a closed economy. Others operate with a mix of state-owned and private enterprises, otherwise known as a mixed economy. Most industrialized nations arguably operate, to varying degrees, within a mixed economy, including the United States, Sweden, France and Mexico.

# The Global Economy

Even with these differing economic models, from a global perspective, trade is relatively open today. Organizations generally have the ability to market and sell products and services around the world with fewer forms of protectionism than ever before. Global trade actually exceeded 30 percent of the world gross domestic product (GDP) in 2006 and accounted for 42 percent of the cumulative growth in world output from 1998 to 2006.[2] Organizations also are forming offshore partnerships and alliances. While the United States once dominated the global marketplace, its share today is about 25 percent. Because of lower trade barriers, international competitors have equal access to the least expensive forms of raw materials, labor and technology. As a result, they benefit from similar economies of scale. According to the World Bank, 20 years ago developing countries supplied 14 percent of the world's manufactured imports to industrialized nations, but today that number is up to 40 percent.[3] Thus, forecasting becomes more complex as organizations struggle to understand the nature of the country's economy in which they conduct business.

Globalization began after World War II in an effort to rebuild Japan and Western Europe. International agreements were created to encourage trade between all free nations. In 1947, the General Agreement on Tariffs and Trade (GATT) was formed, an informal organization that oversaw the multilateral trading system. The United States, Canada and Western European nations then signed the Organisation for Economic Co-operation and Development (OECD) in 1960, which allowed for closer cooperation when economic problems arose (Japan, New Zealand and Australia later signed the agreement). In 1967, a round of multilateral trade negotiations hosted by GATT and known as The Kennedy Round, resulted in agreement among the world's major trading powers to significantly decrease tariffs on all manufactured goods.

The World Trade Organization (WTO) replaced (GATT) in 1995 and has been a catalyst to improve trade relations. The WTO, comprised of 144 member nations, is the only international organization that deals with the rules of trade between countries with the purpose of reducing trade barriers among countries (http://www.wto .org). The WTO also provides a forum for trade negotiations, handles trade disputes, monitors national trade policies and provides technical and trade assistance to developing nations. Its guiding principles are that the trading system should (1) function without discrimination between trading partners; (2) be freer, with barriers coming down through negotiation; (3) be predictable, without arbitrary tariffs or other non-tariff barriers; (4) be more competitive, eliminating export subsidies, product dumping and similar practices; and (5) be more beneficial to less-developed countries. However, while trade barriers have decreased, tariffs and other forms of protectionism such as trading quotas still exist.

## Local Buying Preferences

The issue of local buying preferences has changed over the past decade with the advent of advanced communication technologies and a changing political climate. In general, organizations take a two-pronged approach: standardize where possible while considering local needs. The former German-owned DaimlerChrysler, now Chrysler LLC, for instance, manufactures and sells the Chrysler Sebring model in China, a car originally built and sold in the United States.[4] Wal-Mart's international division, which operates stores in Canada, Central and South America, the United Kingdom, Japan and China, takes its culture and retail concept to each country but "makes a concerted effort to adapt to local cultures and become involved in the local community" according to its Web site.[5] And white-goods manufacturer Whirlpool Corp. launched the Duet washer and dryer in the United States in 2002, which blended the organization's European front-load technology with a U.S. design.[6]

Other global organizations are looking at regional preferences within a specific country and then developing products to meet those needs and desires. Multinational organizations, for example, are looking for ways to market their products to China, a diverse nation with poor rural farmers as well as urban multimillionaires. The affluent accept global marketing and standardized global products but those in the smaller cities do not. The challenge is to adapt to the local preferences of the small cities as market expansion plans continue. According to Deepak Advani, senior vice president and CMO at computer manufacturer Lenovo, products will have to be developed there that appeal to local tastes. Lenovo partners with other organizations such as Disney. As he states, "They [Disney and others] don't take a global marketing campaign or marketing playbook and just execute in China; they really factor in the needs of Chinese consumers and present their value proposition in localized terms."[7]

As organizations develop more complex product lines based on local buying preferences, forecasting becomes more difficult and often less accurate. Some organizations have tried to mitigate this problem by standardizing as much as possible and adapting their manufacturing and distribution systems to market a global product to many country markets. Hewlett-Packard (HP), for instance, delays the final insertion of power supply and user instructions into its printer boxes until right before shipment.[8]

## Risk Factors in the Political Climate

Political factors, either locally or abroad, also can affect demand. New administrations, shifts in the political climate and government takeovers are just a few of the changes that may alter an organization's original demand projections. U.S. medical device manufacturers, for instance, faced great uncertainty in 1999 when the Brazilian government passed stricter laws and created a new medical regulatory body to crack down on drug counterfeiting and other related scandals.[9] Organizations often use published reports to keep informed of changes in political conditions, subscribing to reports by groups such as the Congressional Research Service, a unit of the U.S. Library of Congress that publishes country-specific economic and political reports prepared by specialists. They also often take the predictions of university economics and finance professors and other experts into consideration when estimating future demand.

There is also the potential risk of interruptions in supply because of political problems, such as a change in the government leadership or shifts in political sentiment. While the risk generally is higher in lesser developed countries, disruptions can occur anywhere. Immediately following the terrorist attacks of September 11, 2001, U.S. border security was increased dramatically, creating significant delays at all customs checkpoints. Ford Motor Co. was forced to shut down its plants for several days because of a delayed delivery of engines and drivetrains from Canadian suppliers.[10] Thus, organizations must monitor the political conditions and create contingency plans in the event a disruption in supply occurs.

## Cultural Differences

Organizations also need to consider the cultural differences when expanding globally. Much has been written about what constitutes intercultural competence but disagreement exists. However, it is possible to go to almost any bookstore to find a book that has exhaustive lists on the behavior appropriate for any given country. Because so many different situations exist among and between cultures, a list cannot possibly cover every situation. To adapt to the differences, it is first necessary to understand and value some general differences. In particular, it is important to understand differences in industrial histories, relationships to technology, natural resources, religions and geography.[11]

Cultures also can be defined as high context and low context. According to Heather Keller, "When communicating, people from high-context cultures, such as China, Japan, South American countries and Arab countries, take into account the entire context of the communication event rather than focusing solely on the spoken work. The nonverbal aspects of communication, the relationship with the listener, the situation, the background and the environment are also taken into consideration. People from low-context cultures, such as the United States, Scandinavia, Australia and German-speaking countries, on the other hand, primarily focus on the words being uttered. That is, they use direct, verbal statements to convey meaning."[12] Understanding these differences, then, can enhance the forecasting process.

China's white goods manufacturer, Haier Co., Ltd., recognizes cultural differences as its biggest challenge. The organization has expanded into the United States, building niche markets with niche products. Haier also hires local talent to run local operations. However, as Chairman and CEO Zhang Ruimin says, "When we aimed to be one of the top 10 retailers in the United States, our American managers thought it would be impossible to get there in such a short time." He goes on to say that while localization is good, any gaps in communication or culture need to be addressed quickly to avoid problems later.[13]

## Exchange Rates and Currency Risk

International currency exchange rate fluctuations also play a role in global trade and forecasting. Manufacturers, for example, were closely watching the exchange rates for the Chinese currency, the yuan, in 2006 because a strengthening of the yuan could have made "Chinese goods more expensive to foreigners, allowing other countries to compete better with China's low-cost producers."[14] (The yuan currently fluctuates with the U.S. dollar.)

Another important risk issue in global sourcing is whether the supply management organization should use its own currency or that of the country from which it is making the purchase. Thus, forecasting exchange rates is not uncommon. When payment will be made within a relatively short period of time, the choice is not that important. However, if the relationship with the supplier is long-standing or payments will not be due for an extended period of time, exchange rates can fluctuate considerably, adversely affecting the price that was originally negotiated. The most commonly traded currencies float freely today and rates quickly can be affected by economic, political or psychological factors. Some countries also may choose to impose restrictions or controls on currency exchanges.

German automakers BMW, Volkswagen and Daimler, for instance, have been hurt financially in the U.S. luxury car market by a strong euro against the U.S. dollar. Most production costs are based on the euro, making it difficult to compete on price against Japanese brands Lexus (owned by Toyota Motor Co.) and Infiniti (owned by Nissan). The Japanese yen has been weak against the U.S. dollar, primarily because of slow growth and lower interest rates in Japan. The German automakers have mitigated the problem, although to a small extent, by building cars in European Union countries that have not adopted the euro yet, such as Hungary and Slovakia. Some models are also built in the United States.[15]

The most conservative organizations pay with their own currency so they always know exactly what they're paying. Larger, more aggressive organizations will pay in the suppliers' local currency with caps on the amount of exchange rate fluctuation allowed or they will trade using a *hedging* strategy to help reduce business risk. Hedging involves taking out an investment that will specifically reduce or cancel out the risk in another investment.[16] Global fast-food retailer McDonald's Corp., for example, has a financial markets group, which is responsible for hedging against the risks of international exchange rate fluctuations.[17]

Two types of hedging strategies include the purchase of *forward exchange contracts* and *currency options*. A forward exchange contract is a contract to exchange one form of currency for another at a specified exchange rate on some future date. Currency options give an organization the right to buy a given amount of currency at a specified exchange rate on or before a specified date, but do not require the organization to buy at the end of the period. Currency options offer some flexibility; however, they're more expensive than setting up a forward exchange contract.

## Import/Export Issues

Organizations must consider a number of additional forecasting issues when they choose to buy and sell from others internationally. Sales will be affected first by how easy it will be to sell to international customers. Production costs also will be influenced by how costly and time-consuming it will be to purchase the supply of goods and services necessary to support the demand forecast. However, two other factors must be considered during the forecasting process as well, which increase the complexity of sourcing from international suppliers.

First, a number of costs exist that are not normally incurred in domestic sourcing, such as foreign taxes, payment costs (letters of credit fees, exchange rate differentials and translation costs) and commissions to customs brokers, inspection costs, customs documentation fees and import tariffs. (Tax issues can be extremely complex, so a taxation expert generally should be involved in understanding materials flows between countries and developing the most favorable terms and conditions.) Transportation costs and the additional costs to buy and hold additional inventory to avoid stockouts also will be higher. Additionally, the higher cost of expedited delivery may be necessary at times to maintain production schedules or support service delivery. The risk of obsolescence, spoilage or theft also is naturally greater because more forms of transportation are used and delivery times usually are longer.

While protectionism is on a downward trend, tariffs and surcharges still are used in certain circumstances to protect local industries. For example, certain types of imported stainless steel that contain higher levels of nickel content were subject to a surcharge in the United States in 2007. (Consumer demand for stainless-steel appliances has experienced an upward trend in the United States since 2000.) According to Lawrence Burr, president, Metals Service Center, Atlas Steel Products Co., "With the high cost of 300-series stainless steel, our customers [appliance manufacturers] are asking more and more questions about alternative materials." The Twinsburg, Ohio, organization is getting more requests for the 200-series and 430-series stainless steels that incur a lower surcharge.[18] Supply management professionals must understand and be able to apply the tariff schedules and calculate the tariff duties. There are also the additional costs to maintain the appropriate documentation related to customs requirements, international logistics paperwork and payment transactions. If these additional costs raise the price of a product too much, demand will be lower.

Legal issues also must be considered. In 1988, the United Nations passed the Convention on Contracts for the International Sale of Goods (CISG), which applies to the sale of goods between organizations in participating countries. The CISG differs in some respects to domestic codes such as the U.S. Uniform Commercial Code, so supply management professionals must be aware of international laws pertaining to the specified contract (not all countries have adopted the CISG). Complexities in the law may affect the ability to deliver goods and services.

The previous sections of this chapter allude to the fact that a sound forecasting methodology is needed to help deal with the uncertainty in today's global economy. Effective forecasting begins with a firm understanding of the nature of business cycles. Knowing what economic indicators are important to further that understanding also is important. Lastly, organizations need some sources of information that will improve an organization's chances for creating more accurate forecasts. The remainder of this chapter delves into these topics, beginning with a discussion of business cycles.

## Business Cycles

As mentioned previously in this chapter, every economy, regardless of country, whether free market, closed or mixed, experiences ups and downs. For periods of time, the economy will grow at a robust rate, with household income increasing, consumer spending on the rise and organizations expanding and hiring. There also are periods when the economy will be relatively flat, with little growth in wages, spending or business expansion. A third scenario is *recession,* when the economy is shrinking. Most economists and journalists define a recession as "two back-to-back quarters of negative gross domestic product (GDP) growth."[19] The GDP, according to the U.S. Bureau of Economic Analysis (BEA), "measures the market value of final goods and services produced by labor and property in the United States, including goods that are added to or subtracted from inventories."[20]

Evidence of the business cycle is apparent from changes in the GDP, unemployment rates, price changes and profits. The swings in the economy are known as the *business cycle.* The business cycle has five phases:

1. The highest point of output before a downturn;

2. Recession, or shrinking of the economy;

3. Recession trough, or lowest point in economic activity;

4. Recovery, or resuming growth path; and

5. Expansion, beyond previous high point.

The difficulty lies in predicting a business cycle. Organizations generally use a mix of economic indicators as a basis to forecast long-term growth prospects. More on the economic indicators commonly used today can be found in the next section.

# Economic Indicators

Understanding economic indicators helps supply management professionals identify those market forces that will affect the supply and demand for a particular commodity, product or service. "Economic data can be used to study past economic trends, analyze and understand current movements in markets and predict future market trends," according to an *NAPM InfoEdge* report.[21] As a result, understanding the economic situation leads to more effective material forecasts, supply management budgets and price negotiations. According to Richard DeKaser, senior vice president and chief economist at Cleveland-based financial holdings giant National City Corp., "Keeping abreast of economic developments requires shifting focus to the indicators that best help us understand our position in the business cycle."[22] Some of these economic indicators are discussed in the following sections.

## Leading and Lagging and Coincident Indicators

Because no one indicator can give a true picture of the economy, many are published and then analyzed by businesses and governments. The U.S. Bureau of Economic Analysis (BEA), for example, collects data on 120 indicators in three categories — leading, lagging and coincident — and also develops each set into an *index*. An index is expressed in a way that indicates price changes over time. State and local governments also develop their own indexes for local business use.

A *leading indicator* is a measure of economic activity that changes before the business cycle does and thus indicates its future direction. (*ISM Glossary*, 2006) Some examples include the change in the number of building permits issued in a given period, the money supply (the amount of cash and bank deposits held by organizations and households), inventory level changes, changes in stock prices and the number of unemployment insurance claims. For instance, residential building permits in Utah reportedly dropped 4.5 percent from January 1, 2006, through September 1, 2006, indicating a downturn in the state's economy.[23] Mortgage organizations, construction organizations and subcontractors and appliance manufacturers are just some of the businesses that would use this indicator in their forecasting process. Federal governments also use these indicators to determine whether to raise interest rates.

A *lagging indicator*, on the other hand, confirms that a change has occurred in the economy and tends to follow changes in the economy. In other words, if the economy is improving, the lagging indicators will confirm that phenomenon after the state of the general economy has changed. Some key lagging indicators include labor costs, business spending, prime interest rates, inventory book value, unemployment rates and outstanding bank loans. For example, if business spending is on the increase, this generally confirms that the economy is doing well. Lastly, a *coincident indicator* usually changes concurrently with a change in the economy. Some examples include personal income, nonagricultural employment and industrial production.

Two commonly used U.S. families of indexes are the Producer Price Index (PPI) and the Consumer Price Index (CPI), which are discussed in the following sections.

**Producer Price Index (PPI).** The Producer Price Index (PPI), actually a family of indexes published by many national agencies including the U.S. Bureau of Labor Statistics (BLS),[24] the UK Office for National Statistics (ONS)[25] and Statistics Finland.[26] The PPI, according to the BLS, "measures the average change over time in the prices received by domestic producers of goods and services."[27] The PPI is based on the selling price rather than on the actual cost to produce an item. For manufacturing, these indexes cover the different stages of production — crude goods (raw materials), intermediate goods (work in process) and finished goods, according to the U.S. Department of Labor, which oversees the BLS.[28] More than 8,000 PPIs for individual and groups of products are published each month; they are the first measures of inflation released each month. As of February 2007, the Department of Labor added indexes for the construction, trade, finance, transportation and service industries, a practice already adopted by Japan and currently being tested in the United Kingdom.

The U.S. Bureau of Labor calculates unadjusted indexes for all product groups using actual sales dollars. These indexes typically are used by supply management to predict price trends, determine whether supplier price increases for purchased inputs are equitable and as a basis for contract negotiations. For example, if Pulte Homes, Inc., a U.S. residential home builder, buys preassembled roof frames and the supplier is attempting to raise prices, supply management personnel could review the cost growth of lumber via the PPI to determine if the increase is legitimate. Supply management professionals and their suppliers also use the PPI to predict price inflation and negotiate price escalation clauses. For instance, in 2006, India's Hindustan Construction Company, Ltd., built an escalation clause into some of its government contracts after a review of the PPI for cement costs was found to be increasing.[29]

The PPI for commodities also may be seasonally adjusted when there is some economic rationale for doing so and when statistical tests indicate that there is seasonality present. Adjustments may be made for the normally occurring and repeatable effects such as weather, regular marketing and production cycles, model changeovers, seasonal discounts and holidays.[30] These seasonally adjusted indexes are used to analyze general price trends in the economy. Figure 4-1 illustrates the unadjusted and adjusted change in the U.S. PPI for passenger cars. The unadjusted PPI provides a clearer illustration of seasonal patterns, while the adjusted PPI smoothes out the effects of seasonality.

The disadvantage of the PPIs is that they are less understood and more volatile than the CPI. PPIs also are calculated on a national rather than a regional basis, which limits their applicability for supply management professionals. Lastly, they have been limited in usefulness relative to services, although this is changing.

---

**Figure 4-1    Annual Percent Changes for Passenger Cars, Seasonally Unadjusted and Adjusted PPI**

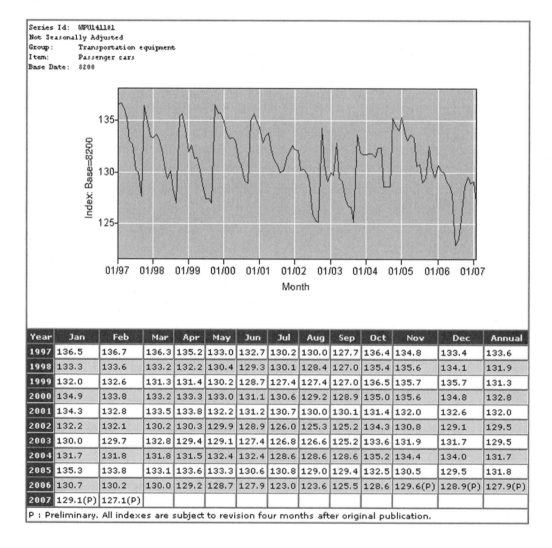

| Year | Jan | Feb | Mar | Apr | May | Jun | Jul | Aug | Sep | Oct | Nov | Dec | Annual |
|---|---|---|---|---|---|---|---|---|---|---|---|---|---|
| 1997 | 136.5 | 136.7 | 136.3 | 135.2 | 133.0 | 132.7 | 130.2 | 130.0 | 127.7 | 136.4 | 134.8 | 133.4 | 133.6 |
| 1998 | 133.3 | 133.6 | 133.2 | 132.2 | 130.4 | 129.3 | 130.1 | 128.4 | 127.0 | 135.4 | 135.6 | 134.1 | 131.9 |
| 1999 | 132.0 | 132.6 | 131.3 | 131.4 | 130.2 | 128.7 | 127.4 | 127.4 | 127.0 | 136.5 | 135.7 | 135.7 | 131.3 |
| 2000 | 134.9 | 133.8 | 133.2 | 133.3 | 133.0 | 131.1 | 130.6 | 129.2 | 128.9 | 135.0 | 135.6 | 134.8 | 132.8 |
| 2001 | 134.3 | 132.8 | 133.5 | 133.8 | 132.2 | 131.2 | 130.7 | 130.0 | 130.1 | 131.4 | 132.0 | 132.6 | 132.0 |
| 2002 | 132.2 | 132.1 | 130.2 | 130.3 | 129.9 | 128.9 | 126.0 | 125.3 | 125.2 | 134.3 | 130.8 | 129.1 | 129.5 |
| 2003 | 130.0 | 129.7 | 132.8 | 129.4 | 129.1 | 127.4 | 126.8 | 126.6 | 125.2 | 133.6 | 131.9 | 131.7 | 129.5 |
| 2004 | 131.7 | 131.8 | 131.8 | 131.5 | 132.4 | 132.4 | 128.6 | 128.6 | 128.6 | 135.2 | 134.4 | 134.0 | 131.7 |
| 2005 | 135.3 | 133.8 | 133.1 | 133.6 | 133.3 | 130.6 | 130.8 | 129.0 | 129.4 | 132.5 | 130.5 | 129.5 | 131.8 |
| 2006 | 130.7 | 130.2 | 130.0 | 129.2 | 128.7 | 127.9 | 123.0 | 123.6 | 125.5 | 128.6 | 129.6(P) | 128.9(P) | 127.9(P) |
| 2007 | 129.1(P) | 127.1(P) | | | | | | | | | | | |

P : Preliminary. All indexes are subject to revision four months after original publication.

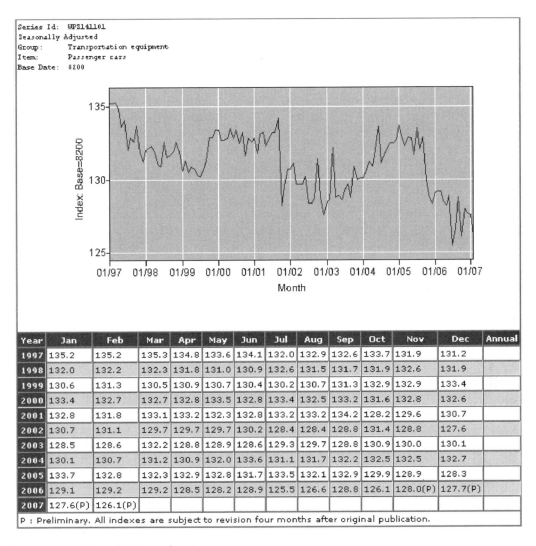

Series Id: WPS141101
Seasonally Adjusted
Group:        Transportation equipment
Item:         Passenger cars
Base Date:    8200

| Year | Jan | Feb | Mar | Apr | May | Jun | Jul | Aug | Sep | Oct | Nov | Dec | Annual |
|------|-----|-----|-----|-----|-----|-----|-----|-----|-----|-----|-----|-----|--------|
| 1997 | 135.2 | 135.2 | 135.3 | 134.8 | 133.6 | 134.1 | 132.0 | 132.9 | 132.6 | 133.7 | 131.9 | 131.2 | |
| 1998 | 132.0 | 132.2 | 132.3 | 131.8 | 131.0 | 130.9 | 132.6 | 131.5 | 131.7 | 131.9 | 132.6 | 131.9 | |
| 1999 | 130.6 | 131.3 | 130.5 | 130.9 | 130.7 | 130.4 | 130.2 | 130.7 | 131.3 | 132.9 | 132.9 | 133.4 | |
| 2000 | 133.4 | 132.7 | 132.7 | 132.8 | 133.5 | 132.8 | 133.4 | 132.5 | 133.2 | 131.6 | 132.8 | 132.6 | |
| 2001 | 132.8 | 131.8 | 133.1 | 133.2 | 132.3 | 132.8 | 133.2 | 133.2 | 134.2 | 128.2 | 129.6 | 130.7 | |
| 2002 | 130.7 | 131.1 | 129.7 | 129.7 | 129.7 | 130.2 | 128.4 | 128.4 | 128.8 | 131.4 | 128.8 | 127.6 | |
| 2003 | 128.5 | 128.6 | 132.2 | 128.8 | 128.9 | 128.6 | 129.3 | 129.7 | 128.8 | 130.9 | 130.0 | 130.1 | |
| 2004 | 130.1 | 130.7 | 131.2 | 130.9 | 132.0 | 133.6 | 131.1 | 131.7 | 132.2 | 132.5 | 132.5 | 132.7 | |
| 2005 | 133.7 | 132.8 | 132.3 | 132.9 | 132.8 | 131.7 | 133.5 | 132.1 | 132.9 | 129.9 | 128.9 | 128.3 | |
| 2006 | 129.1 | 129.2 | 129.2 | 128.5 | 128.2 | 128.9 | 125.5 | 126.6 | 128.8 | 126.1 | 128.0(P) | 127.7(P) | |
| 2007 | 127.6(P) | 126.1(P) | | | | | | | | | | | |

P : Preliminary. All indexes are subject to revision four months after original publication.

*Source:* www.data.bls.gov/PDQ/outside.jsp?survey=wp.

**Consumer Price Index (CPI).** In contrast to the PPI, the consumer price index (CPI) is one of the most popular measures of price inflation for retail goods and services. The CPI also is published monthly by the U.S. Department of Labor and other national agencies. The CPI measures the average change in retail prices over time for a basket of eight major groups with more than 200 categories of various goods and services. Figure 4.2 provides the weightings assigned to each group.

The rate of price inflation is important because it affects everyone, determining how much consumers must pay for goods and services, the cost of doing business and making personal and corporate investments and the quality of life for retirees. It also

Figure 4-2    Sample CPI Weights

| GROUP | WEIGHT |
|---|---|
| 1. Housing | 42.1% |
| Shelter (32.9%) | |
| Fuel and Utilities (4.7%) | |
| Household furnishings and operations (4.5%) | |
| 2. Food and Beverages | 15.4% |
| 3. Transportation | 16.9% |
| Private Transportation (15.8%) | |
| New and used vehicles (8.2%) | |
| Motor fuel (3.2%) | |
| Maintenance and repairs (1.3%) | |
| Used cars and trucks (2.0%) | |
| Public Transportation (1.1%) | |
| 4. Medical Care | 6.1% |
| 5. Apparel | 4.0% |
| 6. Recreation | 5.8% |
| 7. Education and Communication | 5.9% |
| 8. Other Goods and Services | 3.8% |

*Source:* www.bls.gov

helps businesses negotiate labor contracts and governments establish fiscal policy. However, it only represents consumer purchases, does not reflect product or service substitutions consumers might make because of price and is not particularly useful in forecasting. Thus, the CPI should not be used to predict swings in the economy because it is really a lagging indicator.

**Relationship Between the PPI and the CPI.** Supply management professionals also are interested in the relationship between the PPI and the CPI to evaluate their position of strength relative to that of the supplier. Understanding the changes in these indicators is a good way to evaluate that power relationship and is shown in the following example of a fictitious auto manufacturer, ABC Motor Corp. ABC is renegotiating the contract for door panels for one of its midsize models. Steel is a major component of these door panels, so the team reviews the CPI for steel products and the PPI for new cars over the past three years. Figure 4-3 illustrates a comparison between the CPI and the PPI.

While the PPI for steel products has increased significantly over the past three years, the CPI for new automobiles has remained relatively flat. The team uses the table shown in Figure 4-4 as a rule of thumb to determine its negotiating power.

Based on the table, the supply team will likely have less power at the negotiating table. Thus, the team decides to collect more recent price data and develop a cost analysis before entering negotiations with its door panel supplier.

**Figure 4-3    PPI to CPI Comparison**

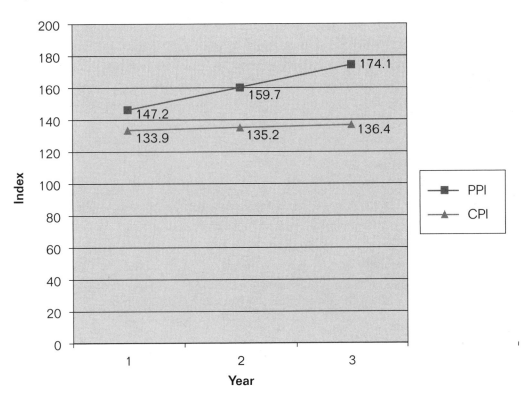

*Source:* Bureau of Labor Statistics.

**Figure 4-4**

| PPI | CPI | BUYING POWER | SUPPLIER POWER |
|-----|-----|--------------|----------------|
| Decreasing | Increasing | Higher | Lower |
| Decreasing | Flat | Higher | Lower |
| Decreasing | Decreasing | Lower | Lower |
| Increasing | Increasing | Lower | Higher |
| Increasing | Flat | Lower | Higher |
| Increasing | Decreasing | Lower | Lower |

*Source:* Adapted from *Supplier Management & Negotiation, Module 1, Research Methods,* developed by Larry Smeltzer for Arizona State University.

In the example, the PPI for steel products has increased significantly over the past three years (producer prices are increasing), while the CPI for new automobiles is relatively flat (prices to the consumer are stable). In this scenario, it will be easier for the door panel suppliers to support an argument for price increases because industry prices for steel products have risen significantly. Thus, the sourcing organization has relatively lower power in a negotiation situation for door panels.

## Implicit Price Deflator

A *deflator* is a value that allows data to be measured over time in terms of some base period. An *implicit price deflator,* a measure of inflation, is a factor used to eliminate price changes in computing a nation's real changes in output. (*ISM Glossary,* 2006) Thus, it is an index of prices for everything that a country produces, making it different from the CPI, which considers consumption only and includes prices of imports. The implicit price deflator was created by the U.S. Department of Commerce and compares the average level of prices in a given year to those of a base year by using the following calculation:

$$\text{Implicit price deflator} = \frac{\text{Current-dollar GDP}}{\text{Inflation-adjusted GDP}}$$

For example, the implicit price deflator for the third quarter of 2006 in the United States was 101.7, indicating that prices in the economy went up 1.7 percent from the third quarter of 2005.[31] Supply professionals, therefore, need to consider the impact of inflation/deflation in the negotiation process.

## Custom Indexes

*Custom indexing* is a professional tool that organizations use to measure, investigate and control price and cost changes within their own organizations. If a supply management professional forecasts an expected upswing in prices for a particular commodity, he or she may be able to find a substitute that meets requirements but is less expensive. Custom indexes are especially useful for commodities that represent a large percentage of total purchases. The supply professional, however, also should be sure to identify any assumptions used to create the index.

A simple price index would be the price of a good or service for a given year divided by the price of that good or service for a base year. The base price is given as 100, and then later comparisons are expressed as a ratio of the later period over the base period multiplied by 100. For example, if the 2006 statistic for wheat was 130 and the base year 2000 statistic is 100, the index would be $(130/100) \times 100 = 130$ and the percentage difference would be $(130/100 - 1) \times 100 = 30\%$. In other words, prices were up 30 percent over the base year. It is always important to report the index periodically and to use the base year for comparison. Often, supply management professionals will create a supplier price index and use it to compare against the producer price index to determine if the supplier is asking for equitable price increases. For instance, if the supplier price index has increased an average of 10 percent annually over the past two years, but the industry producer price index has increased only an average of 3 percent annually, this information can be used in the next round of negotiations to argue for lower prices or for a cost savings clause to be built into the contract.

While indexes are important to the forecasting process, organizations use other nationally published figures to aid them. Two of these are described in the following sections.

## Balance of Trade

The *balance of trade* is the difference between the value of a nation's exports to all other countries and the value of all imports from all other countries over a given time period. If exports are greater than imports, the country's balance of trade is defined as "favorable"; when imports exceed exports, the balance of trade is considered "unfavorable." Some nations, such as Great Britain, also create separate categories for goods and services trade balances, defining each, respectively, as "visible" and "invisible." A significantly large trade deficit may result in higher interest rates, depressed stock prices and lower currency exchange rates because that country will search for foreign capital to finance the deficit. U.S. purchases of industrial supplies, consumer goods and oil in 2005, for example, accounted for a large portion of a negative trade balance, while services were the source of a positive balance (though not nearly enough to offset the former) primarily because of financial services and accounting.[32]

## Balance of Payments

The *balance of payments* is a measure for the difference in the flow of funds across a nation's boundaries. (*ISM Glossary,* 2006) It is an accounting record of a nation's transactions with all other nations during a specific time period, usually one year. The account compares the amount of international currency that is taken into the economy from exports and international investments and the amount of domestic currency that is taken out to pay for imports or investments.[33] The difference between the value of a country's exports and imports is the *balance of trade.*

The account, however, must be in balance. Thus, if a particular nation shows a trade deficit, it must export some of its gold reserves or send some of its currency reserves to those nations with a surplus. If, on the other hand, there is a surplus, that nation must receive an inflow of either or both currency and gold reserves from those nations with a deficit. In the long term, persistent deficits might be corrected through increasing interest rates (making it more difficult to borrow money), lower export prices from the international supplier, an increase in the home country's price of imports through weakening the home country's currency (taking more of the home country's currency to purchase the foreign goods) or adding tariffs or taxes (making these goods and services less attractive). Countries with a surplus also may take steps to maintain healthy global economic conditions. China, for example, with a trade surplus of more than $95 billion, stated in December 2006 that it would work to reduce that surplus to zero by 2010 by cutting back on export growth.[34] Supply management professionals must consider all these issues when making global outsourcing decisions.

# Sources of Data Used in Forecasting

A number of other popular data sources are used to create forecasts, some of which are described in the following sections.

## ISM *Report On Business*® — Manufacturing and Non-Manufacturing

ISM publishes two monthly reports that provide a good overall barometer of current macroeconomic conditions. Macrodata is useful when organizations are forecasting the effects of economic trends on national or worldwide supply and demand. For example, because cotton and polyester are two common textile fibers, any indications of a low worldwide yield for cotton would suggest possible shortages of cotton and thus a shift in demand from cotton to polyester. As a result, cotton shortages might imply an increasing demand for polyester fiber if they are interchangeable and thus an increase in demand for the raw materials used to make polyester. This information would be used by the supply management professional to create a microforecast or an organization-specific forecast.[35]

The Manufacturing ISM *Report On Business*® is based on data collected monthly from manufacturers. As shown in the sample report summary in Figure 4-5, the Manufacturing ISM *Report On Business*® includes a number of factors that affect forecasts,

Figure 4-5    Sample Manufacturing ISM *Report On Business*®

## MANUFACTURING AT A GLANCE

| INDEX | JAN. INDEX | DEC. INDEX | % POINT CHANGE | DIRECTION | RATE OF CHANGE | TREND* (MONTHS) |
|---|---|---|---|---|---|---|
| PMI | 50.7 | 48.4 | +2.3 | Growing | From Contracting | 1 |
| New Orders | 49.5 | 46.9 | +2.6 | Contracting | Slower | 2 |
| Production | 55.2 | 48.6 | +6.6 | Growing | From Contracting | 1 |
| Employment | 47.1 | 48.7 | -1.6 | Contracting | Faster | 3 |
| Supplier Deliveries | 52.8 | 52.6 | +0.2 | Slowing | Faster | 7 |
| Inventories | 49.1 | 45.4 | +3.7 | Contracting | Slower | 21 |
| Customers' Inventories | 49.5 | 51.5 | -2.0 | Too Low | From Too High | 1 |
| Prices | 76.0 | 68.0 | +8.0 | Increasing | Faster | 13 |
| Backlog of Orders | 44.0 | 43.0 | +1.0 | Contracting | Slower | 4 |
| Exports | 58.5 | 52.5 | +6.0 | Growing | Faster | 62 |
| Imports | 52.5 | 48.0 | +4.5 | Growing | From Contracting | 1 |
| **OVERALL ECONOMY** | | | | Growing | Faster | 75 |
| **MANUFACTURING SECTOR** | | | | Growing | From Contracting | 1 |

*Number of months moving in current direction.
Manufacturing ISM Report On Business® data is seasonally adjusted except for Backlog of Orders, Prices, Customers' Inventories, Imports and New Export Orders.

This report reflects the U.S. Department of Commerce's recently completed annual adjustment to the seasonal factors used to calculate the indexes.

*Source:* Manufacturing ISM *Report On Business*® (January 2008 data) Media Release, February 1, 2008.

including changes in new orders, production, employment, supplier deliveries, backlogs of orders, customers' inventories, exports, imports and prices. The *PMI* is a composite index published monthly for the manufacturing sector that can be used to predict future growth or contraction.

A similar monthly report is issued for the non-manufacturing sector, Non-Manufacturing ISM *Report On Business®,* and includes factors such as business activity, new orders, employment, supplier deliveries, inventories, prices, backlog of orders, exports, imports, inventory sentiment and customers' inventories, as shown in Figure 4-6. The NMI (Non-Manufacturing Index), a composite index for the non-manufacturing sector, was established in January 2008.

The individual factors are reported as a *diffusion index*. A diffusion index measures the degree to which a change in something is dispersed, spread out or "diffused" in a particular group. If all members of a group of people (the sample population) are

**Figure 4-6. Sample ISM Non-Manufacturing *Report On Business®***

| SURVEY QUESTION | JAN. INDEX | DEC. INDEX | % POINT CHANGE | DIRECTION | RATE OF CHANGE | TREND* (MONTHS) |
|---|---|---|---|---|---|---|
| NMI | 44.6 | N/A | N/A | Contracting | N/A | 1 |
| Business Activity | 41.9 | 54.4 | -12.5 | Contracting | From Growing | 1 |
| New Orders | 43.5 | 53.9 | -10.4 | Contracting | From Growing | 1 |
| Employment | 43.9 | 51.8 | -7.9 | Contracting | From Growing | 1 |
| Supplier Deliveries | 49.0 | 52.5 | -3.5 | Faster | From Slowing | 1 |
| Inventories | 44.5 | 50.5 | -6.0 | Contracting | From Growing | 1 |
| Prices | 70.7 | 71.5 | -0.8 | Increasing | Slower | 56 |
| Backlog of Orders | 46.0 | 49.0 | -3.0 | Contracting | Faster | 5 |
| New Export Orders | 52.0 | 50.0 | +2.0 | Growing | From Unchanged | 1 |
| Imports | 41.5 | 50.5 | -9.0 | Contracting | From Growing | 1 |
| Inventory Sentiment | 57.0 | 64.5 | -7.5 | Too High | Slower | 128 |
| Customers' Inventories | N/A | N/A | N/A | N/A | N/A | N/A |

*Number of months moving in current direction.
Non-Manufacturing ISM Report On Business® data is seasonally adjusted for the Business Activity, New Orders, Prices and Employment Indexes.

This report reflects the U.S. Department of Commerce's recently completed annual adjustment to the seasonal factors used to calculate the indexes.

*Source:* Non-Manufacturing ISM *Report On Business®* (January 2008 data) Media Release, February 5, 2008.

asked if something has changed and in which direction, they will answer in one of three ways: It has not changed, it has increasedor it has decreased. The diffusion index is calculated by taking the percentage of those reporting "increased" added to half of the percentage of those reporting "no change." Economists and statisticians have determined that the farther the index is away from the amount that would indicate "no change" (50 percent), the greater the rate of change. Therefore, an index of 60 percent indicates a faster rate of increase than an index of 55 percent.

To achieve a valid, weighted sample, survey participants for both the Manufacturing *Report On Business*® and the Non-Manufacturing *Report On Business*® are selected based on each industry's contribution to the gross domestic product (GDP). As a result, there is a correlation between the ISM indexes and the real GDP as shown in Figure 4-7.[36]

Each month, survey participants from both the manufacturing and non-manufacturing sectors are asked to assess their organizations' performance based on a comparison of the current month to the previous month. According to Norbert

**Figure 4.7    Correlation Between Institute for Supply Management Indexes and the Real GDP**

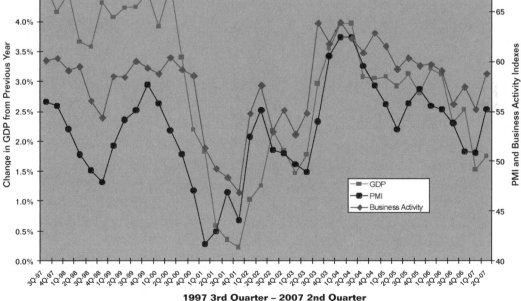

**1997 3rd Quarter – 2007 2nd Quarter**

*Source:* Institute for Supply Management.

Ore, "The greatest value in this type of data may be its ability to recognize change. Understanding the business cycle is important to the financial community, government policymakers and to businesses around the globe. But the early recognition of change in the business cycle plays an even more significant role."[37]

**Application.** The supply management group at Houston, Texas–based Dresser Equipment Group, a division of Halliburton Co., uses the ISM *Report On Business*® extensively in its forecasting efforts, project planning and ongoing communication with both suppliers and customers. According to a supply management professional at Dresser, "Data points are also quite useful in comparing actual versus target pricing levels and in establishing acceptable ranges and/or controls in contracts.

"Regarding forecasting and project planning, a working knowledge of the market and its tendencies is a key to successful project management. [Supply management professionals] record the monthly *ISM Report On Business*® indexes on a spreadsheet, convert the indexes to charts and distribute this information to [the] Procurement and Materials Management team on a worldwide basis. This data is often used in projecting and validating escalations and lead times during long-term projects.

"Regarding communication, the monthly indexes and charts are included as a segment in one of [its] management reports that indicates currency exchange rates, escalations, lead times and production cycle time applicable to major equipment items. Sharing this information with suppliers and customers provides an opportunity to work together to achieve more effective cost management in [the] supply-chain network."[38]

Many countries around the world have adopted the survey methodology used by ISM and publish their own reports. Information from other countries' reports may be helpful if the supply management professional is pursuing sourcing internationally. In addition, data from several countries currently is combined in a monthly global report as well.

## Government Publications

Besides indexes, the U.S. government provides a number of publications that provide useful input in creating a forecast. For example, the Bureau of Economic Analysis, mentioned earlier in this chapter, publishes the *Survey of Current Business,* which is available in pdf format at www.bea.gov/scb/index.htm. This survey reports the monthly GDP and any reasons behind the change from the previous month(s), with supporting data including consumer spending, expenditures on imports and exports, business investment in inventories, government spending and fixed investments in nonresidential property. The BEA also publishes a monthly report on U.S. exports and imports of goods and services, which is based on figures from two months prior. These numbers are used to calculate the net export figure that is used in the GDP account. Another BEA report is *International Transactions,* released quarterly, which reports trade in goods and services, foreign investment that enters the United States and capital that flows out for investment in other countries. This report is important because exports reflect the United States' ability to compete in world trade, improve corporate profitability and create jobs. Imports reflect the strength of demand from U.S. consumers: When demand is increasing, the economy is expanding, although it takes away from GDP growth.

The *Federal Reserve Bulletin,* first introduced in 1914, is a publication designed to present the U.S. Federal Reserve Board's policy issues. Contributors to the *Bulletin* include the Federal Reserve Board's Research and Statistics, Monetary Affairs, International Finance, Banking Supervision and Regulation, Consumer and Community Affairs, Reserve Bank Operations and Legal divisions. The *Bulletin* includes topical research articles, legal developments, a report on the condition of the U.S. banking industry and other general information. As of 2006, the *Bulletin* is published on the board's public Web site on a continuing basis, as it becomes available. The board also prints an annual compendium.[39]

Additionally, the U.S. Bureau of Economics publishes a number of industry-related and other reports that may help an organization in its forecasting process. For example, in August 2004, it published *The Petroleum Industry: Mergers, Structural Change, and Antitrust Enforcement.*[40]

The U.S. Department of Agriculture (USDA) reports on global trading conditions for various commodities. A report on the cotton industry is published every two months. The April 2005 report announced that while exports to Turkey had increased, overall world market share had decreased.[41] In June 2005, the USDA reported, "Bangladesh imports almost all of its cotton needs. India and Pakistan import predominantly only their Extra Long Staple (ELS) and other superior quality cotton needs. The top supplier, the United States, accounted for 30 percent of the region's imports in fiscal year 2003/2004, excluding intratrade (12.7 percent). The need for higher quality cotton is likely to keep the demand for U.S. cotton relatively constant."[42]

Other countries and regions also issue their own national statistics. For example, the Canadian government publishes the *Annual Survey of Manufactures* based on a collection of Canadian financial data and production data. The main financial data are the value of shipments, employment data (the number of employees, salaries and wages), the cost of raw materials and energy consumption. Commodity data (materials and components, goods shipped) also are collected for establishments that are sent long-form questionnaires. The European Union, comprised of 27 member nations (as of 2008), publishes statistics on key economic indicators such as gross national income, balance of imports and exports and gross domestic product (GDP).[43]

## International Publications

Given the global nature of commerce today, supply management professionals also must examine international conditions in the marketplace. International statistics often are segmented by the following classifications: Developed Nation (high-income economies); Developing Nations or Newly Industrialized Countries (such as Hong Kong or South Korea); Big Emerging Markets (including Malaysia, Singapore, Thailand, China); and Poor Third-World Economies (such as Bangladesh and Zaire). Countries within one classification will operate differently from others because of highly varying income levels and the amount of capital available for foreign exchange.

Three international organizations that provide extensive statistical data include the United Nations (UN), the Organisation for Economic Co-Operation and Development (OECD) and the International Monetary Fund (IMF). The United Nations provides international trade statistics and a world economics survey, among other publications. *UN Comtrade,* for example, is a report on global commodity trade statistics for more than 150 countries. Updated daily and available online, it covers more than 5,000 products with options for exploration, data mining and visualization through graphics.[44] The *World Economic Situation and Prospects* is published annually and provides economic growth trends, international trade issues, a projection of international uncertainties and risks and a report on capital flows. The *World Economic and Social Survey* reports annually on issues related to developing countries such as savings, investment and growth; trade; international flows of private cash into developing nations; and systemic issues.[45] The Food and Agricultural Organization of the United Nations also publishes statistical reports regarding agricultural, nutritional, forestry and fishery products.[46]

The Organisation for Economic Co-Operation and Development is a group of 30 governments that have a "commitment to democracy and a [free] market economy." With centers located in countries around the world, member nations work together to address the economic, social and governmental challenges and opportunities associated with globalization. OECD databases cover national accounts, economic indicators, trade, employment, migration, education energy and other areas, most of which is published.[47]

The International Monetary Fund (IMF) is an international organization with 184 member countries. The organization "was established to promote international monetary cooperation, exchange stability and orderly exchange arrangements; to foster economic growth and high levels of employment; and to provide temporary financial assistance to countries to help ease balance of payments adjustment." One of its publications, the *World Economic and Financial Surveys, World Economic Outlook,* contains data on IMF lending, exchange rates, GDP growth, inflation, unemployment, payments balances, exports, imports, external debt, capital flows, commodity prices and more. Published twice a year, the report also can be downloaded at the IMF Web site.[48] For instance, according to the IMF's September 2006 *World Economic Outlook,* Europe's growth was forecast at 2 percent for 2007, down from the 2006 forecast of 2.4 percent. This information suggests that economic conditions will take a downturn. Thus, it is likely that European suppliers will be less inclined to make significant capital investments through 2007; that inventories could be building, increasing opportunities for price concessions; and wage increases are unlikely in the near term so prices should not increase based on that factor.

## Private Publications

Trade magazines and research reports are other good sources of information. *Purchasing* magazine, *Mortgage Banking* and the *Journal of Business Forecasting: Methods and Systems* provide a monthly outlook on U.S. and international business and economic conditions.

Organizations also create and sell reports and research studies that can provide valuable input to a forecast. One such organization is Business Monitor International, which offers a number of services including *Business Markets Online* with intradaily alerts from a treasuries and capital markets team, and comparative risk ratings, macroeconomic analyses and forecasts and industry profiles from a team of country economists; research on 14 industry sectors with five-year forecasts on a number of industry indicators; and specific organization research reports.

Kiplinger Washington Editors, Inc., also provides input to forecasts in the form of several publications, including *The Kiplinger Letter, Kiplinger Business Forecasts* and *The Kiplinger Tax Letter,* which discuss a number of topics such as interest rates, the economy, international issues, costs and employees.

Wachovia, a U.S. financial services provider, distributes a monthly economic outlook report, which analyzes both U.S. and international conditions. A graph of the Eurozone PMI indexes for both manufacturing and services is included in the report. The organization also publishes the monthly *Regional Economic Review* that includes real GDP for each of the 50 U.S. states and special reports on topics such as commodity forecasts, the state of specific industries and inventories.[49]

## Commercial Forecasts

Certain organizations also provide forecasts for specific industries. Connecticut-based Forecast International, Inc., for example, provides market intelligence and analyses for more than 3,000 clients in the aerospace, defense, military electronics and power systems industries. Their products are designed to help corporate executives, military leaders and top government personnel in the strategic planning process and the gathering of market intelligence.[50]

## Regional Surveys

Local and state governments provide forecast information as well. A good example is the Web site provided by the Metropolitan Council, a regional planning agency for the Minneapolis–St. Paul, Minnesota, area.[51] New Zealand's Ministry of Tourism posts forecasts by region with an explanation of its methodology that is useful for local hotels, restaurants and tour operators.[52] University researchers also may survey regional conditions for a specific industry. For example, Professor Ernie Goss, Creighton University, uses the ISM *Report On Business*™ to prepare a monthly *Survey on Economic Conditions for Business in the [U.S.] Midwestern and Mountain States.*[53]

## Internal Historical Data

Organizations often will develop forecasts based on their own internal data. Past forecasts of sales, standard costs, order or production lead times, the seasonality of demand for products and services, current employment levels and turnover rates, specific financial requirements or constraints, among others, may be used as a basis to create a new forecast.

## Industry Sources

A number of industry-specific groups, such as the American Petroleum Institute (API), the International Cotton Advisory Council (ICAC) and the Association of International Automobile Manufacturers (AIAM), provide current and upcoming legislation that will have an impact on the industry and the economic forecast. A number of nonprofit organizations also serve specific industry groups, including the APICS, the Association for Operations Management (www.apics.org/default.htm), the Institute for Supply Management (ISM) (www.ism.ws), the National Association of Manufacturers (NAM) (www.nam.org/s_nam/index.asp) and the National Institute of Governmental Purchasers (NIGP) (www.nigp.org). The United Kingdom's Chartered Institute of Purchasing and Supply (CIPS) (www.cips.org), the Danish Purchasing and Logistics Forum (DILF) (www.dilf.dk), India's Indian Institute of Materials Management (IIMM) (www.iimm.org) and Germany's Association Materials Management Purchasing and Logistics (AMMPL) (http://portal.bme.de/pls/webgui/pk_index .startup?p_language_id=2) are just some of the other organizations worldwide that provide valuable information for their members. Their overall goal is education, but they also provide reports covering the topics of economic conditions and pricing, among others.

### Online Indexes and Search Engines

Lastly, a number of other online resources are available to supply management professionals that have not already been mentioned, which are listed in Figure 4-8. The U.S. Census Bureau, for example, provides statistics on the trade deficit, construction data and median income. The Energy Information Administration Web site includes forecasts and analyses of the worldwide energy supply, demand and prices through 2030.

# Using the Data

If an organization has not had extensive experience in tracking data, it is best to begin by selecting and watching a few key indicators. It also is important to consider the significance of a given product or service that will be purchased. If a good or service is not important to an organization's competitiveness, predictions of economic growth for the next quarter or following year may be enough to make forecasts about price increases and whether it is a buyer's or seller's market. If the purchase is more important to an organization's profitability, more detailed information may be acquired, culled from some of the sources mentioned previously. This information then can be used to develop any forecasting assumptions, thus reducing risk and developing a more accurate prediction.

Global food products manufacturers such as ConAgra Foods draw from a number of sources to make their forecasts. ConAgra provides brand-name food and ingredients to retailers, major food establishments and commercial customers worldwide. Its forecasters begin by evaluating several economic indicators to predict the marketplace, such as GDP growth, CPI, PPI, commodity prices, currency exchange rates, the ISM *Report On Business*®, job growth, productivity changes and restaurant spending. Volatility in commodity prices is a primary concern for ConAgra because commodities make up a large portion of the organization's product spend, making the negotiation process more difficult for supply professionals and naturally affecting product pricing. Thus, commodity prices for dairy, wheat, soybeans, corn, soymeal, meat, pork and poultry are tracked on a regular basis. Another concern is the price of crude oil because it affects production, packaging and transportation costs. Thus, ConAgra closes watches both crude oil futures and natural gas futures (natural gas futures pricing tends to follow crude oil).[54]

**Figure 4-8   Online Resources**

| RESOURCE | WEB SITE |
| --- | --- |
| Securities and Exchange Commission's EDGAR (Electronic Data Gathering, Analysis and Retrieval) database | www.sec.gov/edgarhp.htm |
| Annual Energy Outlook | www.eia.doe.gov/oiaf/aeo/ |
| Bureau of Labor statistics | www.stats.bls.gov/ |
| U.S. Geological Survey (Department of Minerals) | http://minerals.usgs.gov/ |
| U.S. Census Bureau | www.census.gov/ |
| Institute of Business Forecasting | www.ibf.org/ |
| American Institute of Economic Research | www.aier.org/ |
| The Forecasting Institute, Inc. | www.tfiforecast.com/ |
| New York Mercantile Exchange | www.nymex.com/index.aspx |
| U.S. Energy Information Administration | www.eia.doe.gov/ |
| Chicago Board of Trade | www.cbot.com/ |
| Chicago Mercantile Exchange | www.cme.com/ |
| Chicago Board Options Exchange | www.cboe.com/ |
| U.S. Department of Agriculture | www.usda.gov/ |
| Library of Congress databases and e-resources | www.lcweb.loc.gov/ |
| Asian Development Bank | www.adb.org/ |
| Inter-American Development Bank (South America) | www.iadb.org/ |
| Official Statistics on the Web (OFFSTATS) | www.library.auckland.ac.nz/subjects/stats/offstats/ |
| Davidson Data Center and Network | http://ddcn.prowebis.com/ |
| Service Industries Trends (SITrends) | www.sitrends.org/ |
| United Kingdom Statistics | www.statistics.gov.uk/ |

# Summary

To fully understand the forecasting process, supply management professionals need a good background in the economics of forecasting, the global environment in which they work today and sources of information that can help begin the forecasting process. Because global sourcing is on the rise, understanding the generic types of economies in operation is important. From there, understanding country-specific differences that can affect the forecast and the trading process is also essential. A number of resources, including economic indicators, government indexes, surveys and other publications can provide a wealth of information to support the forecasting process. The key is to find the most relevant information that will result in an accurate forecast. Chapter 5 will provide more specific information on developing a forecast using key information and forecast models.

## Key Points

1. Business decisions typically are based on forecasts — a prediction of the future. The overall purpose of the forecast is to minimize uncertainty in the decision-making process.

2. The world operates with a combination of economic markets — free, closed and mixed. Given the global mix of free and mixed economies, trade is relatively open today. While trade barriers have decreased, tariffs and other forms of protectionism such as trading quotas still exist.

3. The issue of local buying preferences has changed over the past decade with the advent of advanced communication technologies and a changing political climate. In general, organizations take a two-pronged approach: standardize where possible, while considering local needs.

4. To manage supplier relationships in different cultures it is first necessary to understand and value some general difference in industrial histories, relationships to technology, natural resources, religions and geography.

5. International currency fluctuations and the additional costs and legal issues associated with international sourcing can impact the ability of organizations to compete effectively, thus affecting a forecast.

6. Every economy experiences swings in the business cycle. Five possible scenarios include: (1) the highest point of output before a downturn; (2) recession, or shrinking of the economy; (3) recession trough, or lowest point in economic activity; (4) recovery, or resuming growth path; and (5) expansion, beyond previous high point.

7. Organizations use leading economic indicators to predict economic change, coincident economic indicators to understand current economic conditions and lagging indicators to respond to the economic environment once a given economic point in an economic cycle has been reached.

8. Good forecasters use a number of resources to help create a forecast, including regional and international publications, industry sources, the ISM *Report On Business®,* private publications, internal historical data and online indices and search engines.

# Forecasting Models and Methods

**A** pilot would never take off without filing a flight plan showing his or her planned route and destination, but organizations often operate without planning demand for the upcoming fiscal year. Demand planning helps ensure a product or service is available when the customer wants it and is the first step of *demand management*. *Demand management,* according to the *ISM Glossary* (2006*),* is "the proactive compilation of requirements' information regarding demand (i.e., customers, sales, marketing, finance) and the organization's capabilities from the supply side (i.e., supply, operations and logistics management); the development of a consensus regarding the ability to match the requirements and capabilities; and the agreement upon a synthesized plan that can most effectively meet the customer requirements within the constraints imposed by supply chain capabilities." As the definition suggests, demand management is the basis for decision-making within the Strategic Supply Management Process. (See Figure I-1 in the "Series Overview" at the beginning of this book.)

Demand forecasts provide estimates for demand planning. A good forecast will help improve customer service, reduce unnecessary inventories and thus working capital needs and lower costs. Although the statement is commonly made that "all forecasts are wrong," a fairly precise forecast is still possible if calculated correctly. This requires a certain degree of analytical skills. This chapter will begin by covering some of the reasons organizations forecast and discuss several factors that affect the demand forecast. The forecasting process then is described, followed by a discussion of the types of forecasting methods typically used by organizations. The important topic of minimizing forecast error is discussed later in the chapter. Finally, sharing forecast information with suppliers is described.

## CHAPTER OBJECTIVES

• Explain why organizations forecast.

• Discuss the factors that affect the demand forecast.

• Describe the qualitative and quantitative methods used in the forecasting process.

• Explain the methods used to detect forecast errors.

• Discuss the value of sharing forecast results with suppliers.

# Why Forecast?

Supply management professionals use forecasts, with other information sources described in Chapter 4, to assist in their planning processes. Good forecasts can be used as a basis to improve a supply management professional's sourcing methods, better identify key suppliers for strategic materials and supplies, improve quality and increase supplier performance levels. The following paragraphs describe in more detail the reasons for forecasting, beginning with the overall purposes of forecasting for organizations, followed by the reasons supply professionals develop forecasts.

## To Estimate Demand

In general, forecasting is a useful planning tool to facilitate future-oriented decisions. More specifically, however, accurate forecasts are needed to help optimize profit levels by tapping into the most lucrative revenue streams. Thus, organizations seek to forecast the sources of those revenue streams to determine where to invest their resources most wisely. For instance, businesses need to predict sales quantities for new and existing products and services, so they develop demand forecasts. While estimating expected sales dollars is common, demand must be predicted in terms of quantity and is needed for operational planning purposes. For example, organizations need to estimate material, labor, transportation, distribution and space requirements for the upcoming year.

Within this context, considering the impact of a *product life cycle* on demand is also important. The concept of the product life cycle is essentially that each product or service goes through several stages, from product development to introduction to a growth stage where sales steadily increase to a maturity stage where sales are relatively flat on to a decline in sales, until finally the product is discontinued. Thus, demand will vary depending on where the product or service is in the product life cycle. For instance, demand for new products to be introduced to the marketplace most likely will be fairly uncertain and therefore difficult to predict, while demand for services in the maturity phase should be relatively stable and easy to estimate.

A forecast also should incorporate the effect of marketing actions on the product's life cycle and on the organization's future share of the market. For example, to temporarily boost sales of a product sliding from the growth phase to the mature phase, an organization may offer a special 10 percent price decrease for sales booked in March or hire a celebrity spokesperson for advertising in the upcoming selling season, which, if effective, may cause a spike in demand.

## To Determine If Supply Can Meet Demand

An organization also must determine whether its demand forecasts are realistic; if there will be enough, too much or not enough industry capacity to meet overall customer demand; and whether it will have the capacity to meet its share of the market. Thus, organizations first create industry *capacity forecasts* by estimating or forecasting the amount of industry capacity and availability.

To create a capacity forecast, an organization evaluates the competition in terms of overlapping product lines and market coverage, and the expected effect on the marketplace. It then estimates capacity for its own organization. U.S. carrier Northwest Airlines, for instance, predicted flat domestic industry capacity (known in the airline industry as available seat miles) for 2005 because of the rising cost of fuel, competitive ticket prices and overcapacity.[1] This information then was used for Northwest's capacity planning.

## To Predict Technology Trends

Organizations also need to forecast *technology trends* and breakthroughs that can impact demand as products and services evolve. In some industries, technological advances have significantly cut product life cycle times. For example, the personal computer (PC) industry is driven by the rapid pace of technological improvements in microprocessors, semiconductors and storage devices where the product life cycle for these components is about six months.[2] If an organization is not ready for those changes, a competitor most likely will be. Senior executives, therefore, must be aware of any technology gaps that may exist within their own organization and the potential threats to revenue or market share if their competitors adopt this new technology.

Forecasting technology trends is typically carried on in an environment of uncertainty. For example, in 1996, Battelle Memorial Institute, an Ohio-based global science and technology enterprise that develops and commercializes technology and manages laboratories with $3.7 billion in annual research, made a prediction of the 10 most innovative products that would be available in 2006. While about half of these products are available today (wireless-access computer data, digital high-definition television, GPS and home health monitors), the other 50 percent have not been realized yet or only with mixed results (pharmaceutical treatments for cystic fibrosis and Lou Gehrig's disease, "smart" construction materials that change color before becoming unsafe, the leasing of appliances and multifuel automobiles).[3]

## To Predict Prices

Supply management also is responsible for performing *price forecasting.* Price forecasting is most commonly used for commodities such as crude oil, metals and other raw materials. For example, appliance manufacturer Maytag, now a part of Whirlpool Corp., predicts the price of cold-rolled steel, a major component of washers, dryers and dishwashers, for the upcoming year to determine product cost. This type of forecasting is important when an organization is a supplier to another industry, especially one that is changing quickly; when the goods used to make a finished product or deliver a service experience volatility in price or availability; or if international conditions have an impact on price or availability of goods or services used. Prices also can be affected by seasonality in demand patterns. Cattle prices, for instance, are known to follow a fairly predictable seasonal pattern, which can easily be incorporated into the price forecast.

## To Predict Dependent Demand

Supply management professionals in a manufacturing environment and in certain service industries (restaurants, for example) also are interested in the need for components that will be used to create their offerings. The demand for these components, which may include raw materials, ingredients, supplies, parts and subassemblies, is known as *dependent demand* because their demand depends on the demand for the finished product or service. For example, McDonald's Corp. estimates the number of Big Macs that will be sold in the upcoming year and uses that forecast to predict dependent demand for the beef patties, buns and "special sauce." A travel agency predicts the number of all-inclusive vacation packages it will sell to estimate the dependent demand for airline tickets, hotel accommodations, cruises and tours. Uncertainty in predicting material needs naturally lies in whether the demand forecast is overly optimistic, a reasonable assumption or overly pessimistic.

As a rule, material specialists will begin with the demand forecast for each finished product as a basis to create these material forecasts. Many manufacturers use a *materials resource plan* (MRP), a software program developed in the 1960s, or *manufacturing resource planning* (MRP II), which links MRP to an organization's financial system and other processes, to calculate demand for these components.[4] An MRP system helps ensure that sufficient quantities of materials are available when needed for production. Two years after Wrigley Co. implemented an MRP system at its UK location, a dramatic improvement in forecast accuracy occurred. As a result, the Chicago, Illinois–based chewing gum and confectionery organization was able to reduce the amount of raw material safety stock and improve quality control of those goods received from suppliers. In turn, higher product quality levels meant lower costs and higher levels of customer satisfaction.[5]

The inputs to an MRP system include a *bill of materials,* a *master production schedule* and an *inventory record database.* A bill of materials is the record of all components that make up a specific finished product, the relationships between each component and the number of each component that will be used (this number will be taken from the engineering and process designs created during the product design stage). The master production schedule provides the details of the quantity of each finished product that will be produced for each time period (an hour, day, week or month) within the planning horizon. The inventory records are the compilation of all inventory transactions such as the release of any new orders, the receipt of orders, inventory withdrawals or order cancellations. The MRP system then uses information from independent demand forecasts for replacement parts and maintenance items, as well as the master production schedule, inventory records that show the amount of inventory on hand and the bill of materials, to estimate the need for all materials, components and subassemblies and at specific times during the planning period. Figure 5-1 provides an illustration of a hypothetical MRP system.

**Figure 5-1    Hypothetical MRP System**

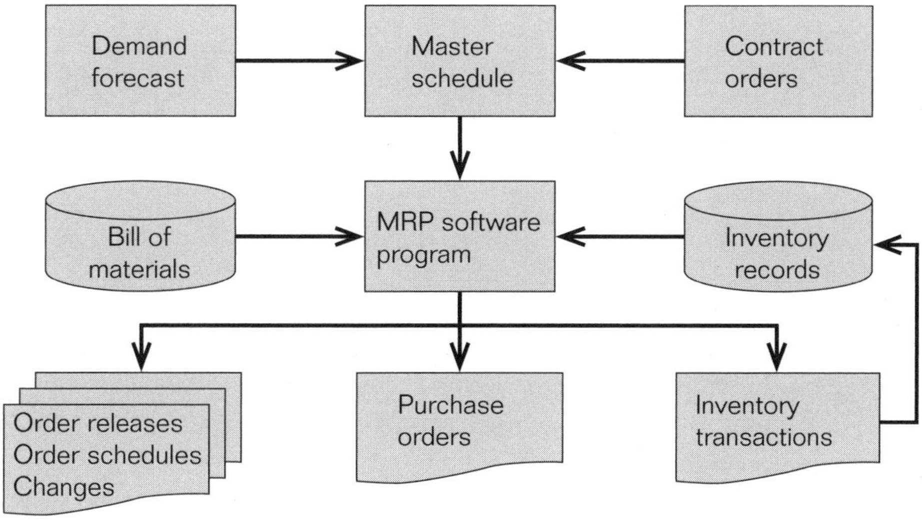

Supply management professionals then can use the results to check component availabilities, estimate price trends and generate purchase orders. Based on this data, inventory policies can be set. For example, if prices are trending down and availability is high, the supply management professional may decide to keep inventory levels to a minimum. Another important part of the process is learning the supplier's expected *order lead times.* Order lead time is measured as the span of time between placing an order with a supplier and receiving the goods. If the organization uses an MRP system, it will use dependent demand figures generated from the MRP system, expected supplier order lead times for each component and expected supplier quality to plan when to place orders. The MRP system then will use this information provided by the supply management professional to create the materials requirements planning record, which indicates when components should be ordered and when they are expected to be received. The following example illustrates how a hypothetical organization uses the MRP record to plan deliveries.

Cox Global Manufacturing, Ltd., makes a product that uses Component A. In its planning session, the manufacturing team calculates its weekly need for Component A based on independent demand forecasts and standing contract orders. The supply management professional has told the team that the expected order lead time is two weeks and lot sizes must be in multiples of 50. The team creates a material requirements planning record based on ordering 150 units every other week and 100 on alternating weeks.

| Item: Component A | | | | | | |
|---|---|---|---|---|---|---|
| Lead time: 2 weeks | Week | | | | | |
| | 1 | 2 | 3 | 4 | 5 | 6 |
| Gross requirements | 160 | 110 | 150 | 180 | 130 | 140 |
| Scheduled receipts | 150 | 100 | 150 | 100 | 150 | 100 |
| Projected on-hand inventory (Beginning inventory = 100 units) | 90 | 80 | 80 | 0 | 20 | (20) |
| Planned receipts | | | 150 | 100 | 150 | 100 |
| Planned order releases | 150 | 100 | 150 | 100 | | |

The record indicates it will run out of Component A in week 6, resulting in a stop in production. As a result, they increase the order for week 4 by 50 units as shown in the following table.

| Item: Component A | | | | | | |
|---|---|---|---|---|---|---|
| Lead time: 2 weeks | **Week** | | | | | |
| | 1 | 2 | 3 | 4 | 5 | 6 |
| Gross requirements | 160 | 110 | 150 | 180 | 130 | 140 |
| Scheduled receipts | 150 | 100 | 150 | 100 | 150 | 150 |
| Projected on-hand inventory (Beginning inventory = 100 units) | 90 | 80 | 80 | 0 | 20 | 30 |
| Planned receipts | | | 150 | 100 | 150 | 150 |
| Planned order releases | 150 | 100 | 150 | 150 | | |

## To Estimate the Supply Management Budget

Supply management professionals must develop a forecast of any actions that need to be taken or resources required to meet their goals over the planning horizon. The forecast will be used as a basis to develop the *supply management budget.* Budgets, in a sense, are forecasts of all monies required to run the supply management organization for the upcoming year. Budgeting also is used to examine and control costs. For example, the supply management group at Universal Music Group used the budgeting process and cross-functional teams to gain control of a large amount of unmonitored spending. Costs had been rising about 20 percent per year while revenues were relatively flat. The UK record organization has a spending budget of approximately £1.5 million ($3.0 million ) with most expenses going toward the purchase of touring-related costs, styling costs, videos, recording studios, session musicians and public relations. As a result, contracts were negotiated for some expenses, while standardized rate cards for 170 areas of spend were developed where costs were the most variable, such as hair styling and makeup.[6]

The supply management budget generally includes four specific types of budgets:

1. *Purchased materials/operations budget.* An estimate of projected operational costs and funds expected to be spent on material and service purchases, which is based on the demand forecast.

2. *Maintenance repairs and operating (MRO) budget.* A budget tied to the expected changes in inventory levels, operating schedules and price levels.

3. *Capital budget.* A budget that covers a multiple-year horizon and is based on expected production or service delivery needs, planned equipment replacements

and special projects and expansion plans, and is tied to the strategic plan for any new mergers/acquisitions, expansion plans, new product or service lines or other capital investments.

4. *Administrative budget.* A budget that identifies all expenses for the supply management function.

While there are many distinct needs for forecasting, the remainder of this chapter will focus on demand forecasting because it has the biggest impact on supply management decisions. The following section begins with a description of some of the factors that affect demand forecasts.

# Factors That Affect Demand Forecasts

It is important to think of the demand forecast as a "living document" and be prepared to adjust the forecast as conditions change. A forecast provides a snapshot of expected future conditions. These conditions, however, can and will change. Some issues that affect economic conditions, such as changes in the money market and global trading conditions, are discussed in Chapter 4. Six other factors that directly impact operations are summarized in Figure 5-2 and described in the following sections.

### Lead Time

Lead time as defined in the *ISM Glossary* (2006) is the time that elapses from placement of an order until receipt of the order, including time for order transmittal, processing, preparation and shipping. Unexpected changes in lead times for order deliveries can adversely affect the forecast. Ideally, customer organizations plan to receive materials as promised, but this is not always the case. Late deliveries can negatively affect an operation, slowing down the conversion and delivery process. Thus, once the forecast has initially been developed, some rethinking and modification will be needed as lead times change. Dallas-based Southwest Airlines, for example, in anticipation of greater than originally projected expected growth in 2007, attempted to place an order for two more airplanes in addition to its original order of 80 from Boeing. However, Boeing had to turn Southwest down, saying delivery was not possible in the near future because of capacity limitations. As a result, Southwest had to adjust its forecast.[7]

### Labor Markets

Labor markets also can affect the forecast. If an organization is experiencing labor shortages, for example, it will be difficult to meet the forecast. The state of Montana, with an unemployment rate of 3 percent, faced severe labor shortages in the fast-food

Figure 5-2    Conditions Affecting a Forecast

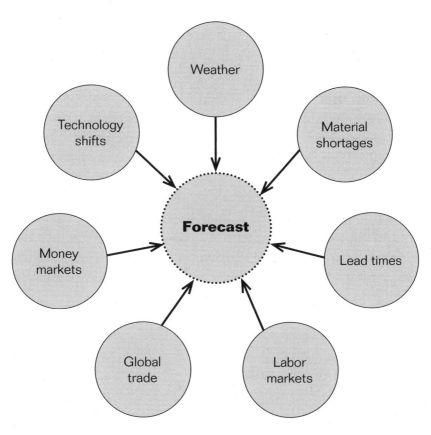

industry during 2006. One A&W Restaurant owner found that employees were leaving for higher-paying jobs in the oil and gas industry and he was forced to close the restaurant during the Wednesday rush hour for two weeks, losing valuable business.[8] New labor contracts or strikes also can have an impact on the forecast. In 2002, for example, 10,000 West Coast labor-union dockworkers were idle for 10 days during a lockout. Hundreds of cargo ships from Los Angeles, California, to Seattle, Washington, were prevented from unloading raw materials and finished goods, resulting in billions of dollars in losses to businesses.[9]

## Material Shortages

As manufacturers move to just-in-time and lean production and service environments (these strategies are discussed in Chapter 1), the chance for supply shortages increases and must be managed effectively. Unexpected events, such as labor shortages or delivery problems as discussed previously or even natural disasters can suddenly create material shortages that impede the ability of an organization to meet demand. In 1999, for example, Apple Computer faced shortages of liquid crystal display (LCD) panels and other components because of an earthquake in Taiwan. As a result, production was delayed for its iBook laptop computer during a period of rapid demand.[10]

## Shifts in Technology

Shifts in technology also impact the forecast, although generally in the long term. As mentioned previously, organizations often will create a separate technology forecast to address these issues. For example, the telecommunication industry is carefully watching new developments in technology that may negatively affect demand for its conventional products and services. A recent report by Heavy Reading, a market research organization, stated that "the business model for conventional telecom voice services (both wireline and wireless) is being unquestionably and permanently dismantled by several technological and market developments, the most important of which are the arrival of voice-over Internet protocol (VoIP) (the technology used to transmit voice conversations over the Internet) as a mainstream service alternative and the growing deployment of WiFi networks by enterprises, local governments and residential users installing wireless home networks."[11] A dual-mode handset that will function as a conventional cell phone but also can be used to handle VoIP currently is being developed.

## Weather Conditions

Climactic conditions, while out of the control of the forecaster, can have an impact on the forecast. In 2005, for instance, Hurricane Katrina shut down the city of New Orleans, severely restricting the ability of oil refineries, gas and timber producers and coffee distributors to meet demand for several months.[12] Some organizations attempt to mitigate this risk by incorporating weather predictions into their forecasts. For example, department stores such as Wal-Mart and Kohl's, rely on independent weather forecasting and advising services as part of their planning process. These quantitative-based forecasts help them set inventory levels, create sourcing and replenishment strategies and are even used to notify downstream suppliers when to start production of a particular product.[13]

While these conditions certainly can alter a forecast and continuity plans are essential, they should not preclude an organization from going through the forecasting process. An effective forecasting framework is essential to minimizing waste. The following section provides a general framework for developing a demand forecast.

# Demand Forecasting Process

In general, organizations go through a five-step process, as illustrated in Figure 5-3, to create a forecast, beginning with the planning process (Step 1) — selecting what will be forecasted, choosing the forecast time horizon and deciding which forecasting model(s) will be used. At this point, it is time to gather any data necessary to create

**Figure 5-3   Forecasting Process**

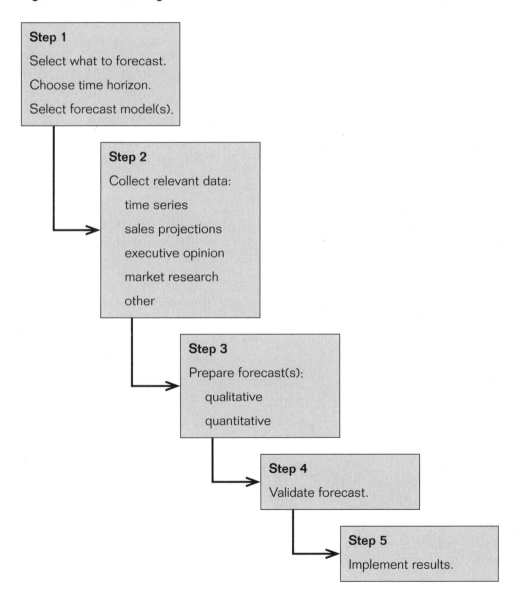

the forecast (Step 2). Once the data is collected and organized, the forecast is created (Step 3). The last steps are to validate the forecast (Step 4) and then implement the results (Step 5).

Brooks Sports, Inc., a U.S. designer of high-performance running footwear, apparel and accessories, changed its forecasting process in 2001 when the organization shifted from selling a broader product line to a set of high-performance products aimed at serious runners. It implemented a collaborative forecasting process that would support the new strategic direction of the organization. Brooks first develops monthly statistical forecasts at the stock-keeping unit (SKU) level based on any trends and seasonal patterns. On a quarterly basis, the sales staff and management prepare a demand forecast for the next 12 months using data collected via the Internet, with a focus on major accounts. Lastly, forecasters compare the statistical forecasts with the sales forecasts, making any necessary adjustments to prepare the final monthly forecast. The organization has found that approximately 90 percent of the final forecasts are similar to the statistical forecasts. Modifications are most often made when a new style is being introduced.[14]

## Length of Forecast

Forecasts typically can be broken down into *long-term, medium-term* and *short-term* timeframes. While there is some argument about the time span that should encompass each of these forecasts, long-term demand forecasts usually are developed for more than one year and are used as a basis for capacity planning, making location decisions and process changes. Medium-term forecasts, varying from three months to one year, help organizations make decisions regarding staffing, production or service delivery, purchasing and distribution. Lastly, short-term forecasts (less than three months) are used as the basis to schedule the workforce, manage inventory, plan production and develop schedules for final product assembly. Senior managers normally will be involved in longer-term demand forecasting; midlevel marketing, supply management, logistics and operations personnel will contribute to medium-term forecasts; and front-line employees will be involved in forecasting shorter-term needs for labor, materials and production.

DNATA, the largest airport cargo transit organization in the Middle East and sole operator at the Dubai Airport with more than 5,000 employees, has used SAS software since 1993 for forecasting. Annually, volume forecasts are created to help plan for expected revenues and expenses. On a daily basis, shop floor managers use forecasting to manage the deployment of resources in their operational areas. Long-term forecasting is used to plan for future facilities and the expansion of current cargo terminal operations. Since formalizing the process, DNATA has reduced forecasting inaccuracies to less than 10 percent. According to Jean-Pierre DePauw, senior general manager, "This [fewer forecasting inaccuracies] has led to a considerable improvement in the decision-making process, particularly in regard to facility expansion and new projects."[15]

The planning horizon for short-term forecasting can vary considerably depending on the type of organization. For example, while DNATA uses daily forecasts, the head nurses at a hospital may forecast in one-hour increments for surgeries, a fast-food franchise manager might create weekly forecasts for workforce needs, a retailer could forecast demand based on the season and a manufacturer might forecast quarterly labor needs.

## Top-Down and Bottom-Up Forecasting

Organizations typically create an annual forecast for planning purposes. They generally begin at the macrolevel with an aggregate forecast for all products and services offered, which is an easier prediction, followed by product lines and then individual items or SKUs. Organizations then generally use either a *top-down* or *bottom-up approach* to allocate demand by location. The top-down approach also is known as the *decomposition approach* because an organization forecasts demand for each product or service and then allocates a percentage of that demand for each retail site, distribution center or manufacturing plant. For example, if a retail clothing chain of 60 stores forecasts overall sales of a particular sweater to be 20,000 units, the forecaster allocates demand by store and provides that information to the chain's distribution centers. The bottom-up approach takes a reverse approach, forecasting demand by store or region, and rolling up those forecasts into an *aggregate forecast*. The demand forecast for all products and services then is used to create an *aggregate plan,* which breaks down all labor and material requirements, usually by quarter.

The top-down approach has been found to be more accurate at the top level and is used for developing strategic plans and budgets. However, forecasting at the lower levels does not tend to be accurate because actual demand fluctuations are not considered. For instance, many retailers have difficulty forecasting the popularity of specific colors or sizes store-to-store. According to a 2005 article by Kathleen Hickey, about 80 percent of retailers "[were] able to forecast a high demand for women's knits [using the top-down approach], but . . . unable to forecast within that category whether long-sleeve shirts or short-sleeve shirts [would] be more popular for that season."[16]

Conversely, the bottom-up approach is recommended for tactical planning and scheduling.[17] It generally results in smaller forecast errors and less bias at the lower levels because it reflects the actual changes in demand. However, higher-level forecasts are generally poorer.

Canadian retailer Northern Group Retail, Ltd., uses the top-down approach and has overcome some of its lower-level forecasting problems by adopting software tools. The software helps the organization "forecast items down to the store and item level" and as a result, it can customize its merchandise store-by-store. Inventory levels have dropped significantly, stores are more productive and gross margins are higher than the industry average.[18]

Ocean Spray, the leading producer of canned and bottled juice drinks, uses both the top-down and bottom-up approach to its advantage. The first week of each month, demand planners use a bottom-up approach, working with the field sales managers to develop a rolling six-month forecast for the top 75 customers (they account for 70 percent of Ocean Spray's revenues), which then are aggregated. The second week, a top-down approach is used in which a series of consensus-building meetings are conducted among managers and directors of sales, marketing and trade marketing. The team reviews forecast error rates and makes adjustments for any upcoming sales promotions. With additional input from demand planning, the final forecast is prepared. According to Paul Gelly, manager of demand planning, "The monthly fluctuations in forecast errors have stabilized significantly — we don't experience wild fluctuations as was the case with our old process."[19]

The types of forecasts an organization uses are related to the time period covered by the forecast, which may be developed using a mix of *qualitative* and *quantitative* methods. Common forecast methods and their applicability are summarized in Figure 5-4 and discussed further in the following section, beginning with a description of qualitative forecasting techniques.

## Qualitative Forecasts

Qualitative, or judgmental, forecasts are known as such because they are developed based on the opinions of others such as managers or other experts, estimates from the sales staff or the results of market research. They are used most often when an organization has no background in quantitative forecasting or when no quantitative data is available for analysis. Qualitative forecasts also are valuable when quantitative forecasts are not particularly accurate and the decision-maker (CEO, president or other senior executive) has a high level of experiential knowledge that is difficult to incorporate into the quantitative forecast. This is often the case when organizations are performing long-range planning or predicting technology trends. Qualitative forecasts also are useful in adjusting for specific events that will take place in the future, such as competitive actions, special promotions and domestic or international political events. Some examples of qualitative forecasts are provided in the next section.

Figure 5-4    Forecasting Methods

| FORECAST METHOD | | TIME-FRAME | | |
|---|---|---|---|---|
| **Qualitative** | **Description** | **Long term** | **Medium term** | **Short term** |
| Sales force composite | A manager reviews each salesperson's best estimate of the expected level of customer demand for his or her region. Forecast then is compiled at the district and national levels for an overall forecast. | X | X | X |
| Market research | Surveys are collected from consumers to estimate the degree of interest in a product or service. | X | X | X |
| Jury of executive opinion | Executive opinion is based on the experience, knowledge and opinions of employees from key areas within an organization and external parties such as customers and suppliers. | X | X | X |
| Delphi method | Moderator collects results from survey sent to panel of experts and then creates a new survey that is sent to the group. This process continues until consensus is reached. | X | | |
| **Quantitative** | | | | |
| Naive forecast | The upcoming forecast is set equal to the most recent period's demand. | | | X |
| Simple moving average | The mean of at least two recent periods of demand data is the basis for the next period's demand forecast. | | X | X |

(continued)

| FORECAST METHOD | | TIME-FRAME | | |
| --- | --- | --- | --- | --- |
| Quantitative (continued) | Description | Long term | Medium term | Short term |
| Weighted moving average | Weights are used on each past demand period to place more emphasis on certain periods based on experience. | | X | X |
| Exponential smoothing | Each forecast is weighted by a given fraction, known as the smoothing constant, of the difference between the most recent actual demand and forecast. | | X | X |
| Multiplicative seasonality | Seasonality is expressed in terms of a percentage of the average demand using an indexing method. | | X | |
| Trend-adjusted exponential smoothing | An exponentially smoothed forecast is adjusted by incorporating a trend value. | | X | |
| Regression analysis | A straight line is fitted to past data using a fitting technique known as the least squares method. | X | X | |
| Box-Jenkins | Complicated yet accurate method estimates a mathematical formula that will approximately generate the historical demand patterns in a time series. | | X | |
| Winter's model | Simultaneously considers the effects of trend and seasonal factors using the exponential smoothing technique. | | X | |
| Single-period model | Past demand data is used to determine how much stock to order based on probability analysis. | | X | X |

## Sales Force Composite

In one commonly used method, each salesperson provides a best estimate of the expected level of customer demand for his or her region. A manager then reviews each forecast to make sure it is realistic. Based on this information, the forecast is compiled at the district and national levels for an overall forecast.

This approach offers several advantages because the sales force likely has the most knowledge on what customers will be buying and in what quantities; regional sales information can be used to manage inventories, distribution and sales staffing; and regional sales can be rolled up into one overall forecast. Marketing organizations frequently share sales force composites with supply professionals to improve forecast accuracy, negotiation capabilities and service to internal and external customers.[20] The downside is that salespeople tend to have their own biases that can adversely affect the forecast. For instance, salespeople may not always be particularly astute in determining what customers will actually buy. Additionally, if performance is based on the forecast, the salesperson may provide an underestimate, working diligently only until he or she has reached his or her projection. Conversely, the salesperson may strive to exceed the projection to look good. To overcome these problems, Sport Obermeyer, a U.S. manufacturer of fashion skiwear, uses independent sales forecasts from a panel of experts for each product as one component in its strategy to improve customer responsiveness and reduce risk. Where forecasts differed significantly, the organization concluded that demand was unpredictable and adjusted production downward. Sport Obermeyer was able to reduce markdowns and increase profitability by two-thirds the first year after implementation.[21]

## Market Research

Market research uses surveys collected from consumers to estimate the degree of interest in a product or service. Surveys may be administered in a number of ways, including by telephone, e-mail, online, regular mail or personal interviews. Marketing personnel attempt to select a sample representing a specific population and then analyze the data using both statistical tools and their own judgment. While market research is used as the basis for short-term, medium-term and long-term forecasting, its accuracy is best for the short term.

Several disadvantages are associated with using surveys in market research. For example, the wording used in survey questions may not always result in learning the true feelings of the consumer. Without actually seeing the product, consumers also may have a difficult time imagining a new product's usefulness. Moreover, if people do respond to a survey, the fact that they say they will use a product or service is no guarantee that they will. Finally, it is difficult to get people to respond to mailed surveys. To resolve some of these issues, some organizations are using Web-based surveys that can be completed quickly and easily. Vermont Teddy Bear Co., a gift delivery service, has started using online surveys that include photographs of product concepts to help develop its demand forecast for new items. This form of market research has worked so well that the results are used to help the organization decide which designs go into production and the production quantities.[22] Organizations also are collecting and organizing customer data by using customer relationship management (CRM) software applications to support the forecasting process. Purchasing and returns transactions, demographic information and responses to marketing promotions can help marketing estimate the future needs of existing and potential customers.

## Jury of Executive Opinion

A forecast employing executive opinion uses the experience, knowledge and opinions of employees from key areas within an organization and external parties such as customers and suppliers. This type of forecast typically is used when past data does not exist, when causal relationships have not been identified, when a forecast is totally out of line with competitors, national or world events are changing or an executive has some information that is not available to the forecaster. For example, executives may adjust a sales forecast for a newly developed sales promotion that has not been released yet. Senior management also may be aware of a new trade agreement that has been signed or a war developing that will open up new selling opportunities. The makers of Tylenol, for instance, had to use a jury of executive opinion to forecast sales for 1983 after a tampering scare in 1982 because demand was highly uncertain. Executive opinion also may be used to develop a forecast for a new product or service without a previous track record. These managers normally hold two or three forecast meetings, perhaps starting with the sales forecast, and work toward consensus.

The advantage of this method is its simplicity and relative ease of use. Thus, it is probably one of the most commonly used forecasting methods today. However, it is subject to a high degree of judgmental bias. These biases often occur because of the dominant positions of some persons such as senior managers, an individual's personal charisma that can sway people, someone who tends to dominate the conversation or the "alleged expertise" of one individual.

## The Delphi Method

The Delphi Method is used to lessen the potential biases commonly found using a jury of executive opinion. A structured approach is used to derive consensus from a panel of experts — usually five to ten — who maintain anonymity. Anonymity is important because it frees each participant to express his or her opinion freely. The Delphi Method also eliminates the need for group meetings. However, it can take multiple iterations to reach consensus and participants may opt to drop out of the process.

A coordinator sends the panel an initial survey, usually asking questions regarding sales revenue estimates including a minimum and maximum, the likelihood that these estimates will materialize and the reasoning behind each participant's estimates. The coordinator then tabulates the results and sends them back along with any anonymous statements. Each participant reviews the results with an option to adjust his or her original estimates based on the opinions of the other respondents, and submits any changes along with the reasons for diverging from the original estimates. This process continues until consensus is reached.

Other uses for the Delphi Method besides sales revenues include long-range forecasting for product and service demand, developing projections for new product demand and predicting technological developments. The results from forecasting societal changes, scientific advances, the competitive environment or government regulation also can be used to help direct the organization's research and development personnel. FedEx, the world's largest express transportation organization, uses the Delphi Method to predict call center usage. Interviews are conducted with internal groups whose initiatives will have an impact on demand, including marketing, information technology, sales and customer service. The results are used with other analytical tools to create a most likely scenario forecast.[23]

While qualitative forecasts are valuable, quantitative methods based on mathematics have their rightful place. If a product has been on the market a long time and demand is relatively predictable, only quantitative forecasts may be necessary. Campbell Soup Co., for instance, has little trouble forecasting demand for its tomato and chicken noodle condensed soups, which have been around for more than 100 years. With relatively recent advances in computer capabilities and software, quantitative forecasting also is much less tedious, allowing forecasters to focus on interpreting the results rather than on assembling the information.[24] The following two sections provide a discussion of two categories of quantitative models: *time series* and *causal analysis.*

# Time Series Forecasting

Time series models use time-based data, which is a set of observations collected at regular intervals over a given time horizon. A clothing retailer, such as Gap, Inc., might collect monthly sales data for each store over the past five years. The data points would be related to specific points in time; thus, the data could be used for time series analysis. The underlying assumption is that a forecast can be created based on patterns observed within the time series data.

Four main patterns may be present separately or in combination:

1. *Horizontal or flat.* Demand data values tend to fluctuate around a mean that does not vary. This pattern is the easiest to predict because of its simplicity. Some examples of horizontal demand include products or services found in the mature stage of their life cycles, such as bread or legal services.

2. *Seasonality.* Any pattern that is observed regularly, occurs for a constant length of time and is influenced by given seasonal factors such as day of the week or a given monthly quarter is considered seasonal. For example, hospitals experience certain peaks in demand for their services during the day. Demand for banking services typically spike on paydays such as Fridays, and on the 15th and 30th of each month.

3. *Trend.* An increasing or decreasing pattern of demand over time is considered a trend. For example, the demand for music DVDs has been on an upward trend since 2004.[25]

4. *Cycle.* A cycle is longer than a season, often a multiyear phenomenon, and is tied to economic fluctuations, such as recessions or inflation. A cycle is probably the most difficult pattern to predict. Economic indicators and indexes generally are used to predict cycles and are discussed in Chapter 4.

A time series is made up of a demand pattern comprised of some combination of these four patterns plus some *random variation,* which is unexplainable and cannot be predicted. Thus, it can be difficult to make a forecast given the number of patterns that may be present. However, several forecasting models are useful in keeping the amount of random variation to a minimum. Models used to predict relatively flat or horizontal demand are discussed in the following section.

## Naive Approach

One of the simplest forecasting methods used is to set the upcoming forecast equal to the most recent period's demand. For example, if Walgreen Co., a U.S. drugstore chain, sells 1,000 bottles of 100-count vitamin C in September, the forecast for October also would be 1,000 bottles. Organizations often use this method as a starting point and then make adjustments based on past experience. This method also can be used as a basis of comparison against more sophisticated models. It is the least expensive, easiest and most efficient method.

## Moving Averages

The *simple moving average* calculates the average of the most current "n" periods. In each recalculation, the most current period's data is added and the oldest data is removed. (*ISM Glossary,* 2006) The forecast typically is based on a calculation of the mean for at least two recent periods of demand data. The data is summed and then divided by the number of time periods used in the calculation. For example, if a forecaster at German retailer Metro Group wants to predict demand for a size 40 (U.S. size 10) woman's dress in a specific style for April using a three-month simple moving average, the calculation would be the average of actual demand for January, February and March. The formula to calculate the moving average is:

$$\text{Moving average} = \frac{\sum\text{demand for past } n \text{ periods}}{n}$$

$\sum$ = a symbol that represents the sum of and
$n$ = number for periods included in the moving average.

Using the Metro example, if actual demand for January, February and March were 2,500, 3,200 and 2,750 dresses, respectively, the forecast for April would be

April forecast = (2,500 + 3,200 + 2,750)/3 = 2,816.7 ≈ 2,817 dresses

As data from a new time period is added, data from the earliest time period is dropped from the average calculation. Again, using the Metro example, when the forecaster wants to predict demand for May, he or she would use actual demand from February, March and April. This method is fairly reliable if the forecaster can assume that demand will remain relatively flat over time.

If a noticeable demand pattern is observed, the forecaster can apply individual weights to each past demand period to place more emphasis on certain periods. For example, an office supply organization might notice that within a three-month period, the most accurate forecast for computer printers is calculated by weighting the most recent month by 50 percent, the second most recent month by 30 percent and the third most recent month by 20 percent. Weights usually are determined based on the forecaster's past experience; there is no set formula. The forecaster often experiments with past demand data to determine the weightings that will provide the most accurate forecast. However, the sum of the weights must equal 1. The calculation of the weighted moving average is as follows:

Weighted moving average = $\sum$ [(weight for period $n$)(demand for period $n$)]

In the following example of an office supply organization such as OfficeMax or Staples, the forecaster collects data on demand for boxes of private-label inkjet paper from April (5,500), May (5,700) and June (5,950). Applying the weighted moving average method, and weights of 20 percent, 30 percent and 50 percent, respectively, the forecast for July would be:

July forecast = (5,500 × 20%) + (5,700 × 30%) + (5,950 × 50%) = 5,785 boxes

The advantage of the simple and weighted moving average methods is the ability to smooth out any unexpected fluctuations in demand so that stable estimates can be made. However, as the number of periods averaged increases, the smoothing effect of the simple moving average method also increases, making these methods less sensitive to actual changes in the data. Another disadvantage of either method is the inability to effectively forecast trends because of the smoothing effect. In the previous example, for instance, although there appears to be an upward trend in demand, the forecast for July is less than the demand for June. Moreover, the simple and weighted moving average methods cannot predict unprecedented events because they are based on historical data. Lastly, both methods require a significant amount of past data to be effective.

## Exponential Smoothing

While the simple and weighted moving average methods require a large amount of past data, the *exponential smoothing method* requires relatively little data and is useful when demand is relatively flat or horizontal. The methodology weights the demand for the most recent period and the forecast for the previous period as a basis for the current forecast. (*ISM Glossary,* 2006) This method is fairly accurate and few calculations are required. However, exponential smoothing is a more sophisticated method than the simple or weighted moving averages, and a qualitative method such as the Delphi Method or managerial experience must be used to set the initial forecast. Exponential smoothing is widely used in wholesale organizations, service organizations and retailing.

Each forecast is weighted by a given decimal value, known as the *smoothing constant,* the difference between the most recent actual demand and the forecast. The smoothing constant will range between 0 and 1 and is determined by the forecaster. The formula to calculate the forecast is

$$\text{Forecast}_{t+1} = \text{Forecast}_t + \alpha(\text{Actual Demand}_t - \text{Forecast}_t)$$

where
$t$ = current time period
$t+1$ = following time period
$\alpha$ = alpha = smoothing constant ($0 \leq \alpha \leq 1$)

The following example illustrates the exponential smoothing method:

JJ International sells patio furniture to retailers in Australia. Susan, the organization's forecaster, has collected the following demand data for one of its tables, as is shown in the following table:

| Month | Demand |
|---|---|
| May | 450 |
| June | 440 |
| July | 420 |
| August | 460 |
| September | 485 |
| October | 435 |

Susan decides to use the exponential smoothing method to calculate the forecast for June, July and August using the exponential smoothing method and a smoothing constant of $\alpha = 0.3$ based on her past experience. She assumes the forecast for May ($F_{May}$) is 450 tables. Given

$$F_{May} = 450, \alpha = 0.3$$

Susan first calculates the forecast for June:

$$F_{June} = F_{May} + 0.3(A_{May} - F_{JMay}) = 450 + 0.3(450 - 450) = 450 \text{ tables}$$

She then calculates the forecast for July:

$$F_{July} = F_{June} + 0.3(A_{June} - F_{June}) = 450 + 0.3(440 - 450) = 447 \text{ tables}$$

Lastly, Susan calculates the forecast for August:

$$F_{August} = F_{July} + 0.3(A_{July} - F_{July}) = 447 + 0.3(420 - 447) = 438.9 \approx 439 \text{ tables}$$

Although any smoothing constant $\alpha$ between 0 and 1 can be used, values closer to 1 more heavily weight the previous period's demand, increasing the responsiveness of the forecast to changes in actual demand. Conversely, an $\alpha$ value closer to 0 weights the previous period's demand less heavily, resulting in a forecast that is less responsive to demand fluctuations. The next example illustrates the effect of different alpha values. Note that while the forecast is most responsive when the alpha value is 0.8, it may not be the most accurate. A comparison of the errors also would be needed to determine which alpha value results in the most *accurate* forecast. More on forecast accuracy is found later in this chapter.

Susan, the forecaster at JJ International, wants to compare forecasts using the exponential smoothing method and different alpha values. She calculates the monthly forecast using alpha values of 0.2, 0.4, 0.6 and 0.8.

An Excel spreadsheet was used for the forecast using Tools, Data Analysis and Exponential Smoothing for each alpha value. The following three spreadsheets illustrate how to set up the calculations based on $\alpha = 0.2$ (complete results are already shown in each example). (In the second spreadsheet, Excel requires the user to enter a *damping factor* rather than a smoothing constant. A damping factor provides the same function as a smoothing constant but is the inverse, $1 - \alpha$. Thus, the damping factor that should be used for calculating the forecast is $1 - 0.2 = 0.8$.) The software also assumes that the first period forecast is equal to the actual demand.

*Step 1. Create a table of the raw data. Select "Tools," "Data Analysis."*

*Step 2. Select "Exponential Smoothing" and "OK."*

*Step 3. Enter input range, damping factor (1 − α) and output range, and select "OK."*

| | A | B | C | D | E | F | G | H | I | J | K | L | M |
|---|---|---|---|---|---|---|---|---|---|---|---|---|---|
| 1 | | | | | | | | | | | | | |
| 2 | | | | | | | | | | | | | |
| 3 | | | | Alpha | Value | | | | | | | | |
| 4 | Month | Demand | 0.2 | 0.4 | 0.6 | 0.8 | | | | | | | |
| 5 | May | 450 | 450 | 450 | 450 | 450 | | | | | | | |
| 6 | June | 440 | 450 | 450 | 450 | 450 | | | | | | | |
| 7 | July | 420 | 448 | 446 | 444 | 442 | | | | | | | |
| 8 | Aug | 460 | 442 | 436 | 430 | 424 | | | | | | | |
| 9 | Sept | 485 | 446 | 445 | 448 | 453 | | | | | | | |
| 10 | Oct | 435 | 454 | 461 | 470 | 479 | | | | | | | |
| 11 | | | | | | | | | | | | | |
| 12 | | | | | | | | | | | | | |
| 13 | | | | | | | | | | | | | |
| 14 | | | | | | | | | | | | | |
| 15 | | | | | | | | | | | | | |
| 16 | | | | | | | | | | | | | |
| 17 | | | | | | | | | | | | | |

Exponential Smoothing dialog:
- Input Range: $B$5:$B$10
- Damping factor: 0.8
- Labels
- Output options
- Output Range: $C$5:$C$10
- New Worksheet Ply:
- New Workbook
- Chart Output
- Standard Errors
- OK / Cancel / Help

*Step 4. Repeat Steps 1 through 3 to develop the other forecasts. A graph then can be created using the spreadsheet results and graphing function.*

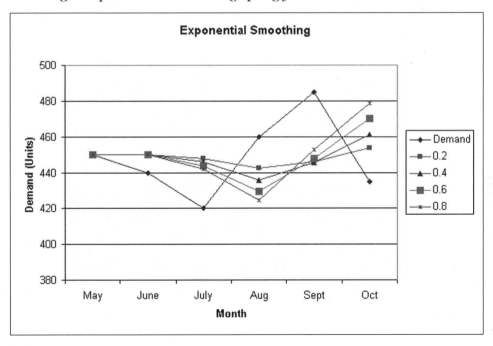

Susan notices that the forecast for $\alpha = 0.2$ is flatter and less responsive to the actual demand, that the forecast is more responsive as the alpha value increases and that the forecasts for $\alpha = 0.8$ is the most responsive to the actual demand. However, all forecasts trail the actual demand. For example, note that the actual demand in July was 420. The forecasts for July are all higher than the demand but closer to the actual demand for June. In August, the actual demand was 460, while all forecasts were less than the actual demand of 460 and closer to the actual demand for July. Similarly, in September the forecasts were all less than the actual demand of 485 but closer to the actual demand for August.

While moving average and exponential smoothing models are good for relatively flat demand, seasonality is common for many organizations, requiring a different forecasting method. The following section provides a discussion of one method commonly used — the seasonal index.

## Forecasting Seasonality

Most organizations will experience some type of seasonal pattern for one or more of their products or services. The goal is to recognize not only when those seasons occur, but how each season's demand exceeds or falls below average demand. While several methods are used to calculate measures to reflect seasonality, this chapter will present one method known as *multiplicative seasonality*, where seasonality is expressed in terms of a percentage of the average demand. This percentage above or below the average is known as the *seasonal index*. For instance, if demand for snow skis in the fall months is 1.5 times the average annual demand, fall demand is 50 percent above the average annual demand.

The steps to calculate a seasonal index are illustrated in the following example. Notice the variation in forecasted demand is based on the season.

Premium Pools builds swimming pools in Phoenix, Arizona, and has been operating for five years. Pat, the owner, has noticed a seasonal pattern in demand each year and would like to use this information to make better supply decisions for the organization's materials. Historically, purchasing policies have been based on obtaining volume discounts and as a result inventory costs have risen significantly in the past year. Following is demand data for the past two years:

| Season | 2005 | 2006 |
|--------|------|------|
| Spring | 200 | 220 |
| Summer | 450 | 465 |
| Fall | 150 | 155 |
| Winter | 90 | 92 |
| Total | 890 | 932 |

To calculate the seasonal index, Pat uses the multiplicative seasonal index method:

*Step 1.* Pat calculates the average demand for each quarter by dividing the total annual demand for each year by 4:

Year 1: 890/4 = 222.5
Year 2: 932/4 = 233

*Step 2.* He then calculates the seasonal index for every season for the past two years by dividing the actual demand for each season by the average demand per season (rounding to three decimal points):

| Season | 2005 | 2006 |
|---|---|---|
| Spring | 200/222.5 = 0.899 | 220/233 = 0.944 |
| Summer | 450/222.5 = 2.022 | 465/233 = 1.996 |
| Fall | 150/222.5 = 0.674 | 155/233 = 0.665 |
| Winter | 90/222.5 = 0.404 | 92/233 = 0.395 |

*Step 3.* The average seasonal index then is calculated:

| Season | Average Seasonal Index |
|---|---|
| Spring | (0.899 + 0.944)/2 = 0.922 |
| Summer | (2.022 + 1.996)/2 = 2.009 |
| Fall | (0.674 + 0.665)/2 = 0.670 |
| Winter | (0.404 + 0.395)/2 = 0.400 |

*Step 4.* Pat expects to build 975 pools in 2007 based on a sales force composite; he calculates the average expected quarterly demand to be 975/4 or 243.75 pools, rounded to 244 pools.

*Step 5.* With this information, Pat forecasts the demand for each season for 2007 (rounded to the nearest whole pool):

| Season | Seasonal Forecast (Pools) |
|---|---|
| Spring | 244(0.922) = 225 |
| Summer | 244(2.009) = 490 |
| Fall | 244(0.670) = 163 |
| Winter | 244(0.400) = 98 |
| Total | 976 |

Note: Because of rounding, the sum of the seasonal forecasts is slightly higher than the expected demand of 975 pools.

Organizations also may also experience demand trends, either up or down. For example, since 2003, computer hardware manufacturers such as IBM and Hewlett-Packard have experienced an upward trend in demand for high-end servers.[26] Armed with this knowledge and a good forecast, supply management professionals can plan and negotiate with suppliers more effectively. The following section provides a description of two commonly used methods to forecast trends.

## Forecasting a Trend

Organizations generally need several periods of data to recognize a trend. Creating a graph of past demand is helpful in providing a visual representation of any demand patterns. When a trend is observed, it is best to adopt a forecasting method that will accurately reflect that trend. Following are two commonly used methods to forecast trends.

**Trend-Adjusted Exponential Smoothing Method.** As described earlier in this chapter, a trend is a consistent upward or downward movement in demand over time. Exponentially smoothed forecasts are not particularly useful when trends are apparent because they always lag reality. However, an exponentially smoothed forecast can be adjusted, to a certain extent, by incorporating a trend component; this is known as *trend-adjusted exponential smoothing*. This method uses two smoothing constants, $\alpha$ and $\beta$. The $\alpha$ value smoothes the initial forecast using the exponential smoothing method, while the $\beta$ value smoothes the trend. $\beta$, similar to $\alpha$, *must* be between 0 and 1. Higher values of $\beta$ (closer to 1) mean the forecaster has placed more emphasis on changes in recent trends, while a small weight (closer to 0) lessens the effect of a current trend. Forecasters generally set the values for the first-period smoothed forecast and trend based on past experience and trial and error. The more periods of demand data that are available to the forecaster, the easier it will be to estimate those values. There are three equations for this method:

1. *Smoothing the initial forecast:* $F_{t+1} = \alpha A_t + (1 - \alpha)(F_t + T_t)$

2. *Smoothing the trend:* $T_{t+1} = \beta(F_{t+1} - F_t) + (1 - \beta)T_t$

3. *Trend-adjusted forecast:* $TAF_{t+1} = F_{t+1} + T_{t+1}$

Where:
$F_t$ = exponentially smoothed average in period $t$
$A_t$ = actual demand in period $t$
$T_t$ = exponentially smoothed trend in period $t$
$\alpha$ = smoothing constant $(0 \leq \alpha \leq 1)$ and
$\beta$ = smoothing constant for trend $(0 \leq \beta \leq 1)$

This method, while useful, is best used with the help of forecasting software because of the extensive calculations required. The next example provides an application of trend-adjusted exponential smoothing using both manual calculations and an Excel spreadsheet.

An upscale restaurant in Calgary, Alberta, Canada, has experienced an upward trend in the sales of one of its menu items, bread pudding. The restaurant's forecaster, Ben, has collected demand data from the past ten weeks to create a forecast using trend-adjusted exponential smoothing, as shown in the following chart:

| Week | Demand | Week | Demand |
|------|--------|------|--------|
| 1 | 51 | 6 | 56 |
| 2 | 54 | 7 | 58 |
| 3 | 53 | 8 | 60 |
| 4 | 55 | 9 | 60 |
| 5 | 57 | 10 | 62 |

Ben decides, based on past experience, to use the following values to calculate the forecast:

Initial forecast (Week 1) = $F_1$ = 50
Initial trend (Week 1) = $T_1$ = 1
Alpha ($\alpha$) = 0.30
Beta ($\beta$) = 0.20

Ben could manually calculate the forecast for week 11. To create the forecast, he must first start by calculating the forecast for week 2 and then progress consecutively through each week until he reaches week 11. Using the initial forecast and trend values for week 1, Ben calculates the forecast for week 2:

1. *Smoothing the initial forecast:*
   $F_{t+1} = \alpha A_t + (1 - \alpha)(F_t + T_t)$
   $= 0.3(51) + (1 - 0.30)(50 + 1) = 15.3 + 35.7 = 51$

2. *Smoothing the trend:*
   $T_{t+1} = \beta(F_{t+1} - F_t) + (1 - \beta)T_t$
   $= 0.20 (51 - 50) + (1 - 0.20)(1) = 1$

3. *Trend-adjusted forecast:*
   $TAF_{t+1} = F_{t+1} + T_{t+1}$
   $= 51 + 1 = 52$

The forecast for week 3 is:

1. *Smoothing the initial forecast:*
   $$F_{t+1} = \alpha A_t + (1 - \alpha)(F_t + T_t)$$
   $$= 0.30(54) + (1 - 0.30)(51 + 1)$$
   $$= 16.2 + 36.4 = 52.6$$

2. *Smoothing the trend:*
   $$T_{t+1} = \beta(F_{t+1} - F_t) + (1 - \beta)T_t$$
   $$= 0.20(52.6 - 51) + (1 - 0.20)(1)$$
   $$= 0.32 + 0.8 = 1.12$$

3. *Trend-adjusted forecast:*
   $$TAF_{t+1} = F_{t+1} + T_{t+1}$$
   $$= 52.6 + 1.12 = 53.72 \approx 54$$

Ben continues these calculations until he reaches week 11. The forecast for week 11 is based week 10's forecast of 60.4 and week 10's trend of 1.1:

1. *Smoothing the initial forecast:*
   $$F_{t+1} = \alpha A_t + (1 - \alpha)(F_t + T_t)$$
   $$= 0.30(62) + (1 - 0.30)(60.4 + 1.1)$$
   $$18.6 + 43.05 = 61.65$$

2. *Smoothing the trend:*
   $$T_{t+1} = \beta(F_{t+1} - F_t) + (1 - \beta)T_t$$
   $$0.20(61.65 - 60.4) + (1 - 0.20)\ 1.1$$
   $$= 0.25 + 0.88 = 1.13$$

3. *Trend-adjusted forecast:*
   $$TAF_{t+1} = F_{t+1} + T_{t+1}$$
   $$= 61.65 + 1.13 = 62.78 \approx 63$$

Alternatively, Ben could use a spreadsheet using Excel, as follows. By graphing the forecast against the actual demand, Ben notices that his forecast appears to be fairly accurate.

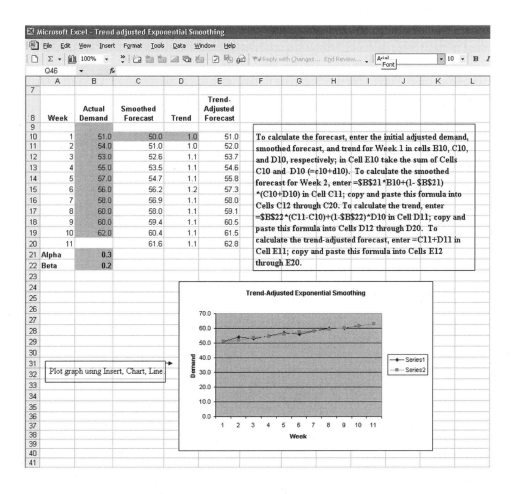

**Linear Regression.** When demand exhibits a clear linear trend either upward or downward, linear regression also can be used with a time series of historical data. Linear regression has been defined as "a causal method in which one variable (the dependent variable) is related to one or more independent variables by a linear equation."[27] The dependent variable is the one that will be forecast, while the independent variable is one that is expected to have a significant effect on the dependent variable. Using linear regression, a straight line is fitted to past data based on a fitting technique known as the *least squares method*. In trend analysis, the dependent variable — demand or price — is expected to change linearly as the independent variable — time or quantity purchased — changes. Supply management professionals may use linear regression, for example, to predict price trends for specific goods or materials based on quantities purchased. The equation used to generate the forecast is:

$$Y = a + bX$$

Where $Y$ = forecast for period $i$

$X$ = time or quantity variable

$a$ = intercept of $Y$ at $X = 0$

$b$ = slope of the line.

The coefficients $a$ and $b$ are calculated (notice that $b$ must be computed first) using the least squares method as follows:

$$b = n \frac{\sum(xy) - \sum x \sum y}{n \sum x^2 - (\sum x)^2}$$

$$a = \frac{\sum y - b \sum x}{n}$$

where

$x$ = independent variable values

$y$ = dependent variable values

$n$ = number of observations

Rather than performing calculations by hand, which can be tedious and subject to error, Excel spreadsheets are simple alternatives. The following example illustrates this method:

Sunshine Shades, a Chinese manufacturer of window shades for automobiles, has been experiencing an upward trend in prices for one of its raw materials. The organization's supply management professional creates a trend line using Excel to predict the next month's price based on past prices.

The following spreadsheet (top of next page) shows the formulas needed to calculate the slope and intercept.

The supply management professional then calculates the forecast for weeks 9, 10 and 11, using the slope and intercept coefficients:

$$\text{Forecast}_{\text{Week 9}} = a + bX = \$4,557.5 + \$85(9) = \$5,322.50/\text{ton}$$

$$\text{Forecast}_{\text{Week10}} = \$4,557.5 + \$85(10) = \$5,407.50/\text{ton}$$

$$\text{Forecast}_{\text{Week11}} = \$4,557.5 + \$85(11) = \$5,492.50/\text{ton}$$

## Simultaneously Considering Trends and Seasonal Patterns

Organizations may realize not only a consistent upward or downward trend in a time series, but also seasonality for a particular item. Hospitals, for example, have always

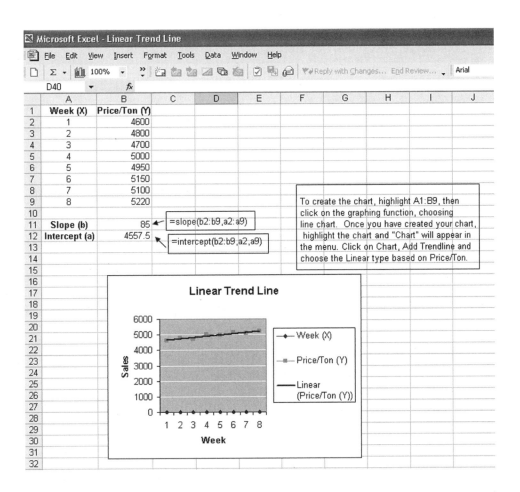

experienced seasonality in demand for emergency room care but in recent years also have noticed a significant upward trend.[28] The data presented in Figure 5-5 provides an illustration where both seasonality and an upward trend are evident. Note that demand in quarter 1 has steadily increased year after year. The same is true for quarters 2, 3 and 4. However, there also appears to be evidence of seasonality each year. The *Winter's Model,* otherwise known as *triple exponential smoothing* or *seasonal exponential smoothing,* is commonly applied in this situation. It uses the trend–adjusted exponential method discussed earlier in this chapter but adds a third parameter, gamma ($\gamma$), to adjust for seasonal factors. As with other more complex methods, Winter's Model should be performed using the appropriate forecasting software. Further discussion of this method is beyond the scope of this text but good forecasting textbooks are available, such as *Business Forecasting* by Wilson and Keating and *Forecasting: Methods & Applications* by Makridakis, et al.

**Figure 5-5  Time Series That Illustrates Both a Trend and Seasonality**

| | DEMAND | | |
| --- | --- | --- | --- |
| | **2004** | **2005** | **2006** |
| Quarter 1 | 148 | 194 | 276 |
| Quarter 2 | 94 | 129 | 158 |
| Quarter 3 | 57 | 77 | 96 |
| Quarter 4 | 135 | 188 | 221 |

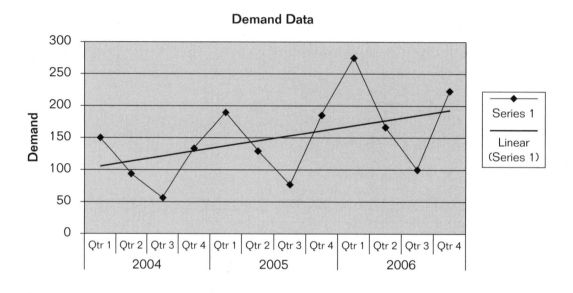

## Box-Jenkins Method

The goal of the Box-Jenkins Method is to find a mathematical formula that will approximately generate the historical demand patterns in a time series. For example, this method has been used to estimate demand for hospital emergency room services, to predict foreign exchange rates and to forecast demand for international tourism services.[29] The advantage of the method is that it can be applied to a variety of modeling situations. However, a large amount of data is required and computer software support, such as that offered by software organization SAS, is required.

The Box-Jenkins Method is a heuristic, which means a few steps are repeated as necessary to develop an accurate forecast. The process involves first identifying the appropriate *ARIMA* process, which then is fitted to the time series data. ARIMA is an acronym that represents an integration of autoregressive (the use of historical data to predict the future) and moving average models. *Fitting the data* means to adjust the data so the time series is relatively flat by removing trends and seasonality through *differencing* (taking the difference between consecutive values that makes modeling easier) and *transformation* (taking the square root or log of each value that helps stabilize the variation when demand changes to a different level) methods.

Graphs of the transformed and differenced data then are used to identify the ARIMA processes that could be a good fit to the data. This analysis is used for *parameter estimation* or, in other words, finding the values of the model coefficients that will provide the best fit for the data. The assumptions of the model then are tested and if the model is not satisfactory, the forecaster must go back and review the graphs again for a more appropriate model. The fitted model then is used as a basis for the forecast.

In some instances, an organization may experience special circumstances that require a different type of modeling process. The single-period model is one method that can be used; it is discussed further in the following section.

## The Single-Period Model

This model is of special importance to businesses that accumulate inventory with a relatively short selling season such as a one-time special event. Past demand data is used to determine how much stock to order based on probability analysis. The assumption is that demand is highly variable but follows a known probability distribution. The goal is to maximize profit, minimize lost sales and avoid an overstocking situation. The following example provides an illustration of the single-period model:

Jeff Jones owns a small Christmas tree lot in Woodland, California. Each year he purchases trees from a local tree farm, but he must place his order in July to have enough trees for sale to his customers. Jeff plans to sell each tree for $45. He pays his supplier $20 per tree, for a net profit of $25. Any trees not sold by December 23 will be sold for $15 (he expects that any trees remaining after December 23 will be sold for the lower price). Jeff usually sells between 50 and 90 trees each year.

He must place his order in multiples of 10. Based on past years' sales, Jeff has estimated the probability of selling the six-foot blue spruce, one of his more popular trees:

| Demand (Blue Spruce) | Probability |
|---|---|
| 50 | .10 |
| 60 | .15 |
| 70 | .35 |
| 80 | .30 |
| 90 | .10 |

There are three possible outcomes in this scenario: (1) Jeff will sell the exact number of trees he ordered, (2) the number of trees he orders will be greater than the number of trees that will be demanded or (3) the number of trees he orders will be less than the number of trees that will be demanded.

The following payoff table summarizes Jeff's calculations:

| | Payoff Table | | | | |
|---|---|---|---|---|---|
| Probability of Occurrence | .10 | .15 | .35 | .30 | .10 |
| Customer Demand (trees) | 50 | 60 | 70 | 80 | 90 |

| Number of Trees Ordered | | | | | | Expected Profit |
|---|---|---|---|---|---|---|
| 50 | $1,250 | $1,250 | $1,250 | $1,250 | $1,250 | $1,250 |
| 60 | $1,200 | $1,500 | $1,500 | $1,500 | $1,500 | $1,470 |
| 70 | $1,150 | $1,450 | $1,750 | $1,750 | $1,750 | $1,645 |
| 80 | $1,100 | $1,400 | $1,700 | $2,000 | $2,000 | $1,715 |
| 90 | $1,050 | $1,350 | $1,650 | $1,950 | $2,250 | $1,695 |

Jeff starts by calculating the payoff when supply equals demand:

Payoff = trees demanded (selling price − unit cost)

For example, when 60 trees are purchased and 60 trees are sold, the payoff is 60 trees × (45 − 20) = $1,500.

He also calculates the payoff when the number of trees ordered is greater than demand:

Payoff = [(number of trees demanded) × (net profit) − (trees ordered − trees demanded) × (net profit)]

Thus, if Jeff orders 70 trees but only 60 are sold before December 24th, the payoff is

(60 * $25) − (10 * $5) = $1,450.

Lastly, Jeff calculates the payoff if the number of trees ordered is less than demand:

Payoff = trees ordered (selling price − unit cost)

For example, if Jeff orders 60 trees but demand that year was for 70 trees, he still can sell only 60 trees and the payoff is:

60 × $25 = $1,500

He then calculates the expected total payoff by multiplying the expected profit for each order quantity by the probability that he will sell that quantity, and then takes the sum of those values. For example, the expected profit for ordering 50 trees is:

($1,250 × 0.10) + ($1,250 × 0.15) + ($1,250 × 0.35) + ($1,250 × 0.30) + ($1,250 × 0.10) = $1,250

The expected profit for ordering 80 trees is:

($1,100 × 0.10) + ($1,400 × 0.15) + ($1,700 × 0.35) + ($2,000 × 0.30) + ($2,000 × 0.10) = $1,715

Jeff reviews the results and decides to order 80 blue spruce trees because the expected profit is the highest.

There are also circumstances when the forecaster is able to identify relationships among demand and other variables. In these situations, causal modeling is commonly used and is described in the following section.

# Causal Modeling

In *causal or associative models,* the dependent variable in the forecast is assumed to be related in some way to other independent variables within the environment. Utility companies, for example, typically forecast sales to commercial customers (the dependent variable) based on the weather, inflation rates, number of customers, electric/gas prices and employment levels.[30] Least squares regression models have been proven to be the best forecasting method when causal linear relationships are evident and thus are discussed further in the following section.

## Least Squares Regression Models

The goal of least squares regression models is to find one or more independent variables that are good predictors of the dependent variable. If there is only one independent variable, the model is known as *simple regression.* When the forecaster finds two or more variables to be good predictors, this is known as *multiple regression.* The parameters *a* and *b* are calculated using the same formulas described in the section for trend analysis. These parameters define a straight line that minimizes the sum of the squared errors, or deviations. In the case of simple regression, the formula is $Y = a + bX$, while the multiple regression model is $Y_i = a + b_1X_1 + b_2X_2 + b_3X_3 \ldots + b_zX_z$. These formulas then are used to make future predictions based on the expected value of the independent variable(s).

Four assumptions or conditions are required to use linear regression:

1.  The independent and dependent variables are linearly related.

2.  The errors are independent of each other or, in other words, there is no serial correlation.

3.  There is constant variance of the errors, or homoscedasticity, versus the prediction.

4.  The errors are normally distributed.

To further understand linear regression, consider the following example:

John and Joan have been mortgage brokers for the past five years. They arrange for home financing using funds from local investors. John and Joan have found that interest rates have an impact on the amount of business they generate each year. They collected the following data for the past five years:

| Year | Average Interest Rate (x) | Loan Value ($000s) (y) |
|------|---------------------------|------------------------|
| 1 | 5.5 | 1,150 |
| 2 | 5.75 | 1,040 |
| 3 | 6.0 | 1,000 |
| 4 | 6.5 | 950 |
| 5 | 6.0 | 990 |

The projected interest rate for year 6 is 5.75 percent.

Using Excel, John and Joan use regression analysis and calculate the slope and the intercept, to estimate their expected loan volume:

| | A | B | C | D | E |
|---|---|---|---|---|---|
| | | **Interest Rate** | **Loan Value** | | |
| 1 | **Year** | **(x)** | **(y)** | | |
| 2 | 1 | 5.5 | $1,150,000 | | |
| 3 | 2 | 5.75 | $  1,040,000 | | |
| 4 | 3 | 6 | $  1,000,000 | | |
| 5 | 4 | 6.5 | $    950,000 | | |
| 6 | 5 | 6 | $    990,000 | | |
| 7 | **Slope (a)** | (188,181.82) | ◄―――=slope(c2:c6,b2:b6) | | |
| 8 | **Intercept (b)** | 2,145,681.82 | ◄― | | |
| 9 | | | =intercept(c2:c6,b2:b6) | | |
| 10 | | | | | |
| 11 | | | | | |
| 12 | | | | | |
| 13 | | | | | |

To forecast their expected loan value for year 6, they use the linear regression equation:

Loan value = a + bx = 2,145,681.82 − 188,181.82(5.75) = 1,063,636 (rounded)

Thus, John and Joan expect to generate $1,063,636 in loans in year 6.

Several forecast models have been described in the previous sections of this chapter. How does one know, however, which of these models will be the best predictor given a particular business environment? The given model will be useful only if the forecasting method is accurate and unbiased. The following section discusses forecast accuracy.

## Forecast Accuracy

ON Semiconductor was experiencing a high error rate in its forecasts, often overstating customer demand by as much as 300 percent for any given year. Because no forecast metrics were used, no one felt pressured to improve the forecasts. However, the organization was losing revenue and customers were dissatisfied. Following a leveraged buyout, the organization refined the forecasting process over a five-year period, integrating its tool sets into an Advanced Planning System with positive results. For example, internal inventories and days of delinquent revenue decreased

14 percent and 25 percent, respectively, and on-time deliveries improved by 15 percent from 2004 to 2005.[31]

The previous example suggests that forecast errors can be costly and forecasters need some measures to estimate and improve forecast accuracy. Forecasters can begin by examining the amount of *forecast error,* defined as the difference between the forecast and the actual demand, for a specified period. In statistics, these errors are known as *residuals.* In other words, for any given period,

Forecast error = Actual demand − Forecast demand

Forecast errors may be either random or biased. *Random errors* are those that cannot be explained by the forecast method. *Bias errors* occur because some type of consistent error is made in the forecast, such as selecting the wrong variables in a regression analysis, using an incorrect trend line or shifting the seasonal demand from where it actually occurs. As a result, purchasing, stocking and labor problems, as well as other issues related to forecast errors, can occur.

Examining forecast errors for a specified time period, for a week or a month, for example, does not provide a complete picture. Rather, the forecaster needs to examine forecast error over several past time periods and, as a further step, use this information to select the "best" forecast by comparing the forecast error between two or more forecasting models.

A second point is that while looking at errors over several time periods is good, errors tend to cancel each other out because some will be negative while others will be positive. For example, if the forecast errors using the exponential smoothing method over the past six months were +1, +6, −2, −6, +2 and −1, the running sum of the errors is 0. At face value, the forecast method appears to be a good one, but in reality, each monthly forecast was inaccurate. Thus, forecasters generally transform each error into an *absolute value* (a positive number) to better understand the magnitude of the errors. Using this same example, and transforming each error to an absolute value, the sum of the errors is now 18 (1 + 6 + 2 + 6 + 2 + 1 = 18).

Forecasters then use the absolute value of each error to create a measure that will be used to evaluate two or more forecasting methods. The *mean absolute deviation* (MAD), the *mean absolute percentage error* (MAPE) and the *mean squared error* (MSE) are three commonly used measures. The MAD is the average of the absolute values over a given number of time periods and is calculated as follows:

$$MAD = \frac{\sum\limits_{i=1}^{n} |A_t - F_t|}{n}$$

where

$A_t$ = Actual demand for given time period $t$

$F_t$ = Forecast for given time period $t$

$n$ = number of time periods included in analysis

| | = a symbol that indicates the absolute value

The MAPE is calculated by dividing the absolute forecast error by the actual demand for each time period. The advantage of this method is that the forecaster has a better idea of the true magnitude of the forecast error. For example, if the error is 20 for a given month, the magnitude is much smaller if the actual demand is 4,000 (0.005) rather than 400 (0.05). The values then are summed, averaged and multiplied by 100. In other words,

$$\text{MAPE} = \frac{1}{n} \sum_{i=1}^{n} \left| \frac{A_t - F_t}{A_t} \right| (100)$$

## Tracking Signal

While the measure of forecast error provides a snapshot of forecast accuracy, the forecaster also needs some assurance that his or her predictions are unbiased over time. One method used to control forecast bias is through the use of a *tracking signal,* which measures how well the forecast is tracking actual upward or downward fluctuations in demand over time. The tracking signal is the running sum of the forecast errors (RSFE) divided by the MAD, calculated as:

$$\text{Tracking signal} = \frac{\sum_{i=1}^{n}(A_t - F_t)}{MAD}$$

The tracking signal is checked each time period to determine whether it falls outside some preset control limits. If the tracking signal is equal to 0, the forecast is equal to the actual demand. A tracking signal greater than 0 indicates the actual demand exceeds the forecast, while a tracking signal less than one indicates the actual demand is less than the forecast. A rule of thumb is to use a tracking signal of $\pm 4$ for inventory items that are carried in higher volumes (or more critical to operations) and $\pm 8$ for lower volume (or less critical) inventories. Forecasters generally plot the tracking signal on a graph to detect any *drift,* or gradual changes. The following example illustrates how to calculate the MAD and MAPE, and includes a calculation of the tracking signal.

Chris, a supply management professional for C&G Supplies, reviews monthly forecasted demand for copy paper. (C&W's forecaster uses the three-period moving average method.) Chris also reviews the calculated MAD, MAPE and tracking signal, as shown in the following Excel spreadsheet.

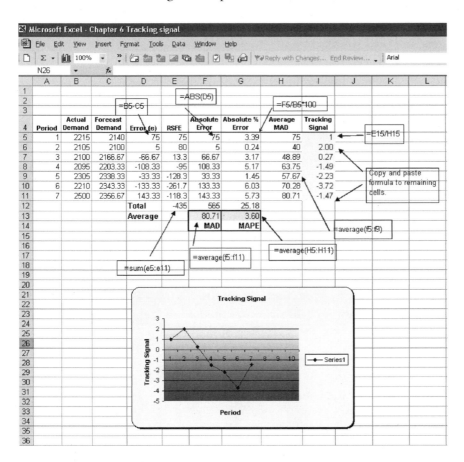

The MAD is helpful when used to compare the MAD for another forecasting method (the smaller the value of the MAD, the more accurate the forecast). However, the MAPE is useful to Chris because it is an indicator of the absolute percentage error. Forecast errors are averaging 3.6 percent, which is relatively small. The tracking signal indicates that the three-period moving average was initially underforecasting and then overforecasting. More data is needed for further interpretation, but at this point in time, there does not appear to be any bias present. The tracking signal also falls between ±4 MADs, which is acceptable for less critical items. Thus, Chris feels comfortable using the three-period moving average to order supplies, although he will continue to monitor the performance indicators closely.

The *mean squared error* is an average of the squared errors. Taking the square of each error prevents positive and negative errors from canceling each other out, and it amplifies the effect of large errors. Thus, this method is useful when large errors are costly or damaging to the organization, such as for an organization that makes expensive surgical replacement parts (hip sockets, pacemakers, etc.). The formula to calculate the MSE is:

$$\text{MSE} \ = \frac{\sum\limits_{i=1}^{n}(A_t - F_t)^2}{n}$$

# Managing Forecast Data With Suppliers

Historically, organizations have created and monitored their own forecasts, using the information to create schedules for manufacturing or service providers, estimate labor needs and place orders with suppliers. A typical scenario might be a manufacturing organization that prepares a forecast to make 50,000 bath towels in several colors, based on past sales data. A schedule then would be sent to the production facility, materials and dyes would be purchased and the towels would be created. However, if customer orders came in and did not match the forecast — perhaps all the orders were for a single color — then more materials and dyes would have to be purchased to meet demand for that one color, and kits with the mix of colors would either sit idle or be "robbed" for parts.[32]

Research has shown that decisions made based on customers' orders only, rather than on actual real-time data, results in the *bullwhip effect*. This term refers to the fact that small changes in customer demand will increasingly become exaggerated as that demand is communicated upstream in the supply chain, from retailers to wholesalers and distributors, all the way back to the manufacturer. Thus, supply management organizations must find a manageable way to share forecast data with their suppliers to minimize inventories and related costs for both parties. From a supply management perspective, suppliers need to be able to forecast demand accurately to deliver the items ordered by their customers in the right quantities at the right times. Information-sharing also helps reduce inventory costs and is essential for those organizations operating in just-in-time or lean environments.

"Forecasting should be used, not to produce a work order, but to give suppliers a [reasonably] accurate estimate of potential," says Drew Curtis, C.P.M., CFPIM. Curtis is manager of strategic sourcing programs for the northeastern United States and Canada, for TTI, Inc., a distributor of electronic components. "Providing the most accurate forecast as possible lays the framework. No matter how automated and streamlined the system, if a supplier had no forecast or history whatsoever and then got a trigger for a year's worth of supply, it wouldn't be prepared. This reinforces the need for integrated relationships and solid two-way communication between supply partners."[33]

Many supply management professionals advocate sharing projections and forecasts with suppliers. Mitchell Millstein, C.P.M., CFPIM, president of Supply Velocity, Inc., a consulting organization based in St. Louis, Missouri, says that if an organization wants to reduce order quantities and on-hand inventory, it must give suppliers forecast information and be responsible for the parts that suppliers build based on the forecast. "Any other method is sticking suppliers with inventory which has to be paid for sooner or later," he says.[34]

*Collaborative Planning, Forecasting and Replenishment* (CPFR) is a term commonly used to describe the information-sharing process. CPFR is "an initiative developed by the Voluntary Interindustry Commerce Standards (VICS) Association that allows collaborative processes across the supply chain. Some of the first applications involved a final retailer sharing its consumer demand forecasts upstream in the supply chain to enable manufacturers of branded goods to produce and distribute their products to the retailer at lower costs." (*ISM Glossary,* 2006) Organizations also may jointly develop production plans, forecasting models and replenishment schedules in an effort to reduce supply-chain costs.

Organizations have adopted CPFR to varying degrees. A division of Baxter Healthcare, a medical products and service provider, works with the Red Cross to obtain forecasts of blood collection products so it can increase its efficiency in inventory planning to meet its customers' needs.[35] In another example, GlaxoSmithKline, a large pharmaceutical organization, and North Carolina–based Mebane Packaging Group developed a system where Glaxo shares forecasting information and production schedules with on-site employees from Mebane. "We improved order patterns and orders come in more effectively in terms of timing and production costs. This initiative led us to reduce costs by 13 percent and lead times by 20 percent," according to George Krall, president of Mebane.[36]

Condis, a large Spanish regional retailer with approximately 3,000 employees; Henkel, a German-based international consumer goods organization with 61,000 people; and Henkel's packaging supplier partnered to fully implement CPFR. Their joint objectives were many: to improve sales growth; reduce costs through a reduction in returns, rush orders, inventory levels, production changes and lead times; improve service levels; reduce stockouts; improve relationships with trading partners; increase the reliability and stability of processes; and improve supply-chain visibility. Henkel initially provided its sales and order forecasts to jointly develop a shared forecast with Condis. Using point-of-sale (POS) data, together they tackled the out-of-stock problems that were occurring by redefining the processes from the regional distribution centers to the POS. Henkel then worked to develop closer relationships with its packaging suppliers for critical items, increasing visibility and efficiency, which enabled suppliers to improve their production planning process. As a result, they saw a significant improvement in forecast accuracy, particularly for promotional products. Henkel improved its service level by 1.5 percent to 99.5 percent and also improved on-time deliveries and deliveries-in-full.[37]

## Overcoming Difficulties

The cited benefits of collaboration include improved forecast accuracy, a decrease in inventory levels and improved service levels.[38] However, there may be initial difficulties in implementing the sharing process. In 1999, Honeywell started transmitting its planning schedule and forecast data to its suppliers and was realizing some of the economies of information-sharing. An EDI (electronic data interchange) Web-enabled process sent forecasted requirements and supplier delivery schedules to Honeywell's suppliers. Unfortunately, supply management employees did not have access to this Web-transmitted data. Instead, they still were relying on a legacy process of printed reports, faxes and phone calls to communicate and collaborate with their suppliers regarding forecasted requirements and supplier delivery schedules. As a result, information often conflicted, confusing their suppliers and resulting in lost productivity.[39]

Another issue, according to a 2006 AMR Research report of consumer packaged goods manufacturers, is that while sales data are more readily available to suppliers today, it is not always transmitted in a timely fashion.[40] To mitigate this problem, demand management teams are overseeing the supply chain more closely and monitoring demand patterns, inventory and activity rates regularly, probably on a weekly basis, with a monthly review. Any upcoming assortment changes, sales or promotions that would increase demand should be shared in advance among the supply-chain members. For example, Litehouse, Inc., a dressings and sauce maker and supplier to Wal-Mart, compares Wal-Mart point-of-sale (POS) data daily against its forecasts using demand-planning software. Litehouse then makes any necessary adjustments in its shipments to Wal-Mart's distribution centers, thus preventing an overstock of fresh supplies that would otherwise spoil. The difference between actual sales and forecasts, which was as high as 60 percent, has been significantly reduced.[41]

Maintaining confidentiality to protect any access to sensitive information from competitors is also a factor. Organizations are working to mitigate this barrier through a process of developing long-term partnerships with key suppliers, using controlled access with firewalled computer software systems and incorporating confidentiality agreements into their contracts.

Lastly, supply management professionals must consider the legal implications of sharing forecast information. Terms and conditions should be specifically included in the contract because they may affect the customer organization's responsibilities. "The obligation to provide forecasts, and the practical consequences that follow as a result, in terms of obligations to acquire and pay for products, may be described in multiple ways," according to a paper presented at ISM's 92nd Annual International Supply Management Conference.[42] For example, forecasting terms may state that supply-chain members should meet at given intervals to share information informally. Conversely, the terms may require some type of materials management system with sharing of sophisticated forecasts.

# Summary

If conducted properly, demand management and forecasting can result in better use of resources and, as a consequence, a more competitive organization. These processes should be used as a basis for budget development, the allocation of resources, labor decisions, technology adoption and work scheduling, among other areas. Moreover, a demand management and forecasting process is most effective when there is a collaborative effort among senior management and multiple functions within an organization, including marketing, operations, finance and supply management.

The starting point for the demand management process is forecasting. Many methods are available to improve forecasting, including both qualitative and quantitative techniques. Qualitative techniques are used when management's insight and experience are required, while quantitative techniques are valuable in their objectivity. However, the best organizations seek a balance between qualitative and quantitative techniques to develop the most accurate forecast. Forecasts are also dynamic documents that must be revised when conditions change, or when the chosen forecast methods no longer produce effective predictions. Tracking forecast errors to determine if the chosen forecast methods still are accurate and viable is important to effective forecasting.

## Key Points

1. Organizations prepare forecasts to (1) estimate demand, (2) determine if supply can meet demand, (3) predict technology trends, (4) predict prices, (5) predict dependent demand and (5) estimate supply management budget.

2. A number of factors can alter a forecaster's original predictions, including (1) lead time changes, (2) changing labor conditions, (3) material shortages, (4) technological shifts and (5) the weather.

3. Organizations generally go through a five-step process to create a forecast, beginning with selecting what will be forecasted, picking the time horizon for the forecast and choose the forecasting model(s) that will be used. Data then is gathered, the forecast is created and lastly the forecast model is validated and the results are implemented.

4. Qualitative, or judgmental, forecasts are developed based on the opinions of others, such as managers or other experts, estimates from the sales staff or the results of consumer surveys. A number of qualitative forecast methods are available, including sales force composite, jury of executive opinion, market research and the Delphi Method.

5. Time series models use a time series, which is a set of observations collected at regular intervals over a given time horizon. A time series may provide evidence of a flat or horizontal demand pattern, seasonality, trends or cycles.

6. Three common and relatively easy-to-use time series models are simple moving average, weighted moving average and exponential smoothing.

7. Seasonality can be forecast using a multiplicative model to create a seasonal index.

8. Trends can be forecast using a linear regression model or trend-adjusted exponential smoothing.

9. The Box-Jenkins Method is a heuristic, where the goal is to find a mathematical formula that will approximately generate the historical demand patterns in a time series.

10. Winter's Model simultaneously considers the effects of time-varying demand levels and seasonal factors and is otherwise known as triple exponential smoothing or seasonal exponential smoothing because it incorporates exponential smoothing.

11. The single-period model uses probabilities to estimate demand for items with a relatively short selling season such as a one-time special event.

12. Forecasters need some measures to determine forecast accuracy and begin by examining the amount of forecast error, defined as the difference between the forecast and the actual demand, for a specified period.

13. Three methods to estimate forecast error are the mean absolute deviation (MAD), the mean absolute percentage error (MAPE) and the mean square error (MSE). Forecasters also estimate bias by using a tracking signal, which is a ratio of the running sum of forecast errors to the cumulative MAD.

**14.** Organizations are adopting collaboration initiatives to varying degrees. Collaborative Planning, Forecasting and Replenishment is one collaboration process by which supply-chain trading partners jointly plan key supply-chain activities from production and delivery of raw materials to production and delivery of final products to end customers.

# 6

# Warehouse Management and Materials Handling

In a perfect world, organizations would be able to precisely predict demand for goods and supplies, and products would be instantly replenished to meet that demand. As a result, there would be no need for storage facilities because inventories would never be held. As pointed out in Chapters 4 and 5, however, demand is subject to a number of uncontrollable factors and even a good forecasting process will not result in perfect predictions. Even if the forecasting process were perfect, organizations still would need perfectly responsive production and absolutely reliable, instant transportation delivery.

In practice, organizations use inventory to improve their ability to coordinate supply with demand and keep transportation and supply costs reasonable. With inventory, effective and efficient warehouses and materials handling systems are needed to facilitate the storage and movement of these materials, goods and supplies to support production and service delivery and the Strategic Supply Management Process (see Figure I-1 in the "Series Overview" at the beginning of this book).

This chapter will focus on warehouse management and materials handling, beginning with some fundamentals including definitions and warehouse types. Next, a description of factors that must be made with respect to locating warehouses and creating a network is provided. A discussion of the need to plan the design of the actual warehouse to meet an organization's needs follows. The chapter concludes with a discussion on current trends in warehousing.

**CHAPTER OBJECTIVES**

• Define the role of warehousing in the supply management process.

• Discuss how warehouses can help meet organizational needs.

- Explore the considerations involved with locating a warehouse.

- Identify various warehouse designs and tracking systems.

- Discuss current trends in warehousing.

# Warehousing Basics

Historically. warehousing has been viewed as a way to meet internal and external customer needs by holding inventory while at the same time avoiding losses that could occur through waste, obsolescence and deterioration. Today's thinking is much more focused on balancing the trade-offs between higher customer service, lower inventory levels and lower operating costs, with international sourcing adding even more complexity. Organizations also realize that value is not created unless inventory is moving toward the customer. Thus, inventory is not sitting in warehouses as long as it used to. Technology is being used to provide real-time information on the location, status and amount of inventory held within a warehouse, which helps facilitate movement. Moreover, business practices such as lean and just-in-time (JIT) production discussed in Chapter 1 are providing impetus to improve warehousing activities to meet faster delivery times.[1]

A *warehouse* is a facility used for receiving, storing and distributing materials in support of organizational strategies. Goods such as those purchased for resale, raw materials, work-in-progress goods, consumable items and finished goods are all held in warehouses.[2] *Materials handling equipment* is used for sorting and placing inventory into the correct location within the warehouse, as well as selecting, picking and moving inventory to the loading areas for shipment.

## Types of Warehouses

Warehouses are used to meet specific organizational needs and can be broken down into the following types:

1. *Commodity warehouses* limit their services to storing and handling certain commodities, such as lumber, cotton, tobacco, grain and other products that spoil easily.

2. *Bulk storage warehouses* offer storage and handling of products in bulk, such as liquid chemicals, oil, highway salts and syrups. They also mix products and break-bulk as part of their services.

3. *Temperature-controlled warehouses* control the storage environment so that both temperature and humidity are regulated. Perishables such as fruits, vegetables and frozen foods, as well as some chemicals and drugs, require this type of storage.

Retailers and distributors also may have a warehouse that contains a temperature-controlled area along with areas for nonperishables.

4. *Household goods warehouses* store and handle household items and furniture as their specialty. Though furniture manufacturers may use these warehouses, the major users are household moving organizations.

5. *General merchandise warehouses* are the most common type and handle a broad range of merchandise. The merchandise stored in this type of warehouse usually does not require the special facilities or the special handling as noted previously.

6. *Miniwarehouses* are small warehouses with unit space varying from 20 to 200 square feet and often are grouped together in clusters. They are designed to provide extra space, and few services are provided. Convenient location to renters is an attraction, but security may be a problem.[3]

## Distribution Center Versus Warehouse

It is important to differentiate between warehouses and distribution centers. The term *warehouse* is broader, referring to a building or structure used to store materials for security, protection and distribution. Materials, such as quarried rock or fermenting wine, in many instances may be stored for long periods of time in a warehouse. Conversely, according to the *ISM Glossary* (2006), a *distribution center* is "a warehouse for (temporarily) storing and shipping material, usually finished goods, often located at a distance from the manufacturing site." A distribution center's main function is specifically to provide a quick throughput of goods to support operations within a region.[4] Organizations may have warehouses that provide both short-term and long-term storage solutions, although it is more common today to physically separate them.

Another difference is that a warehouse normally holds inventory for a single organization or location such as a manufacturing site, while a distribution center typically supports many locations. For example, Wal-Mart manages a large distribution network with its own fleet of trucks to deliver product to its more than 1,000 retail stores in 15 countries. Up to 125 stores are supported by a single distribution center.[5]

Retailers in particular greatly benefit from the use of distribution centers. They allow a store location to stock a large number of products without having to incur high transportation costs. Suppliers deliver in bulk to distribution centers, where they are stored until broken down into smaller quantities and delivered to retail locations. They also may opt to incorporate *cross-docking,* a distribution system in which freight moves in and out of a distribution center or point without ever being stored there. More on cross-docking can be found later in this chapter. Trucking is the most common mode of transportation to move goods in and out of a distribution center, although rail, air or ship combined with short-haul trucking may be used for long-distance or international shipments.

Whether dealing with a warehouse or a distribution center, an important decision organizations must make is location.

# Warehouse Location

For new organizations, the warehouse location decision arises as they determine the number and location of warehouses that will be needed to support production and/or distribution. Essentially, they are designing a new network of warehouses and distribution centers that will support operations. If an organization covers a wide geographic region, it may consider multiple locations for its inventory to save on the cost of transportation. On the other hand, existing organizations that are expanding operations typically face the decision of whether to expand a current facility or add another warehouse to their logistics network. This often occurs because existing facilities do not have enough capacity or customer service is being negatively affected.

Overall, warehouses should be geographically located within an organization's supply and distribution channels so that they support the organizational strategies, maintain business continuity and minimize the total cost of receiving, storing and transporting inventory from suppliers to existing or future production sites, in the case of a manufacturer, and from the organization to distribution centers, retailers and customers. This is not an easy task. If an organization has the wrong number of warehouses and distribution centers, they are in the wrong locations and/or do not serve the intended function, the supply chain will have a suboptimal cost structure and customer service will suffer. A public organization also is likely to consider issues such as service to the general public and location convenience, while a private organization will focus on market position, competition within the region and potential profitability. Regardless of organization type, once an organization determines that it does need at least one new warehouse, several factors should be weighed.

## Financial Considerations

An important consideration is whether the space should be leased or owned. If existing warehouse space is available and affordable, leasing may be the best option, at least in the short term. A *lease* is a contract in which one party obtains use of another party's asset.[6] The immediate ability to have storage capability without a capital investment is an advantage. The purchase of land and buildings can be a substantial investment, particularly for a startup organization. Many organizations, however, opt to own their own structures because of the offsetting benefits of more control and flexibility, lower costs over the long run and tax benefits because of depreciation allowances. Some industry leaders cite the low cost of capital and lack of alternative investments as reasons for an organization to own its distribution center. These same organizations may consider leasing in the future if they have more critical needs for their capital.[7]

The Japanese considered the costs of land when developing the practice of JIT systems, which minimized waste in the supply chain via direct shipments by suppliers. When JIT was being implemented by Toyota, Japan was a poor country that could not afford waste in its manufacturing. High land prices also were a reason for implementing JIT, for many organizations could not afford property for an elaborate warehouse system. As land prices became more affordable in Japan during the 1990s, more organizations began considering warehouse expansions as ways to reduce their transportation costs.[8] By considering various aspects of cost, the Japanese were better able to develop an effective logistics system. They were so successful, in fact, that JIT now is used throughout the world, not just in Japan.

Other major cost considerations are energy, labor and transportation. As energy costs continue to rise, increased local utility costs are an important factor. Labor and transportation are discussed in more detail in the following paragraphs.

**Labor Costs and Availability.** Labor costs are less important today because of the increase in automation, but organizations must take into consideration worker productivity, quality, work ethic and, most important, location. Labor statistics for the areas being considered are readily available and can indicate unemployment rates and regional wages.

Based on the laws of supply and demand, an organization can locate in a high unemployment area and usually have an ample supply of workers available even for modest pay. However, locations where there is a strong union presence, such as in many developed countries, generally means workers will likely vote for representation, resulting in higher wage and benefit costs.

Labor costs can be significant for any organization. To stay competitive, an organization must effectively manage this area. Increased labor costs within the United States, for example, have led many organizations to outsource functions that have been traditionally performed by their own workforces. Supply management professionals should be aware of such trends and their potential impacts to warehousing.

The level of staffing required is another consideration and naturally will vary from one organization to the next. Depending on the type, size and complexity of an operation, positions such as warehouse worker, truck driver and materials manager may be necessary. With the increased use of computer systems for office and floor operations, support staff that is knowledgeable in the technology area is essential. The type and number of personnel required to effectively operate a warehouse must be a prominent part of a warehouse management system plan, for these costs will be ongoing.

**Transportation Costs and Requirements.** Transportation is probably the largest variable cost component in the location decision. For example, if an organization locates a warehouse outside a major metropolitan area because property is inexpensive, it must consider the costs of transporting goods back into the city if that is where the customer base resides.

Planners should begin by determining what modes of transportation will be most practical for the area and will benefit the organization the most. However, they also must consider the available transportation options. Not all transportation providers may serve a location that is under consideration. Thus, supply management professionals can provide the research needed in this area. For example, if an organization ships low-value commodities such as coal or wheat, rail or water transportation is the best option. However, this will require the organization to locate its warehouse near or even at a seaport or rail station. In North America, Kansas City is strategically located in practically the center of the United States. With excellent connections to the highways and rail service that is superior to other locations, this city serves as a distribution center hub for many organizations. Transportation challenges in developing countries require careful consideration and knowledge about the country's infrastructure and transportation providers and schedules. For example, locating a manufacturing facility in a low-cost country may be attractive because of lower construction and labor costs, but a lack of developed roads can make shipping finished goods a problem. More on the advantages and disadvantages of the different modes of transportation available can be found in Chapter 7.

Caterpillar Logistics, a business unit that supports Caterpillar's global service parts business in China, opened a distribution center outside Shanghai in 2005. The director of supply-chain strategy design and transportation chose this location because the adjacent seaport will make it easy to import parts from Japan, Europe and the United States via water transportation. The parts then can be easily transported to nearby manufacturing facilities.[9]

## Environmental Considerations

An organization also should take environmental issues into consideration in its warehouse location decision. In the early 1990s, environmental concerns came to the forefront, as consumers demanded environmentally friendly products and practices from the organizations they bought from. As a result, organizations across the world are making the commitment to be more environmentally responsible for products throughout the supply chain, including the specification of products that are environmentally friendly.[10]

Supply management should be proactive in the environmental areas of logistics, including packaging, remanufacturing, disposal and reuse. In fact, the term *green purchasing* has been coined and refers to "making environmentally conscious decisions throughout the purchasing process beginning with product and process design through product disposal." (*ISM Glossary,* 2006) *Green logistics* also is used and refers to an organization's efforts to measure and minimize the environmental impact of logistics activities. Some environmental issues an organization may consider when deciding on a location include the availability of local recycling programs and cleanup and disposal requirements for hazardous materials and obsolete or out-of-date inventory.

### Governmental Considerations

Local, state and federal government laws and regulations also will likely play a role in locating a warehouse. These often are tied to the goal of keeping the community environmentally safe. Zoning ordinances in the United States are also a consideration for an organization may have to request rezoning, a potentially lengthy process. Building regulations and restrictions vary greatly in other countries. Obviously, an organization must be aware of such restrictions when looking to locate a warehouse in a certain part of the world. For example, in Germany, building and land-use regulations established by the Federal Ministry of Transport, Building and Housing must be adhered to.[11]

### Political Considerations

To bring in new industry and new jobs into their areas, some councils and commissions are willing to offer tax breaks and other financial incentives. Some of these incentives may include corporate income tax credits, ad valorem tax abatements, sales or use-tax exemptions, financial help with land acquisition or site improvements, financing of the facility and assistance with relocation and hiring.[12] Depending on the local politics, officials may be eager to attract new industry, particularly with a declining economy. Others may not be inclined to do so, however, for they may represent constituents who do not wish to see changes in their community.

# Warehouse and Materials Handling Design Factors

In conjunction with the location decision, organizations also must plan and design the warehouse or distribution center in terms of layout and equipment needs that will support their business model, increase productivity and minimize the total cost of operations.

## Facility Design

The design and layout of the warehouse must be orderly so that materials flow efficiently, locations are clearly identified and space utilization is optimal. According to the Chartered Institute of Transport and Logistics in the United Kingdom, the four principal types of warehouse layouts (depicted in Figure 6-1) are as follows:

1.  *Inverted T warehouse flow.* Goods going in and out are located on the same side of the warehouse, with designated areas for bulk storage. Low-use items are placed furthest away from the exit and high-use items nearest. This saves time and minimizes distances traveled for fast-moving stocks.

2.  *Cross-flow warehouse.* This is a one-way system with incoming goods flowing to the left of the entry and into one of three storage areas, depending on usage. This design retains the main advantages of the T system, but removes central aisle congestion.

3.  *Corner warehouse flow.* This design has the incoming and outgoing goods at adjacent sides of the same corner of the warehouse. This layout reduces congestion during times of high throughput activity.

4.  *Through-flow warehouse.* This warehouse design has the advantage of being a flow system with entry and exit points on opposite sides. It achieves good aisle space (i.e., wide), but a disadvantage is that all materials have to travel the full length of the building between receipt and issuance.[13]

Figure 6-1    Warehouse Designs

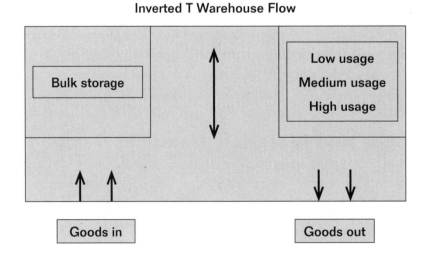

Inverted T Warehouse Flow

## Cross-Flow Warehouse Flow

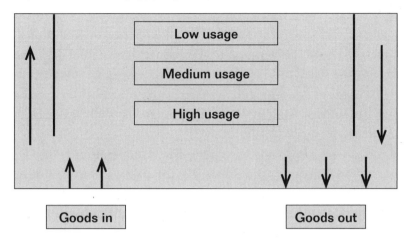

## Corner Warehouse Flow

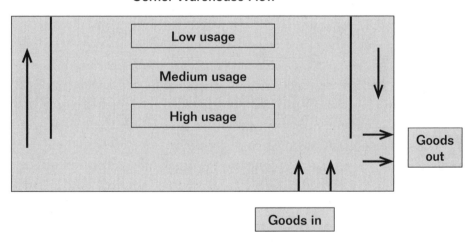

## Through-Flow Warehouse Flow

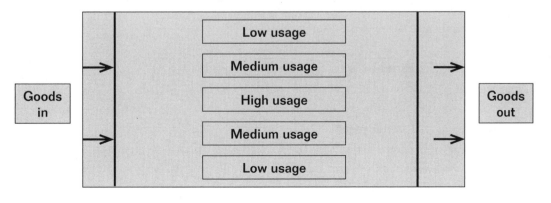

If an organization already owns a facility and wants to increase capacity, it may choose to expand a facility vertically, otherwise known as *build up,* or horizontally, referred to as *build out.* The height of the building will dictate how high shelving can be assembled, which is a key consideration in warehouse design. The higher the shelve racking, the better the space utilization, so in addition to square footage or square meters, it is important to consider cubic footage or cubic meters. Vertical capacity requirements relate directly to the type of equipment that will be needed, which is discussed shortly.

In the past, a newly constructed warehouse or distribution center was expected to support five to ten years of business activities for an organization. Today, more organizations are taking an approach similar to Hewlett-Packard, which expects a facility to last only three years before new processes and products require something different.[14]

## Space Requirements

As mentioned throughout this chapter, when designing the facility, the amount of warehousing and storage space must be determined based on the needs of the organization. For example, overestimating the amount of space needed can result in unnecessary costs in the way of unused space, energy and maintenance. Building services costs represent a significant portion of annual building costs. On the other hand, underestimating space may result in an overcrowded and inefficient warehouse operation. The objectives should be to efficiently use space with the building's cubic footage and achieve balanced traffic flows. If stock movements can be minimized, both in number and distance, then an organization can avoid double handling (a costly practice).

Specifically, the space required for each type of stock needs to be determined, along with the characteristics of the space. Size, shape, weight and the perishable nature of stocks will factor in as well. Lastly, space must be designed to accommodate material handling equipment and personnel requirements. Figure 6-2 lists some reasons why warehouse space requirements may vary.[15]

## Fluctuations in Warehouse Space Required

Two types of storage systems typically are used — fixed and random. A *fixed location* system is one that stores the inventory item in a set physical location. For example, if a certain electrical transformer is stored on aisle 12, shelf A, it can always be found there. This method of storage usually has lower space utilization and higher accuracy. Conversely, *random location* systems store inventory in any available space. As a rule, the use of random locations results in a higher utilization of space, but lower accuracy. In

**Figure 6-2    Reasons for Fluctuations in Warehouse Space Required**

| LESS SPACE REQUIRED | MORE SPACE REQUIRED |
|---|---|
| Decreased production | Growth of market or market share |
| Decrease in number of SKUs | Short product life cycles |
| Less volatile demand | Increase in number of SKUs |
| Longer product life cycles | Direct store delivery to customer |
| Customer takes control of deliveries | Elimination of distributors |
| Smaller manufacturing quantities | Expansion into specialized markets |
| Higher inventory turns | Imported and exported items |
| Smaller purchase quantities (JIT) | Longer production increases |
| Quick response suppliers | Increases in manufacturing quantities |
| Cross-docking | Customer wants fast response times |
| Carriers perform consolidation | Forward-buying |

*Source:* Adapted from T. Hines, *Supply Chain Strategies* (London: Elsevier Butterworth-Heinemann, 2004).

either system, the warehouse location of material should be identified in the inventory records. And, ultimately, organizations must ensure that the needed materials get to the customer. Therefore, they must be aware of how materials can be stored and how they can be accessed quickly. This requires determining specific needs for materials handling equipment.

## Materials Handling Equipment Requirements

Warehousing has its own "tools of the trade," which include various types of equipment to lift and transport materials. Equipment requirements will depend on the type of materials that will be moved. For example, materials such as steel and piping require overhead single and double girder cranes. In the petroleum and chemical industry, drum lifts are commonly used along with forklifts and dollies. A warehouse operation will not typically use any one piece of equipment exclusively, but rather combine a set of manual and automated tools that best fit its operational needs.

A variety of equipment options are available for warehouse operations. These include manual equipment, power-assisted equipment and fully automated and mechanized systems. Manual equipment is flexible, can be used to move a variety of materials and represents a fairly modest investment. It makes sense to use manual equipment when the warehouse holds a variety of different goods. There are some limitations to this equipment, however, including the limited capabilities of the operator with regard to load size and speed. Two examples of manual equipment are two-wheeled and four-wheeled hand trucks and pallet jacks. Pallet jacks, used to manually transport palletized materials, also may be needed, as well as scissor lifts and rolling ladders. For example, employees at West Coast Paper, the Pacific Northwest's largest privately held paper distributor, use pallet jacks to load and unload pallets of copier paper everyday. The equipment is handheld, versatile to operate in tight spaces and can be easily operated by one person.[16]

The output of the warehouse can be increased by using power-assisted equipment. Power-assisted equipment increases the lifting capacity for an operator and allows loads to be stacked. The most common types are forklifts and high lifts. Forklifts are considered standard equipment and can accommodate just about any type of palletized load. While this equipment costs more than manual lifts do, the investment still is quite reasonable and therefore popular. Multistory warehouses with multitiered racking systems will require pneumatic lifts to safely retrieve high-placed items.

Some warehouse and distribution systems essentially are fully automated, using *automated storage and retrieval systems* (AS/RS). With the availability of computer-controlled equipment, bar coding and scanning technology, organizations can operate these systems with minimal staffing. Product orders can be filled by using automated picking systems that retrieve products off the warehouse shelf and place them on a conveyer system to transport them to a loading dock and then on to the customers. These systems are justified when an operation has a substantial and constant flow of goods in and out of the warehouse. Operating costs are lower with automated systems, but the initial investment is high. Failure of automation is always a risk, so ongoing system maintenance is important. HEMA, a large Dutch retailer with more than 300 stores in Germany, Belgium and the Netherlands, expanded its distribution center in 2005 and purchased an AS/RS that has a capacity of 120,000 totes that holds 48 sorting groups of nonfood items. Orders can be shipped within 24 hours, improving speed and accuracy.[17]

**Order Picking System.** Orders also must be picked; this may be performed manually or through an automated process. *Manual order picking* involves warehouse personnel physically retrieving an item from the shelf and bringing it to a staging, distribution or will-call area. Some materials do not require picking equipment, while others will require a forklift or pallet jack. Smaller warehouses with lower volume may be best suited to continue using manual systems and traditional materials handling equipment.

Larger warehouses typically use *mechanized systems* that are automated order-fulfillment systems that use advanced design storage and distribution structures. A *pick module* is a type of mechanized system used in many busy distribution centers. It is designed to pick both bulk items (such as cases of goods) and single items (referred to as "eaches"). The system is constructed of various racking components such as uprights and beams, and includes decking, controls, lighting and conveyor belts. A fully mechanized picking system may be the best choice for a high-volume distribution center. It can create efficiencies as well as improve order throughput time and customer service.

A leading picking technology in the warehouse industry is *voice-recognition* devices. This is increasingly becoming a best practice for distribution and in many cases is replacing traditional handheld devices that scan each item as it is picked. According to Aaron Miller, a principal at Tompkins Associates, Inc., "Instead of having to reach to scan a label when picking, with voice technology a spoken check digit easily confirms the correct location."[18] For example, U.S. Foodservice, Inc., a wholesale distributor to such restaurants as Chili's, Damon's and Pizzeria Uno, has adopted voice-recognition devices. Because of a problem with mispicks in its 82 distribution centers, it incorporated voice-recognition technology within its existing warehouse management system. This resulted in a 75 percent reduction in mispicks and incorrect orders.[19]

In summary, the right level of automation to use in the warehouse takes careful consideration. An organization should consider whether to continue to use the traditional manual system of order picking, which is quite labor-intensive, or look at an automated system that usually requires a sizable initial investment but reduces labor costs and improves accuracy, or a combination of both.

**Docks.** Part of the warehouse design includes the dock configuration. The dock needs to be accessible for both internal and external users, and also have the capacity to meet the traffic needs of each. A *single dock* may be appropriate for a smaller facility with low to moderate shipping activity, while a *two-dock* system can handle a higher-use operation where shipping and receiving are going on simultaneously.

*Cross-docking,* mentioned at the beginning of this chapter, is a distribution system popularized by Wal-Mart, in which goods or materials move in and out of the distribution center, but are not actually stored there for long periods of time. For example, a global consumer products organization such as Procter & Gamble Co., will deliver finished goods from its manufacturing plants to Wal-Mart's distribution centers, where they are unloaded and placed into a number of waiting Wal-Mart trailers and immediately redistributed to retail locations. This eliminates unnecessary storage and handling and reduces costs.[20]

**Security Needs.** Another consideration in designing a warehouse is security. Efforts must be taken by an organization to secure its investment in parts, supplies and equipment through appropriate means. The goal is to adequately protect an organization's fiscal, physical and human resources from theft or harm. All inventories represent a significant investment that must be kept safe and secure.

Proper equipment must be in place to protect the inventory from theft and fire. Local fire codes usually dictate alarm and extinguishing equipment that is appropriate for an industrial warehouse. Security systems with television monitors and badge entry also can be good investments in ensuring warehouse security. For specialized inventory, additional considerations are necessary. Chemical storage, for instance, requires a proper environment and often its own storage room. Perishable items, such as food, may need refrigerated storage to adequately protect it. Businesses such as convenience stores, grocery retailers and pizza chains greatly rely on refrigerated storage. Within the United States, four organizations (AmeriCold Logistics, Burris Refrigerated Logistics, Cold Storage, Inc., and Hal's Warehouse) account for approximately half of the annual revenues for this $2.5 billion industry.[21]

**Physical Tracking Systems.** Numerous tracking systems are available for today's warehouse manager. The use of *bar coding,* an inventory control system that employs machine-readable *bar codes* to identify an organization's inventory, is common today. The bar codes are attached to or imprinted on each box or item and are a pattern of parallel bars and spaces that actually represent specific characters and numbers. The device used for reading the bar code and sending that information to the software system is called a *bar code scanner.* There is a unique standard of bar code that includes code language, print quality and information format for different industries. A lack of a common standard across industries is a challenge for all organizations.[22]

Bar codes can be used in countless applications for they interface with computer software, possess decoding logic and can be easily printed. Bar coding allows for the easy identification of an organization's inventory and interfaces with computerized records. It is highly accurate and can help the warehouse operate more efficiently. Besides assisting with material inventories, bar coding also is useful for keeping track of equipment, furniture and other assets. The use of bar codes in the retail grocery industry has been common for many years. It reduces data-entry errors, which improve processing speed and inventory accuracy. One common application is using a bar code as an *intelligent shipping label.* Within a very small face, information can be stored and accessed, including purchase information, carrier code and freight sort code. Figure 6-3 provides an example of an intelligent shipping label.

A recent trend has been the increasing use of radio frequency identification (RFID), which involves a radio chip attached to an inventory product that allows it to be tracked. RFID has a variety of uses within the supply chain, such as identifying tractors and trailers at a distribution facility and communicating with mobile personnel (drivers). The purpose of an RFID system is to allow data to be transmitted via a mobile device (a tag) that is read and processed according to the needs of the application. Used in the 1930s to identify friendly and unfriendly aircrafts, RFID continues to prove its value. Both Wal-Mart and the U.S. Department of Defense (DOD) require their suppliers to place RFID tags on all shipments to improve performance within the supply chain.

The DOD also uses a *unique identification devices* (UID) system to distinguish one asset from another. *Item unique identification devices* (IUID), a subset of UID, mark tangible items with a *unique item identifier* (UII) in the form of a character string, number or sequence of bits assigned to a discrete entity or its associated attribute. This serves to uniquely distinguish the asset from other like and unlike entities. Each

---

**Figure 6-3    Intelligent Shipping Label**

*Source:* Art Avery and Associates, Reprinted with permission, available from www.elogistics101.com/Article/Barcode%20Secrets.htm.

---

unique identifier has only one occurrence within its defined scope of use, making it useful to track items during their life cycles.[23] They also can be used with RFID bar codes. All DOD suppliers must affix UID labels on items with an acquisition cost of at least $5,000, classified or sensitive items, items that are serially managed or property that is furnished to third parties such as contractors.[24]

**Safety Considerations.** Warehouses and distribution centers must maintain a safe work environment. With the increased use of automated equipment (rollers, conveyors, etc.), if proper precautions are not taken, a hazardous environment can result. Clear policies and procedures must be developed to ensure worker safety, including machinery guards, eye protection, chemical storage and fall protection. Federal and state regulations will guide a supply management professional on minimally accepted procedures, but those should be considered a starting point to develop a specific safety program for an organization's own warehouse. Accident and hazard reporting, equipment operations training and scheduled safety meetings are all part of such a program. A safe and accident-free workplace is obviously a plus for workers, but it also can pay off for the organization as well: claims caused by on-the-job injuries are reduced and workers' compensation insurance rates are lower with a sound safety record.

**Security Issues.** Ever since the events of September 11, 2001, both public and private organizations are aware of the threats surrounding terrorism; most are employing additional security measures at their storage facilities.[25] Prior to that time, supply management professionals may not have perceived much risk, but the world is now a different place. An example of materials that should warrant increased attention during transportation and storage include fertilizer, ammunition and water chemicals.

IBM, the world's largest information technology company with more than 330,000 employees and annual revenues exceeding $90 billion, plays an active role in the Customs-Trade Partnership Against Terrorism (C-TPAT) program within the United States and Canada. Among its many security initiatives is the practice of inspecting empty trailers, including measuring interiors and exteriors to ensure they are not carrying any hidden items that could disrupt the supply chain. According to IBM's vice president of import compliance and supply chain security, Theo Fletcher, these steps allow IBM "to develop a set of consistencies that creates a more efficient, predictable and competitive supply chain."[26] It is certainly a good practice for organizations to embrace the C-TPAT certification program; some industry leaders believe it will become mandatory in the future.[27]

Throughout the world, government agencies are working with industry to ensure safe working environments, including warehousing and distribution. Within the United States, for example, the Occupational Safety and Health Administration

(OSHA) oversees workplace safety, while in China, the State Administration of Work Safety (SAWS) handles this.

**Software Support.** *Warehouse management systems* (WMS) are software packages designed specifically for managing the movement and storage of materials throughout the warehouse. (*ISM Glossary,* 2006) They are readily available today and are used by large and small organizations alike. Off-the-shelf packages can be highly effective, but many organizations choose to make modifications and customizations to better fit their needs. The adoption of this technology is required to keep pace in today's global markets, as a WMS can provide new levels of efficiency and throughput. Although the term *warehouse* still is commonly used, some industry leaders feel the model should be more of a "high-velocity distribution center" with the dominant principle being that products in motion add value.[28] Warehouse management systems can operate on a Microsoft platform and include products such as those from SAP and Oracle, whose enterprise systems contain a materials management module, as well as more specialized packages such as Priya, a WMS by Motek. Priya, which can support more than 400 concurrent mobile users, is highly configurable by the user to accommodate changing customer requirements. It also can support third-party warehouses if necessary.[29]

Organizations in all industries have benefited from the use of a WMS. Core capabilities of these systems (see Figure 6-4) include receiving, replenishment, inventory management, picking and shipping. Many also include enhanced functionality such as labor management, parcel shipping and yard management. New Age & Beyond, a Sydney-based distributor of books, contemporary gift items and housewares, used a WMS to improve the operations and efficiency of its growing organization. Benefits realized with the new system include an increased order accuracy, decreased pick time and improved visibility of real-time inventory levels.[30]

Organizations also may tie their materials resource plan (MRP) or manufacturing resource planning (MRP II) software to their warehouse management systems. MRP (discussed in Chapter 5) is a methodology for defining the raw material requirements for a specific item, component or subassembly ordered by a customer or required by a business process. For example, Boeing, in an effort to better track its consumable parts for its U.S. network of 40 manufacturing facilities, integrated WMS with MRP. As a result, Boeing is able to monitor its parts with better precision and accurately forecast the number of parts that will be needed for a production run instead of using average monthly consumption figures. The integrated system also reaches Boeing's 800-supplier network so the organization can better estimate demand.[31]

In summary, the design and layout of a warehouse facility is critical if the facility is to have effective, efficient flows of inventory. Spending adequate time and

Figure 6-4    Warehouse Management System (WMS) Core Applications

resources on planning a warehouse, based on an organization's projected needs, is certain to pay dividends. Once location and design planning are complete, it is time for implementation.

## Implementation

The final step of any planning process is the implementation of the project. Doing so requires that the business continue to operate effectively during the transition. Test runs or pilot testing of the new warehouse often are performed to ensure there are no disruptions in supply. Experienced workers from existing warehouses also may be brought to ensure continuity.

Similar to any project, the following questions should be considered to successfully add and construct a new warehouses or set of warehouses:

- Who will be responsible for implementation?

- What are the goals of the implementation and how are specific actions aligned with goals?

- What is the timeline for meeting the implementation goals?

- Who is responsible for achieving milestones on the timelines?

- How will business continuity be assured during implementation?

- How will effectiveness be monitored and evaluated?

- What training and development strategies will be used?

- How will rapid changes in technology be dealt with?

- How will funding be provided over the life of the plan?

As with any project, there are some basic rules to successfully implementing and achieving long-range objectives. These can be easily applied to any industry, including materials management and warehouse planning.

1. *Successful efforts involve stakeholders and gain their support.* Planning requires consideration of values and priorities, and should reflect the views of all those involved in the process. Inclusion of stakeholders takes time, but is essential to the success of the effort.

2. *Prioritizing goals is an essential step.* Plans should reflect the priorities of an organization. The most useful plans are succinct and easily translate into effective measures.

3. *Commitment from the top.* The leaders of an organization must commit to the planning effort up front. There also must be a commitment to implement strategies recommended by the committee.

4. *Broad representation.* The planning committee should have representatives from several, if not all, areas of the organization. This ensures the needs of all areas are addressed and will help foster buy-in.

5. *Communication.* All parts of the organization must be made aware of the goals and strategies developed. A committee may have made the recommendations, but it is up to every program area to implement change and also be accountable.[32]

# Warehouse Trends

Because operating a warehouse can be a costly venture, an organization should consider all aspects of warehouse management before making a decision that is right for it. Many organizations are seeing the value of *outsourcing* the warehouse function, which continues to be a viable option within supply management. Many professional organizations specialize in managing inventories for a variety of clients. Often this decision comes down to *value analysis,* which is a systematic evaluation of the value of a good or service. This provides insight into the inherent worth of the service, in this case warehousing, with the objective being to maintain functional suitability while reducing cost. This type of approach to business decision-making is all part of strategic outsourcing, a foundation of supply management.

An example of strategic outsourcing is the approach that Moen, Inc., uses when evaluating its use of suppliers. This well-known manufacturer of plumbing products has developed an internal evaluation tool to aid it in outsourcing decisions:

1. Is the function strategic to the organization?

2. Does the process provide the organization with a competitive edge?

3. Is a performance upgrade needed in the area to separate it from the competition?

When the answer to any of the questions is "No," the organization then considers outsourcing the process. Moen used this tool with a major retail customer in its pallet configuration and determined that outsourcing this function to a packaging design organization was the best approach.[33]

Many organizations are combining JIT (just-in-time) supply contracts with their existing warehouse operations. In many cases, less warehouse space is needed, for materials are delivered directly to the production area rather than being stored in the warehouse. Supply management professionals must attempt to find the right balance between what their own organizations store versus what suppliers deliver when needed.

The term *virtual warehouse* is a valid concept of connectedness that allows an organization to maintain a high level of confidence in its distribution system.[34] Actual buildings and real inventory still exist; at least some is stored and managed by an organization's suppliers. Through the use of the Internet, multiple computer systems are communicating and sharing product information in real time with the supplier network. Orders then are shipped directly from the supplier to the customer, ideally in a seamless and timely manner. The Internet can provide the ideal vehicle for establishing a virtual supply chain.[35]

For example, Robert's Sysco Foods, Inc., a $45 million distributor headquartered in Springfield, Illinois, expanded its product line of 5,500 items through virtual warehousing. Sales representatives determine each customer's needs and if a product is not carried in their own warehouse, they link directly to their partner's — Dot Foods, Inc.'s — virtual warehouse program. Dot Foods, a large redistributor with more than 20,000 products, has distribution centers located across the United States. This partnership has eliminated the need for expanding Robert's Foods' existing warehouse while significantly increasing its offerings. Orders from Dot are packed and shipped to Robert's distribution center, which then are cross-docked and delivered to the customers the following day. As a result, sales have increased more than 16 percent, Robert's has been able to reduce its inventory of slow-moving and special items previously carried in its warehouse and the organization has improved its competitive position.[36]

Other trends include organizations reducing their warehouse space and relying more on suppliers to manage inventories, also known as *supplier managed inventory,* as well as using JIT contracts and the increased use of advanced technology tools in the warehouse.

# Summary

Many considerations go into creating a network of warehouses. Supply management professionals must be aware of the strategic objectives of their organizations, as well as the choices to be made with warehousing facilities. Cost is always an issue, both the initial investment and ongoing costs such as labor and equipment maintenance. It should not be surprising that technology plays a key role in warehousing and logistics. Understanding these technologies and trends and knowing when to incorporate them into an organization will remain a challenge for organizations.

## Key Points

1. Warehouses are facilities used for receiving, storing and distributing materials in support of organizational strategies. They house goods purchased for resale, raw materials, consumable items and finished goods.

2. The basic types of warehouses can be classified as commodity, bulk storage, temperature-controlled, household goods, general merchandise and miniwarehouses.

3. A distribution center provides for a quick throughput of goods to support operations within a region.

4. Materials handling equipment is used for sorting and placing inventory into the correct locations within the warehouse and for selecting, picking and moving inventory to the loading areas for shipment.

5. When designing a warehouse network, there are trade-offs to consider between higher customer service, lower inventory levels and lower operating costs.

6. When adding warehouse capacity, the organization must determine where to locate a new warehouse.

7. The factors that determine the location of a new warehouse include whether to lease or buy, transportation costs, labor costs, supply, environmental issues, governmental restrictions and political incentives.

8. The four principle types of warehouse layouts are inverted T, cross-flow, corner and through-flow.

9. Physical tracking technology, which is common today, includes bar coding, intelligent shipping labels, RFID and UID.

# 7

# Logistics Management and International Transportation

The supply management professional must be aware of the flow and storage of materials throughout the acquisition process, otherwise known as logistics. Logistics is one of the supporting structures of the strategic supply management process. This includes the movement of all raw materials, in-process inventory finished goods and supplies from their origin to the point of final consumption. Typical logistics activities include inbound and outbound transportation, warehousing, fleet management, materials handling, order fulfillment, demand planning and management of third-party logistics providers. Other activities that take place after a product is finished and approved for shipment also are logistics, including selecting distribution outlets, responding to product orders, managing the transportation between downstream parties and overseeing the return of goods. (*ISM Glossary*, 2006) Logistics is one of the key components of supply management as well as a contributor to the economy.[1]

*Logistics management* includes the management of all activities that take place after a product is finished and approved for shipping, including finished goods inventory, selection of distribution outlets, response to product orders and all transportation between downstream parties. (*ISM Glossary*, 2006) In a 2005 ISM survey of managers and above from organizations with revenues of more than $1 billion, 83 percent of the respondents stated logistics was either a part of the individual's personal job responsibilities and/or supervisory responsibilities or the responsibility of someone else in the supply management organization. Supply management professionals work on a variety of logistics activities, including managing the activities associated with inbound and outbound transportation, warehousing, customer services, materials handling, inventory and related information. Logistics activities must be effectively integrated with other key business functions of the organization, such as marketing, sales, manufacturing, finance and information technology, to enhance organizational performance.

For a manufacturer, both inbound and outbound logistics are of concern; not only are raw materials coming into the production facility, but finished goods can simultaneously be going out the other door. Service sectors, including healthcare, education and hospitality services, also have important needs in the area of logistics. Regardless of the organization involved, one organization's outbound logistics is another's inbound.

Many facets of logistics management will be addressed in this chapter: the various modes of transportation, the role of shipping organizations and freight forwarders and traffic patterns will be discussed, as will international transportation and international commercial terms (Incoterms). Whether working in logistics domestically or internationally, the technology impacts are significant. Supply management professionals must be aware of the technology tools available to them, as well as the associated costs and risks. Thorough policies and procedures are important parts of logistics, and transportation restrictions and carrier performance auditing are certainly a part of such policies. Freight claims and damaged shipments also fall in the area of logistics, and supply management professionals must be prepared to resolve these situations. Finally, performance measures and cost savings initiatives will be discussed.

## CHAPTER OBJECTIVES

• Discuss the various functions involved in logistics management.

• Identify the basic modes of transportation along with their respective advantages and disadvantages.

• Explore the issues involved with global transportation including the use of international commercial terms.

• Discuss the options available for supply management professionals to resolve delivery problems.

• Identify ways to measure performance within logistics management.

# History of Logistics

The term *logistics* originated from the Greek word *logistikos* and was used by the Roman armies who identified the military administrative officials as *Logists*.[2] According to S. Tzu and G. Gagliardi (1999), the importance of logistics was noted as far back as 500 B.C. in a book about war strategies.[3] The field of logistics has evolved globally over the years. In the 1970s and beyond, organizations focused on managing logistics costs to stay competitive. Today, logistics is considered an essential operational activity for cost reduction and improved customer service.[4]

Supply-chain management (SCM) evolved in the 1980s and 1990s. This concept included the management of all activities in the supply chain from manufacturer to final customer. SCM was also a realization that all activities must add value to the organization, including logistics.[5] Beginning in the late 1990s through today, the term *supply management* has emerged to best describe the profession that manages the acquisition of goods and services as well as the logistics function. The nature of the supply management profession can be further described as the identification, acquisition, access, positioning and management of resources and related capabilities an organization needs in the attainment of its strategic objectives.[6] The components of supply management include purchasing/procurement, strategic sourcing, logistics, quality, inventory control, materials management, transportation/traffic/shipping, disposition/investment recovery, warehousing, distribution, receiving, packaging, product/service development and manufacturing supervision.

Supply management plays a vital role within an organization, and often lends its expertise in areas such as logistics. All supply management professionals must have a good working relationship with their colleagues who work in the logistics segment of their function and must understand the limitations and trade-offs present in logistical decision-making. The following sections begin with a discussion of the role of transportation.

# Transportation Modes and Roles

## Modes of Transportation

The five basic modes (or types) of transportation are motor carriage, rail, air, water and pipeline. Each of these modes is unique and comes with its own set of advantages and disadvantages. *Motor carriage* is the primary mode of transportation in the United States, with annual operating revenues nearing $250 million.[7] Also known as trucking or highway transportation, this industry consists of both small and large carriers, resulting in a very competitive market. Advantages of motor carriage include a high availability of carriers, prompt transit times and generally reliable service. A disadvantage of using this mode is the geographic limitations of driving on the roadways. For instance, the use of trucking is not feasible for an organization shipping its products from Hawaii to the mainland.

Another important mode is movement by *rail,* which transports materials such as stone, clay and grain. According to the Association of American Railroads (AAR), rail accounts for about 40 percent of all freight transportation each year.[8] During 2004, the railroad industry accounted for 1.6 billion ton-miles of freight.[9] Container shipping, also referred to as COFC (container on freight car), is on the rise because there is less damage, goods can easily be transferred from ships at port and less labor is involved. Rail transportation is considered dependable because the railways are less subject to weather delays, unlike other modes. A prime disadvantage to rail transport is the need for another mode to complete the movement, which is usually trucking.

Movement by *water* is the oldest form of transportation, but still plays a key role in today's global marketplace. This mode includes oceangoing ships as well as barges used on inland waterways. When organizations use ocean shipping, they have the option of using liner service with published rates and schedules or chartering a ship on a contract basis. Some organizations, such as ExxonMobil, own their own vessels. Within the United States, water transportation ships 2.3 billion metric tons of products each year.[10] Shipping by water often is used in strategic areas, such as China, to move low-value bulk materials and heavy items. Water transportation promotes international trade and is essential to industries such as automotive, electronics and heavy equipment, to name just a few. However, it often takes much longer (weeks versus days by truck or hours by air) to ship products by this mode, a noted disadvantage.

Billions of dollars are spent each year on domestic and international *air transportation,* another mode, making it a major component of an organization's logistics program. The demand for air freight carriers continues to increase globally, with air cargo ton miles increasing more than 6 percent in 2006. Fueled in part by growth in Asia, air freight, the Airports Council International predicts, will triple by 2025.[11] Transport by air includes all material shipments made by air cargo carriers devoted to freight only and passenger airlines that carry freight in the belly of the airplane. While the cost of an air shipment is much higher than shipment by truck, a major advantage is that delivery times can be significantly reduced over long distances and the need for trucking is minimal. An overnight cross-country shipment of a component that keeps operations running is well worth the increase in freight costs. Saks Fifth Avenue, for example, contracts for overnight air delivery of its retail items to improve customer service. Using air freight can help organizations reduce their inventories and related carrying costs. In recent years, the use of air carriers for daily shipments has steadily increased, reaching an average of 2.3 million shipments during 2006 (see Figure 7-1).

Pipelines, which have been around since the mid-1800s, are considered the hidden giant of American transportation.[12] This transportation mode is used extensively in the petroleum industry, but also is used to move materials such as coal slurry and natural gas. Pipelines are available throughout the world, with major pipeline projects currently under way in Europe, Africa, Central Asia and the Middle East.[13] In the United States, the Federal Energy Regulatory Commission (FERC) regulates the pipeline industry, which includes more than 100 regulated pipelines within the

Figure 7-1    International Air Express Daily Shipment Volumes

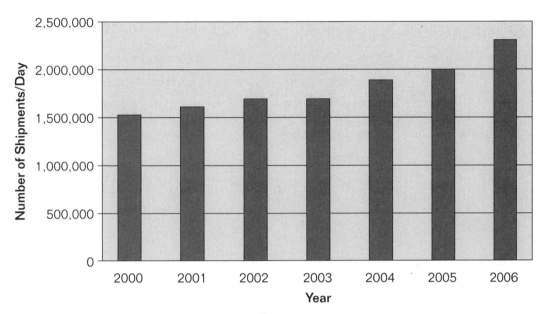

*Source:* Adapted from D. Hannon, "Shippers Leverage Air Cargo As Global Sourcing Extends Supply Chain," *Purchasing* (April 5, 2007), available from www.purchasing.com/article/CA6410204.html.

United States alone. During 2004, this mode remained strong, as it provided more than 2,500 establishments (or transport locations), which resulted in nearly $3 billion in payroll.[14] With its resistance to inclement weather, this mode boasts tremendous dependability. One disadvantage to pipelines is the high initial investment to construct the line and the cost of related equipment.

More often than not, shipments will travel by two or more modes. For example, goods might be shipped to the United States on an ocean liner, then later transferred to a railcar for transport to a train depot, with the final movement made by truck. This is known as a *multimodal shipment.* As a result, supply management professionals often rely on their supplier or a third party to coordinate the transportation of these more complex shipments. More on the use of third parties is discussed later in this chapter.

## Trade-Offs Among Modes

Supply management professionals have a number of choices for transporting materials. No single mode of transportation is best for all deliveries. Each mode has its own characteristics concerning cost, delivery speed, potential for damage enroute and reliability (see Figure 7-2 for a comparison). Air freight is usually the quickest way to

Figure 7-2   Mode Advantages/Disadvantages

| MODE | ADVANTAGES | DISADVANTAGES |
|---|---|---|
| Motor Carriage | High availability<br>Ease of accessibility<br>Reliable service | Impacted by weather<br>Limited international use |
| Air Freight | Faster shipments<br>International use<br>Handle sensitive cargo | Higher shipping costs<br>Requires other modes |
| Rail | Move large volumes<br>Low cost structure | Limited accessibility |
| Water | International use<br>Transport heavy, bulk items | Limited accessibility |
| Pipeline | High dependability<br>Ideal for oil industry | Equipment investment<br>Maintenance costs |

Source: Adapted from Stanley and Matthews, *Logistics and Transportation* (Herndon, VA: National Institute of Governmental Purchasing, 2007), 24.

transport goods, but it is also the most costly. Rail and ocean are the slowest modes of transportation but also the least costly and can move freight types that cannot be moved by air. A supply management professional must consider whether faster delivery warrants the additional cost. In many cases it does. But there are also occasions when longer lead times are acceptable and there is an opportunity to save shipping dollars. Paul Holex, a Dutch flower buyer, purchases more than 200,000 stems at a time and ships them in containers via American Airlines to North America and Japan out of Heathrow Airport, Great Britain. In 2006, he also used ocean containers because it is less costly, there is less handling and temperature control was easier.[15]

## Roles of Third-Party Providers

Supply management is responsible for the on-time delivery of incoming goods; thus, it must ensure a high level of performance from its transportation providers, whether they are internal (also known as private carriers) or external (public or for-hire carriers). The negotiation for, management of and coordination with these third parties often is the responsibility of supply management. As mentioned previously, independent organizations that design and manage some or all of an organization's logistical needs are known as *third-party logistics* (3PL) providers and often are used because of their specialized expertise and experience. The term *third party* or *3PL* originated because these entities facilitate each transportation movement between a purchasing organization and its suppliers without actually taking ownership of a shipment.

While some 3PLs are simply transportation providers or public warehouses, the trend has been to increased consolidation into organizations offering an array of other services, such as information systems, freight bill auditing, inventory management and control and consulting. Organizations such as FedEx Global Supply Chain Services, UPS Supply Chain Solutions and Menlo Worldwide consider themselves solutions providers. A few of these services are described in the following paragraphs.

*Freight forwarders* play an important role in logistics because they provide a transportation service to smaller organizations that want to ship at a competitive rate. The freight forwarder combines these shipments from multiple shippers to make a full carload (CL) or truckload (TL) at a lower freight rate than the shipper could negotiate on its own. Less than carload (LCL) and less than truckload (LTL) rates are logically higher. The rates charged by freight forwarders can be very competitive, particularly when moving goods a long distance. *Air freight forwarders* specialize in the small shipments of air cargo,[16] while *ocean freight forwarders* typically consolidate smaller ocean shipments into containers.

Third parties who act as intermediaries between buyer and seller are known as *brokers.* They represent a carrier as its sales agents and a shipper as its traffic managers. Brokers solicit business from shippers based on the known availability of the carriers they represent. A broker typically will charge the carrier's published rates to the shipper, deducting a certain percentage as its commission (typically 7 percent to 10 percent) and remit the remainder to the carrier.

Shippers also often organize into *shippers' associations,* which are nonprofit cooperatives that negotiate lower rates for their members based on large volumes. They can save their members money by leveraging combined shipments that avoid markups.

A *4PL* is essentially an integrator that brings together the resources and capabilities of its own organization and others to design and operate a comprehensive supply-chain solution. Many service providers may fit within this category, including consultants, IT providers, private organizations and logistics professionals traditionally known for 3PL services. Based on an organization's specific supply-chain initiatives, a 4PL can build a set of activities. Areas such as invoice management, call centers and warehousing facilities are commonly associated with 4PLs.[17]

Understanding the various modes of transportation is important for supply management professionals. Knowing which mode to employ for a particular shipment, the ability to track shipments and when to use third-party support is invaluable. Equally important is an understanding of the role globalization plays in today's markets. Key issues involved with international transportation are covered in the following section.

# International Transportation Issues

## Global Logistics

Globalization is a trend in nearly all markets and is a key issue in supply management. With the ability to rapidly communicate, countries throughout the world are faced with new opportunities for trade. Therefore, many organizations are developing international supply strategies. Global supply chains can provide products that are not available locally when needed.[18] Even when similar goods are available locally, sources in other parts of the world may offer them at more competitive costs, higher levels of quality or with more features.

M. Leenders and colleagues suggest many reasons to do business with global suppliers. These include:

- Lower pricing,

- Improved quality,

- Better availability,

- Reduced cycle time,

- Better technical standards and

- Advanced technology.[19]

However, there also are challenges when dealing in logistics internationally. These include language barriers, quality control differences, foreign laws and political instability.[20]

## Trends in Global Logistics

Several trends are emerging throughout the world that can greatly impact supply management. For example, world commercial services exports rose 11 percent in 2006.[21] By the year 2010, it is estimated that more than half of all organizations will have a global spend of more than 40 percent.[22] Logically, this will lead to the development of international trading partners. Another trend in international trade that directly impacts supply management and logistics activities is the removal of trade barriers. As mentioned in Chapter 4, the World Trade Organization (WTO) includes nearly 150 member nations and functions to resolve disputes, provide assistance and improve trade relations.[23] Trade agreements, in fact, have been established in recent years, including the North American Free Trade Agreement (NAFTA), the Association of Southeast Asian Nations (ASEAN) and the European Union (EU).

According to the *ISM Glossary* (2006), NAFTA, established in 1994, is an international treaty between and among the United States, Canada and Mexico, breaking down trade barriers between these countries. All nontariff barriers to agricultural trade were initially removed and others slated for removal over periods of 5 to 15 years. The United States–Canada Free Trade Agreement of 1989 contains many agricultural provisions that were incorporated into NAFTA.

The ASEAN was established in 1967 in Bangkok by five participating members: Indonesia, Malaysia, Philippines, Singapore and Thailand. Other countries have since joined, with the ASEAN region boasting an annual trade volume of $850 billion. The aim of the ASEAN is to promote economic growth, social progress, cultural development and peace in Southeast Asia. (*ISM Glossary,* 2006) Among its fundamental principles is a commitment to the independence and sovereignty of each participating country.

The European Union (EU) was formed in 1992 with the Treaty of Maastricht. The treaty introduced new forms of cooperation between the participating state governments in Europe. Barriers for trade have been removed slowly to provide a common market in which goods and capital can move about freely. Significant efforts to remove trade barriers actually began in 1958 with the establishment of the European Economic Community (EEC). The agreement between Belgium, France, Italy, Luxembourg, the Netherlands and West Germany abolished trusts and established reciprocal policies on labor, transport and foreign trade. The EEC would later become the European Union.[24] A single European currency was introduced in 1992, the euro, and is managed by the European Central Bank. In 2002, the euro currency replaced the national currencies in 12 of the 15 member countries.

The growth of world trade has remained strong in recent years. During 2006, trade throughout the world grew robustly, as the global gross domestic product increased to 3.7 percent. Merchandise exports within the United States rose 10.5 percent, while Japan, Korea and China recorded even faster growth with their exports during 2006.[25] Members of the European Union have experienced steady growth, and Asia has continued to play a major role internationally with importing, exporting and overall trade value.

In 2005, the global trade fleet was comprised of more than 46,000 ships with a combined tonnage of nearly 598 million gross tons. The fleet is made up of general cargo ships, tankers, bulk carriers, container ships and passenger ships. General cargo ships account for nearly 40 percent of the fleet, while tankers make up 25 percent.[26] (See Figure 7-3.) These ships are technically sophisticated and represent a significant investment, with larger ships costing more than $100 million to build.

## Global Third Parties

Like domestic transportation, a number of third parties play active roles in international shipping. *Foreign freight forwarders* retain experts in global shipping to assist smaller organizations that do not have the necessary experience or expertise. Along with combining smaller loads into containers that can fill a ship, they ensure that all legal obligations are met.

Two examples of third parties specifically related to ocean shipping are ship brokers and ship agents. Sales representatives that work for charter vessel owners,

**Figure 7-3    Global Trade Fleet**

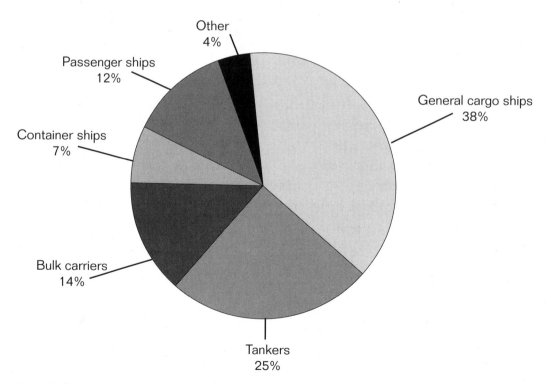

*Source:* Lloyd's Register Fairplay, January 2005, Shipping Facts, available from www.oceanatlas.com/unatlas/uses/transportation_telecomm/maritime_trans/shipping_world_trade/shipping_facts_and_figures.htm#05.

acting as middlemen between the shippers and ship owners, are known as *ship brokers.* *Ship agents* represent a ship operator while the ship is docked in port and manage its arrival, berthing, loading, unloading and customs clearance. They also arrange for the payment of any fees that are due while the ship is in port. Shipping agents can provide the shipper with information on the arrival of the ship that contains its goods and arrange for pickup or delivery.

*Customs house brokers* are licensed to enter and clear goods through customs. They make sure that the documentation necessary for a shipment to clear customs is accurate and complete. The shipper gives a customs house broker power of attorney to pay any import duties that are due with the shipment. The transfer of information for shipment clearance is now performed electronically, reducing overall shipment times. The custom broker's expertise on import regulations or the specific requirements of certain products can be valuable to an organization, especially those with large or unique international shipping requirements.

A shipper also may also require the expertise of an *export packer.* Because of country-specific rules and regulations on packaging, an export packer can hasten the movement of goods through customs. Also, because duties often are based on the weight of the package, an export packer will know what materials and methods will be the least costly to the shipper. Lastly, the export packer will ensure that the shipment receives the right level of protection against climate changes and rough handling.

## Import and Export Documentation

Proper documentation plays a key role for both buyers and sellers involved in international trade. Various documents are used to address issues such as taxation, accounting, bookkeeping and payment. According to E.G. Hinkelman, the most common trade documents fall into these categories:

- *Export documents* are required by the customs office of the exporting country and can vary greatly between countries. License, permits, declarations and inspection certificates are all a part of export documentation.

- Documents issued by a shipping line, air cargo carrier or trucking organization that spell out the terms of the transport are known as *transport documents.* The bill of lading is the most important transport document.

- *Inspection documents* are issued at the request of the buyer to certify the quality and quantity of the materials. These documents also satisfy import and export requirements.

- *Insurance documents* are normally in the form of a policy or a certificate and verify insurance coverage of the goods being shipped.

- *Payment documents* include letters of credit, advices and commercial invoices that address how the payment process will occur.

- Documents that are required by the customs authority of import are known as *import documents*. Minimal documentation includes an entry form and bill of lading, but may include other documents depending on the country of origin and the type of goods being shipped.[27]

## International Commercial Terms (Incoterms)

*International commercial terms,* commonly referred to as *Incoterms,* define the duties of both the buyer and the seller at each state in the movement of goods during international transactions. These terms define who does what as far as transporting, export clearance and import clearance and who absorbs the costs and accepts the risk.[28] These terms were developed by the International Chamber of Commerce (ICC) as a set of uniform rules. Incoterms are not implied in sales contracts. They must be specifically included within the contract if they are to apply. Incoterms are categorized into four groups[29]:

1. *Group E* (EXW). The only term where the seller makes the goods available to the buyer on his or her own premises.

2. *Group F* (FCA, VAS, FOB). Terms where the seller is responsible for delivering the goods to a carrier named by the buyer.

3. *Group C* (CFR, CIF, CPT, CIP). Terms where the seller is responsible for paying for carriage for the goods, but is not responsible for costs of loss or damage to goods.

4. *Group D* (DAF, DES, DEQ, DDU, DDP). Terms where the seller is responsible for all costs and risks associated with bringing goods to their final destinations.

Figure 7-4 describes these groups in more detail.

An example of applying Incoterms might include a German organization manufacturing goods in a Brazilian plant. If an order of goods was set to be delivered to New Jersey, then the contract between the German organization and the U.S. supplier would need to address the specific terms of the transaction. Assuming EXW (Ex Works) was specified in the transaction, the goods would be made available for pickup at the seller's facility and delivery takes place when the goods were released to the buyer's freight forwarder.[30]

## Figure 7-4    International Commercial Terms (Incoterms)

| GROUP | INCOTERM |
|---|---|
| **Group E** Departure | **EXW** – Ex Works (…named place)    *all transportation modes* |
| **Group F** Main Carriage Unpaid    *Buyer insures* | **FCA** – Free Carrier (…named place)    *all modes*  *same*  **FAS** – Free Alongside Ship (…named port of shipment)    *ship*  *ship only*  **FOB** – Free On Board (…named port of shipment) → *vessel loading* |
| **Group C** Main Carriage Paid | **CFR** – Cost and Freight (…named port of destination)    *ocean only*  *buyer insurance*  **CIF** – Cost, Insurance and Freight (…named port of destination)    *ocean only*  *Seller insurance*  **CPT** – Carriage Paid To (…named place of destination)    *all modes*  *Buyer insr*  **CIP** – Carriage and insurance Paid To (…named place of destination)    *all modes*  *Seller insurance* |
| **Group D** Arrival | **DAF** – Delivered At Frontier (…named place)    *Typically rail or motor can be all*  **DES** – Delivered Ex Ship (…named port of destination) → *ocean only*  *unloading by buyer*  **DEQ** – Delivered Ex Quay (…named port of destination) → *ocean only*  *unloading by seller*  **DDU** – Delivered Duty Unpaid (…named port of destination)    *all modes*  **DDP** – Delivered Duty Paid (…named port of destination)    *all modes* |

Note: With EXW (Ex Works), the buyer is responsible for arranging everything, with the supplier only making the goods available. In the case of sea carriage, the supplier delivers to the quay (FAS) or on board (FOB). The ship then leaves at the expense of the buyer. With FCA, the supplier has met his or her obligations as soon as goods have been transferred to the agreed location. The term DAF refers to delivery to the border.

*Sources:* E. Hinkelman, *Dictionary of International Trade,* 6th ed. (Novato, CA: World Trade Press, 2005); A. Van Weele, *Purchasing and Supply Chain Management,* 4th ed. (London: Thomson Learning, 2005).

## Customs-Trade Partnership Against Terrorism (C-TPAT)

A voluntary security initiative through the U.S. Customs and Border Protection (CBP) is the Customs–Trade Partnership Against Terrorism (C–TPAT). This partnership was designed to encourage brokers, carriers and operators to strengthen security practices and improve the integrity of the supply chain. For individual organizations to participate in C–TPAT, they must apply to the CBP. Participants must commit to the following actions:

- Comprehensive self-assessment of their supply chains based on C–TPAT guidelines,

- Completed supply-chain security profile questionnaire,

- Development of a program to enhance their security and

- Communication of C–TPAT strategies to other organizations in their supply chains.

C–TPAT provides organizations an opportunity to actively combat terrorism. Hopefully, the supply chain will be safer for customers, employees and suppliers. The other potential benefits of C–TPAT include the expedited release of shipments, a reduced number of inspections and an emphasis on self-policing.

### Container Security Initiative

Another effective approach to security in global logistics is the Container Security Initiative (CSI), which was developed in the aftermath of the U.S.-based terrorist attacks of September 11, 2001. The purpose of CSI is to protect the global trading system as well as the trade lanes between ports. This initiative was rolled out in 2002, beginning with the international ports that shipped the greatest volume of containers to the United States. A list of the CSI ports currently operating can be found at www .customs.gov/xp/cgov/enforcement/international_activities/csi/ports_in_csi.xml.

# Transportation Policies and Procedures

### Transportation Restrictions

Throughout the world, many rules and restrictions surround transportation. Carriers in the trucking industry, for example, must comply with size and weight restrictions. Because trucks must travel under bridges and overpasses, they are restricted to 13.5 feet in height by the U.S. Department of Transportation. Width and length must comply with appropriate regulations as well to ensure a safe environment on the roadways. Depending on what country or state the truck is traveling in, it may or may not be able to haul multiple trailers. Two trailers being pulled is referred to as a double and three trailers is known as a triple. The latter is prohibited in some U.S. states. In Australia, however, up to four trailers are allowable on the highways.[31]

The federal regulations in Canada are comprehensive in its requirements for transporting dangerous goods. These regulations are enforced by a variety of inspectors, including the Royal Canadian Mounted Police.[32] In China, regulations governing road transportation are implemented by the Ministry of Communications. Rules regarding the licensing, transport and handling of dangerous goods are established by the ministry, as well as policies dealing with load-size restrictions, inspections and border checks.[33]

## Freight Classifications and Rates

Carriers charge line haul rates (or prices) to move goods between two points that are not in the same local pickup and delivery area. With the advent of deregulation, most rates today are negotiated between the shipper and its carriers and set into contract form. The economic basis for setting rates stems from former regulatory standards such as classes and distance. The class system categorizes goods with similar characteristics such as value, density and susceptibility to damage and theft. Most of the 1,000 less than truckload (LTL) carriers that are party to the National Motor Freight Classification (NMFC) system publish their own class rates, which are based on the NMFC classifications.[34]

Today, a carrier commonly evaluates a shipper's goods according to its published rates and then applies a distance cost/rate to them. In many cases, the carrier's published rates are the starting point for negotiating better rates based on other mitigating factors such as total volume with the carrier, favorable directional or seasonal flows, better packaging and faster loading and unloading capabilities.

When setting rates, carriers consider two factors: *cost of service* and the *value of the service.* The first assesses the actual cost of providing the service, while the latter considers the value of the service to the shipper. The intent of the carrier in setting a particular rate is to cover the fixed and variable costs, as well as include a profit margin. *Fixed costs* are not subject to change even if the level of activity changes. Fuel and labor are examples of *variable costs,* for they change based on the level of activity (or output). Higher-value goods often impact the rates charged. The potential of damaging high-cost goods in transit tends to increase insurance costs to protect against the loss. Other factors affecting rates include product weight and density, specialized handling such as refrigeration and various government regulations.

## Freight Terms

Within the area of logistics and transportation there is a unique language. Some of the freight terms that supply management professionals must be familiar with are found in the appendix, "Transportation Terminology," at the end of this chapter. Becoming familiar with the terminology used within the transportation and logistics industry will be of significant benefit to supply management professionals.

# Resolving Delivery Problems

There always will be instances where deliveries are late, goods are damaged or the shipper has shorted or overshipped an order. Poor performance on the part of the shipper or carrier can result in poorly performing customer operations and, as a result, poor customer service. The following sections describe some of the ways these issues often are resolved.

## Delivery Tracking Systems

To prevent delivery problems, more and more organizations are using automated tracking systems for their shipments. This allows users to access real-time information on their products in transit, as well as provide information to customers via online access to organization Web sites. These systems increase operational efficiency with the quality and accuracy of the data provided. International organizations such as United Parcel Service and FedEx use such systems for their package tracking, but with the onset of Internet trade in recent years, even small startup organizations are using tracking systems.

The more sophisticated systems allow for the routing, scheduling, dispatching and territory planning functions. An example of this is a recent partnership between Aramark Corp. and InterGis, a provider of multiuser software systems that automate routing, scheduling and workforce needs. InterGis both provided and implemented the system for Aramark. A national leader in providing uniform and career apparel, Aramark sought to increase efficiency within its delivery routes and reduce costs. After a pilot program at 200 locations proved successful in 2006, Aramark expanded the use of the system to include 3,500 routes. Aramark expects that customer service will be improved and that it will see a return on its investment within six months.[35]

## Visible Versus Latent Damage

As mentioned earlier, damage or loss can occur during the shipment of goods, even with the best efforts of the carrier. Lost goods are items that are missing from a shipment or simply cannot be found while in transit. If the goods actually do arrive at the intended destination but are not in an acceptable condition, they are considered damaged. Damage can be either visible or latent. *Visible damages* are easy to detect during routine inspection. An automobile delivered with a cracked windshield is an example of visible damage. Latent defects, on the other hand, are not easy to detect. A *latent defect* is one that is hidden and is therefore unnoticeable during inspection. An air compressor that looked fine when delivered but was later found to have a faulty electrical switch would be an example of latent damage.

The buyer of the goods has protection in cases of both visible and latent damage. Goods that are visibly damaged can be refused for delivery or can be replaced at no additional cost to the buyer. Latent damages can be a bit more challenging, particularly if the defect is discovered after a lot of time has passed. The buyer, however, still may invoke its warranty rights to replace or repair the item.

The proper receipt of purchased materials is a basic yet important part of supply management. The following determinations should be made for all incoming shipments:

- Whether the goods were actually ordered by the organization,

- If any visible damage occurred in transit,

- That the quantities received are correct and

- That the shipping documentation is complete.[36]

## Freight Claims

Operational error is one of the most common causes of freight claims. The error can be made by the shipper, carrier or buyer in areas such as order processing, packaging, loading or bracing. Damage in transit can occur when materials being shipped are not handled in a safe and reasonable manner or when the proper equipment is not used. Proactive carriers will work to satisfy the shipper's issues immediately. In many instances, however, a freight claim will be necessary.

A freight claim can be filed when any one of the following three conditions exist:

**1.** A party has the legal right to file,

**2.** The time limit for filing has not expired or

**3.** There is clear evidence that the carrier was the cause of the loss.

A claim is based on a party's ability to file a proper freight claim that clearly demonstrates it has suffered a loss because of the fault of the carrier. Only after such a claim is presented can the carrier begin to consider the claim. For motor carriage shipments, the governing regulations can be found in the Code of Federal Regulations (49 CFR Part 370) entitled *Principles and Practices for the Investigation and Voluntary Disposition of Loss and Damage Claims and Processing Salvage.*[37] Although most claims are filed much earlier, a claimant actually has up to nine months from the date of delivery (or the date on which delivery should have occurred) to file a written claim. The carrier then has up to 30 days to acknowledge the claim and assign it a claim number. Within 120 days, the carrier must resolve the claim by paying the amount requested, negotiating a fair compromise or proving it was not liable. The CFR regulations apply within the United States only. Globally, loss and damage claims often are negotiated between the parties involved. For example, a European organization might negotiate lower freight rates by agreeing to limit claims for loss and damage during transit.

## Resolution Process

Logistical conflicts undoubtedly will arise between supply management professionals, suppliers and the logistics providers. Whether the conflicts involve damaged goods, late deliveries or disputed freight rate charges, to name a few, the parties involved must settle the disputes. In the event a freight claim is not settled amicably, the supply management professional may use other means to resolve the issue.

When differences arise, there are three methods of resolution: (1) litigation, (2) negotiation or (3) acceptance.[38] Litigation can be costly and time-consuming for all involved. Although the judicial system is available to all, it often is preferable to resolve differences outside the courts.

Negotiation is a part of everyday life and is a skill that is critical for supply management professionals. Narrowing the differences in a dispute can allow both parties to give a little and arrive at a mutually agreeable resolution. When both parties end a negotiation feeling content with what they have bargained, this is referred to as a *win-win* proposition. The final option is acceptance of the situation, which can be the least desirable approach because it is typically the most costly and sets a bad precedent for future dealings. If a claim is denied or a disagreement in delivery schedule exists, the supply management professional should always work to improve his or her position with the carrier or supplier and not simply accept the situation.

## Freight Auditing

To control transportation costs, organizations need to implement procedures for auditing their freight bills. Many mistakes in billing occur as a result of human error, which can include variances in rates, descriptions, weights and routing. For example, it has been estimated that organizations experience between 3 percent and 5 percent in overcharges to their freight bills each year.[39]

While the auditing function can be performed internally or externally, many organizations find it beneficial to contract out this service. A small organization can find it particularly advantageous to do so, for it likely does not have a staff person for this function. Organizations that perform freight auditing are called *traffic consultants.* They normally provide service on a percentage of the dollars recovered. Larger organizations may have a computerized transportation management system that can perform freight bill audits automatically.

## Carrier Performance Auditing

Management within the supply chain extends beyond the internal operations of an organization. The performance of suppliers and carriers must be optimal to ensure value to the customer. Monitoring, auditing and benchmarking performance can help secure a competitive edge within an industry. It is important to remember, however, that auditing should be carried out in a constructive manner, focusing on improvement rather than taking a punitive approach.

General issues that may need to be addressed include:

- Willingness to work as a partner,

- Commitment to continuous improvement,

- Acceptance of innovation,

- Focus on throughput time reduction,

- Flexibility in logistics systems design and

- Degree of common core values with the customer.[40]

Specific areas of performance that can be audited with a carrier include on-time deliveries, reduction in throughput times, delivery quality, billing accuracy and cost reduction.

# Logistics Performance Measures and Strategies

Up to this point, the focus has been on the planning and implementation of logistics plans. Organizations, however, must periodically preview logistical activities to determine if expected goals are being met. Thus, measurement and control are important for continuous improvement. The following section begins with several common logistics measures and concludes with some general approaches and strategies to manage the measurement process.

## Logistics Metrics

Three areas of concern to logistics are (1) inventory, (2) transportation and (3) customer service. A description of metrics commonly used to evaluate each of these activity areas follows.

**Inventory Turns.** Calculating inventory turns is a key method for determining world-class performance in logistics and supply management.[41] *Inventory turnover* is a measure of the velocity of total inventory movement through the organization, found by dividing annual sales (at cost) by the average aggregate inventory value maintained during the year. The higher the turnover, generally, the more favorable the measure (*ISM Glossary,* 2006). It acts as an overall indicator of material movement within an organization. An item whose inventory is old (or turns over) once a year has a higher holding cost than one that turns over two or three times a year.

**Transportation Costs.** Measuring transportation costs will force an organization to closely look at its actual costs for receiving raw materials and for shipping its products. Therefore, supply management professionals should consider the following questions:

- What are the customer requirements?

- How much time will be taken in transportation?

- What are the costs and benefits of various modes of transportation?

- What are the security or other risk factors?

- What are the storage requirements?

- How well do the transport supplier's systems and standards integrate with your organization?[42]

**Customer Service Measurements.** Several areas that must be measured directly impact customer service. These include speed of delivery, product availability and accuracy of orders. As an organization's service levels increase, so do the costs of storing, processing and transporting orders. So while supply management wants customer service at a high level, there also should be a concern about what this is costing. This is certainly an area to strive for — balance and service level is something that is always subject to adjustment. Overall customer service measurements also are useful. Many organizations use short surveys to gauge customer satisfaction, including Web-based surveys linked to online ordering systems.

## British Airways

Part of the corporate strategy of British Airways (BA) was to build loyalty among its regular fliers, particularly business executives. To do this, it focused on a number of measurements dealing with customer service, procurement activities and supplier performance. This prompted a renewed commitment to customer service through improved supply-chain management. By auditing its food and nonfood suppliers, BA was able to reduce both its supply base and product stocking levels. Within a few months, costs were decreasing, delivery times were improved and customer service ratings were up. While managing a variety of suppliers, the airline was able to greet its executive travelers with quality food, their favorite drinks and current periodicals as they boarded the plane. The project resulted in a five-year savings of more than £50m. This was but one example of supply management professionals playing an integral role in the quality of service delivered. Not only were goals met with regard to acceptable performance levels, but this resulted in an increased awareness of supply management's value in the eyes of corporate executives.[43]

## Logistics As a Profit Center

A progressive approach to controlling logistics is to view it as a potential profit center. Like other areas of an organization, logistics will have capital expenditures and will incur labor and material costs; but it has the potential to add value through its inbound and distribution activities. It also adds value through world-class customer service, which generates revenues and sales.

Thus, the costs of logistics services should be determined; these costs plus an added value or markup becomes the *transfer price.* The transfer price is added to the transfer prices from operations and marketing to estimate the total product price. Once the transfer price for logistics is established, the supply management professional can look for ways to improve profitability of his or her profit center.[44] Organizations also need to ensure that logistics does not profit at the expense of the departments they are serving. As with most things, there is a balance that supply professionals must strive for.

A supply management professional also must have accurate and timely information about performance in to effectively control logistics. This can be accomplished through periodic reviews of logistics activities, also known as *logistics audits.* These audits are necessary to establish reference points for report generation and also to correct errors and misinformation.[45] Logistics audits also can be used as bases to improve an organization's distribution network, customer service and packaging design; reduce inventory requirements; or benchmark against other organizations considered best in class.

## Productivity Reports

While audits may be conducted on an irregular basis, some routine reporting on logistics must be performed to control the function. For example, productivity reports typically are used to measure the efficiency of the various logistical activities. The goal is to put activity performance in relative perspective. Specifically, the output, performance, is treated as the numerator and the input, resources, as the denominator, creating a performance ratio. Productivity reporting is particularly useful when comparing (or benchmarking) one organization to another in the same industry. Many believe that organizations that do such benchmarking and reporting develop a competitive advantage over those organizations that do not. Some of the top evaluation ratios in logistics include the following:

- Logistics cost to sales,

- Activity cost to total logistics cost,

- Logistics cost to industry standard or average,

- Logistics cost to budget and

- Logistics resources budgeted to actual cost.[46]

Figure 7-5 is an example of a logistics productivity report, which can be a valuable tool for senior management in making organizational decisions. For example, if damage claims as a percentage of freight costs were evaluated, one could see that 0.7 percent as reported for the last quarter is nearly twice as high as the industry average (0.4 percent). Therefore, management may want to consider other transportation carriers with better performance histories.

## Using Scorecards

A *scorecard* is simply a form of performance measurement and management that records the ratings from a performance evaluation process. For an organization to improve its performance in supply management, it must first know where it stands as far as activities and outputs. Once this baseline data is established, supply management professionals can set benchmarks for targeted performance. Often, best practices with other comparable organizations are considered when setting these performance goals. Over a set period of time, for instance, quarterly, performance in various supply areas is measured and documented. This data then is used to assess performance in the past and to develop strategies for improved future performance.

The *Supply Chain Operations Reference* (SCOR) model is a process reference model that has been developed and endorsed by the Supply-Chain Council as the cross-industry standard diagnostic tool for supply-chain management. It is a business model process that integrates processes, metrics and best practices (*ISM Glossary*, 2006). This model is further discussed in Chapter 9.

# Summary

Logistics management remains a key area for supply management professionals, both today and in the future. Having a working knowledge of the modes of transportation as well as the advantages of using external resources such as freight forwarders is important. Globalization continues to play a role in all sectors, with international trade

Figure 7-5    Logistics Productivity Report

| Productivity Measure | Current Quarter | Last Quarter | Same Quarter Last Year | Organization Standard | Industry Average |
|---|---|---|---|---|---|
| **TRANSPORTATION** | | | | | |
| Freight costs as a percentage of distribution costs | 33% | 28% | 36% | 30% | 34% |
| Damage claims as a percentage of freight costs | 0.4% | 0.7% | 0.4% | 0.5% | 0.4% |
| Freight costs as a percentage of sales | 9.0% | 9.8% | 11.2% | 9.0% | 8.2% |
| **INVENTORY** | | | | | |
| Inventory turnover | 5.5 | 4.9 | 6.2 | 5.0 | 6.5 |
| Obsolete stock to sales | 0.2 | 0.2 | 0.15 | 0.1 | 0.15 |
| **ORDER PROCESSING** | | | | | |
| Orders processed per labor hour | 52 | 47 | 51 | 50 | 55 |
| Orders processed within 24 hours | 90% | 95% | 89% | 90% | 82% |
| Processing costs to total number of orders processed | $6.50 | $5.95 | $5.80 | $5.85 | $6.60 |
| **WAREHOUSING** | | | | | |
| Percentage of cubes used | 70% | 75% | 65% | 75% | 71% |
| Units handled per labor hour | 207 | 252 | 228 | 225 | 210 |
| **CUSTOMER SERVICE** | | | | | |
| Stock availability | 94% | 89% | 90% | 95% | 88% |
| Orders delivered within 24 hours | 68% | 71% | 70% | 88% | 91% |

*Source:* Adapted from Ron Ballou, *Business Logistics Management* (Upper Saddle River, NJ: Prentice Hall, 1999).

having a language all its own. The use of Incoterms will ensure that both buyers and sellers are on the same page. Ensuring top performance in logistics includes monitoring the work of transportation carriers, as well as measuring the ongoing effectiveness of logistics functions. A number of tools and reports are available to help senior management assess organization performance within the supply chain. By being aware of best practices in their industry, supply management professionals can assist their organizations in making sound decisions.

## Key Points

1. Logistics management includes all activities that occur after a product is finished, including distribution selection, product order response and the return of goods.

2. The five basic modes of transportation are: (1) motor carriage, (2) rail, (3) water, (4) air and (5) pipeline, with each having its own advantages and disadvantages and cost trade-offs.

3. Third-party logistics providers (3PL) provide information, knowledge and valuable services to an organization. Third-party options include freight forwarders, brokers and multichannel merchants.

4. Global logistics is a key issue in supply management because international trade will continue to increase in the years to come. There are many benefits to using global suppliers.

5. The most common freight classifications are class rates and commodity rates, which can take the form of carload (CL) or less than carload (LCL).

6. Logistics and transportation has a language all its own, so supply management professional must be aware of terms such as *cartage, demurrage, dunnage* and *incentive rates.*

7. Damaged and lost shipments can occur, so knowing how to file freight claims and who is responsible for damage are important.

8. Logistics measurements commonly used by organizations include cost to sales, cost to budget, inventory turns and customer service.

## Appendix: *Transportation Terminology*

- **Basing point:** a point at which rates to another destination are computed.

- **Cartage:** local hauling between locations in the same town or city.

- **Charge backs:** costs assumed by the carrier for independent contractors with the understanding that these costs will be charged back later.

- **Classification:** a publication containing a list of articles and the classes to which they are assigned for the purpose of applying rates.

- **Consignee:** the person named in a freight contract that the goods have been shipped or turned over to for care.

- **Demurrage:** the extra charges paid for detaining a freight car or ship beyond the permitted time for loading or unloading.

- **Differential rate:** the amount added or deducted from a through rate to establish a rate.

- **Distance rate:** a charge made on the basis of miles traveled.

- **Dunnage:** the material used to protect or support truck freight and its weight, listed separately on the bill of lading.

- **FAK:** "freight all kinds." It usually refers to full container loads of shipments containing mixed types of freight.

- **Free astray:** shipment that is miscarried or unloaded at the wrong location and then forwarded to the correct location at no charge.

- **Incentive rates:** lower than usual tariff rates assessed because a rail shipper offers a greater volume than specified in the tariff.

- **Joint rate:** a rate for hauling a single shipment over two or more transportation lines (the lines involved cooperate to offer the service).

- **Multiple care rates:** rates established for shippers transporting large quantities of goods that fill up several rail freight cars.

- **Rate basis:** the formula that includes specific factors or elements that control the making of a rate.

- **Released rate:** a lower rate charged if the shipper releases the carrier from loss and damage liability during shipment.

- **Standard rates:** rates established for direct routes from one point to another. Rates by other routes between the same points are set in relation to the standard rate.

- **Through rates:** applicable for transportation all the way from point of origin to destination. A through rate may be either a joint rate or a combination of two or more rates.

- **Volume rates:** used in the trucking industry to refer to a low rate offered to shippers who agree to ship a large quantity of freight over a specified time period.

# 8

# Asset and Inventory Management

To *meet* today's goals of speed, competitiveness, customer service and responsiveness requires that organizations address productivity issues and work to eliminate non–value–adding activities. Inventory management, in particular, has been a target for improvement because of its impact on quality and delivery. Finding ways to improve inventory velocity and increase the frequency of deliveries has been a hot topic in recent years. Just–in–time and lean production, supplier managed inventories and inventory consolidation techniques are some of the methods organizations are using to add value.

Supply management professionals also are concerned with the management of long-term assets for many reasons, although perhaps the most important one is that assets represent a major investment for any organization. Within the public utility industry, for example, net plant assets (plant assets less accumulated depreciation) can account for more than 75 percent of an organization's total assets.[1] Obviously, these assets require proper attention.

This chapter discusses a number of issues related to asset and inventory management, beginning with an introduction to some terms. A brief overview of asset management then is provided, followed by a more extensive discussion of inventory management. The importance of inventory accuracy is addressed and covers such areas as inventory counting, shrinkage and material returns. Replenishment tools are important, for they allow the depleted inventory to be replaced and ready to issue when next needed. This section also covers inventory classification systems, order quantities and addressing slow-moving stocks.

## CHAPTER OBJECTIVES
• Define assets and their role in supply management.

• Discuss the importance of asset management and asset recovery.

• Discuss how inventory can be classified, tracked and reconciled.

• Identify inventory replenishment and priority tools available to supply management professionals.

• Explore current trends in inventory replenishment.

• Identify the types of surplus materials and various methods for disposition.

## Assets Defined

*Assets* are anything of economic value. A tangible asset, such as real estate, a building, equipment or cash, can be touched. An intangible asset, such as a brand, trademark, copyright or patent, cannot be touched. (*ISM Glossary,* 2006) On the balance sheet, real estate, equipment and buildings generally are considered long-term assets, while inventory, cash and receivables fall under short-term assets. Inventory is "any material, component or product that is held for use at a later time." (*ISM Glossary,* 2006) and a special category of assets. As noted earlier in this volume, each item in inventory is typically referred to as a *stock keeping unit* (SKU). A unique number or bar code differentiates each SKU. For example, a shirt style sold at a department store would require a different SKU for each size. All organizations must determine which SKUs are to be stocked. This determination generally is made based on a number of factors, including but not limited to customer preferences, industry trends, product cost, demand forecasts, profitability and storage capacity. More on demand forecasting is found in Chapter 5, and Chapter 6 discusses storage capacity issues.

Cash and receivables also are important to the liquidity of an organization, although not the topic of this chapter. Briefly, when supply management can shorten product cycle times, an invoice can be issued more quickly, resulting in improved cash flow. Additionally, by keeping order quantities and inventories low, an organization can improve its position with current liabilities. These are just a couple of examples of the dividends resulting from greater integration between supply management and operations.[2] In some organizations, supply management may play a support role within the organization, yet it still can effectively reduce costs within the supply chain.[3] In a 2005 ISM survey of supply managers and above from organizations with revenues of more than $1 billion, 81 percent of the respondents stated inventory control was either a part of the individual's personal job responsibilities and/or supervisory responsibilities or the responsibility of someone else in the supply management organization. Figure 8-1 illustrates how the major elements of an organization's balance sheet are linked to supply management.

Figure 8-1　How Supply Management Links to the Balance Sheet

| Balance Sheet Link | Supply Management |
|---|---|
| **ASSETS** | |
| **Short Term** | |
| Cash | |
| | *Order cycle time* |
| Receivables | *Order completion rate* |
| | *Invoice accuracy* |
| Inventories | *Inventory policies* |
| | *Service levels* |
| **Long Term** | |
| Property, plant and equipment | *Distribution facilities* |
| | *Transportation equipment* |
| **LIABILITIES** | |
| Current liabilities | *Procurement policies* |
| Debt | *Financing options for inventory* |
| | *Financing for plant, equipment* |
| Equity | |

*Source:* Adapted from M. Christopher, *Logistics and Supply Chain Management* (London: Prentice-Hall, 2005).

*Asset management,* also known as property management, equipment management and sometimes even inventory control, involves maintaining an accurate accounting of assets, properly identifying each asset and asset recovery.[4] As described in Chapter 6, these fixed assets are used to support the management of inventory. *Asset recovery* is "the re-employment, reuse, recycling or regeneration of something of value (property, equipment, goods and so on) that no longer is necessary for the original intent; the return of environmental conditions to the state they were prior to an action." (*ISM Glossary,* 2006)

*Inventory management* is a subset of asset management and is defined as the business function concerned strictly with planning and controlling *inventory.* Managing an inventory of expendable goods is very different from other assets because inventory is (or should be) transformed (for example, components into finished goods into sold merchandise) or temporarily stored before transformation. Assets, on the other hand, are used to facilitate the transformation. For example, a restaurant building and equipment help facilitate the transformation of raw ingredients into meals for sale to patrons. Forecasting inventory needs also takes place more frequently (monthly or even daily), inventory models are used to determine order quantities and the amount of control varies based on usage and value.

While some may not consider asset and inventory management glamorous, it remains a key function within the supply management profession. It includes many elements considered critical to supply management, for example, data management and analysis, cost management and strategic outsourcing, all of which are key areas within the Strategic Supply Management Process (see Figure I-1 in the "Series Overview" at the beginning of this book). The following sections provide an overview of asset management, beginning with the classification of assets.

# Asset Management

*Fixed assets,* also referred to as *property, plant* and *equipment,* are long-term assets (see Figure 8-2). The *ISM Glossary* (2006) defines fixed assets as assets that last more than a year, have an impact on shareholder value and are considered by management to be worth controlling. *Property,* often referred to as *real property,* can be the most significant investment because it includes land and rights to the land, ground improvements, utility distribution systems and physical building structures such as warehouses and distribution centers that support the management of inventory. Permanent fixtures to an organization's facilities also are considered real property; they include items such as the warehouse itself, delivery dock and parking lot. *Plant* refers to the operational

---

Figure 8-2    Fixed-Asset Classifications

| PROPERTY | PLANT | EQUIPMENT |
|---|---|---|
| Land and rights | Shelving units | Delivery vehicles |
| Ground improvements | Conveyor systems | Forklifts and other lift equipment |
| Utility systems | Picking systems | Computer hardware |
| Buildings, structures | | Bar code readers |
| | | Office equipment |

*Sources:* Adapted from A. Flynn, M.L. Harding, C.S. Lallatin, H.M. Pohlig and S.R. Sturzl, Eds., *ISM Glossary of Key Supply Management Terms,* 4th ed. (Tempe, AZ: Institute for Supply Management, 2006), and M. Christopher, *Logistics and Supply Chain Management* (London: Prentice-Hall, 2005).

---

components such as shelving, conveyors and picking systems that make up the warehouse network. Technically, these may not be part of the real property, but they can be considered semipermanent for they will likely stay in place if the facility is sold and used for a similar purpose. *Equipment* also represents a significant investment and includes items such as delivery vehicles, railcars, computer hardware, office furniture and lift equipment. These articles would be considered portable and are likely to stay with an organization and not with the structure.

## Effective Asset Management Programs

A sound fixed asset management program involves several elements, including a current listing of all assets, a record of their value and a clear delineation of the responsibility for asset management activities. Effective and efficient use of these assets is possible when such a program is in place. The responsibility and accountability of asset management is something that each organization needs to decide for itself. Because supply management is experienced in the acquisition and disposition of assets, and may already participate in the management of expendable inventory, it may oversee this responsibility. In small organizations, supply management often wears many hats, including asset management. A larger organization may have a specialized program for this function within the supply management department. Figure 8-3 shows an example of how an organization might be structured.

Many software programs are available today that deal specifically with asset management and they can be a sound investment for any size organization. These systems include modules for both the management and accounting of fixed assets, as well as help desk functions and preventive maintenance. A recent example of a successful system implementation is ANZ Bank, one of the largest financial institutions in Australia and a worldwide leader. With more than 11,000 assets to be tracked across their

**Figure 8-3    Typical Supply Management Organization**

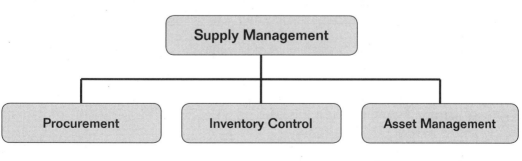

organization, it decided to abandon a manual, paper-based system and partnered with Hardcat, an organization that provides asset management software to organizations in the United Kingdom, the United States and Australia. The system is saving the bank time and resources, and has improved ANZ's accuracy tremendously.[5]

## Asset Recovery

Finding a new use for existing assets is a good business practice. It can minimize environmental impacts and reduce an organization's disposal costs. As explained earlier in this chapter, asset management is a broader term representing a comprehensive approach to acquiring, tracking, managing and reporting on assets. Therefore, asset recovery is an important component of asset management.

Asset recovery applies primarily to an organization's management of its surplus (or idle) equipment. When executed well, it will have a positive impact on return on assets, capital spending and cash flow.[6] Surplus assets can be written off the books for accounting purposes, and when this occurs organizations often look to equipment scrap dealers or an asset recovery organization for any kind of return. It is in this type of instance, however, when a supply management professional can bring tremendous value to the organization. Finding a new use for existing assets is a good business practice and minimizes environmental impacts. By coordinating acquisition efforts throughout the organization and maintaining an accurate asset listing, purchases of new equipment can be avoided. This use of an asset is ideal, but when the equipment is not needed within the organization, supply management should seek to get top value on the open market as a way to maximize the return on invested capital.

Several key factors to success can be found in world-class asset recovery programs. These are:

- An accurate and up-to-date database reflecting all idle or surplus plant, equipment and property with detailed descriptions, asset history and photos;

- Access to the database for all internal users;

- A responsible person at each major location who is designated the asset recovery point person and who functions within the internal network for asset management;

- A professional who is responsible for overseeing the program, the database and the network of internal contacts;

- Internal policies that facilitate the fair value transfer of idle equipment among organization locations;

- Access to market expertise for used equipment or idle real estate through use of a master agreement with an appropriate service provider; and

- Use of the master agreement service provider to determine fair value for internal transfers and to monetize the asset when no internal transfers are appropriate.[7]

As previously mentioned, assets represent a significant investment for an organization. They need to be classified, tracked and monitored during their life cycle, and, when appropriate, need to be disposed of in a manner that results in maximum return. Technology tools and systems that provide the necessary information in an efficient matter must be employed. Involving supply management professionals in the asset classification and disposition process will reap rewards for an organization.

Along with managing an organization's assets, supply management professionals also must handle inventory, which is another area that needs consistent and effective control. The following sections cover this topic in greater detail.

## Importance of Inventory Management

As first mentioned in Chapter 5, the *bullwhip effect* refers to the fact that minor changes in customer demand can become exaggerated as that demand is communicated up the supply chain (retailers, wholesalers, distributors, manufacturers, etc.). These exaggerations, along with the tendency to accumulate safety stock at each point in the supply chain, amplify or intensify for three reasons. First, the bullwhip effect is exaggerated when an organization places the responsibility for meeting demand on the supplier's shoulders, regardless of actual demand fluctuations. Second, carrying too much inventory results when organizations continue with a functional silo mentality, in which each business function optimizes solutions based on its own needs rather than on those of the supply chain. Lastly, when supply management professionals take advantage of pricing discounts, the bullwhip effect is worse because organizations are carrying excess inventory in the system and as a result are increasing the need for warehouse space.

The problem worsens because of the means used to transfer demand and activity data through the supply chain. Typically, demand data is communicated function to function or organization to organization but not necessarily in an accurate manner or with regularity. Activity data, which contains production quantities and the number of product movements within an organization and between supply-chain members, also can contain errors. The combination of errors from these two data sources only compounds the problem. The bullwhip effect is essentially wasteful, occurs because of a lack of information across the supply chain and results in unnecessarily high inventory levels.[8]

Poor inventory policies, along with data inaccuracies, can lead to difficulty in responding to changes in demand and thus trouble scheduling production. As a result, production managers find it hard to manage labor requirements because of the variability in demand. The result is an increase in production costs attributed to overtime and undertime. Data mistakes also result in problems controlling inventory levels and managing warehouse requirements. Additionally, the bullwhip effect can result in customer dissatisfaction because of late or shorted orders. When ordering problems occur, operations spend more time and money to "put out fires" — in terms of expediting costs, additional safety stock and more expensive shipping methods — to satisfy the customer. To improve materials scheduling and customer service and reduce overall supply chain costs, organizations need to minimize the bullwhip effect through more effective inventory management practices and more collaboration with suppliers, as discussed throughout this book. Developing and maintaining relationships with suppliers and internal stakeholders should be viewed as a key to success for supply management professionals.[9]

The following sections discuss the various elements of inventory management, beginning with inventory classification techniques.

## Classifying Inventory

There is an old saying that all inventories are not created equally. This simply means that certain priority items in an inventory warrant closer attention and control by the supply management professional. For example, supply management professionals might classify SKUs as indirect purchases — those that will be used internally by some process or management system — and direct purchases — those items that will be used in production or service delivery and sold to an external customer. Another approach is to classify SKUs by their physical characteristics. Retailers, for example, use category management to classify items as dairy, fresh fruits and vegetables, meat, drugs and so on. Category specialists then oversee the purchase and management of their group. Alternatively, the policy at a given warehouse could be that expensive or critical items are counted more frequently than other materials. Because these items often represent a large annual expenditure for an organization, this only makes sense. Healthcare distributors, for example, track hip replacement parts more closely than bandages.

The book *Inventory Classification Innovation* also offers an intriguing approach to SKUs and how they are differentiated by cost and demand. Cost and demand are considered primary characteristics of all items that can be further broken down into nine types of inventory, as shown in Figure 8-4. Using this classification method, an item of medium cost and demand would be known as a "5," while a low demand and low cost item would be a "1." This matrix could be applied as is or the concept could be expanded with additional categories. It may be desirable to break out cost by more than three categories for instance. If an organization keeps a supply of low-cost inventory

Figure 8-4    InventoryType/Classification for SKU

|  | LOW COST | MEDIUM COST | HIGH COST |
|---|---|---|---|
| **High Demand** | 7 | 8 | 9 |
| **Medium Demand** | 4 | 5 | 6 |
| **Low Demand** | 1 | 2 | 3 |

*Source:* Adapted from Russell Broeckelmann, *Inventory Classification Innovation* (Boca Raton, FL: St. Lucie Press/APICS, 1999).

that is also in low demand (e.g., galvanized nuts and bolts), then that may require less attention than items of slightly higher cost, such as stainless-steel nuts and bolts.

## ABC Classification

Organizations also may use an ABC classification method, based on the Pareto analysis or 80/20 rule. In other words, a small percentage of SKUs should account for a majority of the purchases made. SKUs are divided into three classes, A, B and C. A total value is calculated for each SKU based on annual usage and total purchase dollars spent. For example, if an organization uses 1,000 of an SKU each year and spends $20/unit, the total value equals 1,000 units × $20 = $20,000/year. The SKUs then are ranked high to low.

According to the *Supply Management Handbook,* one of the most useful ways to develop an ABC classification is to begin with an inventory report listing all items in descending order of dollars spent. This will indicate at a glance where the bulk of the dollars reside in an inventory. Normally, the higher value items are considered "A," medium value as "B" and low value items as "C." The smaller percentage items that represent the majority of the dollars (class A) should receive close oversight to maintain scheduled deliveries and minimal inventory. Class B items are reviewed periodically with a normal amount of oversight and only given high priority when the need is critical. The lowest priority of items, class C, would receive minimal attention and could even be ordered in bulk so there is plenty on hand. Procurement cards also are used for C items. Class C items represent only a small percentage of dollars spent.[10] Figure 8-5 provides an example of a typical ABC classification.

As shown in Figure 8-5, the class A items represent just 20 percent of the total items, but account for 80 percent of the dollars spent. This general rule can be applied

Figure 8-5    ABC Classification

| CLASS | PERCENTAGE OF TOTAL ITEMS PURCHASED | PERCENTAGE OF VALUE OF TOTAL PURCHASES |
|:---:|:---:|:---:|
| A | 20 | 80 |
| B | 30 | 10 |
| C | 50 | 10 |

*Source:* Adapted from Tony Hines, *Supply Chain Strategies, Customer-Drive and Customer-Focused* (London: Elsevier, 2004).

to any inventory, even if more than three categories are established. While it may not be an exact science, ABC classification does allow the supply management professional to focus on what is most important.

*Slow-moving stocks* can be a challenge for any supply management professional. These items have low inventory turns and relatively low demand, which may or may not have been anticipated. These stocks should be carefully considered. The first reaction to slow-moving items is often the thought that they are not profitable and should be disposed of. This may or may not be accurate. Even if an item has only two turns in a year's time, it may very well be a mission-critical component that must be kept on hand. Mission-critical means that it is imperative to the success of the organization and its mission, and that not having the item would be disastrous. For example, a U.S. government contractor might consider landing gear axles for a certain helicopter a critical spare part, for it could stop production if it were not available. This could directly impact service delivery and possible future contracts, which is why the U.S. government addresses the issue of critical parts shortages in its business planning.[11]

There can be many reasons for slow-moving stocks, including changes in customer preferences and advancements in technology. In these cases, it may be wise to phase out an item or at least not carry as much in inventory. At some point, a slow-moving item may become obsolete and will need to be dealt with as such.

## Inventory Accuracy and Integrity

Inventory, as mentioned earlier, is a short-term asset but represents a major investment for any organization. Depending on the type and size of the organization, the investment in inventory could easily be in the millions of dollars. Thus, it is incumbent on those who oversee these inventories to ensure that they are well managed. This includes knowing the exact quantity of the materials on hand, as well as the dollar value of the inventory. When inventory records are not accurate, there is an increased chance for unfilled orders resulting in customer dissatisfaction, obsolescence and theft. Also, if inventory records indicate an item is in stock when in fact it either is not or has been misplaced, production delays and additional costs to track and expedite shipments can result.

## Tracking Issues and Returns

The terms *issue* and *return* simply refer to inventory either going out of or coming into the warehouse. The steps normally involved with issuing inventory are picking, staging and delivery. Upon a request from an internal user, for example the sales department, a paper or electronic *pick ticket* is generated in the warehouse identifying the materials needed. The item is then retrieved, or picked, from wherever it resides in the warehouse and then staged for the customer. Staging can be a separate area of the warehouse where materials are housed until they are either delivered or picked up.

Returns can occur for a variety of reasons. Perhaps more material was received than was needed or an incorrect item was received. If a customer does return material to the warehouse, proper procedures must be in place to inspect the item to ensure its condition, as well as adjusting the inventory count. Because a return generates additional costs in labor time and handling, many organizations require a *restocking fee.* It is not unusual for a customer to pay 20 percent of the original purchase price to return an item.

## Verifying Inventory Levels

While most organizations today use computer software that can accurately track what should be in inventory, physically verifying those records still is necessary. This is known as *taking a physical inventory* and refers to the actual counting of the materials on hand in the warehouse. Often warehouse personnel do the counting or in some cases a third-party inventory service is brought in under contract. Count sheets or handheld devices are used to record the actual amount of inventory on hand. Organizations will commonly conduct a physical count at a set period of time, usually at the end of the business year, for instance, to match actual inventory levels against computer records. An annual physical count is a method that many supply managers are familiar with, for this inventory ties into an annual income statement and balance sheet.[12]

**Cycle Counting.** Many organizations in the United States and abroad also verify their inventory through the use of *cycle counting,* which is performed throughout the year. Cycle counting as defined in the *ISM Glossary* (2006) is a physical stock-checking system in which the inventory is divided into groups that are physically counted at predetermined intervals, depending on their ABC classification. Thus, the physical inventory counting goes on continuously without interrupting operations or storeroom activities. This is also referred to as *continuous inventory.* Cycle counting represents a proactive approach to inventory management for inventory records are verified on a frequent basis, not just during a one-time event that "cleans up" an inventory that is inaccurate the rest of the year. It is a best practice that makes inventory accuracy a priority and something to strive for on an ongoing basis. Vodafone Australia, for example, a leading provider of wireless handsets, used cycle counting as part of its expanded logistics program to help expand its network of services in 2005. Increasing its inventory accuracy through cycle counting allowed Vodafone to ship 99 percent of its online orders the same day.[13]

Counting a portion of warehouse items monthly or quarterly is a wise business practice for supply management professionals. It allows for the counting process to be spread out over time by dividing the effort into smaller and more manageable tasks. Cycle counting continues to be the preferred method for ensuring inventory accuracy, for it results in lower inventory write-offs as a percentage of inventory investment.[14]

**Inventory Reporting Measures.** Although any measurement of inventory starts with cycle counting, the reporting format is typically presented in three ways: weeks of supply, average aggregate inventory value and inventory turnover. The *weeks of supply* is calculated by dividing the average aggregate inventory value by sales per week (at cost). The *average aggregate inventory value* is the sum of the dollar values of all items that are held in inventory. *Inventory turnover* measures the velocity of total inventory movement through an organization. As a rule, a higher rate of turnover is better. (*ISM Glossary,* 2006) The formula to calculate inventory turnover is:

$$\text{Inventory turnover} = \frac{\text{Annual sales (at cost)}}{\text{Average aggregate inventory value}}$$

Hopefully, inventory will be sold or turned over multiple times in a year. High inventory turns are desirable for they increase cash flow and reduce the possibility of obsolescence. How many inventory turns are ideal? There is no single best rate for inventory turns, but some industry averages are useful. The inventory turnover is calculated by dividing an organization's cost of goods sold by its average of cost of inventory during the year. Figure 8-6 provides a list of inventory turnover ratios in various industries.

---

Figure 8-6    Inventory Turnover Ratios by Industry Corporations

| INDUSTRY | INVENTORY TURNOVER RATIO |
|---|---|
| Lumber and building materials | 5.2 |
| Hardware stores | 3.5 |
| Grocery stores | 12.7 |
| Gas stations and minimarts | 39.3 |
| Automobile parts | 3.6 |
| Wholesale groceries | 17.8 |
| Wholesale electrical goods | 6.8 |
| Wholesale paper products | 10.7 |
| Wholesale chemical | 9.4 |

*Source:* Adapted from Biz Stats. Com, "U.S. National Averages for Inventory Turnover Ratios," 2003, available from www .bizstats.com/inventory.htm.

---

## Reconciliation

Once an inventory item has been counted and compared against the perpetual records, discrepancies may appear. Less inventory on hand than is expected is referred to as *shrinkage* — a reduction in the amount of inventory on hand for reasons other than issuance or a sale. This can be the result of materials being lost, stolen or misplaced, and also through natural causes such as evaporation and deterioration. Certain materials are more prone to experience shrinkage, such as batteries, drill bits or computer components. If specific items repeatedly experience shrinkage, then policy changes may be warranted. Additional security measures or relocation of the items can help address the problem and reduce theft and pilferage in the future.

These variances normally are noted on *discrepancy reports.* Significant variances that are noted will warrant attention and often result in a recheck of the item and its actual quantity. To settle or resolve these variances is known as *reconciliation.* To reconcile the inventory records, an adjustment will be required. These reports also will serve as an audit trail for the warehouse.

## Measuring Accuracy

*Inventory accuracy* is an important performance measurement because it indicates whether the actual inventory on hand matches the inventory records. Inventory management specialists typically divide the number of SKUs with an accurate count by the total number selected for counting. For example, if 96 SKUs were found to be accurate out of 100 counted, the inventory accuracy would be 0.96 or 96 percent. Making these results known to key warehouse staff on a regular basis can help identify problem areas, as well as keep staff informed when accuracy benchmarks are met. Texas Instruments employed this approach when examining its supply-chain performance. By having its inventory optimization team regularly review both the benchmarks and performance information, it was able to significantly reduce late orders to its customers.[15] Because accuracy is so important, it is imperative that a physical inventory is taken periodically and that it is conducted correctly. This allows for the inventory system to be updated so that it accurately reflects materials available in the warehouse. When a discrepancy occurs, meaning the quantity on hand is different than what the inventory system indicates, a correction then is made through an *inventory adjustment.*

Excess material can result when warehouse inventories are not managed accurately and effectively. In many cases, this excess will need to be disposed of, usually at a loss. Later in the chapter, multichannel disposition plans will be explored, including various methods of disposal or reclamation.

# Inventory Policies and Procedures

The efficient and effective operation of any business function requires sound policies and procedures. Inventory management is no exception. The supply management professional must play a key role in the development of an organization's inventory policies, which also must have the support and buy-in of senior management. Policies should be easily understood by both customers and staff, and should be reviewed and updated periodically. For example, certain inventory issues must be addressed in a warehouse policies and procedures manual. Figure 8-7 provides a list of items that warrant consideration.

The importance of a well-developed policy manual for the warehouse should not be underestimated. It provides a blueprint for the entire organization of its supply management practices and reflects the value of the warehouse operation. World-class organizations inevitably will have sound policies and procedures regarding inventory management, as well as policies on inventory valuation. More on managing the warehouse can be found in Chapter 6.

Figure 8-7    Warehouse Policy Issues

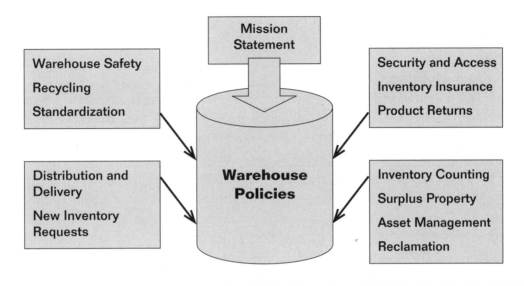

## Inventory Valuation

The three basic methods used to valuate inventory are LIFO, FIFO and average costing. *Inventory valuation* determines the dollar value of inventory on hand at a given point in time.

*LIFO* stands for last in, first out and assumes that items purchased last are sold first. Because these items are likely higher in value in times of inflation or asset appreciation, the remaining inventory is valued at an older price, which gives the organization a lower value for remaining inventory on its balance sheet. *FIFO* means first in, first out and assumes that items purchased first are also sold first. For instance, an electrical component sold out of inventory would be issued at the oldest, or first price.

*Average costing* assigns an inventory value for an item at the average cost paid. So if two air compressors were in inventory, one purchased for $750 and the other for $850, the inventory value for each would be $800.

Organizations also must determine reordering polices, which are discussed in the following section.

# Replenishment and Priority Tools

Knowing when and how much to purchase of a particular item will always serve as a challenge to supply management professionals. To begin this discussion, it is important to understand the costs incurred from owning inventory.

## Inventory Holding Costs

Also referred to as *inventory carrying costs, inventory holding costs* represent what it costs an organization to keep inventory on hand, including the opportunity cost of invested funds, storage and handling costs, taxes, insurance, shrinkage and obsolescence-risk costs. Holding costs typically are stated as a percentage of an inventory item's value over a period of time (e.g., 20 percent per year). (*ISM Glossary,* 2006)

The cost of maintaining an inventory can be substantial for an organization. Surprisingly, inventory holding costs can run between 20 percent and 40 percent, which is considered a conservative range. Some industry experts calculate this number to be even higher. One estimate indicates that when all capital, labor, investment, variable and tracking costs are summed, inventory holding costs can reach 35 percent to 50 percent per year.[16] To assess the true cost of inventory, supply management professionals must look beyond just the cost of the inventory itself. And even though public sector warehouses typically avoid taxes, the holding costs still are considerable.

Following are the components used to calculate the inventory holding costs:

- *Invested funds.* The capital used to purchase the inventory must be considered, whether it is financed through a third party or through the organization's cash flow. This includes lost opportunity costs of capital invested elsewhere.

- *Storage.* The cost for the physical storage of the goods can include rent, utilities, equipment and maintenance costs.

- *Handling.* The cost to handle the inventory, including receiving and picking costs, can be substantial when wages, benefits and other personnel costs are considered.

- *Taxes.* Taxes paid on the value of the inventory on hand, as well as property taxes.

- *Insurance.* Insurance premiums for properly protecting the inventory investment and warehouse facility.

- *Shrinkage.* The loss or shrinkage of inventory, which can be caused by human error or pilferage.

- *Obsolescence.* The losses because of materials becoming out of date.

To assess the true cost of carrying inventory, consider all the costs that go into owning or leasing a warehouse as well as inventory. Only then can the inventory holding costs for an organization be determined. Supply management also should be aware of these costs when placing large orders. The negotiated purchase price may reflect a deep discount, but after factoring in holding costs, the price may not be so attractive. More organizations are moving toward maintaining the smallest amount of inventory possible to meet customer service goals. However, with international sourcing, a new complexity is added to inventory management. Because of some of the risks associated with international sourcing and the need to maintain the continuity of business, many organizations are adding inventory. Recent challenges noted by United Parcel Service (UPS) include longer product lead times from overseas manufacturers. In one case, an organization was seeing 10-week lead times to get products from Chinese manufacturers through customs to its California warehouse and on to multiple customers throughout the United States. Maintaining additional inventory on hand is a natural reaction in such cases, although UPS worked with its client to consolidate direct shipments to reduce delivery time and inventory levels.[17]

## Inventory Ordering Costs

Each time supply management places an order, *inventory ordering costs* are incurred. For the identical item, the costs associated with each order should be the same, no matter what the order size because the same activities will occur.

Some of the costs specifically tied to processing an order include:

- Preparing a material requisition, including phone, fax and e-mail;

- Request for quote process, including quote analysis;

- Price negotiation and order issuance;

- Administrative, expediting and receiving costs; and

- Invoice processing and payables cost.

Once an organization has collected this cost information, it can begin the process of calculating the order size for each item.

## Determining the Order Size

What is the optimum amount of material to order? Some inventory management systems employ a *fixed order quantity* approach in which the amount of material ordered does not vary, only the frequency and timing of the order. For instance, a printing shop may order a certain paper only by the pallet. The order size is always one pallet, but depending on actual demand, the order could be placed monthly or quarterly.

If the fixed quantity is large, then the organization will benefit from a lower purchase price. This also makes the acquisition process more straightforward for the material and quantity are always the same. A potential disadvantage to fixed order quantity is the tendency for higher inventory levels. As previously mentioned, an organization can obtain lower pricing for larger orders, but there is always a cost to handle and store the material. Inventory holding costs are significant and are discussed earlier in this chapter.

For many years, the *economic order quantity* (EOQ) has been used to assist supply management professionals as a starting point to estimate the fixed order quantity. The EOQ formula balances the cost of holding inventory with the cost to order it. The generally accepted formula for calculating the most basic EOQ is:

$$EOQ = \sqrt{\frac{2(\text{Annual usage in units})(\text{Order Cost})}{(\text{Carrying Cost})}}$$

Notice that annual usage is expressed in units and is based on the forecasted usage. As mentioned earlier, the order cost is the sum of all fixed costs incurred when an item is ordered, and the annual holding cost is the cost associated with having inventory on hand.

The EOQ is a viable tool for the supply management field; often it is a built-in function of many automated materials management systems. The formula gives the supply professional valuable information prior to order placement. The EOQ value often is adjusted to accommodate such issues as factory packaging, shipping requirements and quantity discounts.

Figure 8-8 provides an example of an EOQ calculation based on the frequency and size of the order. For purposes of this example, the acquisition cost is $33.33; the annual use is $5,000 and the carrying costs are at 12 percent. Based on this information, the optimum value is reached with three orders per year. At that frequency, the carrying and acquisition costs are balanced.

**Deciding When to Reorder.** Once the EOQ has been determined, inventory levels are monitored. When inventory levels reach the reorder point, an order for the EOQ is triggered. A reorder point is a predetermined inventory level that triggers an order. (*ISM Glossary,* 2006) Where should the reorder point be set? Generally, the supply management professional will set this so that enough material is on hand to meet the demand until the new order is received. A number of factors are considered when determining the reorder point. These include the importance of the item (will it stop production?), the anticipated demand (how much is needed?) and the supplier lead time (how long will it take?).

## Figure 8-8    EOQ Model

| | NUMBER OF ORDERS PER YEAR | | | | |
|---|---|---|---|---|---|
| | 1 | 2 | 3 | 6 | 10 |
| $ Per Order | $5,000 | $2,500 | $1,667 | $834 | $500 |
| Average Inventory | 2,500 | 1,250 | 883 | 417 | 250 |
| Carrying Costs | $300 | $150 | $100 | $50 | $30 |
| Acquisition Costs | $33 | $67 | $100 | $200 | $333 |
| Total Cost | $333 | $217 | $200 | $250 | $363 |

*Source:* S.H. Corwin, *Intermediate Public Procurement,* 2nd ed. (Herndon, VA: National Institute of Governmental Purchasing, 2000).

## Variable Order Systems

Organizations also may opt to preset a maximum inventory level needed to run operations efficiently and a reorder point, and then review inventory levels periodically. When inventory reaches the reorder point, enough inventory is ordered to bring levels back up to the maximum. This type of system is common when review and ordering costs are relatively high.

## Safety Stock

Whether a fixed or variable order system is used, *safety stock* is always a consideration. Safety stock is sometimes referred to as *buffer stock* because additional inventory is held as a safeguard against fluctuations in either the supply or demand of an item or delivery risk, such as with the use of international suppliers. In the event of a spike in demand, safety stock can become quite valuable for it prevents a stockout or a total depletion of material on hand. Depending on the importance of the item in question, the safety stock literally can save the day and keep a production line running or ensure valuable goods are ready for delivery to the final customer.

The challenge with this concept is carrying an ample amount of safety stock without stockpiling it unnecessarily. The latter can be costly. Normally, the level of adequate safety stock can be determined by knowing the supplier's lead time to acquire an item. For example, if three days are required to secure the materials, then having an average of three days' usage of safety stock in the warehouse makes sense. An experienced supply management professional will use this information, along with his or her experience, to determine an appropriate safety stock level.

Another important consideration is the type of control system that should be adopted.

## Inventory Control Systems

Inventory managers monitor and control inventory in two common ways. With a perpetual inventory control system, an organization's inventory values are kept continuously in line with its actual inventory on hand. After each purchase, withdrawal and sales transaction, the inventory records are updated. If inventory levels for an item have fallen below a set amount, more will be ordered. The ability to maintain continuously updated records is possible with inventory management software. A perpetual inventory management system still requires an organization to periodically take a physical count to ensure that the computer records are accurate. The EOQ model typically is used in perpetual inventory management systems. Wal-Mart uses a perpetual inventory system. Through the use of bar code scanners and computerized inventory systems, it can tell how many items are in stock currently, how many were sold last week or even how many are on hand at individual stores.[18]

This differs from a *periodic inventory* system, where transactions are recorded in an account as purchases, withdrawals and sales are made. However, inventory is only reviewed on a periodic basis (e.g., weekly, monthly, quarterly) to determine if more should be ordered from the supplier. A periodic inventory system generally is used by smaller organizations or those where inventory withdrawals are infrequent. A variable order system is commonly used with a periodic inventory control system. ABC Building Services, a locally owned maintenance company, uses a period inventory system. Supplies and materials are purchased throughout the year to perform its work, but the inventory account is updated only at the end of each quarter to reflect actual inventory on hand.

Other inventory control considerations may include:

- Should the inventory be held in-house or by a supplier?

- What inventory items receive top priority and attention?

- How can one ensure that inventory levels remain relatively low?

There is no single correct answer for any of these questions, but by becoming aware of the tools available, supply professionals can best position themselves and their organizations for success. The next section begins with a discussion of inventory costs.

# Trends in Inventory Replenishment

A supply management professional may save acquisition costs because of negotiated volume discounts, which at first glance may seem attractive. A retailer such as Home Depot, for example, could decide to place one large order for a particular style of refrigerator to realize a savings on the total purchase cost. However, carrying and handling costs will be high and probably will not offset the savings. Organizations are increasingly finding ways to reduce the amount of inventory carried.

## Inventory Consolidation

In recent years, private and public organizations alike have worked toward maintaining a leaner inventory. This includes reducing the amount and types of inventory on hand, as well as consolidating inventories at multiple locations. By reducing the number of locations, organizations are experiencing cost savings in several areas. Operational costs can be reduced with fewer sites, and inventory levels also are reduced. One of the other prime areas where organizations see savings is in the reduction of their safety stock. Inventory usage may be consistent, but fewer sites mean less overall safety stock.

With multiple locations, leads times for each facility can vary, even for the same product. This type of decentralization can make forecasting requirements quite challenging. When selecting the appropriate facility for consolidating inventory, key considerations include which sites have the lowest lead time and the best operational efficiency.[19] When Boeing merged with McDonnell Douglas, the largest aircraft manufacturer in the world was faced with the need to reduce costs within its inventory warehouses. In an effort to drive costs down, the organization consolidated its inventory locations for the C-17 aircraft, which was made up of more than 4,000 parts and took two years to build. By upgrading its storage equipment, rearranging stocking locations and using a warehouse management system (WMS, further covered in Chapter 6), Boeing was able to make significant improvements. Picking productivity improved, labor costs were trimmed and a total of 70,000 square feet of warehouse was freed up.[20]

## Just-in-Time Inventory Management

The Japanese have held that excess inventory equates to waste and is not a good use of an organization's resources. Perhaps as a result of the scarcity of industrial space in their country, the Japanese developed the *kanban system* to ensure low levels of inventory.[21] The word *kanban* is Japanese for the type of card that originally was used in manufacturing environments. Kanban is defined in the *ISM Glossary* (2006) as a printed card that contains specific information such as part name, description, quantity and so on that signals a cycle of replenishment for production and materials. It is an order release mechanism. Toyota has successfully employed kanban in its production scheduling system. By requesting a predefined standard quantity of a component or subassembly, Toyota work centers can better ensure low setup costs and short lead times.[22] Production personnel use the kanban to convey to supply management that additional inventory is needed. Placed in the bin, the kanban card is removed when the inventory is depleted, and the card then is given to the supply management professional. This action prompts a replenishment order for the item and helps keep inventory levels low. The kanban system is most effective for small lot sizes of items that are high volume and low value.[23]

For instance, a quantity of roller bearings is used up on the production floor and kanban will ensure it is replenished only at the time it is needed and not before. This prevents a buildup of inventory, which, in turn, reduces costs. This is consistent with the philosophy behind kanban, which is to maintain a well-balanced supply chain.

## Inventory Scheduling

*Flow manufacturing,* or flow production, is a term used to describe a "one-piece flow" business strategy that allows an organization to establish a continuous sequencing of product, within a flow process, that is replenished either from external suppliers or other internal processes based on actual customer demand and works hand in hand with just-in-time. Contrary to traditional manufacturing methods, individual units of production "flow" directly through the manufacturing process without the time delays associated with batching. Traditional manufacturing practices include batching of partially completed parts into lots, waiting in front of another manufacturing process for further processing. Traditional factories also move in-process inventories extensive distances from one manufacturing process to another. By reducing or eliminating batching and unnecessary routing, lead times can be reduced and the cost of work-in-process and finished goods is reduced. Because there are less materials on the shop floor, material control is simplified in terms of tracking and management activities. A manufacturer also can move from a build-to-stock to a build-to-order environment.

Founded in Japanese manufacturing principles and specifically the pulling of materials through production based on actual customer demand, organizations using a flow manufacturing strategy typically create manufacturing cells, which are u-shaped physical layouts of manufacturing equipment to manage the flow of materials. Within the cells, all manufacturing steps are carried on for similar parts, and workers are trained to operate all equipment within the cell. The u-shaped design eliminates much of the waste in production because workers travel less between unfinished and finished product, and virtually all work-in-process is eliminated.

Part of flow manufacturing is *level scheduling* of production, defined as a technique to balance production throughput at each workstation to meet expected *cycle times*. The cycle time is a measure of how frequently each unit will be produced. Important to the success of flow manufacturing is converting suppliers to the same business strategy.

The flow manufacturing strategy originated from a methodology created in the 1980s by the John Costanza Institute of Technology (JCIT International). JCIT International (now DemandPoint, 2007) develops and delivers educational programs to those in the manufacturing industry. The organization also developed the Demand Flow® Technology (DFT) model, which is a mathematical set of tools used to design flow lines and processes to lessen manufacturing lead times by reducing waste. Ultimately, the goals are to increase manufacturing speed, responsiveness and flexibility.

## Supplier-Managed Inventory

The traditional method for replenishing inventory was to simply place an order with a supplier when materials were depleted as needed. Suppliers were given no advance knowledge of the customer's requirements, often resulting in rush orders, increased freight costs and delays in production.

*Supplier-managed inventory* (SMI) is a progressive approach to controlling inventory. Formerly referred to as vendor-managed inventory, this concept gained ground in the 1990s as organizations focused on reducing supply-chain costs. The *ISM Glossary* (2006) states a supplier is responsible for ensuring that stock is maintained at appropriate levels in the supply professional's facility and for replenishing items when these levels drop. With SMI, the supplier receives information about the needs of the customer, including historical usage, current inventory levels, material forecasts and promotional products. This information then allows the supplier to assume responsibility for inventory management. Suppliers assume the risks of having the necessary levels of inventory on hand. Upper-stock and lower-stock levels are conveyed by the customer, but the task of inventory replenishment falls to the supplier. In many cases, the supplier owns the inventory being managed until the product is issued.

There are many benefits to supplier-managed inventory. These may include:

- Partnership is formed between the parties.

- Communications are improved.

- Order processing speed is improved.

- Purchases are generated on a predefined basis.

- Improvement occurs in fill rates.

- Decrease in stockouts exists.

- Increase appears in inventory turns.

- Planning and order costs are decreased.

- Overall service level is improved.

SMIs offer numerous advantages to both the supplier and the customer. Both may have their own reasons for embarking on the partnership, but ultimately SMI must be beneficial for all. A recent study by the Electronics Supply Chain Association on the use of supplier-managed inventory offered some interesting findings regarding the reasons for participating in SMI as illustrated in Figure 8-9.

A recent example of a successful SMI program was Boeing's partnership with a key supplier of raw materials, Alcoa. Boeing sent weekly forecasts and inventory counts to the supplier, which allowed Alcoa to make better internal production decisions, resulting in improved ordering and product deliveries. Ultimately, both parties found SMI to be a win-win proposition. Boeing and Alcoa noted the following as key factors to their success:

- Team members from each organization were willing to make changes to their current processes.

- Senior management from both organizations supported the process, which included a charter statement signed by both parties.

- Both organizations displayed an ability to put everything on the table.[24]

SMI does have its limitations, however. Some organizations may hesitate to implement such a program for fear they are losing control of their inventories. An increased dependence on the supplier also may be perceived as a disadvantage of SMI.

# Inventory Disposition

While it is easy to see the value in concentrating on the "front end" of inventory management, such as material forecasts and order quantities, it also is important to properly deal with obsolete and damaged stocks at the "back end." Leading organizations have begun to pay more attention not only to their purchasing practices but also to the disposal of surplus material, which can turn the idle equipment into value.[25]

## Investment Recovery Principles

*Investment recovery* is defined in the *ISM Glossary* (2006) as a systematic, centralized organizational effort to manage the surplus/obsolete equipment/material and scrap recovery/marketing/disposition activities in a manner that recovers as much of the

## Figure 8-9    Reasons for SMI Participation

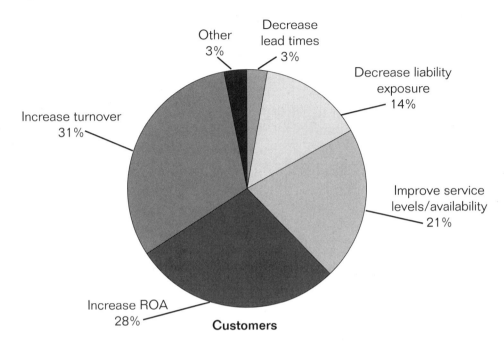

**Customers**

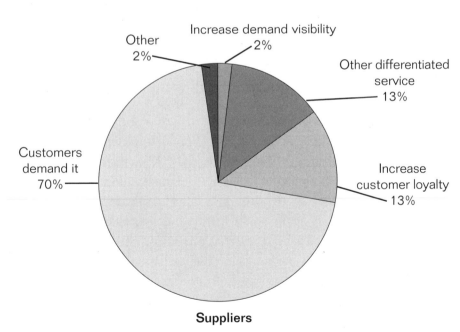

**Suppliers**

*Source:* C. Roberts "The Rise of VMI, Asia Pacific Development," available from www.gdsinternational.com/infocentre/artsum.asp?mag=10&iss=43&art=1926.

original capital investment as possible. An organization's inventory and assets continue to have value when they reach the end of their useful lives. Very often it falls to the supply management professional to properly dispose of these assets and to do so with maximum investment recovery in mind. Supply management is most knowledgeable of the markets an organization buys in, as well as the supplier base of potential interested parties. The following should be kept in mind when disposing of an organization's assets:

- Items must be disposed of in a timely manner for there is a cost to keeping them on hand.

- Whatever disposal method is employed, it should attempt to maximize proceeds for the organization.

- When unneeded assets are converted to cash, they should be used to offset the cost of operations or invested in new assets.[26]

This chapter covers the area of asset disposition related to inventory. Assets also can include capital equipment and computer hardware, which are covered in Chapter 7.

Reverse logistics is a broad and evolving field. *Reverse logistics* is defined as "the term most often used to refer to the role of logistics in product returns, source reduction, recycling, materials substitution, reuse of materials, waster disposal, and refurbishing, repair and remanufacturing."[27] In recent years, successful reverse logistics programs have improved customer service as well as financial performance. An example of such success is the U.S. Postal Service, which created Parcel Return Service, a division that provided retailers with a convenient way to handle returns that uses a third-party logistics provider, Newgistics, Inc., to work directly with USPS customers in addressing their reverse logistics needs.[28] An example that further demonstrates commitment on a global scale is Hewlett-Packard (HP), which provides recycling services for computer equipment, printing supplies, batteries and even cell phones. HP's efforts resulted in the recovery of 187 million pounds of electronics globally during 2006.[29] Members of the supply chain, along with logistics service providers, must be committed to establish good reverse logistics programs. Therefore, it should be a part of an organization's current and future supply strategies.

A *multichannel disposition plan* will allow an organization to use a variety of approaches to dispose of its excess inventory and even finished goods if they become damaged. Such a plan will consider a number of factors to ensure that a disposition method is appropriate for the material at hand. These factors include market demand, the condition of item, marketing opportunities and market trends.

One method fits all circumstances — a multichannel disposition plan. Products such as bicycles may have a high consumer demand and be sold off through online systems like eBay. Raw materials would likely be more specialized, so a negotiated sale to another manufacturer may be more appropriate. For instance, a mechanical contractor with a large quantity of steel plate left over from a completed project may be able to sell the material to a railcar manufacturer that uses the same material in its processes.

## Surplus Material Categories

Surplus materials can come in many shapes, sizes and varieties. *Surplus property* is a term used to describe materials and assets that no longer are needed by an organization. They can include inventory items as well as noninventory assets that may fall under the control of supply management. These items may become available for many reasons and fall into the following general categories.

*Damaged* stock is material that has suffered some type of damage or neglect and is therefore not fit for its intended use. This damage can occur because of defective manufacturing, improper handling or inadequate packaging. Material that arrives at the warehouse damaged should be refused or returned to the supplier. However, if the damage is not apparent and only discovered at a later time, the buying organization may have to take responsibility. To avoid damaging goods during handling, warehouse personnel should be well trained in proper materials handling procedures. Materials such as metal or wood that have no utility value are considered *scrap*. Scrap can be generated by an organization and can include material left over from special projects or normal production. Often scrap includes nonferrous metals such as copper, aluminum and brass. In recent years, the recycling of scrap metals has continued to grow. Because of tight markets, increased values and organizational commitment to sustainability, more than 4 million tons of aluminum and 1.5 million tons of copper are recycled each year.[30]

Inventory items subject to *spoilage* are those that deteriorate or rot over time. These items include food products, chemicals or rubber products that have limited shelf lives. Spoiled items do not normally have any value. Local bakery outlets, however, can offer discounted breads and pastries to consumers. They still are within their product expiration dates but usually are closer to the date than the same products on shelves of major grocery retailers.

*Obsolete* stocks are inventory items that no longer can serve their intended purpose because of market or operational changes.[31] As technology advances in every industry and market, products can become obsolete quickly. This can be a challenge faced by supply management professionals, whether their inventory consists of ship repair parts or high-tech computer equipment. These stocks have outlived their useful lives and are not likely to be sold at their full value. However, every effort should be made to get as much value out of the inventory as possible. The Ann Arbor District Library manages a surplus property program that offers outdated and obsolete equipment to the highest bidder. As an example, a laminating machine that originally cost hundreds of dollars was recently offered for $15. With changing technology, the older machine was not worth much on the open market, but the agency made a sincere attempt at recovering what it could.

## Disposal Marketplace

An important part of an organization's disposition process is a sound knowledge of the disposal marketplace. Many options are available for the supply management professional to dispose of surplus property. More than likely an organization will use experts in a given industry that provide disposition services and are neither the buyer nor the seller, otherwise referred to as *third-party specialists.* One type of third-party specialist is the *broker,* an intermediary who brings the buyer and the seller together. They do not take ownership of the goods, but provide brokerage services for a fee. Payment arrangements are handled between the buyer and the seller. Another option is the *dealer* who specializes in buying and selling, but actually takes ownership of the goods and resells them at a profit. Supply management professionals, again, must be knowledgeable and connected in the industries in which they work, and be able to employ the services of an outside party that is most beneficial to their organization. Public Surplus is an organization that sells all types of equipment on behalf of government agencies (www.publicsurplus.com), while Surplus Record serves as a directory of surplus electrical equipment (www.surplusrecord.com). Both use the Internet as a prime marketing tool to provide disposition services to their clients.

Other organizationss are emerging in the marketplace that not only serve as a resource for disposition of assets, but for developing sustainable strategies that can be considered at the start of the acquisition process. Interface, Inc., offers sustainable floor covering and interior fabrics for the commercial market. The organization is committed to sustainable business practices that minimize the impact on our environment. For Interface, these types of practices are not just sound business practices, but rather a corporate philosophy that resonates from the chief executive throughout the organization.[32]

## Disposition Methods

Numerous avenues are available for disposing of surplus property. If other departments in the organization do not have a need for the item (reuse within the organization generally is preferable), then the following methods should be considered.

An *auction* is a type of public sale where the goods are sold to the highest bidder. Heavy equipment and motor vehicles often are sold through an auction process. In recent years, many organizations have used *electronic sales,* where items are sold online via the Internet. Many commercial sites exist, such as eBay, that list and sell all types of goods and materials. The advantage of an online sale is that more potential buyers will see the wares, which often results in higher sale prices. Applying the value of existing equipment against the purchase of new is referred to as a *trade-in.* An organization is in a better position to leverage a higher price from a buyer when a potential new sale is on the line. Disposing of equipment separately can result in a lower financial return.

Similar to the method of procuring a new item, a *bid* process also can be used to dispose of property. Interested buyers submit written bids to the organization, which then selects the most advantageous offer. This method often is employed in the public sector. *Retail sales* can be a viable means of disposal if the value and quantity of the equipment are high enough. Because retail space is required to display the sale items, this can be relatively costly. When surplus equipment is offered to an organization's staff through an *employee sale,* then certain benefits can be realized. For example, when Brigham Young University is ready to "retire" any of its fleet of vehicles, it first offers them to employees at wholesale places.[33] This is a great deal for the employees and saves the organization significant transactions costs associated with disposal in the marketplace. Preset prices can ensure that the organization gets a fair market value, and it avoids the time and expense of dealing with outside parties. This is a common private sector practice that also is used by some public agencies.

Donation and discard are methods that will not realize revenue for an organization. A *donation* is the transferring of property to another party at no cost to the party. Often, not-for-profit organizations are the recipients of these donations. A lack of revenue does not necessarily mean there is no value or return for the donating organization. The demonstration of goodwill through a community donation certainly can be beneficial, as well as tax deductible in many cases. *Discard* refers to literally throwing away an item of no value. This is a last resort and should be used only if there is truly no value in the item and no demand for it.

A prime objective when disposing of surplus property of any type is to obtain maximum value. Hard-earned capital was used to purchase the inventory item, so naturally an organization wants to recoup as much of the original investment as possible.

One of the first steps is to establish a baseline value for the item. In some industries, published guides can be used to assist with this value determination. The automotive and RV industries use such guides, including books and Web sites to gauge current value. For more than 80 years, the *Kelley Blue Book* has provided market pricing for all types of motor vehicles and is used extensively in the automobile in-dustry (www.kbb.com). Additionally, the National Automotive Dealers Association began publishing the *NADA Guide* in 2000, which serves as an appraisal guide for autos, motorcycles and recreational vehicles (www.nadaguides.com). The *book value* of an asset is calculated on its original value less the accumulated depreciation to date. Past or current sales figures also can be used as a resource. The price that an item can command on the open market is referred to as its *fair market value.* Figure 8–10 can serve as a general guideline when establishing an item's potential value, with the factor serving as the multiplier against its original cost.

Disposition methods of surplus materials are important, but the area of physical storage cannot be overlooked. The following section deals with issues related to estab-lishing a physical warehouse to house materials, including surplus.

## Value Stream Mapping

*Value stream mapping* (VSM) was originally a lean manufacturing technique in which the transformation of materials is traced from beginning to end to determine if there is waste in the process either in the form of a step where no value is added or a point of "wait time" when material is being stored to await further value-adding transfor-mation. This concept also is applied to services. (*ISM Glossary,* 2006) Value stream mapping, which is similar to flow charting or process mapping, objectively looks at a process to determine value-added and non-value-added components. This technique

Figure 8-10    Value of Surplus Material

| TYPE | CONDITION | FACTOR |
|---|---|---|
| New | In original container | 1.0 |
| Excellent | Like new condition | .90 |
| Good | Solid working condition | .85 |
| Fair | Needs refurbishing | .50 |
| Poor | Needs complete rebuilding | .40 |
| Scrap | Appropriate for salvage | .30 |

*Source:* Chandrashekar, A and Dougless, T. "Asset Recovery: New Dynamics for Purchasing Organizations," *International Journal of Purchasing and Materials Management,* (September 22, 1997).

can be useful in many areas of supply management, including warehousing or services purchasing. J. Womack and D. Jones define the value stream as "a set of all actions, both value and non-value-added, required to bring a specific product [whether a good, a service or some combination of the two] through the [critical] main flows."[34] Organizations can have several value streams, including investment recovery for surplus materials. When this or any other business process is mapped, an organization can determine what steps do not add value and consider eliminating them. VSM is an effective tool that provides material processing steps with information flow and allows an organization to make the best use of its resources.

One of the easiest ways to create a VSM is to create a cross-functional team from managers and nonmanagers throughout the organization. For supply management processes, this team likely would include operations, purchasing and customer service groups. An ideal size team is between seven and ten members. The first step for the VSM team is called a *kaizen,* which is Japanese for "change for the better." With an experienced facilitator, the group can work through the four steps of VSM, which are:

1. Determine the process family.

2. Draw the current state map.

3. Determine and draw the future state map.

4. Draft a plan to arrive at the future state.

The VSM process can help organizations build improvements and efficiencies in their processes. It requires a dedicated team of professionals who are willing to think beyond their current practices.[35]

## Summary

Asset and inventory management continues to play a valuable role within the supply management field. Whether in the areas of supplier relationship management, cost management or social responsibility, the supply management professional certainly contributes toward organizational success. The importance of inventory management is addressed in this chapter, as well as what it takes to maintain an accurate inventory.

Today's warehouses rely on various third parties for both inventory management and distribution support, as outsourcing continues to face all areas of an organization. Being aware of industry trends, disposition channels and virtual warehouses will ensure the inventory function continues to add value.

## Key Points

1. Assets are property that retain their value over a period of time. These can include vehicles, building structures and equipment, for each has an economic life along with a residual value. The management of these items is known as asset management, which is a segment of materials management. The three categories of fixed assets are property, plant and equipment.

2. The three ways to valuate inventory are LIFO, FIFO and average costing.

3. Supplier-managed inventory (SMI) is a growing trend and can offer many benefits to both the customer and the supplier.

4. A small portion of the items in an inventory represent the largest investment and should therefore be monitored more closely through the use of ABC classification.

5. Because inventory holding costs are high, organizations should attempt to balance their acquisition and holding costs by applying the EOQ formula.

6. Inventory turnover measures the velocity of total inventory movement through an organization.

7. Flow manufacturing is a term used to describe a "one-piece flow" business strategy that allows an organization to establish a continuous sequencing of product that is replenished either from external suppliers or other internal processes based on actual customer demand.

8. Manual order picking involves the use of warehouse personnel to physically retrieve an item, while mechanized systems automate the order fulfillment process.

9. Value stream mapping is a technique that evaluates a process and identifies both value-added and non-value-added activities.

10. Organizations should consider a number of factors when developing a multi-channel disposition plan, including market demand, item condition and marketing opportunities.

11. When disposing of surplus materials and inventory, the supply management professional should attempt to obtain the maximum value for the organization.

9

# Quality in Supply Management

The issue of quality has evolved greatly within the field of supply management and in recent years, its importance has continued to grow. Industrial and commercial products were traditionally acquired based on unit price, while other factors such as quality, availability and after-sale service often were overlooked. No longer can supply management professionals afford not to rank quality at the top of their priority lists. Quality should be viewed as a critical factor in the sourcing decision.[1]

Earlier in the book, the strategic procurement process was depicted, and it is evident that quality impacts many areas of supply management. When considering strategic outsourcing and supplier relationship management, it is critical to maintain a high standard of quality.

This chapter will reflect on the importance of quality by first looking at several key definitions (see Figure 9-1) and their applications to the supply management profession. Also covered in this chapter will be various quality programs and tools that can be used to make a positive impact on poorly performing processes. Improving supply management also is important, so appraisal processes are discussed. Lastly, given the amount of outsourcing today, techniques and methods to improve supplier performance are covered.

## CHAPTER OBJECTIVES

• Discuss supply management's role in assuring quality.

• Identify the quality improvement models that can help improve the competitiveness of organizations.

• Explore how the use of quality tools can be used within supply management.

• Explore the processes that can help improve performance within supply management.

• Discuss how supplier performance can be measured and improved.

# Defining Quality and Its Role in Supply Management

*Quality* can be described as a precise and measurable variable that is inherently present in the characteristics of a product or service. It also has been defined as synonymous with "innate excellence." A high-quality product or service should be superior to other like items. *Quality management* is the function of planning, organizing, controlling and improving the quality of products and processes. (*ISM Glossary,* 2006)

*Quality assurance* is a management function that includes establishing specifications that can be met by suppliers; using suppliers that have the capability to provide adequate quality within those specifications; applying control processes that assure high-quality products and services; and developing the means for measuring the product, service and cost performance of suppliers and comparing it with requirements. (*ISM Glossary,* 2006) A function of quality assurance is quality control. *Quality control* is responsible for measuring quality performance and comparing it with specification requirements as a basis for controlling output quality levels. (*ISM Glossary,* 2006) Another related term is *quality improvement,* which is a systematic approach to remove waste, loss and rework to make a process more effective and efficient. (*Glossary of Quality Management,* 2006)

---

**Figure 9-1    Quality Terminology**

| | |
|---|---|
| **Quality** | A precise and measurable variable that is inherently present in the characteristics of a product or service. |
| **Quality Management** | The function of planning, organizing, controlling and improving the quality of products and processes. |
| **Quality Assurance** | Postproduction inspections to ensure the quality of a good or service; an end of process activity to control quality. |
| **Quality Control** | Compares actual quality received with the intended goals and defines appropriate steps to correct deficiencies. |
| **Quality Improvement** | Systematic approach to remove waste, loss and rework to make the process more effective and efficient. |

*Source:* A. Flynn, M.L. Harding, C.S. Lallatin, H.M. Pohlig and S.R. Sturzl, Eds., *ISM Glossary of Key Supply Management Terms,* 4th ed. (Tempe, AZ: Institute for Supply Management, 2006).

---

## Supply Management's Role in Quality Assurance

The role of supply management in assuring quality is to ensure that the goods and services acquired meet quality expectations and that they support the strategic objectives of the organization. This includes identifying products, determining customer needs, identifying the right suppliers and establishing metrics to verify the quality of services and products.[2] A product that simply conforms to a specification or standard may be minimally acceptable, but that does not mean it is quality.

Whether it is hiring a consultant to support a service provider's operations or acquiring raw materials to be used in the manufacture of finished goods, the supply professional plays a key role in ensuring quality. For many U.S. organizations, more than 50 percent of the final price of a product is the cost of the purchased goods, and in Japan it often is even higher. Thus, when supply management delivers quality through its suppliers, an organization's competitiveness is improved.[3]

Research indicates that organizations will rely even more on supply management in the future. Supply managers must continue to play active roles for their organizations in securing quality goods and services. By developing and executing value acquisitions, supply management can ensure maximum return for their organizations.[4] In a 2005 ISM survey of supply managers and above from organizations with revenues of more than $1 billion, 83 percent of the respondents stated quality was either a part of the individual's personal job responsibilities and/or supervisory responsibilities or the responsibility of someone else in the supply management organization. Because it may interact with any part of an organization on a given project, supply management has the opportunity to make a positive impact on a daily basis. By assuming a leadership role and employing the tools discussed in this chapter, supply management professionals can best add value to their organizations. This new, advanced responsibility means that supply management must take responsibility not only for negotiating the equipment purchase, but also for the performance of the equipment and the supplier throughout the entire life cycle. To achieve this, supply management must monitor and improve the performance of its suppliers.

Supply management, however, also must realize the risks of overspecifying quality. Developing product requirements that are excessive can result in additional costs and delays. To ensure an appropriate level of quality, a *performance specification* should be considered. This approach simply details the performance criteria required for a particular product or service. (*ISM Glossary,* 2006) For example, by using a performance specification, the Queensland Government in Australia determined that BMW motorcycles were the best value for its police officers.[5]

# Quality Models

A number of improvement models and programs are being used by organizations today to increase quality and competitiveness; several have proved to be tried-and-true by some leading organizations such as Toyota, Bank of America, Deere & Co. and Target. The following section will address current processes that can increase quality, beginning with Six Sigma.

## Six Sigma

A leading quality improvement model for many organizations today is *Six Sigma*. As briefly discussed in Chapter 1, this is a disciplined methodology that uses relevant data to eliminate defects in a process. The objective of Six Sigma is the implementation of a measurement-based strategy aimed at reducing variances and improving processes. Organizations that implement Six Sigma are striving for a level of quality that is near perfection. For a process to achieve Six Sigma status, it must produce no more than 3.4 defects per million opportunities.[6,7]

Six Sigma programs have been used to develop new processes for manufacturing and service sectors, as well as to improve existing processes in need of improvement. When General Electric's former CEO Jack Welch needed a methodology to benchmark business performance, he implemented Six Sigma and in one year alone improved the bottom line by $600 million.[8]

Services organizations, such as Bank of America Corp., have adopted Six Sigma to improve their supply management process. Bank of America handles more than $7 million annually in services, which accounts for 60 percent of its overall spend. Using the DMAIC process (defined in the following paragraph), the financial services provider improved an established sourcing process to convey clear expectations to service providers, as well as its business objectives. Using what it refers to as a supplier relationship management (SRM) system, Bank of America now appoints trained professionals to oversee supplier performance. The key objective with its outsourced services has been to establish key relationships that result in cost savings and faster service deliveries.[9]

DMAIC and DMADV are two Six Sigma processes that organizations commonly used to improve performance. DMAIC (define, measure, analyze, improve, control) is used for existing processes in need of incremental improvement, while DMADV (define, measure, analyze, design, verify) applies to either new or existing processes requiring more than just incremental improvements (see Figure 9-2).[10]

In addition to improving quality in the supply management processes, Six Sigma can be effectively applied to project management. As supply professionals continue to

Figure 9-2    DMAIC Versus DMADV

| DMAIC<br>Improve *existing* processes incrementally | DMADV<br>*New* processes or improve existing processes more than incrementally |
|---|---|
| **D** – Define project deliverables and customer goals. | **D** – Define project deliverables and customer goals. |
| **M** – Measure the process to determine current performance. | **M** – Measure and determine customer's needs and specifications. |
| **A** – Analyze and determine the root causes of any defects. | **A** – Analyze process options that will meet the customer's needs. |
| **I** – Improve the process by eliminating defects. | **D** – Define the process in detail to meet the customer's needs. |
| **C** – Control future process performance. | **V** – Verify design performance and ability to meet customer's needs. |

*Source:* Adapted from SixSigma, www.isixsigma.com/dictionary/DMAIC-57.htm.

lead projects for their organizations, this can be an extremely effective tool. The project management process was covered in more detail in Chapter 2.

## Standardization Programs

Standardization of materials is also a trend that improves quality and leads to efficiencies and cost savings. Establishing an organization's consistent physical and functional characteristics for its materials is known as *standardization*. The standardization process can take place at different levels: across an organization, throughout an industry, across a nation and around the world. (*ISM Glossary,* 2006) Such efforts, at least at the organizational level, must involve supply management. Standardization, for example, is a driving factor for organizations that operate in a just-in-time (JIT) environment.

Many organizations have a recurring need for the same or similar products over time, and it is those organizations that can benefit greatly from a standardization program. A standard is a product that an agency consistently specifies, for it meets its operational needs and is a result of a standardization effort. When specific design, size, color, quality and material criteria are used, this is referred to as a standard specification. Even if multiple manufacturers can provide products that meet all the criteria, an acquired product still is considered standard if the good or service complies with the organization's requirements. The use of specific components and manufacturing methods are the basis for establishing certain products as accepted standards.[11]

Standardization has several advantages, as well as some disadvantages. The advantages include:

- Fewer varieties of products being purchased,

- Lower product costs because of volume increases,

- More timely sourcing process,

- Reduced inventory of product types and

- Reduced operational and administrative costs.

The downside to standardization, actual or perceived, can include:

- Potential reliance on fewer suppliers, therefore limiting competition,

- Missed opportunities for considering new product developments and

- Potential limitation of customer choices.[12]

A well-conceived *standardization program* can result in cost reduction for an organization, as well as lead to efficiencies in procurement, inventory control, training and maintenance. Proper testing methods must be established to ensure that products provided are of acceptable quality. The use of a standardization committee is key to such a program. Besides supply management, which often assumes a leadership role with standardization, other departments to involve include engineering, operations, maintenance, sales and production. Some of the activities and deliverables of a *standards committee* are:

- Developing organizational standards and product or service specifications,

- Establishing policies and procedures for administering a standard program,

- Evaluating exception requests to established standards,

- Maintaining ongoing participation with suppliers to provide input to the program and

- Establishing benchmark criteria for the program.[13]

What areas are prime candidates for standardization? Just about any good or service that an organization buys can benefit from standardization. This certainly includes high-volume items that can result in leveraged pricing from a single supplier. For example, if several thousand light fixtures are purchased in a given year, selecting a standard fixture type for quality and appearance could be a very attractive opportunity for a lighting distributor. The opportunity for reduced pricing based on exclusive use could benefit both buyer and seller. Other areas, including the procurement of facilities and maintenance/repair/operating (MRO) supplies, should also be considered.

Standard specifications can include the designation of specific brand names, such as Hewlett-Packard printers. They also can result in generic requirements that include product features and are open to any manufacturer that can meet those requirements. The other outcome could be the establishment of a *qualified products list* (QPL), where multiple brand names have been accepted as meeting the standard.

In addition to effects within an organization, material standardization can have an impact on national and international fronts. As markets continue to globalize, the need for universal standards becomes even more important. As reported by the Slovenian Institute for Standardization, international standardization includes such fields as technology, heavy metals, textile, packaging, telecommunications and transportation. When nonharmonized standards exist in various countries or regions, this results in trade barriers. Numerous professional standards groups develop and maintain standards, such as the American National Standards Institute (ANSI), the American Society for Testing and Materials (ASTM), the Canadian General Standards Board (CGSB) and the International Organization for Standardization (ISO).[14] ASTM E2500, for example, is the standard for the design of pharmaceutical manufacturing equipment. This standard was established by the ASTM in cooperation with the U.S. Food and Drug Administration (FDA) and the International Society for Pharmaceutical Engineers (ISPE).[15]

Standard specifications also can prompt communication among designers. This can assist them with increasing the ratio of products to parts. For instance, an organization may have 50 products that are created from 500 unique parts, which results in a products-to-parts ratio of 0.1. If the same 50 products are created from 400 parts, then the ratio is improved to 0.125 and results in a higher standardization. This type of product standardization is a key part of just-in-time (JIT) inventory systems.[16]

A key component of a material standardization program is the cost benefit analysis. This can help in "selling" the effort to senior management as well as justify the decisions made by the standards committee. A *cost benefit analysis* is a thorough examination of an alternative course of action, including the identification of all costs and benefits. This will assist an organization in determining whether or not to pursue such action. In the case of a standardization program, the benefits described earlier in this chapter would be included, as well as the projected cost savings from reduced inventory and standardized training. When product standards are implemented, then only those subcomponents that support the particular product are necessary to have on hand in inventory. Logically, this saves time and money when fewer items are stocked. With a reduced need for training internal staff on maintaining multiple products or systems, additional efficiencies and savings are gained. Material standardization is likely to cost an organization up front as far as time and resources committed, but in the long run it can pay dividends with the efficiencies created.

When Deere recognized that up to 70 percent of the manufactured product costs occurred externally, it aggressively pursued material standardization. This effort included the reduction of its standard shipping containers from 43 to 3. By taking aggressive steps early on in the process, it was able to reduce its supply-chain costs significantly. By employing this and other lean supply strategies, Deere moved closer to one of its overall goals: to design products that delight its customers at the lowest total cost.[17]

While standardization certainly can result in holding fewer items, it differs from simplification. When an organization reduces the number and design of items (or stock keeping units) it uses, this is referred to as *simplification*. (*ISM Glossary*, 2006) A good example of simplification is 3M's wheel weight system, which was designed to meet precision wheel balancing requirements. This allows organizations to reduce their costs by eliminating traditional wheel weight inventories of various sizes.[18]

## International Organization for Standardization (ISO)

*ISO* is the International Organization for Standardization, a network of the national standards institutes in 157 countries worldwide. A nongovernmental organization, ISO is based in Geneva, Switzerland, and offers one membership per country. In the United States, this member organization is the American National Standards Institute (ANSI). It acts as a bridging organization for the public and private sectors, while addressing the needs of business and consumers alike. The ISO is the world's largest developer of standards, realizing the importance of quality and standards in products and services of all types. When there is an absence of standards, products can be of poor quality or incompatible with existing equipment. The ISO standards contribute toward making the supply of products and services consistent, efficient and safe. The term used throughout the world is always *ISO,* even though the organization may have various abbreviations in different languages. For instance, the United States may use *IOS* for the International Organization for Standardization in English, while France and Canada would translate it as Organization Internationale de Normalistion or *OIN*.[19]

To promote and develop global standards, third-party registration and accrediting councils evaluate an organization's quality systems. Throughout the world, organizations are widely adopting ISO 9001:2000, which now is considered the global standard for providing assurance about an organization's ability to satisfy quality requirements and enhance the customer–supplier relationship.[20] Many industry leaders view ISO 9001:2000 as a fundamental shift in the approach to quality management by the ISO. Rather than focus on complying with a series of regulations and procedures, organizations are determining customer needs and expectations and developing management systems that address those needs. Through collaborative leadership, a systemwide approach is created that strives for continual improvement that benefits all parties involved. The objectives of the ISO management system standards include:

- Providing assurance about quality in supplier-customer relationships;

- Operating in an environmentally sustainable manner;

- Unifying quality, environmental and information security requirements in sectors and areas of activity;

- Qualifying suppliers in global supply chains;

- Providing technical support of regulators;

- Giving organizations in developing countries a framework for participating in global supply chains, export trade and outsourcing;

- Assisting in the economic progress of developing countries and transition economies;

- Transferring good managerial practices; and

- Encouraging the rise of services.

The 2006 ISO Survey of Certifications reports that the number of organizations obtaining ISO 9001 certification for quality management increased by 16 percent. This demonstrates the growing acceptance of ISO standards throughout the world.

The ISO 14001:2004 certification addresses an organization's quality systems and practices in the area of environmental management. In today's world of sustainability promotion and corporate social responsibility, many organizations have committed to minimizing activities that are harmful to the environment. Through 2006, certificates had been issued in 140 countries and economies for ISO 14001:2004, with the services sector accounting for 27 percent of all certificates.[21] (Social responsibility also is discussed in Volume 1 of the ISM Professional Series *Foundation of Supply Management.*)

Quality assurance is a key issue for supply management professionals and ISO standards can assist both internally and externally. Organizations that practice processes such as production and raw materials acquisition can be registered as ISO, as can outside suppliers. With more and more organizations throughout the world focusing on quality throughout the supply chain, ISO may very well be the most important standard for supply management.[22]

# Quality Tools

The enemy of quality within the supply chain is inconsistency. By applying the quality tools discussed in the following sections, supply management professionals can achieve a consistent level of quality for their organizations.

## Plan-Do-Check-Act Cycle

W. Edward Deming's four-step plan for process improvement is known as the plan-do-check-act cycle (PDCA). The improvement cycle may seem intuitive, but it nevertheless has proved to be very effective as a problem-solving tool for countless organizations. A quality team begins by selecting a process that is flawed and documents it based on collected data. Once the team has prepared a cost/benefit analysis, it creates an improvement plan. It then implements the plan and measures the effect of the changes. The results then are measured against the original goals and, if deemed successful, the new process is standardized in the organization.[23] Kaoru Ishikawa further developed Deming's plan and created the six steps for quality improvement that are illustrated in Figure 9-3.[24]

**Figure 9-3    Ishikawa's Six Steps**

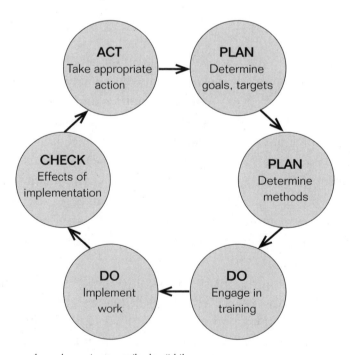

*Source:* Adapted from www.skymark.com/resources/leaders/ishikawa.asp.

## Histograms

A histogram as defined in the *ISM Glossary* (2006) is a diagram of values being measured versus the frequency with which each occurs. When a process is running normally (only common causes are present), the histogram is depicted by a bell-shaped curve. A histogram is a useful tool for summarizing and displaying the distribution of a process data set. It is a simple graph that can be constructed by segmenting the range of data into equal-size groups. The vertical axis is labeled "frequency" and the horizontal access is labeled with the range of the variable being reported. A histogram conveys the most common response in the system as well as what distribution the data takes (varied, centered, etc.). Figure 9-4 provides an example of a basic histogram.

## Pareto Analysis

Throughout history many have played a significant role in the development of quality management principles. Vilfredo Pareto was an Italian economist who studied the distribution of wealth. What he found was that a relatively small amount of the population (20 percent) controlled the majority of the wealth (80 percent). This has come to be known as the Pareto analysis or the 80/20 rule. As mentioned in Chapter 8, his theory was the basis for the ABC inventory classification system, but it also played a

**Figure 9-4    Histogram**

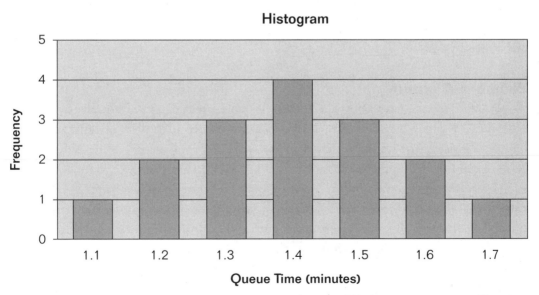

*Source:* Adapted from K. Simon, "Histogram," iSixSigma.com, May 27, 2001, available from www.isixsigma.com/library/content/c010527c.asp.

significant role in quality management. Essentially what Pareto contended was that a vital few have the greatest impact on the whole; in other words, about 80 percent of the problems often result from only 20 percent of the potential causes. For example, most of the problems with suppliers may come from a small percentage of the supplier base, or just a few production areas can account for the largest share of defective products.

In the 1930s, Dr. J.M. Juran conceptualized the Pareto analysis, which allowed millions of managers to help differentiate the vital few from the useful many within the organization. His *Quality Control Handbook* still serves as a valuable reference for supply management professionals, for it provides guidance on how quality goods and services can lead to improved performance. The three management processes Juran believes are essential for all organizations are: (1) quality control, (2) quality improvements and (3) quality planning.[25]

W. Edward Deming is considered one of the 20th century's leading authorities on quality. Deming contended that management actually controls 85 percent of the process while operations controls only 15 percent of the improvement. For instance, management has the ability to replace machinery if a current machine cannot consistently produce conforming products. It also has the authority to revise the acceptable tolerances within a specification.[26] An operator certainly plays a key role in the manufacturing process, but it is actually an organization's management team that has the greatest ability to improve quality. Deming's teachings stressed the need to constantly strive for improved quality and productivity. By monitoring the way a process works, rather than conducting mass inspections, an organization can improve productivity and lower its costs.

## Fishbone Diagram

The *fishbone diagram* (also known as the "cause-and-effect diagram" and discussed in Chapter 2) was developed by Kaoru Ishikawa as a way to identify root causes of problems in a process that results in delays and waste. The problem itself is identified in the head of the fish while major causes are noted at the major bones (see Figure 9-5). For each cause, the question of "Why" is asked up to five times. These answers are the root causes that allow an organization to identify existing problems and ultimately improve quality. Ishikawa and Deming were colleagues and both used this diagram when working with organizations to improve their management policies and practices.

## Run Charts

A *run chart* as illustrated in Figure 9-6 is a graphic representation of system performance over a period of time. The X axis is time and the Y axis is the attribute being

**Figure 9-5    Fishbone Diagram**

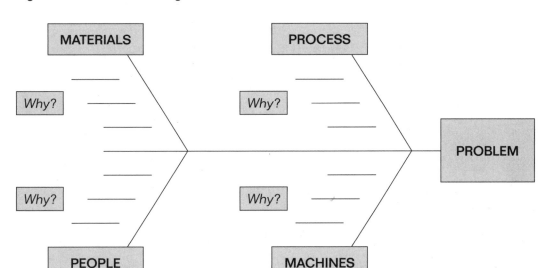

measured. With sufficient data, upper and lower control limits can be statistically derived that will indicate if future data points are in or out of control. (*ISM Glossary,* 2006) The run chart can help determine if the system is stable and can offer data against which to make future changes. By understanding what is a normal, predictable variation, an organization can avoid undercontrolling or overcontrolling a process. Each improvement effort should include a team that evaluates system performance to assemble baseline data that changes can be evaluated against. The following steps are useful in constructing a run chart:

1. Plan how and where data will be obtained by writing an operational definition.

2. Complete the chart-identified information, including what is measured, dates, locations, collector and other relevant data.

3. Calculate the process average.

4. Calculate the upper and lower control limits.

5. Determine the scaling for the chart.

6. Interpret the chart.

Figure 9-6    Sample Run Chart

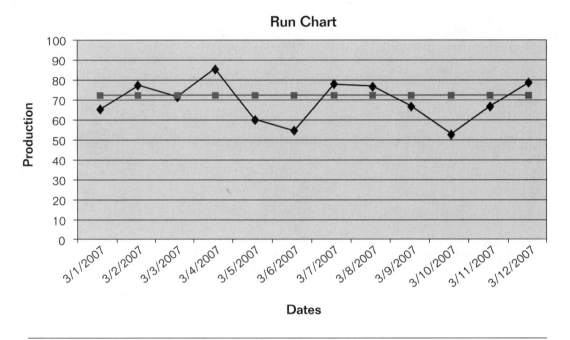

When interpreting the run chart, an organization should look for the following results, for they can indicate an unstable process or one that is not in control:

- A point outside the limits (99.7 percent should fall within the limits);

- A run of seven points: above the center line, below the center line, going in one direction up, going in one direction down; or

- Nonrandom patterns: cycles (may indicate too many data are combined–shift, equipment, etc.), too close to average (center line), too far from average (center line).[27]

## Statistical Process Control

*Statistical Process Control (SPC)* is a quality control method employed primarily in manufacturing that uses control charts to detect whether a process is under control. SPC uses the application of statistical control charts to measure and analyze the variation in processing operations. The methodology monitors the process to determine whether outside influences are causing the process to go "out of control." The objective is to identify and correct such influences before defective products are produced, and thus keep the process "in control." (*ISM Glossary,* 2006) Service providers such as

Taco Bell, Domino's and the Ritz-Carlton, however, also use SPC to improve operations. This method was originally used by Deming to assist the American war effort during World War II by improving industrial production methods. Deming introduced SPC to industry leaders in Japan after the war. He created a basis for the control chart and developed the concept of statistical control through a series of experiments. SPC is quite different than traditional quality control, where all finished products are inspected for conformance with predetermined specifications. Using statistical tools, SPC observes the performance of a production line to predict problems that can result in inferior products.

An example would be a production facility that fills plastic containers with liquid hand soap. When production is running as planned, the containers receive 10 ounces of product within certain tolerances. If the environment changes so can the inputs; if a belt pulley wears out it may dispense 10.5 ounces. Left unchecked, each overfill can result in waste and lost profits. By using statistical tools, such problems can be detected by quality personnel. When the root cause of such a variation is detected, it can be corrected before it becomes a larger problem. Many organizations require proof of SPC from suppliers, particularly for manufactured products they deem critical. Motorola, Inc., is an example of a supplier that has successfully applied SPC techniques. Within its Tactical Electronics Division, it used a team of engineers trained in SPC to review design prints and move quickly into full-scale production.[28]

## Capability Indexes

Variations can occur in any manufacturing process, because each machine is different as is each component that is produced, even if the differences only are detectable by a microscope. The key is to ensure the variations stay within an upper and a lower specification limit. The capability of a process must be examined to see if it can produce within the required parameters on a consistent basis. Once any abnormal causes have been eliminated from the process, it is considered to be in statistical control. *Cp* and *Cpk* are two common ways to measure capability. Each of these methods compares the process spread with the specification spread and measures the variation. Cpk measures how well centered on the desired value the process spread is, as well as the tightness of the variation. For example, a food manufacturer might measure the exact weight of a product and compare it against the desired weight using a capability index.

Figure 9-7 illustrates the normal variation for a custom manufactured bushing, which has a specification spread of 1.500 inches ± 0.010. This means the dimension should be 1.500 inches but can be as much as 1.510 inches or as little as 1.490 inches and still be within an acceptable tolerance. When a run of 50 bushings is produced, the results are noted, which represent normal variations.

**Figure 9-7    Example of Normal Variation**

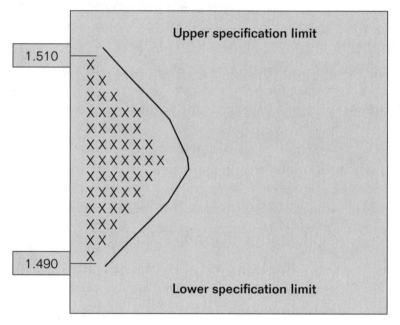

*Source:* Adapted from Greg Hutchins, *Purchasing Strategies for Total Quality* (Homewood, IL: Business One Irwin, 1992).

The middle of the range is known as the specification target. Ideally, these occurrences are minimized when the process spread is within the specification spread, and maximized when the process spread is outside the specification spread. When the bell curve is centered in the middle of the specification and is narrow (as shown in Figure 9-7), this indicates a quality process that is in control. When production units are not centered on the specification target, and more of the occurrences are outside of the set tolerances, that target is deemed unacceptable (see Figure 9-8). In this example, too many occurrences are falling within the upper end of the specification limit, which is why the bell curve appears higher than normal. These situations require attention, for the cause must be determined to correct production. Reasons for unacceptable production outputs can include an inexperienced operator, inferior properties of raw materials or a procedural change in methods between work shifts.

While these tools can be used to improve specific supply management activities and processes, a broader goal often is to assess and advance the supply management function. The following section describes the use of capability maturity models to

**Figure 9-8    Example of Unacceptable Variation**

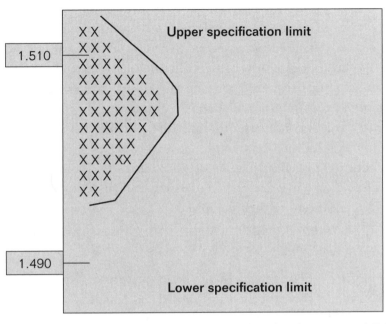

*Source:* Adapted from Greg Hutchins, *Purchasing Strategies for Total Quality* (Homewood, IL: Business One Irwin, 1992).

appraise the current state of an organization's supply management capabilities and use that appraisal as a baseline for such advancement.

# Improving Supply Management Performance

The *capability maturity model* (CMM) is an appraisal process that was developed to measure and improve an organization's critical core capabilities. Mark Paul and a team of researchers at Carnegie Mellon University's Software Engineering Institute (SEI) developed the CMM in the 1980s to help military officers quickly assess and describe a contractor's ability to deliver the specified software on time. While the original intent was to measure the maturity level of the software development processes, several other process areas have since been added to the model. Although similar to ISO 9001, which sets a minimum standard to specify manufacturing and service industry quality levels, CMMs are more explicit in defining *how* to achieve continuous improvement within an organization. A CMM also confirms the progress an organization is achieving with its processes and helps make the benefits of process improvement visible to other employees. ADP Securities Industry Software, an IT service provider within the security brokerage industry, implemented CMM as part of its quality processes and, ultimately, ADP achieved ISO 9001 certification.[29]

The appraisal process is used to assess any needs within a customer–supplier relationship. It also can be used to help motivate and facilitate buy-in from various stakeholders within and outside an organization. Essentially, the capability maturity model is one tool that can help organizations determine the current maturity of their processes, identify the ones that need improvement and then support their move to the next level of excellence through continuous improvement practices. CMMs provide a place to begin the road to improvement for a given process by bringing together the organization's past experiences. The model then allows team members to work within a structured framework to prioritize their actions and come up with a definition of what improvement means to their organization. Lastly, a maturity model can be used as a benchmark against other organizations.

Organizations generally go through five levels of process maturity:

1. *Initial.* The sourcing process is considered ad hoc, chaotic and hectic. Management understands the value of this process; it is accepted and practiced among the majority of organizations within a given industry. However, the life cycle of sourcing is not completely understood and the organization does not know any part of the process in any level of detail. Process documentation is used infrequently and on an ad hoc basis. Employees are not held accountable for using the process or following standard operating procedures.

2. *Repeatable.* The sourcing process has moved from the initial stage to where it is used more repeatedly because of external pressures. Parts of the process have been improved such as supplier assessment or contract management, but minimal improvement is evident over the initial stage for the entire sourcing process. There is no policy that requires the consistent use of the process or set standards.

3. *Defined.* The sourcing process is basically defined as a standard business process and required to be used by all levels of the organization. The sourcing activities are linked together and the process is more focused. People inside the organization now understand the effect of each activity on other activities. Formal documentation now has been created to standardize the process. Some metrics to measure performance begin to emerge.

4. *Managed.* The sourcing process is now an organized, standard business process, and management and measurement take place. The process has been fully integrated with all other core processes and a supply management department

emerges that is responsible for outsourcing. Metrics are used periodically to measure the process and make decisions.

5. *Optimized.* To remain at this stage the organization must seek process improvements and optimization in a formal continuous manner. Metrics are used systematically to measure process quality, efficiency and effectiveness. Continuous improvement practices are in place to improve the sourcing process. Process streamlining initiatives also are being implemented to improve the process.

The original CMMs have since been more fully developed into the capability maturity model integrated, which is discussed further in the following section.

## Capability Maturity Model Integrated

The *capability maturity model integrated* (CMMI) is a collection of best practices that aid organizations in improving their processes. Released in 2001, CMMI integrates the CMM software used for the original capability maturity model, Electrical Industry Alliance Interim Standards, and Integrated Product Development CMM into one framework. Thus, CMMI can address several areas of improvement at the same time, rather than as separate initiatives, over the product development life cycle. The Standard CMMI Appraisal Method for Process Improvement (SCAMPI) uses oral presentations, demonstrations, surveys and databases and other instruments to rate the strengths and weaknesses of a given process based on the CMMI models. An appraisal team, which often is outsourced to third parties, makes the assessment. A CMMI product suite is available that provides a framework, models and appraisal methods and materials.

CMMI also has been applied to the acquisition process for systems or services to improve supplier capabilities, which, in turn, can help them deliver products at a higher quality more quickly, at a lower cost, using the most suitable technology.[30] Known as CMMI-ACQ, it covers six process areas:

1. Solicitation and supplier agreement development,

2. Acquisitions management,

3. Acquisitions requirements development,

4. Acquisitions technical solutions,

5. Acquisitions validation and

6. Acquisitions verification.

These six process areas are supplemented by 16 other process areas, such as project management, organization and support.

## Contract Management Maturity Model

Effective contracts depend, to a great degree, on the processes used to create them. Thus, to award and successfully manage contracts, an organization should have processes in place that are disciplined and capable. Another tool developed in 2006 is the *contract management maturity model* (CMMM), which measures an organization's contract management process capability against the five levels described earlier and then uses the evaluation as a guide to continuously improve process capability. The key contract management areas are: (1) procurement planning, which identifies the business needs that will best be met by outsourcing; (2) solicitation planning, the preparation of documents to support the solicitation process; (3) solicitation; (4) source selection; (5) contract administration; and (6) contract closeout. These areas are all part of the strategic supply management process identified earlier in the book.[31]

There are five levels of contract management process maturity, as described in Figure 9-9. At the ad hoc level (Level 1), rudimentary contract management processes exist with some informal documentation but there is no accountability for not following the standards and processes. The better organizations transition through the second level (basic) to fully established and required processes throughout their organization as defined in the structured level (Level 3). At this point, senior management is providing direction and approval for the contracting strategy, decision-making process, required documents and the terms and conditions. The best organizations attain an integrated (Level 4) or an optimized level (Level 5), using performance metrics regularly to measure contract management processes. Continuous improvement efforts are in place by which the organization applies lessons learned from past experiences and establishes a set of best practices.[32]

Once some form of capability maturity model analysis is complete, organizations can engage in a two-pronged strategy: (1) continuous improvement activities and (2) breakthrough improvement initiatives such as Six Sigma. Beyond performance assessment, organizations also must find ways to improve supplier performance to fulfill their missions and visions. More on initiatives to make improvements can be found in the following section.

# Improving Supplier Performance

To improve supplier performance, organizations must first develop, measure and evaluate their own quality requirements, as discussed earlier in this chapter. Only by

Figure 9-9    Contract Management Maturity Levels

| MATURITY LEVEL | | DESCRIPTION |
|---|---|---|
| 1 | Ad hoc | Contract management processes exist and are accepted and practiced. Management understands the benefits of a contract management process. It includes some informal contract management process documentation and is used on an ad hoc basis. Managers and personnel are not held accountable for not following standards. |
| 2 | Basic | Some basic contract management processes and standards are in place but only required on complex, critical and highly visible contracts. Consistent policies and standards do not exist on other contracts. Processes and standards exist but have not been institutionalized throughout the organization. |
| 3 | Structured | Contract management processes have been fully developed, institutionalized and mandated throughout the organization. Formal documentation has been developed and some processes may be automated. The processes and documentation can be tailored for the unique aspects of each contract. Senior management provides guidance, direction, approval of contracting strategy, decision, documents and terms and conditions. |
| 4 | Integrated | Contract management processes have been fully integrated with the organization's core processes and the end user or customer. Performance metrics are used periodically to measure the contract management process and make related decisions. |
| 5 | Optimized | Contract management processes are fully integrated with the organization's core processes and end user or customer. Performance metrics are used systematically to improve process quality. Contract management personnel apply lessons learned and develop best practices. Continuous improvement efforts are used to improve and streamline contract management processes. |

*Source:* Adapted from G.A. Garrett and R.G. Rendon, *Contract Management: Organizational Assessment Tools* (Asburn, VA: National Contract Management Association, 2005).

becoming aware of internal standards for quality can an organization realistically set the mark for its suppliers.

To determine the requirements and expectations of the final customer, an organization can use customer surveys and interviews.[33] A survey can be a formal instrument, either written or electronic, or a less formal means of feedback such as personal conversations or correspondence. Whatever method is employed, the important thing is to obtain accurate and relevant responses from the customer base. Once the survey results are tallied, they can be analyzed to develop product specifications. These can include acceptable levels of performance, use, safety and reliability. The selected suppliers then will need to comply with these requirements. Under the leadership of R. David Nelson, C.P.M., both Honda Motor Co., Ltd., and Deere & Co. employed such quality programs to improve supplier performance and reduce product defects. These practices were used with suppliers throughout the world to increase the competitiveness of both Honda and Deere in their respective markets.[34]

## Focus Groups

When individuals are brought together for a facilitated exchange of ideas about a specific topic for purposes of gaining perspective to influence decision-making, this is referred to as a *focus group. (ISM Glossary,* 2006) This process allows organizations to research issues related to the products and services they provide in a market and to assess the needs of their customers. Focus groups can help them better provide existing services, as well as gauge how well a new product or service will be received. For example, an organization that specializes in data storage may use a focus group to gather feedback on the direction of data storage within the healthcare sector. This can help position it to expand into a new market with new customers, but it also can assist it with serving the needs of its existing clients.

Focus groups include a series of interviews with up to a dozen people at the same time. A great deal of information is gathered during these interview sessions. To prepare, an organization must identify the major objectives of the sessions. Carefully developing the questions that will be asked of participants is an important part of the planning process. Of course, participants must be identified and provided with information about the session. This can include sharing the agenda, the questions to be asked and how participants can obtain the results of the focus group effort. Whether provided by an internal or external source, an experienced facilitator is key to a productive process. He or she can keep participants involved and moving in the right direction. Summary results in the form of a report will come out of the process, which will be forwarded to management so that decisions can be made.

## Gauge Internal Requirements

It is also important to remember that supply management plays a key role within the organization. Thus, it is critical that effective relationships be built with internal customers, and that supply management professionals clearly understand their needs and requirements. The following represent ideal organizational characteristics:

- Working closely with the immediate customer on supply-chain design, cost and customer issues;

- Understanding the end customer's wants/needs;

- Understanding market trends; and

- Recognizing the importance of communicating customer needs throughout the organization.[35]

Today's markets are more competitive than ever, so organizations must take advantage of any and all opportunities to improve their competitive advantage. Because most organizations rely on their suppliers more than in past years, developing performance measurements for suppliers is necessary to ensure competitiveness. One of the hardest tasks an organization faces, however, is establishing its internal requirements and determining what to measure. A measurement must be meaningful while at the same time achievable. A key is to establish benchmarks today with goals and objectives that can be accomplished tomorrow. The ability of an organization to measure is a key to its success.[36]

Scorecards can assist an organization in determining how well internal requirements are being met. A *scorecard* is a performance measurement and management document that records the ratings from an evaluation process (*ISM Glossary,* 2006). *Benchmarking* involves selected practices and measurements that are compared from one organization to another. Organizations look at other organizations considered to be world-class and compare their practices with their own. Xerox Corp. was the first organization to use *competitive benchmarking* back in 1976. (Xerox collected data from several other organizations and generated a report that compared it to the aggregated data from the other "best firms."[37]) Since then, benchmarking has been used to measure performance throughout an organization, including manufacturing, marketing and supply management. Measurement areas to gauge supplier performance include the following:

- Order cycle times,

- Delivery reliability,

- Frequency of delivery,

- Stock availability,

- Documentation quality,

- Order completeness and

- Technical support.[38]

The Supply-Chain Council offers a measurement model called *Supply Chain Operations Reference* (SCOR) that is widely used. This is a cross-industry diagnostic tool for supply management professionals that uses processes, metrics, best practices and technology to enhance supply performance (*ISM Glossary,* 2006). SCOR considers the following:

- All customer interactions, from order entry through paid invoice;

- All product transactions, from a supplier's supplier to a customer's customer, including equipment, spare parts, bulk products, software, etc.; and

- All customer interactions, from the study of aggregate demand to the fulfillment of orders.

Organizations using SCOR that have been recognized for their operational excellence include the Lockheed Martin Aeronautics Co. and the Swiss Federal Institute of Technology. By using the SCOR model, these organizations were able to define an efficient modeling approach for their supply chains. The metrics employed with SCOR included order fulfillment cycle time and cost of goods sold. This allowed the supply management professionals to simulate the current and future state of their supply chains, which helped them better evaluate both cost and performance.[39] Figure 9-10 offers a perspective on what an organization can benchmark using the SCOR model.

## Developing Supplier Measures

Organizations throughout the world are working to improve their relationships with key suppliers. One of the most important decisions for them is which concept to apply when measuring the performance of the supplier. A concept that has been successfully employed time and time again is the *balanced scorecard* (BSC). Developed by Robert Kaplan and David Norton in the early 1990s, the BSC links performance measures to each other and also to the organization's vision and strategy. The key performance categories are financial, customer knowledge, internal business processes and learning and growth.[40]

A supplier rating system is a method used to evaluate and rate suppliers' performance, which generally emphasizes quality, service, delivery and price. Rating formulas vary depending upon the nature of the item being purchased, the quality required and competition within the supply industry. More formalized systems require internal stakeholders to assign a weight (often out of 100 percent) to each key performance

Figure 9-10    SCOR Model Benchmarks

| METRIC | OUTCOME | DIAGNOSTIC |
|---|---|---|
| Customer Satisfaction | Perfect order fulfillment<br>Customer satisfaction<br>Product quality | Delivery to commit date<br>Warranty costs<br>Returns<br>Customer response time |
| Time | Order fulfillment lead time | Source cycle time<br>Supply-chain response time<br>Product plan achieved |
| Cost | Total supply-chain costs | Value-added productivity |
| Assets | Cash-to-cash cycle time<br>Inventory days of supply<br>Asset performance | Forecast accuracy<br>Inventory obsolescence<br>Capacity utilization |

*Source:* Adapted from Tony Hines, *Supply Chain Strategies* (Burlington, MA: Elsevier Butterworth-Heinemann, 2002).

indicator. A supplier rating system can be developed to evaluate performance areas such as service quality, product defects, and on-time deliveries. A set amount of points are possible to earn, with deductions for occurrences such as product failures and late deliveries attributable to the supplier. Figure 9-11 represents a typical system for rating suppliers.

The goal of product quality is always zero defects. A *material reject rating* (MRR) divides the total number of rejected products by the total units received, calculating a percentage of reject materials. Considerations that go into delivery performance include cycle time reduction, delivery dates kept, short lead times and quick deliveries for urgent needs. When evaluating a supplier's cost performance, the *total cost of ownership* should be evaluated, including all costs associated with the acquisition of the good or service as well as any additional costs incurred before or after product or service delivery (*ISM Glossary,* 2006).

Many things are involved when evaluating a supplier's performance, so there can be potential distortions. For example, the subjectivity of the end user can impact supplier rating in the areas of product quality and customer service. The expertise and

Figure 9-11    Supplier Rating System

| Supplier Name: Ace Electrical | | |
|---|---|---|
| INDICATOR | POSSIBLE | SCORE |
| **Product Quality** | 30 | 26 |
| Fitness for purpose | | |
| Durability | | |
| End customer satisfaction | | |
| Packaging | | |
| **Service Quality** | 25 | 21 |
| On-site service | | |
| Installation | | |
| Training | | |
| Warranty response | | |
| **Delivery Reliability** | 20 | 18 |
| On-time deliveries | | |
| Late shipments | | |
| Carrier consistency | | |
| Over/under shipments | | |
| **Customer Service** | 15 | 12 |
| Responsiveness | | |
| Flexibility | | |
| Designated account manager | | |
| Problem solving | | |
| **Financial Administration** | 10 | 7 |
| Price competitiveness | | |
| Invoicing procedures | | |
| Timely payment to subs | | |
| Financial stability | | |
| **Overall Rating** | 100 | 84 |

training of the internal staff also can be a factor. And as with any process, the quality and validity of the data must be sound to be of value.

## Effect of Legal Requirements

Part of the responsibility of supply management is to be aware of the legal requirements and obligations of its suppliers. Effectively communicating and negotiating with supplier representatives is certainly of value when managing performance, but at times, it is necessary for an organization to claim its legal position.

Terms that are negotiated into a supplier contract can certainly be beneficial. Provisions that offer protection with regard to set delivery times, zero-defect product guarantees and on-site services are just a few examples. By being aware of these contractual requirements, the supply management professional can better position himself or herself during discussions of supplier performance. When a term or provision is included within the contract, the supplier has a legal obligation to perform. In most instances, the supply professional can leverage these terms to prompt supplier performance. There are, of course, legal remedies available through the judicial system when other, less formal means are unsuccessful. When legal remedies are pursued, it is wise for organizations to use legal counsel. Whether an organization employs in-house attorneys or secures these services through a contract, supply management professionals must be ready to work with legal counsel when dealing with complex issues. This is especially true in disputes arising with global suppliers when differences in languages, laws and business practices can create additional challenges.

## Supplier Selection Factors

Supplier selection (or sourcing) has been identified as a best practice in supply management.[41] Because it significantly impacts supply-chain quality, supplier selection must be given top priority by supply management. This may be the best opportunity to pursue both prevention and quality at the source. Prevention deals with taking a strategic approach to avoid defects and problems before they occur. Ideally, this can be accomplished at the same time quality is being assured. When taking the lead in supplier selection, supply management professionals must consult with other business areas such as engineering, manufacturing and quality assurance. By gathering input from others and diligently evaluating potential suppliers, an organization can best position itself for top supplier performance.

As organizations of all types increase their reliance on outside suppliers, it becomes even more important to properly select quality suppliers. Supply management professionals aim to meet organizational needs through the use of suppliers, and ensure attributes such as quality, capability, technology and service. For example, a supplier's ability to fulfill customer requirements at a high level, and do so while simultaneously working with other customers, is an indicator of its *capacity* (see Chapter 3 for additional discussion). This characteristic moves beyond its experience and expertise and measures its ability to take on additional clients. If an organizational consultant is the best in its field, but is a two-person team booked across the country, it simply may not have the ability (or capacity) to fulfill the requirements of an organization seeking its assistance. The issue of *capability* looks at a supplier's experience and expertise, which verifies it is qualified within its area and has performed successfully for an extended period of time for other organizations. Therefore, it is important to assess both the capacity and capability of a supplier before considering it, as both are directly related to the quality the supplier can deliver.

Today's best practices include the development of key suppliers into partnership status. Toyota is a good example of an organization that actively works with key suppliers to ensure quality. Personnel from the automobile manufacturer went into the supplier facility to explain exactly what was needed with regard to materials. These visits helped the suppliers identify waste and inefficiencies in their own systems and gave them an opportunity to improve them. This type of on-site collaboration was a departure from traditional negotiations, which were viewed as adversarial. This approach by Toyota provided benefits for both parties and was truly viewed as a win-win situation.[42] The services and products provided by supplier partners are done so in a seamless manner, and a great deal of confidence is instilled in them. These supplier partners are capable and mature and they have proved themselves by delivering the highest quality of services at competitive prices. Most organizations possess only a handful of these partners. Figure 9-12 illustrates the evolution of candidate suppliers to supplier partners.

**Weighted Average Method.** Many factors can be involved in supplier selection and these can vary from organization to organization. Cost, availability, technology, past performance and financial stability are some of the common issues of concern to supply management professionals. Once these factors are selected, organizations often use some form of a *weighted average method* for evaluation purposes. Each factor is assigned a weight based on its relative importance to the acquisition. The ultimate goal is to enter into an agreement with a qualified supplier who provides quality goods and services. To help ensure such quality, a review of a supplier's past practices in this area is a good idea. A buying organization can look at its own experience with a supplier (has it provided quality in the past?), as well as the experience of other customers. By reviewing a supplier's quality assurance policies and even visiting its facility, quality practices can better be determined.

**Figure 9-12 Supplier Capability and Maturity**

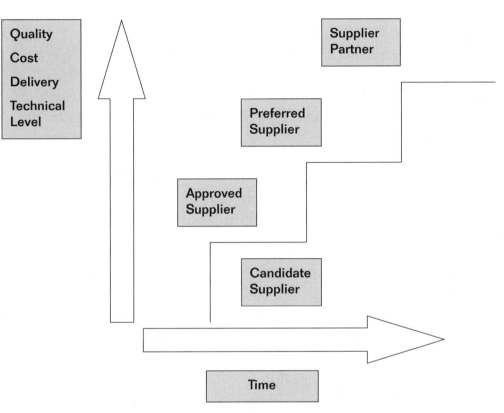

*Source:* Adapted from G. Hutchins, *Supply Management Strategies* (Portland, OR: Quality Plus Engineering, 2002).

This is also an area where certifications and registrations from third parties can prove beneficial. As discussed earlier in this chapter, an ISO certification is a strong indicator of a supplier's commitment to quality processes. *Good Manufacturing Practices* (GMP) is another program regulated by the U.S. Food and Drug Administration. This requires that domestic and foreign manufacturers maintain quality systems for furnishing medical devices for distribution in the United States. GMP covers the design, manufacture, packaging, labeling, storage, installation and services of these devices. The FDA tracks problems with medical devices and can inspect the operations of a manufacturer to ensure compliance with the GMP.

**Supplier Testing.** A determination should be made about the extent of testing that will be conducted, as well as what test methodologies will be used. A competitive and widely used measurement in certain industries is *parts per million* (PPM), which refers to the average number of defective parts produced out of one million. Many organizations consider 1,000 to 10,000 to be an acceptable quality level for their component suppliers.[43] Earlier in this chapter, the Six Sigma program was discussed, which requires a level of 3.4 PPM defect levels. This achievement of quality certainly is world-class.

Regardless of the testing method or standard, the purchasing organization and the supplier must be in agreement. For both the testing methods and the results, there should be congruence. Motorola is an example of a supplier that has taken steps to ensure quality in its operations and has been recognized as such. In 2002, Motorola received the Malcolm Baldrige National Quality Award, which is given each year by the president of the United States to organizations that demonstrate outstanding performance and results. A global supplier of radio networks and systems, Motorola was recognized for employee productivity, customer satisfaction, return on assets and recycling.[44]

Quality often is associated with parts and components, but it is equally important when acquiring services. Many organizations ensure service quality through the use of service level agreements, which are addressed in the following section.

## Service Level Agreements

The services sector, one of the fastest growing areas of supply management, includes all types of contracted services. Health, financial, entertainment and consulting are but a few examples of service areas being used by leading organizations. The services sector has been identified as the area of fastest growth within the gross domestic product (GDP) by the U.S. Bureau of Economic Assessment. Services represent more than 80 percent of regional and national growth.[45] A *service level agreement* (SLA) is a common tool used within the service sector. It defines the work scope, sets the expectations and defines the relationship between the organization and the service provider. The SLA also addresses what the provider is promising, how the services will be performed, the means of measuring performance and any long-term aspects of the agreement (*ISM Glossary,* 2006).

An SLA will assist both parties in better understanding the roles and responsibilities of each other. It can lead to increased customer satisfaction, as well as improved lead times and on-time deliveries. The agreement spells out an organization's expectations and what can happen if they are not met. If properly established, it can greatly benefit the buying organization in managing supplier performance in the areas of cost and quality. The goal when monitoring cost performance is to obtain the best cost/performance relation possible. Cost performance includes two factors: relative direct cost in comparison to other service providers and relative cost trend in comparison to an industry index. Criteria for evaluating cost performance can be a comparison to other sources within the industry for the same product or service (or against cost of in-house services), as well as the price tendency, which is the frequency of increases or decreases in cost.[46]

The quality of a service provider can be measured in a number of ways and, whichever method is employed, it should be spelled out in the SLA. Metrics that assess quality include:

- Product quality performance,
- Production line performance,
- Reliability performance,
- Customer returns,
- Corrective action responsiveness,
- Parts per million levels (Six Sigma),
- Reject of materials,
- Production stoppages,
- Quality of performance,
- Accuracy,
- Completeness of work product,
- Customer service and
- Customer availability.[47]

**Inspection and Testing.** When an organization is having services provided through an SLA, it may very well include a provision for inspecting and testing the quality being provided. *Inspection* is the act of checking the quality of a good or service to determine whether or not it meets the necessary specifications. (*ISM Glossary,* 2006) In an information technology service arena, for instance, the quality of computer components may be subject to inspection on an intermittent basis. Likewise, the quality of the service could be inspected, including a key requirement for system uptime. There may even be a penalty in the SLA for downtime outside of an acceptable level. Although 100 percent uptime may be every organization's goal, 99+ percent is more realistic as far as a standard to hold a service provider to.

An SLA can help the parties better communicate and manage each other's expectations. The SLA is considered a key document within an outsourcing agreement, for it defines the required service the supplier has to provide.[48] To truly establish a win-win relationship, the following steps should be considered:

1. *Gather background information.* Before asking for commitments from its supplier, an organization must carefully review its needs and priorities. Also, the supplier should assess its service history and realistically determine the level of service it can provide.

2. *Ensure agreement about the agreement.* Sometimes the parties to an agreement can have very different views of what can be accomplished. Before developing the SLA, it is a good idea to have a candid discussion to ensure there is basic agreement about the SLA.

3. *Establish ground rules for working together.* The parties need to discuss and agree on the division of responsibility for tasks, scheduling and potential impediments. Identifying communication styles and preferences also can minimize conflict.

4. *Develop the agreement.* This is an important step, but certainly not the only step. With assistance from each organization, the agreement must be debated and negotiated with regard to content. This step can take several weeks or even several months.

5. *Generate buy-in.* Before finalizing the SLA, all stakeholders must weigh in and make suggestions. Besides gathering team buy-in, this step also will improve the quality of the final agreement.

6. *Complete the preimplementation tasks.* Identify and complete the tasks that need to precede implementing the agreement. This may include developing tracking and reporting mechanisms, as well as training.

7. *Implement and manage the agreement.* A point of contact should be established for problems, maintenance of ongoing communication, service reviews and implementing modifications.[49]

The management of an SLA is a key function and requires a variety of skills. One must be knowledgeable of the operational needs of its organization, but must also be familiar with the other party's business practices. Being skilled in communications and negotiations is important, as well as being able to commit the necessary time and energy to the agreement. Serving as the point of contact for any problems or concerns and regularly assessing how the relationship can be improved also is important.

Intuit, Inc., a premier provider of tax preparation and personal finance software with operations in the United States, the United Kingdom and Canada, uses service level agreements for its outsourcing. During 2007, Intuit generated more than $2.7 billion in revenues and the majority of its purchasing spend was on services.[50] The supplier selection criteria employed by Intuit included:

- Technology

- Quality

- Responsiveness

- Delivery performance

- Cost competitiveness

- Business ethics and viability

Intuit's use of service level agreements includes a clear statement of work (SOW), along with key expectations for its suppliers. Figure 9-13 illustrates a standard agreement used for call center providers.[51]

## Minimizing Risk of Counterfeit Components

A growing risk is the use of *counterfeit components,* which are items produced by an unlicensed manufacturer that are labeled and marketed as genuine. In many cases, these components are indistinguishable from the real parts, but are of inferior quality. Depending on the application, these counterfeit components could fail and cause major problems for an organization. There has been increased use of counterfeits in the technology industry; even the U.S. government purchased new computer equipment containing these components. This is another area for ensuring quality from a supplier, particularly those who provide customers a finished product comprised of many subcomponents acquired from second-tier and third-tier suppliers. Prime suppliers should be questioned about their quality control practices in these areas, and specifically how they ensure quality from their own supplier base. Verification of policies and practices that prevent the use of counterfeit components are likely to become more common in the future. A world leader in the automotive industry, DaimlerChrysler AG, has taken the issue of counterfeit parts very seriously. With recent increases in fake parts such as windshields and brake linings that can threaten passenger safety, DaimlerChrysler joined forces with other automobile manufacturers to form the Automotive Brand Protection Coalition. This group's mission is to eradicate the use of fake parts so that public safety is protected, as well as the quality of their products.[52]

**Figure 9-13    Service Level Agreement Template**

1. **Services** — Covers services to be performed by supplier, including SOW.

2. **Buyer's obligations** — Obligations and responsibilities of the buying organization, such as supplier training, software and support.

3. **Business turndown/upturn** — Expectations of the supplier when significant turns in business occur, including disasters.

4. **Compensations and payment** — Payment terms are outlined such as early payment discounts and invoice disputes.

5. **Quality control/gain share support** — Requirements for supplier's quality control processes, and the potential for sharing benefits for process improvements.

6. **Term/termination** — Specifies the term of the agreement and what events are required to end the agreement early.

7. **Ownership** — Property rights for software and work products.

8. **Confidential information** — Both parties agree to keep agreement terms and shared processes confidential.

9. **Representations/warranties** — Establishes that the supplier and its services and processes are in good standing.

10. **Indemnification** — Supplier protection from third-party claims.

11. **Insurance** — Supplier must maintain certain types and levels of insurance, including workers' compensation and commercial general liability.

12. **Limitation of liability** — Limits supplier's liability to certain monetary thresholds.

13. **Dispute resolution** — Methods by which disputes and issues are jointly resolved.

14. **General** — Other miscellaneous clauses such as media notices and assignments.

*Source:* Adapted from: IT Service Level Agreement, Portland Public Schools, Oregon; and "Establishing Service Level Agreements," Naomi Karten, available from www.nkarten.com/sla.html.

# Summary

Ensuring quality throughout the acquisition process has become an important focus for today's supply management professional. In all industries and sectors, supply management professionals must be familiar with quality processes and realize they need to play a key role in matters relating to supplier quality. As strategic outsourcing and relationship management continue to grow in use, the opportunity will continue for supply management to increase its value to its organization.

Feedback from final customers can assist with developing requirements and specifications. Supplier relationships are managed in accordance with these requirements to ensure that products and services are provided in a timely manner. Organizations must realize that markets are competitive today, and that by focusing on issues of quality they can be positioned for success.

## Key Points

1. Quality management ensures that all activities to design and implement a service are effective and efficient.

2. Quality control compares the actual quality received with the intended goals.

3. Six Sigma is a quality process that strives for a measure of quality near perfection and uses relevant data to eliminate defects.

4. ISO is the International Organization for Standardization, with the American National Standards Institute serving as the U.S. member.

5. The capability maturity model is an appraisal process that was developed to measure and improve an organization's critical core capabilities.

6. The capability maturity model integrated can address several areas of improvement at the same time over the product development life cycle.

7. The Contract Management Maturity Model measures an organization's contract management process capability against five levels, and then uses the evaluation as a guide to continuously improve process capability.

8. The SCOR model is a diagnostic tool that uses processes, metrics, and best practices to benchmark an organization's performance.

9. The balanced scorecard, developed by Kaplan and Norton, links performance measures to each other and also to the organization's vision and strategy.

10. According to Deming, management has the ability to control the majority of a process improvement.

11. Service level agreements are commonly used within the service sector. An SLA defines the work scope, sets the expectations and defines the relationship between the organization and the service provider. It also addresses what the provider is promising, how the services will be performed and the means of measuring performance.

# 10

# Performance Evaluation

**A** challenging task for any organization is determining what to measure. By focusing on a particular issue or process, an organization can better identify what needs to be done and then do it. Many industry leaders feel that an organization's ability to measure is a key to its success. Once measurements have been selected, then performance must be evaluated against those measurements. This includes performance within an organization, as well as the performance of key suppliers.

This chapter will address the issue of identifying which performance measurements to employ and how to create them. Performance results must be evaluated and performance corrected, to meet stakeholder needs. One of the ways to measure performance is by using key performance indicators. A corrective action process will take the results of a performance evaluation and make the necessary changes for improvement.

Creating measurements to evaluate the performance of suppliers also is important. This allows an organization to identify areas for supplier improvement. Such a program includes audit and validation processes, reporting and supplier training. Supplier Relationship Management is a key part of the Strategic Supply Management Process (see Figure I-1 in the "Series Overview"), so, naturally, supplier performance evaluation is very important. Compliance metrics for organizational policies will be discussed, which can include issues such as supplier diversity and social responsibility. Supply management professionals also must be aware of various management reporting requirements, including those of the ISO, GAAP and Sarbanes-Oxley.

The final section in this chapter covers the evaluation of employees, whose objectives must be aligned with organizational goals. Criteria for their success must be determined and appropriate appraisal factors developed. Multiple sources of feedback are available for evaluating employees, including peers, customers and suppliers. With the continued advancement of the supply management profession, and the increased importance of supply management in the organization, professional development becomes more important than ever. Many opportunities exist for lifelong learning.

Whether evaluating performance internally (i.e., systems, employees) or externally (i.e., suppliers, customers), it is important to understand the major steps in the process. Figure 10-1 depicts the steps involved in performance evaluation.

## CHAPTER OBJECTIVES

• Discuss how supply management can create and employ performance measurement.

• Define performance measurement and discuss the interrelation of measurements.

• Explore how performance measurements and audits can aid in supplier development.

• Discuss social responsibility and its importance to supply management.

• Identify the appraisal and evaluation tools that can improve employee performance.

• Discuss the importance of professional development and education for supply management professionals.

**Figure 10-1    Performance Measurement Steps**

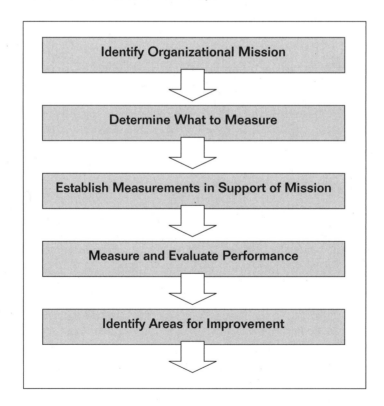

# Establishing Performance Measurements

The process of assessing progress toward achieving predetermined goals is called *performance measurement* and includes information on the efficiency with which resources are transformed into goods and services (outputs), as well as the results of an activity compared to its intended purpose (outcomes). A *performance measure* addresses the type of activities conducted (process), the products or services delivered by a program and the results of those products and services.[1]

## What to Measure

Numerous measurements can be considered, so the key is to find those that are meaningful for an organization, particularly as they relate to supply management. A heavy equipment manufacturer will likely have measurements that differ from those of an electronics distributor, but there are some common attributes of good performance measures. Among other things, they need to be customer-focused, credible, cost-effective and comparable. Figure 10-2 illustrates the criteria for good performance measures.

**Figure 10-2    Criteria for Good Performance Measures**

*Source:* C. Stoffle and S. Phipps, "Creating a Culture of Assessment: The University of Arizona Experience," *ARL Bimonthly Report,* No. 230.321 (October/November 2003), 26–27.

Measurements, first and foremost, must support the strategic objectives of the organization. Just as supply management serves to achieve the organization's mission, so do the performance measurements that are put in place. This is a direction that top leaders must both set and support. Leading organizations that have been successful in measuring performance have created a culture of participation and continuous improvement. In the past several years, the University of Arizona has integrated a performance management program that ensures services delivered to its library system customers are of the highest quality. The performance effectiveness management system (PEMS) was designed to align individual, unit and organizational efforts with the strategic goals set for the organization. Its goal was to institute measurements that indicated success, progress and improvement. Guided by facts, research and analysis, its services were delivered to maximize positive outcomes for customers and stakeholders. The university encouraged the staff to:

- Care about the results it produced,

- Value the impact it had on the process and

- Know how its results related to use expectations.[2]

This is an example of the kind of organizational commitment necessary to ensure ongoing assessment of its services, and the use of tools and data for continuous improvement. Arizona's experience used both contracted services and internal resources to improve performance. Supply management professionals can find this example valuable, for it was successful in integrating performance measurements that focused on organizational outcomes. By determining appropriate activities, setting quality standards and establishing measurements, the university was able to meet its objectives. Such efforts can be successful in other industries, including information technology. Hewlett-Packard (HP) uses performance measurements within its manufacturing facilities in China. To ensure key issues are properly addressed, HP procurement and supply management professionals integrate performance measurements into its suppliers' overall management systems. Benchmarking metrics such as annualized return rate, annualized failure rate and defects per million, the organization is better able to monitor activities that impact quality. These efforts have resulted in tangible benefits for both HP and its suppliers. With improved performance, the suppliers are given preference in the sourcing process, while HP has seen improved service quality and reduced risk.[3]

## Interrelation of Measurements

Measurements also must be interrelated, so that they contribute to the flow of smooth operations within supply management. For example, hard dollar cost savings, percent of direct and indirect spend addressed or supplier on-time deliveries are examples. Therefore, these measurements would be interrelated. When measurements interface and complement each other, it is certainly an ideal situation. If the accuracy of a sales forecast can assist production by adjusting inventory on hand, this is an indication that the right measurements are in place.

## Measurement Creation

Traditional measurements focused heavily on labor productivity and often over-looked true cost drivers such as product design, process complexity, quality issues and manufacturing flexibility. Measurements today need to focus on two critical areas: the customer and the competition. This typically involves measures of throughput and lead times, as well as financial measures such as asset utilization and profitability.[4] Many experts feel that if something cannot be measured, then it cannot be managed. Of course, when determining which measurements are needed, an organization must always keep in mind the needs of the customers, for they will ultimately determine the organization's success and performance, whether it offers a product or a service. Measurements must not only address the current needs of the customers, but also must be able to change as customer needs and demands change. This is why performance evaluation should be considered an evolving work in progress. Measurements and metrics that are effective today are likely to be modified or replaced in the future.

No matter the size, sector or specialization, organizations normally focus on the same general aspects of performance:

- Financial considerations,

- Customer satisfaction,

- Internal business operations,

- Employee satisfaction and

- Community and shareholder satisfaction.[5]

For private organizations, a principle measure of success is monetary profit. While public sector agencies may not be striving for profit, they should be looking to maximize performance. They are accountable for the achievement of program goals and service delivery by legislators, suppliers and the general public. Publicly held corporations are accountable to their shareholders and public agencies to their tax-payers, but most world-class organizations place customer service at the top of their measurements.[6]

## Results Evaluation

Once performance has been evaluated, the results must be acted on. The performance information first is formally reviewed and management is provided feedback on how future performance plans might be adjusted. An organization's performance information is used to perform benchmarking against its predetermined goals, as well as a comparative analysis against other organizations. This comparison will help identify opportunities for re-engineering and reallocation of resources. Top organizations that are industry leaders that are profitable year after year must be doing something right. Reviewing their best practices in the area of performance evaluation can serve as good indicators of how they achieve such success.

The results of performance evaluation should be reported throughout the organization. By sharing the performance data internally, management can continue to build a level of trust and a culture of continuous improvement. Sales performance for the global organization, for instance, can be shared with the organization's locations throughout the world. Technology can serve as a great communications tool, such as posting performance information on an intranet.

Performance results also must be communicated externally. Customers and shareholders will find this information quite valuable. Many organizations share performance data through annual reports that are made available to shareholders, executives, even industry associations and the general public. Hopefully, sharing quality information can help enhance performance in the future. It can help set priorities and decision-making down the road, for the feedback from shareholders and customers influences strategic decision-making. Once performance is evaluated and reported for a set time period, then the performance measurement process starts again for future periods.

## Key Performance Indicators

*Key performance indicators* (KPIs) can assist an organization in defining and measuring its progress. KPIs are quantifiable measurements of the improvement in performing an activity that is critical to business success. A KPI needs to complement the overall targets of an organization and relate to its key activities. These will differ based on the type and size of the organization, but examples can include increases in international orders, help desk calls resolved promptly or percentage of on-time customer deliveries. Financial KPIs focus on gross sales, costs or working capital while allowing the organization to monitor and control its cash flow and profitability. Used as a performance management tool, a KPI can measure factors such as employee turnover, which can be an indicator of stability in the workforce.

Each KPI will need a title, definition, method of measurement and target. The number of KPIs should be limited and allow for the achievement of business goals. This keeps everyone focused on the key objectives and makes performance monitoring easier. How does an organization choose the right KPIs? The indicators chosen must:

- Reflect the goals of the organization,
- Be critical to its success,
- Be measurable and comparable and
- Allow for corrective action.[7]

Figure 10-3 includes some KPIs that can be used within a supply management organization.

## Performance Management Systems

An *earned value management system* (EVMS) is used to establish a relationship between the cost, schedule and technical aspects of a project. It measures progress, accumulates actual costs, analyzes deviations from original plans and forecasts the completion of

**Figure 10-3    KPIs for Supply Management**

| TITLE | DEFINITION | MEASUREMENT |
|---|---|---|
| Customer Service | Satisfaction of final customers for services and good received | Percentage of customer responses that rate services good or excellent |
| On-Time Delivery | Requested products delivered within requested timeline | Percentage of orders delivered by customer requested date or earlier |
| Inventory Accuracy | Actual inventory on hand correctly reflected in inventory records | Percentage of inventory counted that matches computerized record |
| Purchased Materials Cost | Total cost of materials purchased for a program or project | Percentage of cost reduction from prior purchase or budgeted amount |
| Quality of Goods | The quality of the goods, materials and services received | Level of quality, reject rate of materials |
| Lead Time | Time spent in the acquisition process | Percentage of lead time reduced in acquisition cycle |

*Source:* Adapted from A.J. Van Weele, *Purchasing & Supply Chain Management,* 4th ed. (London: Thomson Learning).

events. It also can make sure changes in a project are incorporated in a timely manner. (*ISM Glossary,* 2006) Advantages of using an EVMS as a project management tool include improving the definition of the work scope, preventing scope creep, communicating progress to stakeholders and keeping the project team focused on achieving progress. Essential features of any EVMS implementation include:

- A project plan that identifies work to be accomplished,

- A valuation of planned work, which is called a plan value (PV), and

- Predefined earning rules or metrics to quantify the accomplishment of the work, which is called earned value (EV).

For large or more complex projects, the EVMS implementation may include additional features, such as indicators of cost performance (is the project over or under budget?) and schedule performance (is the project ahead or behind schedule?). At the turn of the 20th century, EVMS was employed in the industrial manufacturing sector, and later by the U.S. Department of Defense (DOD) in the 1960s. Its use expanded in the 1980s and 1990s to include procurement and supply management applications as ways to manage and measure performance. EVMS, however, does have limitations. While indicating whether a project is on time, on budget and work scope is completed, it does not necessarily measure quality. It is, still, a valuable tool for supply management.

*Value stream mapping* can be applied to either goods or services as a technique to determine if there is waste in a process. It was originally used in manufacturing where the transformation of materials was traced from the beginning of a process to the very end. Waste can include a step of the process where no value is added or a point in the process where material is being stored to await transformation. This "wait time" effectively results in waste. (*ISM Glossary,* 2006)

A method of measuring an organization's activities in terms of its vision and strategies is the *balanced scorecard* (BSC). This gives management a comprehensive view of business performance at a glance. It focuses not only on financial outcomes but also on the human issues that can drive the outcomes. Implementing the scorecard typically involves four steps:

1. Translating the vision into operational goals,

2. Communicating the vision and its link to individual performance,

3. Business planning and

4. Feedback and adjusting the strategy accordingly.

Organizations use BSC to clarify and update their budgets, identify and align strategic initiatives and conduct performance reviews to improve strategies.[8] This process views an organization from four different perspectives: (1) customer, (2) financial, (3) internal business processes and (4) learning and growth. Metrics are developed and data is collected and analyzed from each perspective. The U.S. Department of Energy employed BSC in its Office of Procurement and Assistance Management to meet both organizational objectives and customer expectations. As a result of BSC, improvements were made in procurement processes, customer services and budget performance.[9] Figure 10-4 illustrates the balanced scorecard.

**Figure 10-4    Balanced Scorecard**

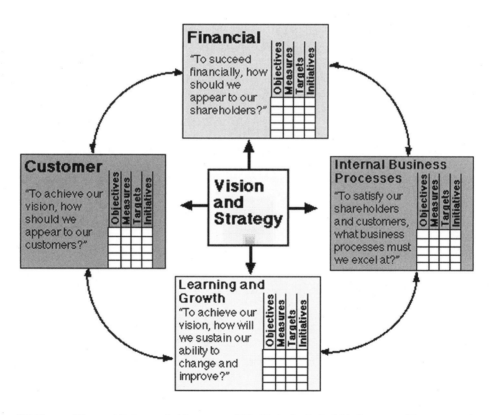

*Source:* "12 Manage, Rigor and Relevance in Management," The Netherlands. Available from www.12manage.com/methods_balancedscorecard.html. Reprinted with permission.

## Corrective Action Process

The performance measurement tools discussed so far in this chapter can assist supply management professionals in recognizing good performance as well as poor performance. Once a group of qualified individuals has identified performance problems, the logical next step is determining the appropriate action for correcting the problem. A *corrective action process* is a means to identify, analyze and correct problems in process or performance. Conversely, a *preventive action* occurs when proactive steps are taken to avoid a problem. Before a problem can be solved, it must be understood. One of the first steps a team must take is to fully describe the problem in measurable terms. Often, short-term corrective actions can be put in place until a permanent solution is implemented. Verifying the root causes of a problem is important to prevent their reoccurrence. National Semiconductor Corp., an industry leader in electronics manufacturing, has instituted many quality systems including the *8D* problem-solving process by which eight disciplines are used to identify, correct and eliminate the recurrence of quality problems. This organization also recognizes an overlooked step in quality processes — recognizing the team's achievement. The 8D process includes the following disciplines (see also Figure 10-5):

1. *Use a team approach.* Establish a small group of people with the knowledge, time, authority and skill to solve the problem. The group must select a team leader.

2. *Describe the problem.* Describe the problem in measurable terms. Specify the internal or external customer problem by describing it in specific terms.

3. *Implement and verify short-term corrections.* Define and implement those intermediate actions that will protect the customer from the problem until a permanent solution is implemented. Verify the effectiveness of these actions with data.

4. *Define and verify root causes.* Identify all potential causes that could explain why the problem occurred. Test each potential cause against the problem description and data. Identify alternative corrective actions to eliminate the root cause.

5. *Verify corrective actions.* Confirm that the selected corrective actions will resolve the problem for the customer and will not cause undesirable side effects. Define other actions, if necessary, based on the severity of the problem.

6. *Implement permanent corrective actions.* Define and implement the permanent corrective actions needed. Choose ongoing controls to ensure the root cause is eliminated. Once in production, monitor the long-term effects and implement additional controls as necessary.

**Figure 10-5    8D Problem-Solving Process**

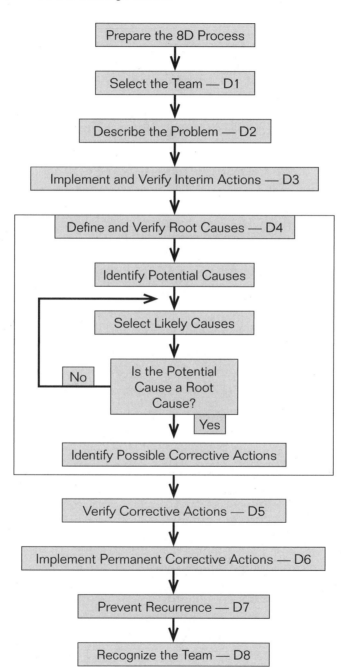

*Source:* Adapted from National Semiconductor, "Quality Network, Eight Disciplines Problem-Solving Process," available from www.national.com/quality/8d.html.

7. *Prevent recurrence.* Modify specifications, update training, review workflow and improve practices and procedures to prevent recurrence of this and all similar problems.

8. *Congratulate the team.* Recognize the collective efforts of the team. Publicize the achievement and share the knowledge and learning.[10]

## Measuring and Evaluating Supplier Performance

Organizations today are relying on external suppliers more than ever, and this is expected to increase in the future. By developing strategies to align and manage supplier relationships, organizations can increase their ability to stay competitive. *Supplier performance measurement* is the process of measuring, analyzing and managing supplier performance for the purpose of reducing costs, mitigating risk and driving continuous improvement. With growing global competition, mass customization, increased customer expectations and harsh economic conditions, organizations are counting on their suppliers to furnish larger portions of parts, materials and assemblies formerly provided internally.[11]

There is definitely a cost associated with failing to adequately manage a supplier's performance. It is estimated that billions of dollars are lost as a result of poor supplier performance. A prime example of this was the Ford Motor Co., who lost $3 billion after it had to recall more than 13 million defective tires provided from one if its key suppliers.[12] If this can happen to a large organization, there are certainly risks for smaller organizations.

While it may not be practical to closely monitor all suppliers, it is important to focus on key suppliers. Most organizations monitor the performance of suppliers that meet one of the following criteria:

- Represent the largest portion of total spend,
- Produce a critical product or
- Maintain a critical supply relationship.[13]

A manufacturer of healthcare equipment may use a performance management system only on those suppliers on which it spends more than $500,000 annually. This may represent only 25 percent of its supplier base, but it is concentrating its efforts on the relationships that have the biggest strategic and financial impact on its organization. Figure 10-6 illustrates how organizations decide which suppliers to measure.

**Figure 10-6    Determining Which Suppliers to Measure**

| BASED UPON: | PERCENTAGE: |
|---|---|
| Portion of total annual spend | 72.4% |
| Type or nature of the product | 65.8% |
| Nature of supplier relationship | 52.6% |
| Size of the supplier | 10.5% |
| Geography of supplier | 9.2% |

*Source:* Adapted from Aberdeen Group, "The Supplier Performance Measurement Benchmarking Report," December 2002, available from www.peoplesoft.com/media/en/campaigns/srs4/3531_supplier_rating_system_03_ft/aberdeen_spm_0103 .pdf.

## Performance Measurements

After deciding which suppliers to monitor, an organization next must determine which areas of performance to measure. To initiate a process of continuous improvement, measurements and benchmarks must be created. This system also will indicate how quickly the improvement should occur. Several of the more common areas of supplier performance measurement are:

- Process capability,

- Life cycle costs,

- Service levels,

- Defects per product,

- Late or rejected shipments,

- Production stoppages,

- Final customer satisfaction and

- Warranty costs because of product failure.

As an international leader in the area of quality improvement, Federal Express Corp. (FedEx) has identified several measurements that are key to customer satisfaction. An internal team works continually to reduce failures in areas such as damaged packages, missing proof of delivery, invoice adjustments and lost packages. These activities support FedEx's commitment to speed and reliability, both of which are key to staying competitive in its industry.[14]

## Supplier Audits

When determining the capability of a supplier, many indicators must be considered. A potential supplier may have a long history of performance, operate state-of-the-art facilities, possess ISO registration and have the desire to partner on a long-term basis. These are all positive signs indicated that a supplier is considered world-class, but additional evaulating still may be necessary. Using *supplier audits* is another helpful tool in supplier selection and monitoring. A supplier audit is an objective examination and verification of a supplier's capabilities measured against set criteria. It can include a review of documents, processes and facilities to affirm compliance with legal and contractual requirements.

There are three basic types of supplier audits. They are:

1. *Systems audit.* Checks internal documentation of compliance audits.

2. *Process audit.* Checks the supplier's cost, quality and delivery and other critical processes for capability and improvement.

3. *Product and service audit.* Checks the supplied product or service for conformance to technical standards and performance standards.

Normally, audits are formal and highly structured, beginning with an early discussion of the purpose and scope of the audit. Based on the scope and intent of the audit, an organization may investigate the following areas:

- Quality manual, procedures and work instructions,

- Organizational structure,

- Logistics processes,

- Cost sharing,

- Technical capabilities,

- Web or business to business (B2B) capabilities,

- Training and certifications,

- Documentation,

- Final product test and evaluation,

- Corrective and preventive actions,

- Measuring equipment and calibration and

- Storage and delivery.[15]

An audit is a snapshot in time of a supplier and its performance. Efforts should be made to ensure the picture is accurate and that it is done in a nonthreatening manner. Strategic partnerships with key suppliers should be viewed as long-term relationships that are mutually beneficial. An audit, therefore, should not be seen by either party as anything other than an opportunity to make improvements.

Waters Corp., a scientific instrumentation organization in Massachusetts, used supplier auditing to support its global strategies in recent years. It was able to identify potential problems with suppliers prior to production, which greatly assisted the outsourcing efforts of this $1.2 billion corporation.[16] Additionally, supplier auditing was a key part of Textron, Inc., while expanding the capabilities of a key equipment supplier in the Czech Republic. Its approach was to look at a supplier's "total package," keeping in mind both current and future requirements. This was part of Textron's standard evaluation and rigorous audit program for its potential suppliers.[17]

A certain amount of preparation can pay off in an audit. This can include a discussion with the supplier that produces valuable background information such as financial statements, previous audits, bills of materials, test reports, etc. Ground rules for the audit can be established at a preliminary conference. Questions and misconceptions also can be addressed. Acquiring the sought-after data is the next step, and this requires the auditor to interview personnel, review policies and specifications and assess technical capabilities.

Once data has been collected, it then must be interpreted. This may be a time-consuming process, but it can pay dividends when it leads to improved performance. The audit team attempts to identify variations, risks or waste and then recommends corrective actions. In a closing conference, early problems and recommendations can be reviewed, and if there is disagreement, the supplier may want to appeal its case.

As a final step, the supplier is notified in writing of the audit results and recommendations. Deficiencies then are corrected prior to the next product shipment. Any root causes of problems are eliminated, which should happen with each critical process step that has a noted deficiency. The owner of the process is still the supplier, and the supply management professional for the auditing organization serves as an adviser.[18]

Results of supplier performance must be used constructively. Figure 10-7 illustrates the most common use for this data.

At times, an audit may identify a need for supplier training. This can include remedial training on an existing process or requirement. When a remedy or corrective

Figure 10-7    Uses of Supplier Performance Data

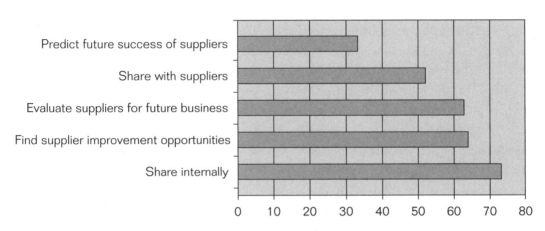

*Source:* Adapted from Aberdeen Group, "The Supplier Performance Measurement Benchmarking Report," December 2002, available from www.peoplesoft.com/media/en/campaigns/srs4/3531_supplier_rating_system_03_ft/aberdeen_spm_0103 .pdf.

action is needed, *remedial training* should be used. Supplier training can be provided by an organization's staff or by qualified third parties. Depending on the nature of the training, it may make sense to conduct it at the supplier's facility.

Supplier workshops are helpful and allow for a healthy exchange of information and ideas. Attended by new suppliers hoping to learn more about doing business with an organization, these workshops can explain the requirements and expectations for suppliers. These workshops often are used to promote diversity in the supplier pool.

## Supplier Development

It is important for suppliers to perform at an appropriate level, whether it is for goods, services or both. Supply management's effort to strive for continuous improvement includes the extension of such expectations to its suppliers. The process of elevating a supplier's performance and quality to acceptable levels is known as *supplier development*. Supplier development as defined in the *ISM Glossary* (2006) is a systematic effort to create and maintain a network of competent suppliers and to improve various supplier capabilities that are necessary for the supply management organization to meet its competitive challenges. There is always room for improvement and that includes small suppliers new to an organization, as well as large suppliers who have been in business for years.

This type of development takes a commitment from both sides, and particularly buy-in from the supplier's senior management. JAMAK Fabrication, Inc., is an example of such an organization. This international manufacturer, whose clients include Delphi Corp., Chrysler LLC and General Electric Co., actively works with suppliers in their development and even assists them with securing ISO certification (www .jamak.com). Team leaders should be selected from both the purchasing organization and the supplier to make the effort successful. The selected team members can concentrate on the development areas and then identify a process that makes the most sense. The team leader from the purchasing organization must actively participate with the supplier team, conducting meetings and inspections at the supplier facility. Any changes recommended to improve practices should be driven by data and objectivity, for the approach must be justified to each side.

Once the changes are implemented, the aim is to be able to demonstrate a visible improvement. This can include factors such as cost savings, increased efficiency, reduction in waste or improved quality. When this point is reached, an organization's team leader can leave the ongoing, improved process in the hands of the supplier. This model for supplier development is shown in Figure 10-8.

The development of international suppliers, however, does present challenges. The outsourcing of services such as call centers and software help desks may be tempting because of the low wages of offshore suppliers. Some organizations have seen positive results, such as reduced costs and consistent service levels. Potential risks for these arrangements also should be considered; these include:

- Supply disruption risk,
- Extended lead times,
- Confirming supplier capabilities,
- Differences in business ethics,
- Foreign currency issues and
- Differences in productivity.[19]

## Compliance Metrics

Many organizations follow unique policies based on the requirements established by organizational leaders and stakeholders. These requirements are extended to their suppliers along with performance metrics and compliance measures. *Supplier diversity programs* are common to both public and private sectors. They promote the use and development of small businesses including minority-owned and women-owned organizations. Nike is an example of an organization that uses its size and resources

Figure 10-8    Supplier Development Model

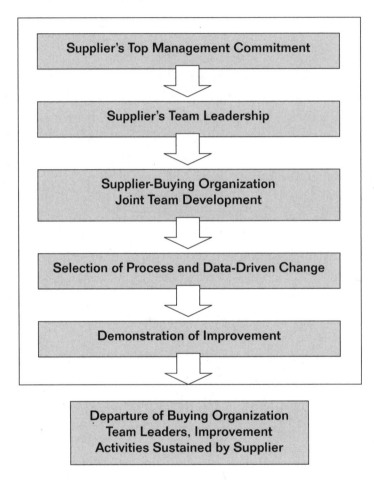

*Source:* L. Ellram and T. Choi, *Supply Management for Value Enhancement* (Tempe, AZ: Institute for Supply Management, 2000)

to make a difference. Deemed as a priority from its board of directors, Nike works diligently to position contracts in a manner that best fits small emerging businesses. It actively seeks out qualified organizations to contract with directly, as well as to connect them with its larger, existing suppliers. For example, a large contract with an office supplier may include a requirement to subcontract with minority-owned and women-owned organizations for up to 10 percent of the contract value. Compliance is verified through prime contractor reporting and documentation from subcontractors. With minorities accounting for nearly half of its retail footwear sales, Nike realizes the value of providing opportunities to minority-owned businesses. Believing that supplier diversity represents a sound business practice, Nike looks to increase its business opportunities for small organizations. These efforts to reach out to the same groups that make up a large share of its retail buyers have garnered them recognition from minority-owned business associations.[20] Metrics in supplier diversity include the percentage of contract spend with minority-owned and women-owned businesses, and the number of subcontracts or second-tier suppliers over a given period of time.

Similar programs occur at all levels of government, including federal, state and local agencies in the United States. While set-aside programs for minorities and women have been challenged in the courts, it is still common to see the use of aspirational goals (sometimes referred to as targets) in public sector contracts. This requires large prime contractors to provide opportunities and outreach to small businesses to earn a subcontract. While not technically a requirement, the government agency will evaluate the prime contractor on its efforts and results. The diversifying of contract dollars to minority-owned, women-owned and emerging small businesses is referred to as minority, women and emerging small business (MWESB) utilization.

Organizations in all sectors are seeing the value of supplier diversity. Senior management seems to realize that sourcing with minority-owned businesses makes sense, as they represent an increasing customer base. In 2004 alone, U.S. organizations spent more than $60 billion with minority-owned and women-owned businesses, and with minority groups expected to grow to 37 percent of the population by 2020, this annual spend is likely to increase.[21] Developing a supplier diversity program demonstrates an organization's awareness of local demographics, and also allows it to take a leadership position in doing the right thing. This corporate thinking expands into other parts of the world as well. In recent years, the European Union (EU) has begun developing programs that positively impact the financial position of ethnic minorities.

Through local workshops in the region, the port of Portland, Oregon, is able to showcase its nationally recognized Small Business Program. Opportunities for prime contractors as well as first-tier and second-tier suppliers are discussed, which has increased the use of disadvantaged business for the agency.[22] Private sector organizations that have strong supplier diversity programs and participate in supplier workshops include Nike, Office Depot, and the Starbucks Corp.

Supplier diversity is also a key strategy within the service industry. Bank of America, Turner Construction Co. and Accenture are very successful service providers that incorporate diversity as part of their mission and strategies. Hilton Hotels is also committed to providing opportunities for women-owned and minority-owned suppliers through open access to its supply management programs. Hilton pledges that the diversity of its supplier base will reflect the diversity of the communities it serves.[23]

*Social responsibility* (SR) (also known as corporate social responsibility or CSR) is an emerging trend for organizations in all parts of the world. It is identified by ISM as a key part of the Strategic Supply Management Process (see figure I-1 in the "Series Overview" at the beginning of this book). So what is social responsibility? It is best defined as a framework of measurable policies and resulting behavior designed to benefit the workplace, the individual, the organization and the community in the following areas: community, diversity, environment, ethics, financial responsibility, human rights and safety. (*ISM Glossary,* 2006) The supplier diversity issue, discussed previously, is certainly a component of social responsibility. SR also expands to other areas of expectations for suppliers, such as commitment to human rights and their policies on environmental health and safety. Hewlett-Packard has been a leader in SR, publicly stating that one of its organizational objectives is global citizenship. It requires a standard of conduct for its suppliers, verifying compliance with child labor laws and environmental requirements. Figuring that the environmental performance of a product can best be addressed at an early stage, HP designs products with snap fits, which reduces the need for solvents and simplifies the disassembly process.[24]

Compliance is not limited to areas such as diversity and social responsibility. Supply management professionals must continually assess supplier compliance in areas such as product quality, contract delivery times, service response and even customer satisfaction. Metrics established up front will be used to determine whether or not a supplier's performance complies with the agreed-on standards. Monitoring compliance can help improve supplier performance by identifying and correcting deficient service areas. (More information on social responsibility can be found in the *Foundation of Supply Management,* Volume 1 of the ISM Professional Series.)

## Supply Management Audits

Supply management professionals receive various types of reports and audits. These documents must be carefully read, and any issues raised must be resolved in a timely manner. All audits should be viewed as opportunities to identify areas for improvement in an organization. Regardless of the reason for the audit, supply management professionals can consider them as another tool to help improve performance.

An organization that possesses ISO certification has to prove via an audit process that production processes are in accordance with its quality management manual. An *ISO audit* verifies that processes such as the following are in full accordance with applicable documentation:

- Production processes are in compliance.

- Employees are properly informed of processes.

- Continuous quality improvement is in place.

- Process changes are handled appropriately.

- Changes are properly shared with employees.

ISO standards traditionally have been linked to products and manufacturing processes. However, service providers also can achieve ISO certification. Therefore, the same standards for evaluation and auditing can be applied to services in any sector of activity.[25] (The ISO standardization program and its relationship to quality are discussed further in Chapter 9.)

Corporate Express, an international leader in the office supply and computer products industry, maintains ISO 9001 certification in most of its 40 distribution centers, which span over 8.1 million square feet. With one of the most advanced distribution infrastructures in the industry, including over 1,100 delivery vehicles, they deliver an average of $13 million in daily orders throughout the United States (www .corporateexpress.com/fact_sheet.html). As an organization, Corporate Express is committed to quality improvement in their practices and processes (see Figure 10-9), evidenced by the fact they have achieved ISO 9001 and are pursuing 14001 certification.[26]

---

**Figure 10-9    ISO Quality Policy**

### ISO Accreditation

**Corporate Express**

**Policy and Position on Quality**

We believe corporate activities should be transparent. Standing by our responsibilities as a company, a group, and as individuals is of high priority.

We subscribe to internationally recognized standards such as ISO 9001 (Quality Management System) and ISO 14001 (Environmental Management System).

Submitting our practices and processes to ISO scrutiny is one element of sound corporate social responsibility.

Our policies represent a positive differentiator and are designed to meet high standards of quality.

We are progressively auditing each link in the value chain of the products we sell.

*Source:* Adapted from Corporate Express, Corporate Responsibilities, available from www.cexpgroup.com/eng/about_us/ corporate_responsibilities/our_position.aspx.

---

**GAAP.** GAAP stands for *generally accepted accounting principles,* which are the practices that govern financial reporting as determined by the Financial Accounting Standards Board (FASB). The purpose of a financial audit is to determine whether or not an organization's financial statements are prepared in accordance with GAAP. Management of an organization is ultimately responsible for preparing these financial statements, which can be prepared internally or by an outside accounting organization. When financial statements are formally audited, the auditor in charge of the process has a responsibility to issue an opinion on the accuracy and fairness of the financial statements in question.

The U.S. Securities and Exchange Commission (SEC) discovered some interesting practices when investigating corporate fraud in the 1990s. Noted audit deficiencies included a very common practice of auditing organizations failing to gather sufficient evidence to evaluate such areas as asset valuation and asset ownership. Surprisingly, nearly half of the audits failed to follow GAAP standards or applied them incorrectly. Other areas of concern included failure to demonstrate an appropriate level of skepticism or professional care.[27]

**Sarbanes-Oxley.** In the wake of accounting scandals at several U.S. organizations, the *Sarbanes-Oxley Act* (known as SOX) was passed in the United States in 2002. Sponsored by Senator Paul Sarbanes and Representative Michael Oxley, this legislation requires all publicly traded organizations to submit reports to the SEC on an annual basis, verifying the effectiveness of their internal accounting controls. These reporting requirements, as well as the penalties for noncompliance, went into effect in 2006. Based on the nature of the offense, penalties can include up to $15 million in fines and 25 years in prison.

The SOX legislation brought about a need for corporate transparency in the area of financial reporting. It also looked to restore confidence with both investors and the general public. The six main areas of SOX are as follows:

1. *Audit committees.* Organizations must establish fully independent audit committees.

2. *Waiting period.* A minimum of one year must pass before an audit engagement member can be hired as a CEO, CFO or CAO.

3. *Loan prohibition.* Organizations may not extend loans to directors or corporate officers.

4. *Reporting.* Annual internal control reports must be produced.

5. *Disclosure.* Organizations must disclose information regarding material changes on a real-time basis.

6. *Protection.* Whistleblower protection must be provided for its employees.

During the past two years, the focus has shifted from the finance and accounting areas of an organization to other functional areas, including supply management. Since SOX raised the bar in the financial control area, inventory accuracy and inventory value are more important than ever. Segregation of duties must be ensured, which can include supply management. For instance, individuals authorized to procure goods and services should not be the same ones receiving and paying invoices. This limits the opportunity for fraud. Off-balance sheet obligations also must be considered. Supplier-managed inventories and equipment lease agreements have financial implications to an organization and therefore must be reported. This new level of scrutiny actually provides the supply management professional with an opportunity to work with senior management and corporate finance officers more than in past years. It also serves as an opportunity for supply management professionals to demonstrate excellence and value.[28] DHL International, Ltd., developed new standard operating procedures for sourcing, distribution and inventory control as a result of SOX. With multiple business units working together, including supply management, the organization was able to better ensure compliance while continuing to serve its customers throughout the world.[29]

Internationally, a growing number of corporate governance controls are being initiated. Corporate governance controls are an evolving worldwide trend, with SOX-like laws expanding into Europe and Japan. Similar to the U.S. legislation, these laws address professional ethics, objectivity, auditing procedures and reporting requirements.[30]

## Validation of Current Policies and Procedures

In the wake of recent problems and deficiencies, certainly some lessons can be learned. Organizations of all sizes must be aware of established regulations, whether they are ISO, GAAP or SOX requirements. Experience has proved that both organizations and individuals can pay a significant price for noncompliant practices. Every organization should evaluate its policies, processes and procedures. It should emphasize the importance of proper planning, supervision and review of corporate operations, particularly in the financial area. This validation of the current landscape should be an ongoing effort.

Audits should be welcome. External parties can play a valuable role in lending their expertise to an organization through an audit. The advantage to being an "outsider" is that no preconceived notions or assumptions exist. The audit needs to be conducted professionally, objectively and honestly. Audit reports inevitably will find deficiencies that an organization needs to address, and often the recommendations include the corrective action needed, the priority the and necessary timeline.

Both internal and external audits are performed at set frequencies. For instance, some ISO audits are required every year and some every three years. Likewise, a financial audit may be required each year. Special audits do not have set intervals but are important nonetheless. The goal for senior management must be to establish an organization that is continually improving its policies and processes to get them in full compliance.

# Evaluation of Employees

One of the primary ways of maintaining a high-performance work team within supply management is through the diligent evaluation of employee performance. The goal of employee evaluation is to ensure personal accountability to the goals of an organization. It is crucial to use a performance evaluation technique that supports achievement of organizational goals, and also to link employee expectations to its mission. When employees understand the goals of the employer, they are better able to understand their specific roles in supporting those goals. It also is important that employees understand the purpose and value of evaluations. Communication is certainly a key to such understanding. Evaluations can assess either individual or team performance, with the former being the most common. While each organization has its own evaluation technique, these techniques generally fit within two broad categories. *Summative evaluations* are intended to rate the strengths of an employee. They assess performance over a set period of time, most often the preceding year, and recognize accomplishments and successes. The tools used to diagnose weaknesses in employees' performance are referred to as *formative evaluations.* They identify areas for improvement for a specified period of time in the future.[31] For example, if supplier negotiation skills were identified as a supply professional's weakness, and a plan was made to obtain negotiation training within six months, this is an example of formative evaluation.

An organization can use a performance evaluation system to accomplish its mission, and to improve employee performance through some type of incentive program. This can include a performance bonus that is considered on an annual basis. If an employee achieves set objectives for the year, receives high ratings from peers and consistently performs at a high level, he or she can earn additional compensation via a cash bonus. While more money always sounds good, it is not always the prime motivator for employees. Figure 10-10 offers some ideas for nonmonetary rewards.

Figure 10-10    Nonmonetary Employee Motivators

| | |
|---|---|
| **Flexible work arrangements** | Allowing employees some flexibility in their work schedule or the ability to do special projects from home. |
| **Opportunity to participate** | Asking an employee to participate in a special project, such as an employee committee or budget team. |
| **Recognition** | Everyone likes a pat on the back and public acknowledgment for a job well done. This can be a formal presentation or a verbal acknowledgment. |
| **Development opportunities** | Sending employees to internal training can help them develop their skills at little or no cost. |
| **Challenging assignments** | Assignments that are new or unique can be appealing, such as new software or a design-build project. |

*Source:* Adapted from International City/County Management Association, *Human Resource Management in Local Government* (Washington, DC: ICMA, 1999).

Part of motivating employees is valuing them as a resource within the supply management group. Every employee appreciates a pat on the back for a job well done, but this must be sincere and specific. Rather than saying "You're great," make the acknowledgment fit the accomplishment. Saying "Great job on securing that secondary supplier for electric motors" will better convey appreciation. Managers should strive to set up their employees for success and motivate them to perform at a high level. A willingness to value employees and communicate effectively will help build a positive work environment and, ultimately, a flourishing business.[32]

For each position, an organization should determine what the factors are for success in that position. To define the critical success factors of a position, a supply management professional can ask the following questions:

- What are the competencies and skills of a successful individual in this job?

- What skill weaknesses contributed to failure in the past?

- What is the person in this job required to do on a regular basis to succeed?

- What performance factors will align individual and team behavior with the organizational goals and objectives?[33]

## Determining Appraisal Factors

The choice of the appraisal factors used in evaluating employee performance depends on the purpose of the evaluation. Most organizations aim to accomplish several objectives simultaneously. These often include improved employee performance, detection of nonperformers, identification of areas for employee development and improving employee retention. Organizations also must decide whether a single appraisal system is appropriate for all employee groups or if it should consider several parallel systems that align with the needs of each work group. There are many types of appraisal systems and factors for appraisal. They can include both quantitative and qualitative factors.

*Quantitative factors* are statistical in nature, often resulting in numbers. An example of a quantitative factor for employee performance might be the number of supplier contracts negotiated or the dollar value of inventory reduced. These results can be compared against previously determined goals, industry averages or the performance of other employees. *Qualitative factors* are somewhat more subjective and are based on customer feedback and a supervisor's observations. Factors such as responsiveness to customer needs or ability to learn new tasks would be considered qualitative. Technical expertise and professional judgment are employed in qualitative evaluations, while quantitative evaluations rely on the analysis of statistical data.

## Conducting Interviews

An effective manager must use his or her interview skills to gain information about employee performance. Evaluation forms and customer surveys are effective, but at times, personal conversations are best. An interview can give a supervisor the opportunity to gain information firsthand, either from an employee or a customer. Personal interviews can be valuable, for people tend to be more forthright in person, and even share information they may be uncomfortable putting on a survey. An interview should be open, with both sides communicating. Providing feedback also is important. This is the first step in using the information gained during the interview. For example, a major customer may convey concern to the warehouse supervisor about the level of service being provided by distribution personnel. Besides the immediate feedback given to the customer thanking him or her for the information, the supervisor should close the loop with the affected employee and discuss the matter with him or her.

There are numerous sources from which to receive feedback regarding an employee's performance. Traditionally, an employee's direct supervisor has single-handedly conducted the performance evaluation. Today, in addition to their supervisor, employees often are evaluated by their peers and coworkers. These can include members of their work team, who likely know better than anyone the level of a team member's performance, or other peers within the organization. A peer review could be from anyone else in the organization, perhaps an accounting professional holding a comparable position in the controller's office. Disadvantages of peer reviews include the difficulty in maintaining anonymity, and the fact that they are generally unpopular with employees.

An evaluation tool that has been used more in recent years, including by supply management, is *self-assessment.* This is an opportunity for employees to evaluate their own performance against set objectives. An effective way to increase employee participation in the evaluation process, self-assessment establishes clear communication between supervisor and employee. A downside is that it can be subject to bias and inflated ratings, for the employee ratings tend to be higher than those of the supervisor. Self-assessment requires time and commitment from both the employee and the supervisor. (See Volume 3 of the ISM Professional Series, *Leadership in Supply Management,* for a discussion on skills needed in the current environment.)

Internal customers can provide valuable input on employee evaluations, particularly those who work closely with the employee. Accuracy can be less reliable if obtained from sources that are distant or occasional customers. For supply management staff, internal customers could include customers or end users in marketing, finance, production, maintenance or sales. This can be a form of peer review, but the supervisor gathers information specifically from individuals within the organization that receive services from supply management.

Obtaining feedback from the supplier community is not as common as a peer review, but it can still be just as effective. More than ever, supply management professionals are interacting with suppliers. These relationships are key to organizational success and will continue to grow in the future. Similar to an internal customer, a supplier can see firsthand the quality of an employee's performance. When this information is solicited in a professional manner, it can greatly aid a supervisor in evaluating an employee's performance. An example of this is the supplier roundtable project launched by Toyota Motor Engineering & Manufacturing North America, Inc. (TEMA). By soliciting direct feedback from groups of 10 to 15 suppliers, management obtains candid information about supply management's performance and learns what must be changed for the suppliers to operate most effectively.[34]

Employees must be accountable for meeting their performance goals and objectives. When this does not occur, a supervisor can use certain tools to attempt to improve performance. A *performance improvement plan* is a formal document that identifies deficient areas of performance for an employee, methods to measure the needed improvement, as well as the repercussions if acceptable improvement is not made. This type of plan can be used when routine training, on-the-job experience and verbal instructions do not result in acceptable employee performance. This will put the employee and supervisor on the same page as far as job expectations and can create necessary documentation for future personnel action (demotion, termination, etc.).

## Staff Development

Some studies indicate significant differences in the human resources management practices between the United States and China. When faced with the threat of labor uncertainties, organizations within the United States exhibit somewhat rigid behavior. This includes reducing their investment in employee development and limiting the decision-making process to central management. Conversely, Chinese organizations lean toward a greater reliance on its employees and consider them an integral part of the organization. This results in increased training for employees and an emphasis on the use of performance assessments.[35]

The professional development of staff will continue to be crucial to the advancement of the supply management profession. Those new to the profession, as well as seasoned veterans, need to hone their knowledge and expertise to increase their value. CAPS Research, working in partnership with its global network of executives and academics to disseminate supply management best practices, has identified continual learning as an attribute of world-class supply management professionals.[36] In-house training programs, technical seminars and college coursework all play key roles in professional development. Countless opportunities exist for supply management professionals to develop their portfolio of skills. Organizations of all types will need to develop a multipronged approach to develop and retain supply management professionals. This includes ongoing training of existing staff in a fiercely competitive job market.[37]

More and more organizations are financially supporting supply management professionals in this area. They see the value of the investment in training for their team, realizing it will pay dividends for the organization. For instance, having a certified supply management professional on staff can be just as valuable as employing a registered architect or a certified public accountant. The new qualification for supply management professionals is Certified Professional in Supply Management (CPSM), which will become the premier designation for the profession. Even when individuals within the profession pay for professional development out of their own pockets, it is money well spent. Countless times such investments have paid off in the way of promotions and upgrades.

Finally, higher education continues to become more and more important to supply management. Today's professionals see the value of possessing a college degree, and many earn their degrees in supply management or a related field. Other areas such as finance, business and project management have degree holders within the supply management ranks. In the coming years, accredited college degrees will likely become requirements for supply management professionals and not just desirable credentials. What is the value of a degree in supply management? Top-level schools such as Arizona State University, Michigan State University and Howard University are examples of universities offering excellent programs. Through progressive curriculum, faculty with industry experience and internship opportunities, many students have job offers in hand on graduation.

# Summary

By establishing measurements for performance, supply management can help set the bar for an organization. This applies to internal operations, such as marketing, production and sales, as well as its extended enterprise of suppliers. There are many ways in which to measure and evaluate performance, with the key being to determine those measurements that are most appropriate. They must be realistic and achievable and help the organization continually improve.

Suppliers must be managed so they develop into key sources of supply for the organization. As more organizations increasingly rely on suppliers for goods and service, the role of supplier relations becomes more important for supply management. Suppliers also must be familiar with the various audits that can impact their organizations.

Effective management and evaluation of employees is important, so the techniques and skills in human resources management must be developed. Supply management professionals must be concerned with evaluating and improving staff performance, as well as how to use professional training to develop employees in their areas of improvement.

## Key Points

1. Performance measurement is the process of assessing performance toward a predetermined goal; it can be qualitative or quantitative.

2. Suppliers that make up a large portion of annual spend, provide a critical product or hold a critical relationship should have their performance evaluated.

3. Once supplier performance has been evaluated, the information must be reviewed by management, shared with other stakeholders and then acted on to ensure improvement in performance.

4.  Key performance indicators are quantifiable measurements of the improvement in performing an activity critical to business success and include value stream mapping and the balanced scorecard (BSC).

5.  Supplier performance measurement is the process of measuring, analyzing and managing supplier performance for the purpose of reducing costs, mitigating risk and driving continuous improvement.

6.  Common areas of supplier performance measurement include process capability, life cycle costs, service levels, defects per product, late or rejected shipments and production stoppages.

7.  A supplier audit is an examination and verification of a supplier's capabilities against set criteria. The three basic types of supplier audits are systems audit, process audit and product audit.

8.  Supplier development is the process of elevating a supplier's performance and quality to acceptable levels.

9.  Audits that impact supply management include ISO, GAAP and SOX audits.

10. The goal of employee evaluation is to ensure personal accountability to the goals of an organization.

11. Summative evaluations are intended to rate the strengths of an employee and assess performance over a set period of time. Formative evaluations are used to diagnose weaknesses in an employee's performance and identify areas for improvement in the future.

12. Quantitative factors are statistical in nature and can be compared against previously determined goals, industry averages or the performance of other employees. Qualitative factors are subjective and based on customer feedback and a supervisor's observations.

13. Self-assessments are evaluation tools that allow employees to rate their own performance. Understandably, employees often rate their performance higher than their supervisors do.

# 11

# Knowledge Integration

It is often said that knowledge is power. Organizational knowledge is transferred through multiple mediums including face-to-face meetings, e-mail, organization newsletters and Web portals, among others. One of the key issues today is effectively transferring that information without the associated problem of information overload. A related issue is making that information easily accessible and useful for decision-making. Information may be transmitted in the form of raw data or consolidated reports. Supply management professionals must access, analyze and manage various forms of data, including inventory forecasts, supplier cost proposals and distribution schedules. Data must be analyzed across the organization and each business unit must contribute its knowledge for the good of the whole.

Knowledge can be used strategically, improve organizational efficiency, and become a source of competitive advantage for organizations today.[1] For example, Toyota, the world's most profitable automaker, relies on its employees for ideas to improve efficiency and quality. In 2006 alone, employees generated more than 560,000 improvement ideas.[2] However, the challenge is putting those systems in place to effectively integrate this knowledge. Data management and analysis supports knowledge integration and is a key process in strategic supply management, as discussed in Chapter 1. This chapter covers the topics of knowledge management and knowledge integration and the role they play in sharing information within and across organizations. Systems employed by leading organizations will be discussed, including MRP, MRP II, ERP and ERP II. Other tools and processes, also covered in this chapter, include customer relationships, distribution planning and system development life cycle. This chapter begins with several definitions.

## CHAPTER OBJECTIVES

• Explore how knowledge is transferred throughout an organization and discuss how it can be used strategically.

- Define current terminology employed within knowledge management.

- Discuss information technology systems and the various steps of system development.

- Define enterprise resource planning and material requirements planning and explore their role within supply management.

- Discuss how an organization can expand its technology systems to its suppliers and customers.

- Identify emerging trends in technology that impact supply management professionals.

# Definitions

*Knowledge* can best be described as "familiarity and understanding that is gained through experience or study."[3] Employees who possess a desirable knowledge, for example in the area of contract negotiations, and are hired for their mental skills (as opposed to physical skills) are sometimes referred to as *knowledge workers.* Organizational-specific knowledge develops from combining individual knowledge into collective knowledge. Knowledge is also transferred from one subunit to another along two dimensions, technical and social. For technical information transfers to successfully occur, the source and the recipient of the information must have the necessary capabilities to recognize the value of the new information, be able to assimilate it and then apply it to a relevant business purpose, otherwise known as *absorptive capacity.* The social dimension refers to the level of knowledge sharing within the social context of an organization.[4]

The term *knowledge management* developed in the 1990s and, according to ISM, is the attempt to collect and make effective use of the information contained in sources such as documents, reports and plans, as well as the know-how residing in the heads of knowledge workers. (*ISM Glossary,* 2006) Knowledge is not useful unless it is applied, managed and integrated. Thus, knowledge management helps organizations use their collective knowledge to their best advantage. This is accomplished by working to improve the synergies between the data-processing capabilities of their information technologies with the creativity and innovativeness of their employees. Collaboration and cooperation are critical to knowledge integration, requiring organizations to develop those necessary skills and experience that will allow for efficient and effective knowledge transfers. This is especially important when operations are in distant geographic locations. As knowledge exchanges improve, more system innovations, faster technical problem-solving and increased headquarters-subsidiary patenting often result.[5]

The Illinois Department of Central Management Services (CMS), for example, created a knowledge management system that consolidated data resources for its procurement office. The computer-based system was developed in partnership with Microsoft Corporation and Kanalytics, and allowed staff from across the state to access information and communicate with their peers. Through a Web-based portal, procurement and supply management professionals can easily access industry data, product information, policies and procedures and contract proposals.[6] The Illinois knowledge management model is depicted in Figure 11-1.

The importance of knowledge management to the supply management professional should be evident. To make sound business decisions, knowledge throughout the organization must be transferred to the decision-makers. The Strategic Supply Management Process (see the "Series Overview" at the beginning of this book) notes that data management and analysis is a key process step for supply management professionals, who in many cases are these decision-makers. Supply management

**Figure 11-1    Knowledge Management Model**

**Illinois Department of Central Management Services**

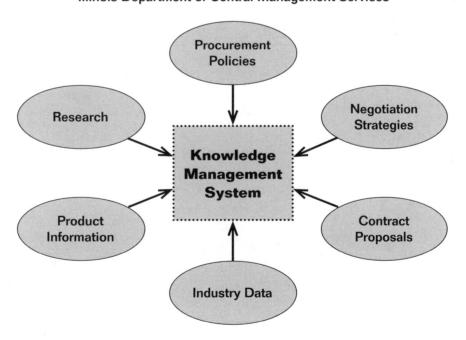

*Source:* Microsoft Corp., "Knowledge Sharing Across Agencies and States Provides for Smarter Procurement," March, 2006, available from www.microsoft.com/windowserver/compare/casestudydetails.mspx?recid=57.

professionals must understand the concept of knowledge management and its importance to the organization, but equally important is the ability to apply the available technologies that share this knowledge. Proficiency in technology use has been identified as a key attribute for supply management professionals, both now and in the future.[7] The following section covers information systems, which are the tools for collecting and transferring this data.

# Information Technology Systems

The world of technology continues to reshape the supply management profession. Organizations of all sizes and sectors are using technology more than ever in their daily operations. *Information technology* refers to the set of electronic tools used by world-class organizations to generate, process, transfer, interpret and use information. These tools include computer hardware, software, databases and networks. (*ISM Glossary,* 2006) A recent study by Computer Sciences Corp. found that industries from chemical distribution to telecommunications were using various IT systems to advance their supply chains.[8] Figure 11-2 identifies some of the technologies these organizations are using to drive results.

**Figure 11-2    Technologies Used to Advance Supply Chains**

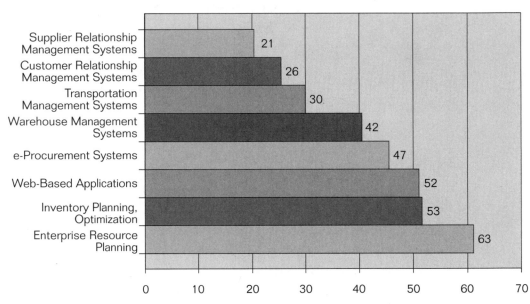

*Source:* Adapted from C. Poirier, *Calibrating Supply Chain Management* (Waltham, MA: Computer Sciences Corp., CSC, 2003), available from www.csc.com/features/2003/106.shtml.

Information systems link business operations, such as production, supply management and logistics, with both the supplier's operation and the customer. They offer organizations the advanced tools to manage and integrate data into business processes. The trend has been for organizations to move away from independent or *legacy systems* for business applications and use integrated systems with a single database. Many organizations use this shared information for replenishing products in the workplace with their upstream operations and those of their key suppliers. For example, Bhs Ltd., a large UK department store chain, uses its information system to replenish store inventories as the daily information is gathered from point-of-sale terminals. Corporate headquarters then transmits this information to the supplier, which packages individual store requirements into bar-coded parcels. These parcels are taken by a logistics service provider to a transshipment center, where they are sorted for store delivery. Essentially, a just-in-time (JIT) delivery is achieved that enables low levels of inventory to be carried in the stores.[9] This replenishment system, made possible by the use of an integrated information system, is shown in Figure 11-3.

The process of developing information systems through investigation, analysis, design, implementation and maintenance is known as the *system development life cycle* (SDLC). Also referred to as information systems development or application development, it covers the entire spectrum of an information system, from requirements

**Figure 11-3    Replenishment Order System**

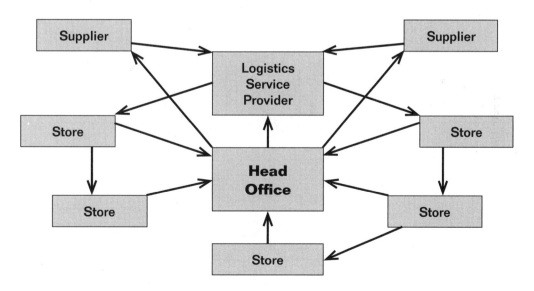

*Source:* Adapted from M. Christopher, *Logistics & Supply Chain Management* (London: Financial Times Prentice Hall, 2005).

analysis to systems testing. There are five phases in the SDLC, with each phase containing several steps and considerations, as shown in Figure 11-4. A description of each step follows.

1. *Software concept.* This first step includes identifying the need for a new system, determining whether a business problem exists, conducting a feasibility study to determine the cost effectiveness of the solution and developing a project plan. This phase of the process involves end users working with information systems staff to improve their work, with all participants keeping in mind the strategic objectives of the organization. Prior to budget approval for the system development, management approval will be needed.

2. *Requirements analysis.* This is the process of analyzing the informational needs of end users, the organizational environment and any present systems in use. Ultimately, the functional requirements of the system must be developed based on

**Figure 11-4    System Development Life Cycle**

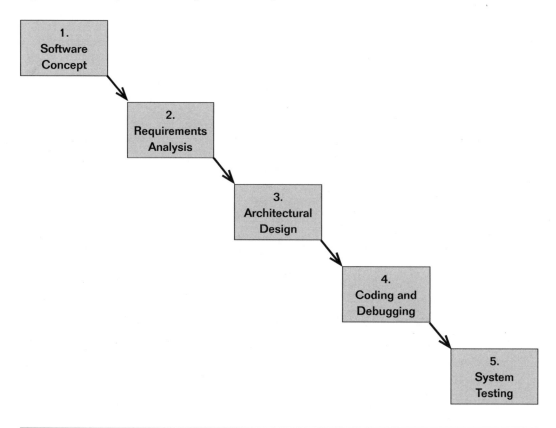

user needs. Requirements of the system can be documented with the use of interface storyboards or executable prototypes. This documentation will be referred to throughout the system development process to ensure the project aligns with identified needs and requirements.

3. *Architectural design.* Once requirements have been determined, an organization can determine the specifications for hardware, software, data resources and information products that are needed. The design will serve as a system blueprint with the goal of detecting problems and errors before they are built into the final system.

4. *Coding and debugging.* Coding and debugging is the process of creating the final system. The identification and removal of bugs will allow the system to function smoothly and as planned. This phase is completed by information systems professionals.

5. *System testing.* All systems must be tested to evaluate their actual functionality as compared to the intended functionality. Other issues to consider during this phase are the conversion of old data into the new system and training of employees on system use. End users are important in helping to determine whether the developed system meets the intended requirements.

## Other Considerations

There are other issues to consider in the SDLC process. Within supply management, there is the insource/outsource decision or, more specifically, "Do we purchase an existing software product, develop our own customized system or use an application service?" The system development life cycle does not actually change with an off-the-shelf program; it is merely adjusted. Concepts for the software still must be considered, as well as the analysis of an organization's requirements. The coding and debugging process is replaced with the evaluation of potential purchased products. Coding also may be required for the necessary interfaces between the new software with existing systems.

The planning stages of the SDLC are of prime importance, for requirements analysis and architectural design must be performed properly to ensure success downstream. Good planning helps reduce errors and the chances for missing production schedules. It is estimated that an undetected design error can take 10 times longer to fix during the debugging stage than if it had been detected during planning.

A business case and project plan should be created during the concept stage. These are formal, written documents that clearly lay out the justification for the project and related investment, as well as a plan that specifically identifies how the project will be accomplished. The project plan is continually refined during the SDLC as users and developers gain a clearer idea of the project scope. Management will need to review both the business case and the project plan to determine whether resources should continue to be committed to the project.[10] Project management was covered in greater detail in Chapter 2.

As mentioned earlier in this chapter, IT is reshaping the organization and changing the nature of the linkages between organizations. While information sharing has long been central to efficient supply management, the advances in technology are the driving force behind competitive strategies.[11] Today's leading organizations increasingly use information technology to improve responsiveness; an IT-enabled supply chain has even been referred to by industry leaders as an important weapon to achieve a competitive advantage.[12]

An important piece of the supply chain as it relates to the use of technology is the implementation of xRP systems. In the acronymn xRP, which stands for *extended resource planning systems,* the *x* may be materials, enterprise or distribution. (*ISM Glossary,* 2006) These systems will be discussed in the following sections, beginning with an overview of enterprise resource planning (ERP).

# Enterprise Resource Planning

According to the *ISM Glossary* (2006), *enterprise resource planning* "usually refers to a particular type of computer software package that integrates various functions within an organization. It may be used to enable processes such as forecasting, materials management and purchasing." One of the fastest growing markets in the software industry, enterprise resource planning is expected to experience strong growth in the next several years, evolving into a $32 billion industry by 2010.[13]

The goal for ERP adopters is to integrate all data and processes of an organization into a single system. Typically, these systems use multiple components of software and hardware to achieve integration. One of the key elements of an ERP system is the use of unified databases to store data for the various modules of the system. The motivators for this shift toward extended resource planning are listed in Figure 11–5.

## Materials Resource Plan

Prior to ERP, other systems had been developed to achieve some form of integration within an organization. *Materials resource plan* (MRP) is a software program originally developed in the 1960s to define the raw material requirements needed for a specific item, component, subassembly ordered by a customer or required by a business

Figure 11-5    ERP Motivators

| MOTIVATOR | PERCENTAGE |
|---|---|
| Improved operational efficiency | 82% |
| Improved management information | 73% |
| Cost savings | 64% |
| Better service to customers | 34% |
| Better link to suppliers | 30% |

*Source:* Adapted from C. Mills, "ERP Leads Fight Against Information Overload," PMP Research, October, available from www.pmpresearch.com/downloads/PMPResearch_ERPLeadsFight.pdf=.

process (additional discussion of MRP is included in Chapter 5). Many MRP software applications can automatically place the raw material orders to the preferred supplier via fax, e-mail or electronic data interchange (EDI). In 1981, MRP was extended to *manufacturing resource planning* (MRP II).

MRP II is an extension of the materials resource plan, which is a closed–loop system (it does not interface with other systems). MRP II is used by organizations to effectively plan all its resources used in manufacturing products. It addresses operational planning in all units and financial planning in dollars, and has a simulation capacity to address "what if" questions. MRP II (according to the *ISM Glossary,* 2006) is comprised of a variety of functions that are linked together, including:

- Business planning,
- Sales,
- Operational planning,
- Production planning,
- Master production scheduling,
- Material requirements planning,
- Capacity requirements planning and
- Execution of support systems for capacity and materials.

ERP has a much broader scope than MRP or MRP II, covering basic functions of all types within an organization. Major corporations, governments, nonprofits and healthcare providers are examples of large organizations using ERP systems. These systems provide benefits that range from increased standardization and lower maintenance costs to better reporting capabilities from having a single database rather than multiple databases.

For a software package to be considered an ERP system, it must provide functionality in a single system that would normally be covered by two or more systems. Intuit® QuickBooks® is a simple example of such a system, for it provides both accounting and payroll functions. More commonly, ERP systems include more broad-based applications that eliminate the need for external interfaces between multiple systems. Some of these business applications include manufacturing, customer relationship management, supply chain, financials, human resources and warehouse management. ERP systems sometimes are mistakenly identified as *back office systems,* which are systems that do not directly involve customers and the general public. However, ERP also may include *front office systems* that deal directly with customers and suppliers. Customer relations management (CRM) systems and supplier relationship management (SRM) systems connect with electronic business systems such as e-Commerce and e-Government. The New Zealand Post was able to better control its procurement spend and improve supplier performance when it implemented an SRM system. By consolidating its pool of suppliers and improving spend monitoring, the state-operated postal service was able to improve its level of customer service.[14]

The multiple applications offered by an ERP system are shown in Figure 11-6; those related to supply management are discussed in the following section.

## Add-On Modules

Add-on modules are multiple add-on applications (or modules) to ERP systems. Each organization must evaluate its operational needs and determine if additional ERP modules can meet those needs. For example, a *continuous replenishment program* (CRP) is an inventory management program where information is submitted electronically from the customer to the supplier. This enables the supplier to maintain a sufficient level of inventory for the customer. CRP is a basic system but can result in very positive outcomes, which is why organizations use it for replenishing commonly used components and raw materials. (*ISM Glossary,* 2006)

A *warehouse management system* (WMS) is designed specifically for managing the movement and storage of materials throughout the warehouse. By providing information to warehouse management, a WMS can assist with inventory control, distribution activities and personnel administration. A WMS can provide completed production

**Figure 11-6    Enterprise Resource Planning Systems**

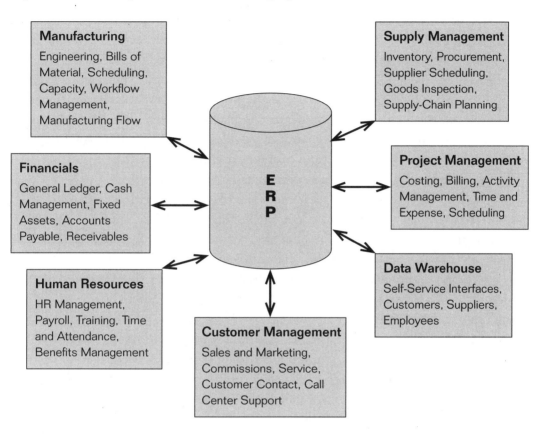

units, while a time and attendance system can offer payroll and departmental transfer data. The information from both systems can combine to provide an overall picture of warehouse operations and related costs.[15] Del-Nat Tire Corp., a tire distributor based out of Washington, D.C., uses an integrated WMS solution with handheld bar code scanners in its tire warehouses. This automation with its tire-picking process allowed Del-Nat to improve efficiency and accuracy within its warehouse operation and improve order fulfillment by 35 percent.[16]

*Customer relationship management* (CRM) refers to systems that manage and deal with customer needs via Web access. They can help an organization manage its call center or e-mail response system, but they cannot help leverage customer information or analyze customer profitability. With CRM, the goal is to provide 24-hour access to customers, both new and existing. It allows for improved retention of customers through better relationship management and niche marketing. When operating effectively, CRM can reduce the cost of sales by allowing customers to handle sales themselves. Customers can access products at any time and even configure their own orders. The ultimate goal is to secure a competitive advantage. Some CRM applications are considered analytical for they allow an organization to analyze customer data to determine buying habits. This can lead to better sales forecasting and improved profitability. CRM systems are growing in popularity and importance. In a recent survey, 25 percent of respondents indicated their organizations had completed a CRM implementation, while another 20 percent were in the process of implementation. Another 10 percent will initiate CRM applications in the next year.[17]

As organizations move toward more strategic relationships with suppliers, many are employing *supplier relationship management* (SRM) modules within their ERP systems. An SRM can offer many benefits, including the ability to source and select materials quickly and to monitor supplier quality. SAP offers an SRM application that helps an organization manage supplier spend, which can lead to increased profitability. The application simplifies and automates the procurement and contract negotiation process through a single analytical framework.[18] These types of systems can greatly assist supply management professionals with *spend management,* which is a process organizations use to control and optimize the money they spend. It may involve cutting operating and other costs associated with doing business. According to CAPS Research, up to 50 percent of an organization's indirect dollars are spent on maverick buys,[19] which reinforces the need for spend management.

*Distribution requirements planning* (DRP) is a supply management term for the time-based demand from the distribution center to balance the customer fill rate against inventory investment. This will inform the organization about what products are on hand to fulfill existing requirements and what needs to be shipped from the distribution center. *DRP II* is *distribution resource planning* and is more sophisticated, for it uses a computerized inventory system for replenishment at multiple warehouse sites. Planning for warehouse space, personnel requirements, transportation alternatives and financial flows are also functions of DRP II.

## Supply Management and ERP

The supply management module of an ERP system is certainly an important tool for today's supply management professional. Depending on the system, this may be referred to as supply management, materials management or procurement, but the essential functionality should be consistent: order placement, master contracts, inventory control, materials forecasting and replenishment. A key consideration with ERP is that it is simply another tool for the supply management professional to ensure timely delivery of quality goods and services when needed. Software interfaces, customer reports and data analysis become important only when they help supply management meet organizational objectives and improve profitability. The future appears to be bright for ERP systems, particularly in manufacturing where communications and data visibility can be improved. According to Christopher Loch, writer and editor for *CIO* magazine, ERP technology allows organizations to "integrate all departments and functions across a company into a single computer system that can serve all those different departments' particular needs."[20]

## ERP Implementation

ERP software systems are complex and usually require significant changes to an organization's business practices. When an ERP project is launched, the internal business units must be committed, but they also must be adaptable to the resulting work flow and process changes that will occur. The amount of time a system implementation takes will vary based on the complexity of the system and the size of the organization. A smaller organization with a basic ERP system may take as little as three months for implementation, while large organizations with complex systems can take years. Large organizations with superior in-house IT skills sometimes choose to implement portions of ERP systems. They then develop interfaces to other ERP or stand-alone systems that meet their business needs.

It is very common to use both internal technical staff and third-party consultants to handle the implementation. The project manager should come from within the organization and, of course, be willing to take complete ownership of the project. The third-party consultants will provide services under the oversight of the project manager. These services may come from the ERP system supplier or other organizations that specialize in systems implementation and are authorized by the ERP supplier.

Services provided from third parties fall into three basic areas: (1) consulting, (2) customization and (3) maintenance/support. Consulting services include initial implementation and tailored service required to activate the system. Additional product training, creation of process triggers and workflow, report writing and complex data extracts often are part of this phase. Consultants also are responsible for planning and jointly testing the implementation, which is a key part of the project. Documentation is sometimes overlooked on implementations, particularly with customizations. Project managers must ensure adequate documentation is received. Customization refers to changing how the ERP system works based on unique client needs. This occurs when the consultant writes new user interfaces and underlying application codes.

SAP's manufacturing and customer relationship modules may be deemed to be the best fit for those areas, while human resources and materials management are handled by Oracle modules. Both are world leaders in the ERP software industry and most commonly provide a single system and database for their clients. At times, however, using multiple systems makes sense, such as with a retailer who uses a discrete point-of-sale (POS) product along with a specialized application for warehousing and merchandising. Nearly 70 percent of large and 42 percent of midsize organizations have more than one ERP system. Additionally, more than 25 percent of large manufacturing organizations have more than four systems, many of which are a result of mergers and acquisitions.[21]

After implementation is complete, it may be wise to enter into a support agreement. This will ensure that the ERP system operates properly, the internal staff receives adequate support and the rights to system patches for the current version and future releases are specified. It is not unusual for the cost of implementation services to match or exceed the cost of the ERP licensing. A large organization with multiple business sites, even in different countries, may spend several times the cost of the ERP system on the implementation. When extensive customization is required, project costs understandably increase. Support and maintenance services can cost up to 25 percent of the amount of ERP licensing.

## ERP Challenges and Limitations

Organizations also should be aware of the challenges and limitations associated with ERP systems. The success of an ERP project relies on the skill and experience of the workforce, which makes system training a key factor. Inadequate investment in an ongoing training program can lead to problems later on. Both small and large organizations have a tendency to cut training budgets, which is a concern. The stability of the workforce also can be a problem. Hiring organizations and consultants both have the same challenge of attracting and retaining staff with a high level of experience and expertise. The top performers may be headed to leading organizations for top pay on new projects. Commitment for system success must be organizationwide. Because many integrated links need a high level of data accuracy for other applications to work effectively, an ERP system may be only as strong as its weakest link.

# Beyond ERP to ERP II

MRP, MRP II and ERP have focused on internal needs, but organizations now see the necessity to expand their practices to include customers and suppliers. While ERP generally focuses on integrating general accounting, distribution and logistics, manufacturing, plant maintenance and human resources within one organization, resource planning systems that extend to the integration of supply-chain partners in real time have been developed more recently and include supply chain management, e-commerce and customer service management. These systems are more commonly referred to as ERP II, although the acronyms xRP and enterprise commerce management (ECR) also are used. For organizations that currently possess at least a basic ERP system, ERP II can build on existing structures and help develop a valued supply network.

## Strategies for ERP II

Leading organizations in many instances are discovering the value of ERP II systems, and see this as a source of competitive advantage. Implementing new business strategies and streamlining processes are prime concerns, and potentially can be addressed through the use of ERP II. Dell, Inc., has sought out process efficiencies and increased customer service. By using ERP II, it can better manage the organization and flow of economic activities — supply, demand and value exchanges — within its organization.[22]

While organizations are realizing that opening up business processes and systems to outside partners is a best practice, they also must ensure that strategic thinking is a part of these advancements. Regardless of how thorough an implementation is, it must be of strategic value to be worthwhile. Where an organization is and where it wants to be in a market must first be determined before it decides the best way to get there. Technology should be considered an enabler and not a final solution. If business strategies can be defined and developed, then it is likely a technology tool can help deliver it. An ERP II application of note is one implemented by the John Crane Group, now a member of Smiths Group PLC, a $1 billion manufacturer of sealing products in the United Kingdom. Through the use of an online supplier portal, it was able to bring together its internal ERP system with both its EDI and non-EDI suppliers. This enables Crane and its suppliers to improve productivity and planning accuracy.[23] This type of forward thinking has helped Crane stay highly competitive in the sealing industry, even earning the Breakthrough Product of the Year for its corrosive resistant mechanical seals in 2006.[24]

The sharing of information is a valuable tool for improving relations with suppliers and customers. Organizations are opening up their networks to increase value, offer better service and reduce communication time. Not only can customer orders be placed online for Amazon.com, but the shipments also can be tracked online.[25] This provides instant information for users and reduces the need for attended call centers. Likewise, potential suppliers can register for state business at the Oregon Procurement Information Network (ORPIN).[26] Countless public and private organizations have developed enterprise systems that provide access to information and opportunities to interested suppliers.

ERP II is a demonstration of knowledge management and integration in action. Traditional ERP business areas still are maintained within an organization's business enterprise, but many areas are extended to supplier and customer bases. By taking advantage of ERP II technologies, organizations can increase their competitive edge while decreasing their costs. Figure 11-7 illustrates the common areas of information that are shared.

Many organizations do not possess the internal expertise to fully integrate an ERP II and instead contract with third parties that bring the required technical expertise. Philippines-based Wohldorf Systems, Inc., for example, is an ERP II solutions

**Figure 11-7    ERP II — Extension of Traditional ERP Systems**

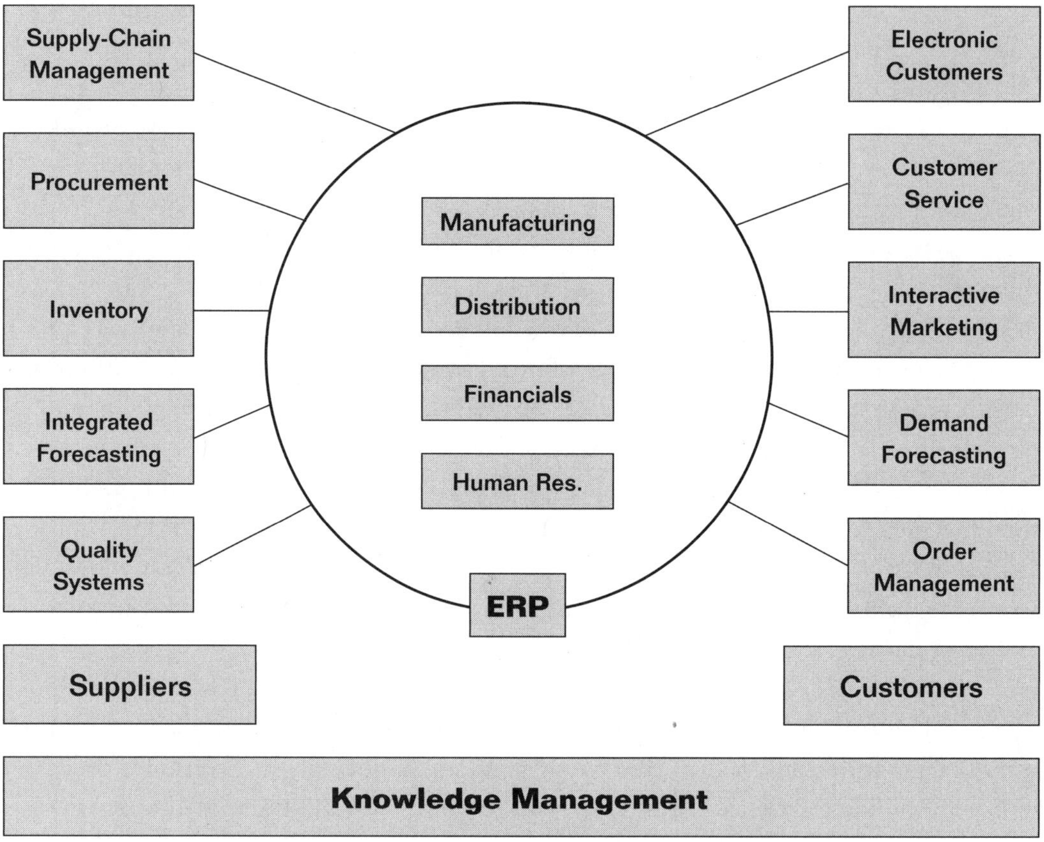

*Source:* Adapted from R. Coomber, "From ERP to XRP," *Telecommunications* 34:12 (December), 72.

provider. It offers systems development and implementation services, as well as training and e-business consulting. Organizations such as Wohldorf work with clients to get the most out of proven third-party systems like PeopleSoft-Oracle.[27]

Caterpillar Logistics Services, Inc., a division of Caterpillar International, is another third-party organization that provides supply management solutions to a large client base. Working with Hyundai, it was able to implement a logistics services system that allowed the client to reduce IT costs and support staff in Korea. Based primarily on a need for increased customer satisfaction, Cat Logistics helped Hyundai improve parts availability and overall service.[28]

# Technology Trends in Supply Management

The advancement of Internet technologies has resulted in significant improvements in business communications. This has been seen in the United States, Japan, Italy and France, among other countries, and has resulted in advancements in their ERP and supply-chain management practices. These impacts can be summarized as follows:

- Better relationships with business partners,

- Increased customer satisfaction, and supply and demand chain costs are being reduced,

- Organizations around the globe are reassessing themselves in terms of threats and opportunities,

- Improved transparency of workflow systems and their coordination,

- Better flexibility of the system with regard to business decisions and

- Well-informed decision-making; new quality in planning and forecasting.[29]

Supply management will continue to rely heavily on information technologies in the future. Over the past several years, CAPS Research has continually stressed the importance of technology's role in the profession, even citing IT proficiency as a critical skill for world-class professionals.[30] The need for such skills will only increase in coming years.

It is anticipated that both ERP and CRM applications will become mainstream for leading organizations, particularly medium-size businesses (MB). In a 2006–2007 survey by AMI Partners, Inc., MBs reported that currently one-third are employing ERP and 25 percent intend to do so in the next year. Small businesses, on the other hand, are likely to proceed cautiously in this area. While nearly 75 percent currently use business accounting software, only 11 percent intend to use ERP in the next 12 months. Manufacturing and service sectors are spending more on ERP systems than other sectors are. In the CRM market, the services industry outpaces all other sectors in both adoption and spending.[31]

Spend management technology is a growing area for many organizations, which certainly impacts supply management. This includes e-procurement systems that allow online, retail shopping catalogs, as well as e-sourcing and spend analysis. Modules that handle spend analysis allow organizations to segment purchases by commodity, supplier and amount, so informed decisions can be made with procurement strategies. ERP products will continue to break new ground in the areas of supplier performance, financial forecasting, sourcing and bid optimization.[32]

## Summary

Supply management professionals must be aware of the importance of the proper management and analysis of data. It is imperative that the knowledge gained from this data is used to improve business practices. The knowledge also must be shared throughout the entire organization. As supply management aligns its strategies with those of the organization, it must play an active role in the sharing of data and information with other business units.

Numerous information systems are available and must be selected based on the needs and goals of the organization. Integrated systems are much more efficient than independent systems used in past years. The use of these systems is a way to efficiently manage knowledge within an organization, as well as extend knowledge to suppliers and customers. There is a life cycle for system development that supply management professionals must be familiar with, for they are an integral part of any major systems acquisition. Information technologies are a reality in today's markets and will only become more important in the future. Supply management professionals must pay close attention to these advancements and how they can benefit an organization. If they do not do so, then they and their organizations risk being left behind.

The role of supply management continues to evolve in all business sectors. More and more, the profession is viewed as a critical and strategic player by leading organizations throughout the world. The use of technology tools that share data and knowledge across the organization will only aid this evolution. While knowledge integration is the last chapter in this book, supply management professionals should consider the concept as just the beginning. Understanding how knowledge is integrated, and how technology is used to do so, will allow supply management professionals to move forward and add even more value to the organization.

This book has covered numerous key areas of supply management, including its role in planning, product development, project management, forecasting, logistics, inventory management and quality assurance. Each of these areas is important, but combined they represent a full spectrum of knowledge for today's supply management professional.

## Key Points

1. Knowledge management is the attempt to collect and make effective use of the information contained in documents, reports and plans and the knowledge residing in the heads of subject matter experts. Knowledge workers are employees who possess such knowledge and are hired for their mental skills.

2. Information technology refers to the set of electronic tools used to generate, process, transfer, interpret and use information. These tools include computer hardware, software, databases and networks.

3. Materials resource plan (MRP) is a method used for defining the raw materials needed for a specific item, component or subassembly ordered by a customer or required by a business process.

4. Manufacturing resource planning (MRP II), an extension of material requirements planning, is a method used by organizations to effectively plan all its resources used in manufacturing products.

5. Enterprise Resource Planning (ERP) is a software system that integrates various functions within an organization. It can be used to enable and improve business processes and integrates all processes of an organization into a single system.

6. Warehouse management system (WMS) manages the movement and storage of materials throughout the warehouse.

7. Customer relationship management (CRM) systems manage and deal with customer needs via Web access and automated systems.

8. Supplier relationship management (SRM) is an ERP system module that can allow an organization to quickly source and select materials, as well as monitor supplier quality.

9. Extended resource planning (xRP) systems include the functions of ERP, such as general accounting, distribution, manufacturing, plant maintenance and human resources, but also supply management, e-commerce and customer service management.

10. System development life cycle (SDLC) is the process of developing information systems through investigation, analysis, design, implementation and maintenance.

# Endnotes

## Chapter 1

1. Cherish Karoway, "The 21st-Century Purchaser," *Purchasing Today* (February 1996), see www.ism.ws/.

2. A.T. Kearney, "Creating Value Through Strategic Supply Management," (2004), www .atkearney.com/main.taf?p=5,3,1,115,1.

3. Robert M. Monczka, Robert J. Trent and Kenneth J. Petersen, *Effective Global Sourcing and Supply for Superior Results* (Tempe, AZ: CAPS Research, 2006), 8.

4. Mickey North Rizza, "Supply Management Breakthrough Coming?" *Supply Chain Management Review* (May/June 2006): 13.

5. Roberta J. Duffy, "One on One: An Interview With Patricia Hanson," *Journal of Supply Chain Management* (Winter): 2.

6. Francis J. Quinn, "The Power of Procurement," *Supply Chain Management Review* (December 2005): 7.

7. Jill Schildhouse, "Corporate Ethics: Taking the High Road," *Inside Supply Management* (March 2005): 31.

8. www.ism.ws/SR/content.cfm?ItemNumber=4762&navItemNumber=4887.

9. R. Dan Reid and Carl D. Riegel, *Purchasing Practices of Large Foodservice Firms* (Tempe, AZ: CAPS Research, 1989), and Institute for Supply Management, *ISM Principles of Social Responsibility,* www.ism.ws/SR/content.cfm?ItemNumber=4767&navItemNumber=5503.

10. Peter Kraljic, "Purchasing Must Become Supply Management," *Harvard Business Review* (September–October 1983): 109–17.

11. Johan Beer, Alex Giacomini and Lufthansa, "Lufthansa: Setting a New Course for Purchasing," *Efficient Purchasing* 3: 34.

12. Linda P. Michels and Traci G. Elkhart, "Methods of Supplier Investigations," *NAPM InfoEdge* (August 2000), see www.ism.ws/.

13. Johan Beer, Janne Danielsson, Anna Reinberg and Holger Staffansson, "Building Better Procurement," *Efficient Purchasing* 3 (2006): 44.

14. Bronson Methodist Hospital Malcolm Baldrige National Quality Award Summary (2005), www.quality.nist.gov/PDF_files/Bronson_Methodist_Hospital_Application_Summary.pdf.

15. Rochelle Rucker, "Six Sigma at Citibank," *Quality Digest* (December 1999), www.qualitydigest .com/dec99/html/citibank.html.

16. C.J. McNair, "Beyond the Boundaries: Future Trends in Cost Management," *Cost Management* (January/February 2007): 15.

17. Ayon Chakrabarty and Kay Chuan Tan, "The Current State of Six Sigma Application," *Managing Service Quality* 17(2) (2007): 194–208; T.N. Goh, "A Strategic Assessment of Six Sigma," *Quality Reliability Engineering International* 18(5) (2002): 403–10.

18. S.F. Gale, "Building Frameworks for Six Sigma Success," *Workforce* (May 2003): 68–9.

19. Peter Coote and Stathis Gould, "Lean Management," *Financial Management* (September 2006): 26.

20. A.T. Kearney, "Creating Value Through Strategic Supply Management."

## Chapter 2

1. *A Guide to the Project Management Body of Knowledge,* 3rd ed. (Newtown Square, PA: Project Management Institute, 2004), 5.
2. *A Guide to the Project Management Body of Knowledge.*
3. John A. Kuprenas, "Implementation and Performance of a Matrix Organization," *International Journal of Project Management* 21 (2003): 51–62.
4. Joel Makower, "Supply and Da Man," *Superfactory* (August 2006), www.superfactory.com/articles/Makower_Supply_Da_Man.htm.
5. "Six Sigma: Defining the Problem Statement" (November 27, 2006), www.anticlue.net/archives/000750.htm.
6. Jerry B. Harvey, "The Abilene Paradox: The Management of Agreement," *Organizational Dynamics* (Summer 1974): 63–80.
7. Paul Evans, "Performing a SWOT Analysis of Tesco PLC" (December 2006), www.321books.co.uk/catalog/tesco/swot-analysis.htm.
8. Charles H. Kepner and Benjamin B. Tregoe, *The New Rational Manager* (Princeton, NJ: Princeton Research Press, 1981).
9. Kepner-Tregoe, "Interbake Foods: Integrating Two Acquisitions While Driving Bottom-Line Results," (2006), www.kepner-tregoe.com/PDFs/CaseStudies/InterbakeMailerKL545.pdf.
10. Jason Westland, *Project Management Life Cycle* (London: Kogan Page, 2006), 17.
11. Samuel J. Mantel Jr., Jack R. Meredith, Scott M. Shafer and Margaret M. Sutton, *Project Management in Practice* (New York: John Wiley & Sons, 2001), 56–7.
12. "Project Management for Modern Managers," *PC World* (September 9, 1999), www.pcworld.com/article/id,12660/article.html; James R. Bourk, "A New Look at Your Old Project Management Methods Can Promote Your Advantages," *Infoworld* (January 15, 2001): 52.
13. Jason Kemow and Francine Holloway, "Bringing Control to Global Supply Management: Business Process Management (BPM) and Advanced Project Management Practices," *Proceedings of the 90th Annual International Supply Management Conference,* May 2005.
14. *A Guide to the Project Management Body of Knowledge.*
15. Jennifer Koppy, "IT Leasing Case Study: Metro Health" (2006), http://h20330.www2.hp.com/hpfinancialservices/downloads/203910%20-%20IT%20Leasing%20Case%20Study.pdf.
16. James P. Lewis, *Project Planning, Scheduling and Control* (New York: McGraw-Hill, 1995), 230.

## Chapter 3

1. Steven Wheelwright and Kim Clark, *Leading Product Development: The Senior Manager's Guide to Creating and Shaping the Enterprise* (New York: The Free Press, 1994), 5.
2. Michiel Leenders, P. Fraser Johnson, Anna Flynn and Harold E. Fearon, *Purchasing and Supply Management,* 13th ed. (New York: McGraw-Hill, 2005).
3. P. Teague. "Product Development: Material and Supply Join Design Teams," *Purchasing Magazine Online* (September 1, 2005), www.purchasing.com/article/CA6250272.html?q=.
4. Dan Dimancescu and Kemp Dwenger, *World-Class New Product Development* (New York: AMACOM, 1996), 41–42.
5. "Management by Web," *BusinessWeek OnLine* (August 28, 2000), www.businessweek.com/common_frames/ma_0035.htm?/2000/00_35/b3696011.htm.

6. Kenji Hall, "A Mobile Gizmo With Ginza Info," *BusinessWeek OnLine* (March 7, 2007), www .businessweek.com/globalbiz/content/mar2007/gb20070306_237395.htm?chan=top+news_ top+news+index_global+business.

7. www.apple.com/services/consulting/.

8. www.http://www.ideo.com/about/.

9. www.spectrafund.com/sf/appmanager/spectraportal/welcome/.

10. www.triodos.com/com/international_funds/renewable_energy/?lang=/.

11. Rhoda Miel, "Supplier Goes Straight to the Designers," *Automotive News* 12(3) (August 10, 2006): 14.

12. Glenn H. Mazur, "Doubling Sales With Quality Function Deployment," *Proceedings of the 5th Annual Service Quality Conference,* September 16–7, 1996, Las Vegas.

13. Robert G. Cooper and Scott J. Edgett, "Ten Ways to Make Better Portfolio and Project Selection Decisions," *Visions* (June 2006), www.pdma.org/visions/june06/better-portforlio.php.

14. Joan M. Lang, "Simple Seafood Makeover," *Seafood Business* (October 3, 2007), www .seafoodbusiness.com/index.asp?ItemID=3504&rcid=191&pcid=190&cid=191.

15. David Smith, "Fair Wind for World's First 5 MW Turbine," *Modern Power Systems* 23(10) (October 2003): S11–3; "Repower 5M: Successful Offshore Premier," Repower Systems AG press release, www.repower5m.com/index_flash_uk.htm.

16. Boeing Corporation, "Computing and Design/Build Processes Help Develop the 777," www .boeing.com/commercial/777family/pf/pf_computing.html.

17. "Dairy Fresh Farms Announces Results of New Generation Milk Test Market Launch in Western Canada," *Business Wire* (November 8, 2005), www.lexisnexis.com.ezproxy1.lib.asu .edu/us/lnacademic/results/docview/docview.do?risb=21_T2460020731&format= GNBFI&sort=RELEVANCE&startDocNo=1&resultsUrlKey=29_T2460020741&cisb=22_ T2460020740&treeMax=true&treeWidth=0&csi=7924&docNo=1.

18. Jerry W. Thomas, "Product Testing" (1993), www.decisionanalyst.com/publ_art/prodtes1.dai.

19. Michael E. Porter, *Competitive Strategy* (New York: The Free Press, 1980).

20. Stanley Holmes, "Adidas: The Machine of a New Sole," *BusinessWeek* (March 14, 2005): 99; "Full Year 2006 Results," Adidas press release, www.adidas-group.com/en/home/welcome.asp.

21. Edward H. Phillips, "American Absorbs Reno Air," *Aviation Week & Space Technology* (September 6, 1999): 32.

22. "DeBeers Introduction and Profile," www.debeersgroup.com/debeersweb/About+De+Beers/ De+Beers+Structure/INTRODUCTION+AND+PROFILE.htm.

23. Lee J. Krajewski and Larry P. Ritzman, *Operations Management: Strategy and Analysis* (Upper Saddle River, NJ: Prentice Hall, 2001), 334.

24. Ibid., 334.

25. Jeffrey A. Trachtenberg, "Borders Business Plan Gets a Rewrite," *Wall Street Journal* (March 22, 2007): B-1.

26. "Look Before You Leap," *Business 2.0* (April 2005): 128.

27. "Hitachi's Drastic Reorganization of Its Global Logistics System in Alliance With DHL," Hitachi news release (October 23, 2003), www.hitachi.com/New/cnews/031028.html.

28. Jean V. Murphy, "Logistics Plays Key Role in Success of New Product Introductions," *Global Logistics & Supply Chain Strategies* (August 2006): 58.

29. Dennis Kneale, "Whitacre's Way," *Forbes* (January 8, 2007): 84–90.

30. Murphy, "Logistics Plays Role in Success of New Product Introductions," 58.

31. Murphy, "Logistics Plays Role in Success of New Product Introductions," 57.

32. "What's the Best Way to Measure a Supply Chain? At Lexmark, Cash Is King," *Global Logistics & Supply Chain Strategies* (December 2005): 32–7.

33. Stephen Blake, "Technology: Food Packaging in a Modern World," *Just — Food* (December 2005): 7, http://galenet.galegroup.com.ezproxy1.lib.asu.edu/servlet/BCRC?as1=technology&JN=JustFood&locID=azsulibs&ai2=KE&srchtp=adv&c=1&dfd=01&ab1=AND&ab2=AND&dtm=12&ai1=KE&aca=nwmg&docNum=A140659976&bConts=2&dty=2005&dtd=30&ste=31&tbst=tsVS&tab=2&ai3=KE&dfy=2005&dfm=09.

34. Murphy, "Logistics Plays Role in Success of New Product Introductions," 57.

35. Andy Reinhardt, "Nokia's Magnificent Mobile-Phone Manufacturing Machine," *BusinessWeek OnLine* (August 3, 2006), www.businessweek.com/globalbiz/content/aug2006/gb20060803_618811.htm.

36. Michele J. Flynn, Nancy J. Hite and Michael J. Stanly, "Identifying a Product's Raw Materials," *NAPM InfoEdge* (August 2001), www.ism.ws/pubs/InfoEdge/InfoEdgearticle.cfm?ItemNumber=11862.

37. Robert B. Handfield, Gary L. Ragatz, Kenneth J. Petersen and Robert M. Monczka, "Involving Suppliers in New Product Development," *California Management Review* 42(1) (1999): 59–82.

38. Debra Leitka, "Challenges of Component Obsolescence," *Inside Supply Management* (November 2002): 10, www.ism.ws/pubs/ISMMag/ismarticle.cfm?ItemNumber=12195.

39. Nicolette Lakemond, Ferrie van Echtelt and Finn Wynstra, "A Configuration Typology for Involving Purchasing Specialists in Product Development," *The Journal of Supply Chain Management* (Fall 2001): 11–20.

40. E.E. Scheuing, I. Wirth and D. Antos, "Early Involvement of Purchasers Saves Time and Money," *PM Network* (March 1996): 30–3.

41. J. Carbone, "Buyers Link Hands With Designers," *Purchasing Magazine* (March 16, 2006): 34–9.

42. M.A. McGinnis and R.M. Vallopra, *Purchasing and Supplier Involvement: New Product Development and Production/Operations Process Development and Improvement* (Tempe, AZ: CAPS Research, 1999), 10.

43. L.M. Ellram, "Taking Aim at Target Costing," *Purchasing Today* (February 1999): 65.

44. Institute for Supply Management, *ISM Principles of Social Responsibility,* 2004, www.ism.ws/SR/content.cfm?ItemNumber=4767&navItemNumber=5503.

45. S.V. Walton, R.B. Handfield and S.A. Melnyk, "The Green Supply Chain: Integrating Suppliers into Environmental Management Processes," *International Journal of Purchasing and Materials Management* 34(2) (1998): 2–11; Stephan Vachon, "Green Supply Chain Practices and the Selection of Environmental Technologies," *International Journal of Production Research* (September 2007): 4,357–79.

## Chapter 4

1. www.state.gov/r/pa/ei/bgn/2698.htm.

2. Stephen S. Roach, "The Lessons of 2006," Morgan Stanley's Global Economic Forum (January 3, 2007), www.morganstanley.com/views/gef/.

3. Merrell Tuck, "Growth Prospects Are Strong But Social, Environmental Pressures From Globalization Need More Attention," World Bank press release 2007/159/DEC (December 13, 2006), http://web.worldbank.org/WBSITE/EXTERNAL/NEWS/0,,contentMDK: 21157190~pagePK:64257043~piPK:437376~theSitePK:4607,00.html.

4. "Chrysler Group's Global Alliance Strategy Builds on Solid Sales Momentum in Canada, Mexico and International Markets," *Motor Trend* (January 4, 2007), www.motortrend.com/features/newswire/91/25445/.

5. www.walmartstores.com/GlobalWMStoresWeb/navigate.do?catg=369.

6. "Whirlpool Corporation Today — Building Customer Loyalty Worldwide," www.whirlpoolcorp.com/about/history/today.asp.

7. "Selling to the Local Chinese Market: An Interview With Lenovo's Deepak Advani and BCG's Hal Sirkin" Knowledge@Wharton (October 16, 2006), http://knowledge.wharton.upenn.edu/article.cfm?articleid=1575.

8. Hau L. Lee, Corey Billington and Brent Carter, "Hewlett-Packard Gains Control of Inventory Through Design for Localization," *Interfaces* 23(4) (1993): 1–11; Hau L. Lee and Corey Billington, "The Evolution of Supply-Chain-Management Models and Practice at Hewlett-Packard," *Interfaces* 25(5) (1995): 42–63.

9. "Brazilian Medical Device Market in Flux," *Medical Device Translation News* (Winter 1999), www.luz.com/mdtn_archives/brazil.html.

10. Charla Griffy-Brown, "Just-in-Time to Just-in-Case: Managing a Supply Chain in Uncertain Times," *Graziado Business Report* 6(2) (2003*)*, Pepperdine University, http://gbr.pepperdine.edu/032/supplychain.html#return6.

11. Larry R. Smeltzer, "Managing Cultural Differences in Buyer-Supplier Relationships," *Proceedings of the 81st Annual International ISM Conference,* 1996, Chicago.

12. Heather R. Keller, "Soft Skills for Global Managers," *Inside Supply Management* (September 2007): 26.

13. "Haier, Already a Success, Aims Higher," Interview with Zhang Ruimin, Knowledge@Wharton (April 5, 2005), www.knowledgeatwharton.com.cn/index.cfm?fa=viewfeature&languageid=1&articleid=1111.

14. "What's Ahead for 2007? Knowledge@Wharton Network Surveys the Globe" (December 13, 2006), http://knowledge.wharton.upenn.edu/article.cfm?articleid=1621.

15. Jeremy van Loon and Chad Thomas, "BMW, Mercedes Struggle With Lexus in U.S., Hampered by Euro," Bloomberg.com (January 19, 2007), www.bloomberg.com/apps/news?pid=20601170&refer=special_report&sid=aW80HKOCkdew.

16. U.S. Commodity Futures Trading Commission, *CFTC Glossary,* www.cftc.gov/educationcenter/glossary/glossary_h.html.

17. Financial CAD Corporation, "Increasing the Effectiveness of Hedging Interest Rates and Foreign Exchange Rates: A Case Study" (2002), www.comsol.ch/comsol/pub/media/pdf/fincad%20mcdonalds%20new.pdf?PHPSESSID=756548398b06241d145dde710ca3e575756548398b06241d145dde710ca3e575.

18. "The Materials Market Still Packs a Punch," *Appliance Magazine* (January 23, 2007), www.appliancemagazine.com/editorial.php?article=1656&zone=1&first=1.

19. B. Baumohl, *The Secrets of Economic Indicators* (Upper Saddle River, NJ: Wharton School of Publishing, 2005), 18.

20. U.S. Department of Commerce, Bureau of Economic Analysis, www.bea.gov/national/pdf/nipa_primer.pdf.

21. Wade C. Ferguson and Jeffrey A. White, "Negotiating to Prevent Cost Increases," *NAPM InfoEdge* (May 1996), www.ism.ws/pubs/InfoEdge/InfoEdgeArticle.cfm?ItemNumber=10131.

22. "Speaking of … Economic Indicators," *Purchasing Today* (August 2001): 56.

23. Dave Anderton, "Housing Boom May Be Cooling Off in Utah," Deseretnews.com (November 14, 2006), http://deseretnews.com/dn/view/0,1249,650206905,00.html.

24. Indexes for other countries can be found at the U.S. Census Bureau Web site, www.census.gov/main/www/stat_int.html.

25. www.statistics.gov.uk/StatBase/Product.asp?vlnk=790.

26. www.stat.fi/til/index_en.html.

27. www.bls.gov/.

28. www.bls.gov/ppi/.

29. K. Muthukumar and Amit Bhandari, "Infrastructure Companies Look at Cement Imports to Cut Raw Material Costs," *The Economic Times* (June 6, 2006), http://economictimes.indiatimes.com/articleshow/1621524.cms.

30. www.bls.gov/ppi/ppifaq.htm.

31. *Economic Indicators* (Washington, DC: U.S. Superintendent of Documents, November 2006), 1.

32. David J. Lynch, "U.S. Trade Deficit Balloons to $805B," *USA Today* (March 14, 2006), www.usatoday.com/money/economy/trade/2006-03-14-econ-usat_x.htm.

33. Actually there are two accounts: (1) the current account, which includes transactions from commodity exports and imports of goods and services, and (2) unilateral (one-way) transfers, which include foreign-aid grants.

34. "Goal Is to Cut Surplus to Zero by 2010," *World Trade* (December 2006): 20.

35. H.E. Lewis, "Forecasting in the Purchasing and Supply Arena," *NAPM InfoEdge* 3(11) (July 1998).

36. Current monthly reports and more detailed information can be found at www.ism.ws/.

37. Norbert J. Ore, "Assessing Global Economic Performance," *Inside Supply Management* (October 2005): 20.

38. Norbert J. Ore, "The Value of the ROB," *Purchasing Today* (April 1999): 26.

39. R. Avery, K. Brevoort and G. Canner, "The 2006 HMDA Data," (December 21, 2006), www.federalreserve.gov/pubs/bulletin/.

40. Federal Trade Commission, Bureau of Economics, "The Petroleum Industry: Mergers, Structural Change and Antitrust Enforcement" (2004), www.ftc.gov/os/2004/08/040813mergersinpetrolberpt.pdf.

41. USDA, "Cotton: World Markets and Trade," Circular Series FC 04-05 (April 2005).

42. USDA, "Cotton: World Markets and Trade," Circular Series FC-06-05 (June 2005).

43. Http://epp.eurostat.ec.europa.eu/portal/page?_pageid=1090,30070682,1090_33076576&_dad=portal&_schema=PORTAL.

44. Http://comtrade.un.org/.

45. www.un.org/esa/desa/.

46. www.fao.org/waicent/portal/statistics_en.asp.

47. www.oecd.org/.

48. www.imf.org/.

49. www.wachovia.com/small_biz/page/0,,447_5164_5171,00.html.

50. www.forecastinternational.com/.

51. www.metrocouncil.org/metroarea/stats.htm.

52. www.tourismresearch.govt.nz/Analysis/Forecasts+and+Trends/.

53. www2.creighton.edu/business/economicoutlook/regional/mountainstates/surveymethodology/index.php.

54. Http://investor.conagrafoods.com/phoenix.zhtml?c=97518&p=irol-homeprofile; Bill Lapp, "Economic and Commodity Review," *Presentation made to the ISM FoodService Purchasing Manager's Conference,* May 21, 2004, www.ism.ws/files/secure/index.cfm?FileID=3366.

## Chapter 5

1. "Northwest Airlines Adjusts Domestic Capacity Forecast for 2005," *Airline Industry Info* (March 15, 2005), http://findarticles.com/p/articles/mi_m0CWU/is_2005_March_15/ai_n13249215/.

2. Kenneth L. Kraemer, Jason Dedrick and Sandra Yamashiro, "Refining and Extending the Business Model With Information Technology: Dell Corporation." *The Information Society* 16(1) (2000): 5.

3. "Battelle Predicts Ten Most Innovative Products by 2006," 1996 press release, www.battelle.org/forecasts/innovations.stm.

4. An MRP system also may be a module within an enterprise resource planning (ERP) system. More on ERP can be found in Chapter 11.

5. Phil Robinson, "Business Excellence at the Wrigley Company Using BPCS Software" (September 1998), www.bpic.co.uk/cases/wrigley.htm.

6. Emma Clarke, "Fire and Brimstone," *Supply Management* (April 27, 2006): 26–7.

7. Ben Mutzabaugh, "Boom Forces Boeing to Say, 'Sorry, We're Sold Out'," *USA Today* (November 28, 2006), http://blogs.usatoday.com/sky/2006/11/boeing.html.

8. D. Berta, "QSRs Rethink Employment Strategy During Labor Shortage," *Nation's Restaurant News* (August 28, 2006): 1.

9. B. Breen, "Living in Dell Time," FastCompany.com (November 2004): 86, www.fastcompany.com/magazine/88/dell.html.

10. Griffy-Brown, "Just-in-Time to Just-in-Case."

11. Heavy Reading Worldwide Research, "Wireless VoIP and the Future of Carrier Voice Services Executive Summary" (2006), www.heavyreading.com/details.asp?sku_id=1309&skuitem_itemid=972.

12. Caryl Fagot and Debra Winbush, "Hurricane Katrina/Hurricane Rita Evacuation and Production Shut-in Statistics Report as of Wednesday, February 22, 2006." *U.S. Government Minerals Management Service* (February 22, 2006), www.mms.gov/ooc/press/2006/press0222.htm; "Hurricane Katrina Impacts Coffee and Sugar Industries," *Food & Drink Weekly* (September 5, 2005), http://findarticles.com/p/articles/mi_m0EUY/is_32_11/ai_n15403154/.

13. Kimberly Morrison, "Forecast Business Is No Fair Weather Friend," *The Morning News* (November 6, 2007), www.nwaonline.net/articles/2007/11/06/business/110707weather.txt.

14. Business Forecast Systems, "Collaborative Forecasting Running Smoothly at Brooks Sports," *Trends* (March 2006): 5–6.

15. "A Business in Transit," www.sas.com/success/dnata.html.

16. Kathleen Hickey, "Retailers Starting to Get It Right — at the Store Level," *Global Logistics and Supply Chain Strategies* (April 2005), www.supplychainbrain.com/content/headline-news/single-article/article/retailers-starting-to-get-it-rightat-the-store-level/.

17. K.B. Kahn, "Revisiting Top-Down Versus Bottom-Up Forecasting," *Journal of Business Forecasting* 17 (Summer 1998): 14.

18. Hickey, "Retailers Starting to Get It Right."

19. Paul Gelly, "Managing Bottom-Up and Top-Down Approaches: Ocean Spray's Experience," *Journal of Business Forecasting* (Winter 1999/2000): 3–6.

20. Alvin Williams, Larry Giunipero and Tony Henthorne, "The Cross-Functional Imperative: The Case of Marketing and Purchasing," *International Journal of Purchasing and Materials Management* 30 (Summer 1994): 28.

21. Marshall L. Fisher, Janice H. Hammond, Walter R. Obermeyer and Ananth Raman, "Making Supply Meet Demand in an Uncertain World," *Harvard Business Review* (May–June 1994): 83–92.

22. "Vermont Teddy Bear Zooms into New Product Designs," http://info.zoomerang.com/stories/study-vermontTB.htm.

23. Weidong Xu, "Long-Range Planning for Call Centers at FedEx," *The Journal of Business Forecasting* (Winter 1999/2000): 1–4.

24. Dave Blanchard, "Food for Thought," *Logistics Today* (June 2006): 1–2.

25. Mike Snider, "Trend Toward Music DVDs Starts to Amplify," *USA Today* (January 27, 2006), www.usatoday.com/life/music/news/2006-06-26-dvd-chuckberry-main_x.htm.

26. R. Waters, "Pick-Up in Server Market Lifts Fortunes of Tech Companies," *Financial Times* (March 29, 2007): 29.

27. Lee J. Krajewski and Larry P. Ritzman, *Operations Management: Processes and Value Chains*, 7th ed. (Upper Saddle River, NJ: Pearson Education, 2005): 544.

28. K. Krizner, "Report Shows Rise in Emergency Room Visits Puts Pressure on Hospitals," *Managed Healthcare Executive* (September 2006): 40–41.

29. R. Champion, L.D. Kinsman, G.A. Lee, K.A. Masman, E.A. May, T.M. Mills, M.D. Taylor, P.R. Thomas and R.J. Williams, "Forecasting Emergency Department Presentations," *Australian Health Review* (February 2007): 83–90; H. Fang and K.K. Kwong, "Forecasting Foreign Exchange Rates," *The Journal of Business Forecasting* (Winter 1991/1992): 19; Clark Hu, "Advanced Tourism Demand Forecasting: Artificial Neural Network and Box-Jenkins Modeling, a Dissertation" (2004), Purdue University, http://proquest.umi.com.ezproxy1.lib.asu.edu/pqdweb?index=0&srchmode=1&sid=1&vinst=PROD&fmt=6&startpage=-1&vname=PQD&did=764941521&scaling=FULL&pmid=66569&vtype=PQD&rqt=309&TS=1196119303&clientId clientId=25164.

30. George C.S. Wang, "Forecasting Practices in Electric and Gas Utility Companies," *The Journal of Business Forecasting* 25 (Spring 2004): 11–5.

31. Tim Williams, "Forecasting Journey at On Semiconductor," *The Journal of Business Forecasting* 25 (Spring 2006): 29–32.

32. This example was adapted from Roberta J. Duffy, "The Future of Purchasing and Supply: Demand-Pull Possibilities," *Purchasing Today* (January 2000): 48.

33. Ibid.

34. Nandita Ravulur, "Come Out, Come Out Wherever You Are," *Purchasing Today* (February 1999).

35. Institute for Supply Management Satellite Series, *Logistics in Supply Management Program Handbook* (Tempe, AZ: Institute for Supply Management, February 5, 2004): 3–10.

36. Ravulur, "Come Out, Come Out Wherever You Are," 53.

37. "European CPFR Insights" (2002), Accenture and ECR Europe, www.ecrnet.org/ 04-publications/blue_books/pub_2002_cpfr_european_insights.pdf.

38. KJR Consulting, *CPFR Baseline Study, Manufacturer Profile* (Washington, DC: Grocery Manufacturers of America, 2002): 5, www.gmabrands.com/industryaffairs/docs/cpfr.pdf.

39. Robin Giebner and Carole A. Baggerly, "Revolutionizing E-Procurement: Honeywell Decreases Lead Time, Implements Multi-Tier Supplier Collaboration," *Presentation at the 86th Annual ISM Conference,* 2001.

40. D. Hofman and L. Cecere, "Consumer Products: Insights on Benchmark Costs and Results," *AMR Report* (2006), www.amrresearch.com/Content/Search_Results.asp?No=100&N= 4294967174.

41. Galen Gruman, "Supply on Demand — Manufacturers Need to Know What's Selling Before They Can Produce and Deliver Their Wares in the Right Quantities," *InfoWorld* (April 18, 2005): 9.

42. J.K. Winn and C. Kunz, "Can Lawyers Add Value to the Value Chain?" *Proceedings of the 92nd Annual International Supply Management Conference,* May 2007, 5, www.ism.ws/files/Pubs/ Proceedings/BMWinnKunz.pdf.

## Chapter 6

1. K. Lysons, *Purchasing and Supply Chain Management,* 5th ed. (London: FT Prentice Hall, 2000).

2. T. Hines, *Supply Chain Strategies, Customer-Driven and Customer-Focused* (London: Butterworth-Heinemann, 2003).

3. R.H. Ballou, *Business Logistics/Supply Chain Management,* 5th ed. (Upper Saddle River, NJ: Pearson Education, 2004).

4. J. Nagel, ed., *Supply Chain Management: A Procurement* (Melbourne: Hargreen Publishing, 2003).

5. V. Govindarajan, "Tuck School of Business at Dartmouth, Case Study: Wal-Mart Stores, Inc." (2002), http://mba.tuck.dartmouth.edu/pdf/2002-2-0103.pdf.

6. L.M. Ellram and T.Y. Choi, *Supply Management for Value Enhancement* (Tempe, AZ: National Association of Purchasing Management, 2000).

7. T.A. Foster, "Developers of DCs Have Become Key Strategic Partners," *Global Logistics and Supply Chain Strategies* (June 2004), www.supplychainbrain.com/.

8. F.A. Kuglin, *Customer-Centered Supply Chain Management* (AMACOM, 1998).

9. T.A. Foster, "Logistics Inside China: The Next Big Supply Chain Challenge," *Global Logistics and Supply Chain Strategies* (September 2005), www.supplychainbrain.com/content/ headline-news/single-article/article/logistics-inside-china-the-next-big-supply-chain-challenge/.

10. K. Babich and C. Pettijohn, *Sourcing in the Public Sector* (Herndon, VA: National Institute of Governmental Purchasing, 2004).

11. Http://plannet.difu.de/2001/reports/pdf/germany.pdf.

12. N. Bauhof, "Logistics Distribution and Warehousing 2006: Network Optimization," *Area Development Online* (2006), www.areadevelopment.com/specialPub/aug06/supplyChainOptimization.shtm.

13. Hines, *Supply Chain Strategies, Customer-Driven and Customer-Focused*.

14. D. Hale and A. Van Bodegraven, "Planning DCs for an Unknown Future," The Progress Group, www.theprogressgroup.com/publications/wp16_planningdcs.html.

15. Hines, *Supply Chain Strategies, Customer-Driven and Customer-Focused*.

16. www.wcpc.com/page.cfm?page_id=258&site=1&section=7&subsection=79&find_me=&start=0.

17. L. Kempfer, "European Retailer Expands DC, Adds AS/RS," *Materials Handling Management* (March 2005): 30–31.

18. T. Keyan, "Improving Warehouse Picking Operations: Voice Recognition Systems Offer Advantages That Scanning Technology Can't Touch," *Frontline Solutions* (2004), http://findarticles.com/p/articles/mi_m0DIS/is_5_5/ai_n6121010.

19. K. Blanchard, *Supply Chain Management Best Practices* (Hoboken, NJ: John Wiley & Sons, 2007).

20. R. Schonberger, "Supply Chains: Tightening the Links," *Manufacturing Engineering* 137(3) (September 2006), www.sme.org/cgi-bin/find-articles.pl?&ME06ART61&ME&20060917&&SME&.

21. www.researchbuy.com/marketwikis/Perishable_Food_Storage_Market_Research.

22. L. Stanley and D. Matthews, *Logistics and Transportation* (Herndon, VA: National Institute of Governmental Purchasing, 2007).

23. Epic Data, Inc., "UID Dictionary," www.epicdata.com/uid/uid-dictionary.php.

24. www.acq.osd.mil/dpap/UID/.

25. G. Gianakis and D. Matthews, *Warehousing and Inventory Control* (Herndon, VA: National Institute of Governmental Purchasing, 2008).

26. J. Yuva, *Inside Supply Management* (Tempe, AZ: Institute for Supply Management, 2006).

27. J. Brady, "Trends in Transportation and Their Impact on Supply Management," *Inside Supply Management* (February 2006): 31.

28. J. Krusinko, "Delivering the Goods: The Rise of High Velocity Distribution Centers," *Professional Report* (Winter), www.siordata.com/publications/Krusinski%20-%20winter%2005.pdf.

29. www.motek.com/product/index.html.

30. N. Ayub, "Case Study: New Age and Beyond Warehouse Management System," (August 10, 2007), http://blogs.ittoolbox.com/supplychain/wms/archives/case-study-new-age-beyond-warehouse-management-system-wms-18446/.

31. C. Trunk, "High-Flying Productivity, Material Handling in America's Best Plants" (March), www.mhmonline.com/nID/2921/MHM/viewStory.asp.

32. www.gse.hardvard.edu and www.fpm.iastate.edu.

33. Blanchard, *Supply Chain Management Best Practices*.

34. H. Richardson, "Virtually Connected, Transportation and Distribution" (March), http://findarticles.com/p/articles/mi_hb3566/is_200003/ai_n8386603.

35. M. Christopher, *Logistics and Supply Chain Management* (Upper Saddle River, NJ: FT Press, 2005).

36. C. Perkins, "Robert's Foods Links Up With Virtual Warehouse," *Nation's Restaurant News* (May 24), http://findarticles.com/p/articles/mi_m3190/is_21_38/ai_n6051877.

## Chapter 7

1. "CSMP's State of Logistics Report," Council of Supply Chain Management, http://cscmp .org/Resources/SOL.asp.

2. P. Cuviello, "Adapting Logistics Capabilities to National Security Requirements," 21st Annual National Logistics Conference, National Defense Industrial Association (NDIA), March 2005, www.dtic.mil/ndia/2005logistics/tuesday/cuviello.pdf.

3. S. Tzu and G. Gagliardi, *The Art of War: In Sun Tzu's Own Words* (Seattle, WA: Clearbridge Publishing, 1999).

4. Hines, *Supply Chain Strategies, Customer-Driven and Customer-Focused.*

5. A.J. Van Weele, *Purchasing & Supply Chain Management,* 4th ed. (London: Thomson Learning, 2005)

6. J. Cavinato, *An Analysis of the Expansion of the Purchasing Field Into New Value-Added Roles in Organizations* (Tempe, AZ: Institute for Supply Management, 2001).

7. www.bts.gov/publications/national_transportation_statistics/2006/html/table_truck_profile .html.

8. www.aar.org/AboutTheIndustry/AboutTheIndustry.asp.

9. Bureau of Transportation Statistics (2006), www.bts.gov/publications/national_transportation _statistics/2006/html/table_rail_profile.html.

10. U.S. Maritime Administration, Office of Data and Economic Analysis (2006), www.marad.dot .gov/MARAD_statistics/2007%20STATISTICS/USWTSR%20bOOKLET.pdf.

11. D. Hannon, "Air Cargo to Triple Globally by 2025," *Purchasing* (March), http://findarticles .com/p/articles/mi_hb3381/is_200703/ai_n18889108.

12. Stanley and Matthews, *Logistics and Transportation.*

13. www.gasandoil.com/gpm/samples/welcome.html.

14. U.S. Department of Transportation, Bureau of Transportation Statistics, "Pipeline Transportation Establishments and Employment: 2004," (September 26, 2006), www.bts.gov/ publications/state_transportation_statistics/state_transportation_statistics_2006/html/table_ 06_06.html.

15. T. Foster, "A Dutch Solution to the Distribution Challenge in the E.U.," *Global Logistics & Supply Chain Strategies* (July 23, 2007), www.supplychainbrain.com/content/headline-news/ single-article/article/a-dutch-solution-to-the-distribution-challenge-in-the-eu-2/.

16. E.G. Hinkelman, *Dictionary of International Trade,* 6th ed. (Novato, CA: World Trade Press, 2005).

17. "What Is 4PL?," (August 4, 2003), www.supplychain.ittoolbox. com/documents/popular-q-and-a/what-is-4pl-2083#.

18. Hines, *Supply Chain Strategies, Customer-Driven and Customer-Focused.*

19. M. Leenders, H. Fearon, A. Flynn and P. Johnson, *Purchasing and Supply Management,* 12th ed. (Boston, MA: McGraw-Hill Irwin, 2002).

20. R. Lewicki, D. Saunders, J. Minon and B. Barry, *Negotiation,* 4th ed. (New York: McGraw-Hill Irwin, 2003).

21. WTO World Trade Report 2007, www.wto.org/english/res_e/booksp_e/anrep_e/wtr07-1a_e.pdf.

22. R. Duffy, "Global Sourcing on the Rise," *Inside Supply Management* (September 2006).

23. www.wto.org/english/thewto_e/whatis_e/whatis_e.htm.

24. P. Lagasse (ed.), *The Columbia Encyclopedia,* 6th ed. (New York: Columbia University Press, 2007), www.bartelby.com/65/eu/EuropnUn.html.

25. WTO World Trade Report 2007.

26. Lloyd's Register Fairplay, "Shipping Facts" (January 2005), www.oceanatlas.com/unatlas/uses/transportation_telecomm/maritime_trans/shipping_world_trade/shipping_facts_and_figures.htm#05.

27. Hinkelman, *Dictionary of International Trade.*

28. Hines, *Supply Chain Strategies, Customer-Driven and Customer-Focused.*

29. Hinkelman, *Dictionary of International Trade.*

30. P. Lopata, "Insight Into Incoterms," *Inside Supply Management* 17 (2) (February).

31. Http://en.wikipedia.org/wiki/Semi-trailer_truck/.

32. www.assembly.nl.ca/legislation/sr/statutes/d01.htm.

33. Hong Kong Trade Development Council, "Regulations Governing International Road Transportation" (2005), www.tdctrade.com/report/reg/reg_050903.htm?w_sid=194&w_pid=703&w_nid=&w_cid=&w_idt=1900-01-01&w_oid=180&w_jid=.

34. R. Bohman, "Take Advantage of LTL Weight Breaks," *Logistics Management* (August 1, 2006), www.logisticsmgmt.com/article/CA6360554.

35. "ARAMARK Chooses Intergis Solution to Automate Routing, Scheduling and Dispatching Functions," www.intergis.com/news_aramark.html.

36. M. Leenders and A. Flynn, *Value-Driven Purchasing: Managing the Key Steps in the Acquisition Process* (New York: McGraw-Hill, 1995).

37. www.access.gpo.gov/nara/cfr/waisidx_07/49cfrv5_07.html#301.

38. G. Hutchins, *Supply Chain Strategies for Total Quality* (Homewood, IL: Business One Irwin, 1992).

39. Ballou, *Business Logistics/Supply Chain Management.*

40. Christopher, *Logistics and Supply Chain Management.*

41. Blanchard, *Supply Chain Management Best Practices.*

42. Hines, *Supply Chain Strategies, Customer-Driven and Customer-Focused.*

43. Van Weele, *Purchasing & Supply Chain Management.*

44. Ballou, *Business Logistics/Supply Chain Management.*

45. Ibid.

46. Ibid.

## Chapter 8

1. W. Brady, *Managing Fixed Assets in the Public Sector: Managing for Service Excellence* (Boca Raton, FL: Universal Publishers, 2001).

2. Christopher, *Logistics and Supply Chain Management.*

3. L. Ellram, *Strategic Cost Management in the Supply Chain: A Purchasing and Supply Management Perspective* (Tempe, AZ: CAPS Research, 2002), www.capsresearch.org/publications/pdfs-public/ellram2002es.pdf.

4. Brady, *Managing Fixed Assets in the Public Sector.*

5. *Case Study: ANZ Bank*, www.hardcat.co.uk/casestudyanz.html.

6. Rudski, et al., *Straight to the Bottom Line: An Executive's Roadmap to World Class Supply Management* (Fort Lauderdale, FL: J. Ross Publishing, 2006).

7. Ibid.

8. C. Atkinson, "More on Wal-Mart, Bullship and Vinson," (May 19, 2006), www.inventorymanagementreview.org/2006/05/index.html.

9. P. Carter, et al., *Succeeding in a Dynamic World: Supply Management in the Decade Ahead* (CAPS Research, Institute for Supply Management and A.T. Kearney, 2007).

10. J. Cavinato, A. Flynn and R. Kauffman, *Supply Management Handbook,* 7th ed. (Tempe, AZ: Institute for Supply Management, 2006).

11. U.S. General Accounting Office, *Defense Inventory: Several Actions Are Needed to Further DLA's Efforts to Mitigate Shortages of Critical Parts,* Report to the Chairman, Subcommittee on Defense, Committee on Appropriations, House of Representatives (2003), www.gao.gov/new.items/d03709.pdf.

12. Arizona State University, "Inventory Policy, FIN 402: Inventory" (March 1, 2005), www.asu.edu/aad/manuals/fin/fin402.html.

13. Brightpoint, Inc., "Vodafone Australia Case Study," www.brightpoint.com/Brightpoint/Global/26/English/73/Vodafone/12030.html.

14. T. Hurlbut, "Cycle Counting," Inc.com (June 2005), www.inc.com/resources/retail/articles/200506/counting.html.

15. i2 Technologies, Inc., *Improving Service and Market Share With i2 Inventory Optimization,* October White Paper (2005), Dallas, Texas, www.i2.com/assets/pdf/WPR_inventory_optimization_WPR7178.pdf.

16. L. Buddress, "Getting the Most From Your Indirect Purchasing Dollar," *Proceedings From the 2006 ISM Annual Conference* (Tempe: Institute for Supply Management, 2006)

17. D. Zamsky, *Inventory in Motion: a Direct Alternative to Global Fulfillment,* UPS Supply Chain Solutions White Paper (2005), www.sups-scs.com/solutions/white_papers/wp_inventory_in_motion.pdf.

18. D. Kieso, J. Weygandt and T. Warfield, *Fundamentals of Intermediate Accounting* (Hoboken: John Wiley & Sons, Inc., 2005), www.wiley.com/college/sc/kiesofund/samp/chpater8.pdf.

19. Hines, *Supply Chain Strategies, Customer-Driven and Customer-Focused.*

20. Boeing, "Catalyst International Milwaukee," www.catalystinternational.com/content/why_catalyst/case_studies/boeing.asp.

21. Christopher, *Logistics and Supply Chain Management.*

22. Ballou, *Business Logistics/Supply Chain Management.*

23. Hines, *Supply Chain Strategies, Customer-Driven and Customer-Focused.*

24. V.A. Micheau, "How Boeing and Alcoa Implemented a Successful Vendor Managed Inventory Program," *Journal of Business Forecasting* 24(1) (Spring 2005): 17–9.

25. Rudski, et al., *Straight to the Bottom Line.*

26. Brady, *Managing Fixed Assets in the Public Sector.*

27. J.R. Stock, "Reverse Logistics in the Supply Chain," *Global Purchasing and Supply Chain Strategies* (Boston: World Market Research Centres, 2001).

28. www.usps.com/parcelreturnservices/features.htm.

29. www.hp.com/hpinfo/globalcitizenship/environment/recycle/index.html?hpr_R1002_USEN.

30. Ezinarticles.com/?Metal-Recycling-Resultsin-in-Big-Benefits&id=812958.

31. Gianakis and Matthews, *Warehousing and Inventory Control.*

32. www.interfacesustainability.com/comp.html.

33. Brigham Young University, Purchasing Department, *Surplus Sales Information,* www.surplus .byu.

34. J. Womack and D. Jones, *Lean Thinking* (New York: Free Press, 2003).

35. T. Manos, "Value Stream Mapping: An Introduction," *Quality Progress* 39(6) (June 2006): 64–9.

## Chapter 9

1. T. Stundza, "Assured Quality Critical in Global Sourcing," *Purchasing* 136(11) (August 16, 2007).

2. Blanchard, *Supply Chain Management Best Practices.*

3. G. Hutchins, *Supply Management Strategies, Quality Plus Engineering* (Portland, OR: Working It, 2002).

4. Carter, et al., *Succeeding in a Dynamic World.*

5. R.W. Linton, "Specifications of Procured Goods," *Supply Chain Management* (Melbourne: Hargreen Publishing, 2003).

6. Six Sigma is the abbreviated form of six standard deviations from the mean and mathematically translates to about two defects per billion, which, strictly speaking, would be a pure Six Sigma process. Because no organization is nearly perfect enough to achieve such level of quality, the term *Six Sigma* has taken on the equivalent defect rate of 3.4 part per million, which takes into account + or – standard deviations of a specified average (www.siliconfareast .com).

7. Blanchard, *Supply Chain Management Best Practices.*

8. D. Shand, "Six Sigma," *Computerworld* (March 5, 2001): 38.

9. L. Ellram and W. Tate, "Bank of America: Services Purchasing and Outsourcing," *PRACTIX,* CAPS Research 9 (May 2006).

10. R. Aguayo, *The American Who Taught the Japanese About Quality* (New York: Simon & Schuster, 1991).

11. Babich and Pettijohn, *Sourcing in the Public Sector.*

12. Ibid.

13. Ibid.

14. Ibid.

15. ASTM International, "ASTM E2500-07, Standard Guide for Specification, Design, and Verification of Pharmaceutical and Biopharmaceutical Manufacturing Systems and Equipment," www.astm.org/cgi-bin/SoftCart.exe/DATABASE.CART/REDLINE_PAGES/E2500 .htm?E+mystore

16. Ellram and Choi, *Supply Management for Value Enhancement.*

17. R.D. Nelson, "John Deere Optimizes Operations With Supply Management Efforts," *Journal of Organizational Excellence* 21(2) (February 2002).

18. http://multimedia.3m.com/mws/mediawebserver?66666UuZjcFSLXTtmxfcnXfEEVuQEcu ZgVs6EVs6E666666--

19. www.iso.org/iso/about.htm.

20. "Latest Issue of the ISO Survey Shows 16% Rise in ISO 9001 and ISO 14001," International Organization for Standardization Press Release (November 23, 2007), The ISO Survey of Certifications 2006, www.iso.org/iso/pressrelease.htm?refid=Ref1089.

21. The ISO Survey of Certifications 2006.

22. Hines, *Supply Chain Strategies, Customer-Driven and Customer-Focused.*

23. W.E. Deming, *Out of Crisis* (Cambridge, MA: Massachusetts Institute of Technology Center for Advanced Engineering, 1986).

24. K. Ishikawa (D.J. Lu, trans.), *What Is Total Quality Control* (Englewood, CA: Prentice Hall, 1985).

25. www.juran.com/who_sub_our_founder.asp.

26. G. Hutchins, *Purchasing Strategies for Total Quality* (Homewood, IL: Business One Irwin, 1993).

27. N. Tague, *The Quality Toolbox,* 2nd ed. (Milwaukee, WI: ASQ Quality Press, 2004).

28. Motorola, Inc., "A Case Study: Statistical Process Control," www.mpcps.com/ACaseStudy.pdf.

29. www.remedy.com/solutions/documents/success-stories/BMC_SS_ADP.pdf.

30. Kathryn M. Dodson, Hubert F. Hofman, Gowri S. Ramani and Deborah K. Yedlin, "Adapting CMMI for Acquisition Organizations: A Preliminary Report," *Special Report CMU/SEI-2006-SR-005* (Pittsburgh PA: Carnegie Mellon and Software Engineering Institute, 2006).

31. G.A. Garrett and R.G. Rendon, *Contract Management: Organizational Assessment Tools* (Asburn, VA: National Contract Management Association, 2005).

32. Ibid.

33. Kuglin, *Customer-Centered Supply Chain Management.*

34. A.K. Reese, "An Interview With Manufacturing's Number One Purchasing Professional," *Fabricating and Metalworking* (April 9, 2001), www.fandmmag.com/web/online/Metal-Forming-and-Fabricating/An-Interview-with-Manufacturings-Number-One-Purchasing-Professional/2$267.

35. Ellram, *Strategic Cost Management in the Supply Chain.*

36. T. Kivisto and V. Vivolainen, *Benchmarking Municipal Public Procurement Activities in Finland, Challenges in Public Procurement: An International Perspective* (Boca Raton, FL: PrAcademics Press, 2005).

37. J. Blakeman, *Benchmarking: Definitions and Overview* (Milwaukee, WI: Center for Urban Transportation Studies, University of Wisconsin-Milwaukee, June 2002), www.uwm.edu/Dept/CUTS/bench/bm-desc.htm.

38. Hines, *Supply Chain Strategies, Customer-Driven and Customer-Focused.*

39. P. Schosleben and R. Hieber, "ETF Zurich: Performance Management in Partner Networks," www.supply-chain.org/galleries/default-file/ETH%Zurich%20-%20Academic.pdf.

40. L. Kaufman, "Measuring the Performance of Truly Strategic Supplier Relationships," *PRACTIX,* CAPS Research 7 (March 2004).

41. Blanchard, *Supply Chain Management Best Practices.*

42. Hines, *Supply Chain Strategies: Customer-Driven and Customer-Focused.*

43. Hutchins, *Supply Management Strategies.*

44. www.quality.nist.gov/Contacts_Profiles.htm.

45. www.bea.gov/newsreleases/regional/gdpstat/gsp_newsletter.htm.

46. Institute for Supply Management, "2007 Semiannual Economic Forecast," www.ism.ws/about/MediaRoom/NewsReleaseDetail.cfm?ItemNumber=17369.

47. L. Marin and J. Miller, *Contracting for Public Sector Services* (Herndon, VA: National Institute of Governmental Purchasing, 2006).

48. Hutchins, *Supply Management Strategies.*

49. Van Weele, *Purchasing & Supply Chain Management.*

50. N. Karten, "Key Steps in Establishing a Service Level Agreement" (2003), www.nkarten.com/slaservices.html.

51. Intuit, Inc., *2007 Annual Report,* http-download.intuit.com/http.intuit/CMO/intuit/investors/annual_reports/Intuit_2007_Annual_Report.pdf.

52. Ellram and Tate, "Bank of America."

53. H.Y. Al-Shamsi, M.A. Khan and M. Al-Bachari, "Daimler Chrysler Case Study, Fighting the Counterfeit Spare Parts Market," www.dubai-ethics.ae/derc/PDF/DaimlerChryslerReportCaseStudy.pdf.

## Chapter 10

1. N. Kingsbury, *Performance Measurement and Evaluation, Definitions and Relationships* (Washington, DC: U.S. Government Accountability Office, 2005), www.gao.gov/news.items/d05739sp.pdf.

2. C. Stoffle and S. Phipps, "Creating a Culture of Assessment: The University of Arizona Experience," *ARL Bimonthly Report* 230.321 (October/November 2003): 26–7.

3. M. Varmazis, "How HP Measures Supplier Performance and Compliance," *Purchasing* (September 21, 2006), www.purchasing.com/article/CA6372376.html.

4. Hines, *Supply Chain Strategies, Customer-Driven and Customer Focused.*

5. A. Gore, *Serving the American Public: Best Practices in Performance Measurement,* National Performance Review Benchmarking Study Report (June 1997).

6. Ibid.

7. W. Trevett, "Measure Performance and Set Targets," Business Link, Cranfield University School of Management (2007), www.businesslink.gov.uk/bdotg/action/detail?type=reousrces&itemid=1079681286.

8. K. Schwartz, "ABC: An Introduction to Balanced Scorecard," *CIO* (July 13, 2007), www.co.com/article/123750/ABC_Intro_To _ Balanced_Scorecard/.

9. U.S. Department of Energy, "The Balanced Scorecard Program," http://management.energy.gov/about_us/726.htm.

10. National Semiconductor, "Quality Network, Eight Disciplines Problem-Solving Process," 2006, www.national.com/quality/8d.html.

11. T. Minahan and M. Vigoros, "The Supplier Performance Measurement Benchmarking Report: Measuring Supply Chain Success" (December 2002), Aberdeen Group, Inc., www.aberdeen.com/summary/report/other/iSource_SPM.asp.

12. E. Kay, "Ways to Measure Supplier Performance," *Purchasing Magazine OnLine* (February 3, 2005), www.purchasing.com/.

13. Minahan and Vigoros, "The Supplier Performance Measurement Benchmarking Report."

14. C. Freeland and A. Ward, "FedEx Founder Credits Supply Chain Flexibility," *Financial Times*, (November 17, 2006).

15. Hutchins, *Supply Management Strategies.*

16. D. Hannon, "Technology Firm Minimizes Supplier Risk in Global Sourcing," *Purchasing* (February 15, 2007), www.purchasing.com/article/.

17. S. Avery, "Transforming Textron," *Purchasing* (October 10, 2002), www.purchasing.com/article/CA250886.

18. Hutchins, *Supply Management Strategies.*

19. Rudski, et al., *Straight to the Bottom Line.*

20. B.J. Back, "Nike Wants Its Suppliers to Reflect Ethnic Diversity," *Portland Business Journal* (March 25, 2002), http://portland.bizjournals.com/Portland/stories/2002/03/25/focus3.html.

21. Rudski, et al., *Straight to the Bottom Line.*

22. www.portofportland.com/SROS_Home.aspx.

23. https://cvmas02.cvmsolutions.com/hilton554/

24. www.hp.com/hpinfo/globalcitizenship/environment/productdesign/index.html.

25. www.iso.ch/iso/iso_catalogue_ics.htm.

26. www.cexpgroup.com/eng/about_us/corporate_responsibilities/our_position.aspx.

27. M. Beasley, J. Carcello and D. Hermanson, "Top 10 Audit Deficiencies, Lessons From Fraud-Related SEC Cases," *Journal of Accountancy* (April 2001), www.aiepa.org/pubs/jofa/apr2001/beasley.htm.

28. R. Engel, "Sarbanes-Oxley Impact on Supply Chain Management," *Proceedings of the 2006 Annual Conference of the Institute for Supply Management* (Tempe, AZ: Institute for Supply Management, 2006).

29. N. Shister, "Logistics Outsourcing Meets Sarbanes-Oxley," *World Trade* 18(10) (October 2005).

30. www.european_sarbanes_oxley.com.

31. D. Javitch, "Establishing an Employee Review System," *Entrepreneur* (April 5, 2007), www.entrepreneur.com/humanresources/employeemanagementcolumnistjavitch/article70172.html.

32. N. Nelson, "Valuing Employees," *HR Magazine* 51(2) (February 2006).

33. Metro Human Resources, *Hiring and Retaining Top Performers* (Portland, OR: METRO, 2005).

34. G. Migliore, "Toyota Creates Roundtables to Gain Supplier Feedback," *Automotive News* (September 5, 2005), www.highbeam.com/doc/161-135935915.html.

35. D. Fields, A. Chan, S. Akhtar and T. Blum, "Human Resource Management Strategies Under Uncertainty," *Cross-Cultural Management* 13(2) (2006): 171–86.

36. "Succeeding in a Dynamic World," *Inside Supply Management* 18(5) (May 2007).

37. Ibid.

## Chapter 11

1. R. Andreu and S. Sieber, "Knowledge Integration Across Organizations," *Knowledge and Process Management* 12(3) (2005): 153–60.

2. G. Hamel, "Management Innovation," *Leadership Excellence* (January 2007): 5.

3. *American Heritage Dictionary,* 4th ed. (Boston: Houghton Mifflin Company, 2006).

4. T. Frost and C. Zhou, "R&D Co-Practice and Reverse Knowledge Integration in Multinational Firms," *Journal of International Business Studies* 36(6) (November 2005): 676–87.

5. Ibid.

6. Microsoft Corporaton, "Customer Solutions Case Study," Illinois Department of Central Management Services (2003), www.microsoft.com/windowserver/compare/casestudydetails.mspx?recid=57.

7. L. Giunipero and R. Handfield, "Purchasing Education and Training II," CAPS Research, www.capsresearch.org/publications/pdfs-public/giunipero2004es.pdf.

8. C. Poirier, *Calibrating Supply Chain Management* (Waltham, MA: Computer Sciences Corporation, CSC, 2003), http://www.csc.com/features/2003/106.shtml.

9. M. Christopher, *Logistics and Supply Chain Management*.

10. Virginia's Community Colleges, VCCS Procedures for Initiation of Technology Projects, January 12, 2005, http://system.vccs.edu/its/procedures/procdocs/Procedure-Initiation_of_Technology_Projects.doc.

11. Christopher, *Logistics and Supply Chain Management*.

12. R. Seethamraju "Utilizing Enterprise Resource Planning in the Supply Chain," in *Supply Chain Management: A Procurement Perspective,* (P. Nagel, ed.) (Melbourne: Hargreen Publishing, 2003).

13. J. Maguire, "The Future of ERP," *IT Management* (November 15, 2006), http://itmanagement.earthweb.com/erp/article.php/3643966.

14. "Oracle Customer Study," *New Zealand Post* (2005), www.oracle.com/customers/snapshots/new_zealand_post_03_0505.pdf.

15. D. Cook, "Separate but Equal: Warehouse and Labor Management Systems," *Multi-Channel Merchant* (September 13, 2006), www.multichannel.com/opsandfulfillment/advisor/warehouse_labor/index.html.

16. Blanchard, *Supply Chain Management Best Practices.*

17. S. Patton, "CRM: Are Companies Buying It?" *CIO,* CIO Research Reports (January 7, 2002), www.cio.com/article/31031/Get_the_CRM_You_Need_at_the_Price_You_Want.

18. www.sap.com/solutions/business_suite/srm/index.epx.

19. T. Purdum, "Managing Maverick Spend," *Industry Week* 255(12) (December 1, 2006).

20. C. Koch, "ABC: An Introduction to ERP," *CIO* (2007), www.cio.com/article/40323/.

21. K. Parker, "The Paradoxes of ERP-Based Productivity," *Manufacturing Business Technology* (September 1, 2006), www.mbtmag.com/article/CA6369603.html.

22. C. Moller, "ERP II: A Conceptual Framework for Next-generation Enterprise Systems?" *Journal of Enterprise Information Management* 18(4) (2005): 483–97.

23. Editorial Staff, "John Crane Gets Visibility Into Order Life Cycle," *Supply & Demand Chain* (February 15, 2005), www.sdcexec.com/online/article.jsp?id=6517.

24. D. Volden, "John Crane Today News," (January 10, 2007), www.johncranetoday.com/.

25. www.amazon.com/.

26. www.oregon.gov/das/ssd/spo/index.shtml.

27. www.wohldorf.com/.

28. "Cat Logisitcs, Case Studies, Enabling Growth in Europe for Hyundai," http://logistics.cat.com/cda/components/fullArticle?m=119073&x=7&id=377557.

29. V. Vuksic and M. Spremic, "ERP System Implementation and Business Process Change: Case Study of a Pharmaceutical Company," *Journal of Computing and Information Technology* 13(1) (2005): 11–24.

30. Carter, *Succeeding in a Dynamic World.*

31. D. Panek, "CRM and ERP Becoming Mainstream for U.S. Medium Businesses," *CRM Manager Magazine* (February 26, 2007), www.crmmanager.net/magazine/news.

32. C. Dominick, "Spend Management Technology Trends" (June 28, 2005), www .nextlevelpurchasing.com.

# References

## Chapter 1

DeFeo, J.A. and W.W. Barnard. *Juran Institute's Six Sigma: Breakthrough and Beyond,* McGraw-Hill, New York, 2004.

Flynn, A., M.L. Harding, C.S. Lallatin, H.M. Pohlig and S.R. Sturzl, (Eds.). *ISM Glossary of Key Supply Management Terms,* 4th ed., Institute for Supply Management, Tempe, AZ, 2006.

Leenders, M.R., H.E. Fearon, A.E. Flynn and P.F. Johnson. *Purchasing and Supply Management,* 12th ed., McGraw-Hill, New York, 2002.

Monczka, R., R. Trent and R. Handfield. *Purchasing and Supply Chain Management,* 2nd ed., South-Western, Mason, OH, 2002.

Womack, J.P. and D.T. Jones. *Lean Thinking,* The Free Press, New York, 2003.

## Chapter 2

Flynn, A., M.L. Harding, C.S. Lallatin, H.M. Pohlig and S.R. Sturzl, (Eds.). *ISM Glossary of Key Supply Management Terms,* 4th ed., Institute for Supply Management, Tempe, AZ, 2006.

*A Guide to the Project Management Body of Knowledge (PMBOK® Guide),* 3rd ed., Project Management Institute, Newtown Square, PA, 2004.

Kepner, C.H. and B.B. Tregoe. *The New Rational Manager,* Princeton Research Press, Princeton, NJ, 1981.

Lewis, J.P. *Project Planning, Scheduling and Control,* McGraw-Hill, New York, 1995.

Mantel, Jr., S.J., J.R. Meredith, S.M. Shafer and M.M. Sutton. *Project Management in Practice,* John Wiley & Sons, New York, 2001.

Pennypacker, J.S., (Ed.). *Principles of Project Management,* Project Management Institute, Newtown Square, PA, 1997.

Verma, V.K. *Organizing Projects for Success,* Project Management Institute, Newtown Square, PA, 1995.

Westland, J. *Project Management Life Cycle,* Kogan Page, London, 2006.

## Chapter 3

Dimancescu, D. and K. Dwenger. *World-Class New Product Development,* AMACOM, New York, 1996.

Flynn, A., M.L. Harding, C.S. Lallatin, H.M. Pohlig and S.R. Sturzl, (Eds.). *ISM Glossary of Key Supply Management Terms,* 4th ed., Institute for Supply Management, Tempe, AZ, 2006.

Krajewski, L.J. and L.R. Ritzman. *Operations Management: Straegy and Analysis,* Prentice Hall, Upper Saddle River, NJ, 2001.

Leenders, M., P.F. Johnson, E. Flynn and H.E. Fearon. *Purchasing and Supply Management,* 13th ed., McGraw-Hill, New York, 2005.

Porter, M. *Competitive Strategy,* The Free Press, New York, 1980.

Wheelwright, S. and K. Clark.*Leading Product Development: The Senior Manager's Guide to Creating and Shaping the Enterprise,* The Free Press, New York, 1994.

## Chapter 4

Baumohl, B. *The Secrets of Economic Indicators,* Wharton School Publishing, Upper Saddle River, NY, 2005.

Flynn, A., M.L. Harding, C.S. Lallatin, H.M. Pohlig and S.R. Sturzl, (Eds.). *ISM Glossary of Key Supply Management Terms,* 4th ed., Institute for Supply Management, Tempe, AZ, 2006.

Leenders, M.R., H.E. Fearon, A.E. Flynn and P.F. Johnson. *Purchasing and Supply Management,* 12th ed., McGraw-Hill, New York, 2002.

## Chapter 5

Chase, R.B., F.R. Jacobs and N.J. Aquilano. *Operations Management for Competitive Advantage,* 10th ed., McGraw Hill-Irwin, Boston, MA, 2004.

Flynn, A., M.L. Harding, C.S. Lallatin, H.M. Pohlig and S.R. Sturzl, (Eds.). *ISM Glossary of Key Supply Management Terms,* 4th ed., Institute for Supply Management, Tempe, AZ, 2006.

Heizer, J. and B. Render. *Principles of Operations Management,* 6th ed., Prentice Hall, Upper Saddle River, NJ, 2006.

Krajewski, L.J. and L.P. Ritzman. *Operations Management: Processes and Value Chains,* 7th ed., Pearson Education, Upper Saddle River, NY, 2005.

Makridakis, S.G., S.C. Wheelwright and R.J. Hyndman. *Forecasting: Methods & Applications,* 3rd ed., John Wiley & Sons, New York, NY, 1997.

Wilson, J.H. and B. Keating. *Business Forecasting,* 5th ed., Irwin/McGraw-Hill, Burr Ridge, IL, 2007.

## Chapter 6

Ballou, R.H. *Business Logistics/Supply Chain Management,* 5th ed., Pearson Education, Upper Saddle River, NJ, 2004.

Bauhof, N. "Logistics Distribution and Warehousing 2006: Network Optimization." *Area Development Online,* August/September, www.areadevelopment.com/specialPub/aug06/supplyChainOptimization.shtm.

Blanchard, K. *Supply Chain Management Best Practices,* John Wiley & Sons, Hoboken, NJ, 2007.

Christopher, M. *Logistics and Supply Chain Management: Creating Value-Adding Networks,* 3rd ed., FT Press, Upper Saddle River, NJ, 2005.

Ellram, L.M., and T.Y. Choi. *Supply Management for Value Enhancement,* National Association of Purchasing Management, Tempe, AZ, 2000.

Flynn, A., M.L. Harding, C.S. Lallatin, H.M. Pohlig and S.R. Sturzl, (Eds.). *ISM Glossary of Key Supply Management Terms,* 4th ed., Institute for Supply Management, Tempe, AZ, 2006.

Foster, T.A. "Logistics Inside China: The Next Big Supply Chain Challenge," *Global Logistics and Supply Chain Strategies,* September, 2005, www.supplychainbrain.com/.

Foster, T.A. "Developers of DCs Have Become Key Strategic Partners," *Global Logistics and Supply Chain Strategies,* June, 2004, www.supplychainbrain.com/.

Gianakis, G., and D. Matthews. *Warehousing and Inventory Control,* National Institute of Governmental Purchasing, Herndon, VA, 2008.

Gilmore, D. "Welcome to the Intelligent Warehouse," *Supply Chain Manufacturing and Logistics,* 1999.

Hines, T. *Supply Chain Strategies, Customer-Driven and Customer-Focused,* Butterworth-Heinemann, London, 2003.

Kempfer, L. "European Retailer Expands DC, Adds AS/RS," *Materials Handling Management,* March 2005, pp. 30–31.

Keyan, T. "Improving Warehouse Picking Operations: Voice Recognition Systems Offer Advantages That Scanning Technology Can't Touch," *Frontline Solutions,* May, 2004, http://findarticles.com.

Kuglin, F.A. *Customer-Centered Supply Chain Management,* AMACOM, New York, 1998.

Lysons, K. *Purchasing and Supply Chain Management,* 5th ed., FT Prentice Hall, London, 2000.

Nagel, J., (Ed.). *Supply Chain Management: A Procurement Perspective,* Hargreen Publishing, Melbourne, 2003.

Perkins, C. "Robert's Foods Links Up With Virtual Warehouse," *Nation's Restaurant News,* May 24, 2003, http://findarticles.com/p/articles/mi_m3190/is_21_38/ai_n6051877/.

Richardson, H. "Virtually Connected," *Transportation and Distribution,* March, 2000, http://findarticles.com/p/articles/mi_hb3566/is_200003/ai_n8386603.

Trunk, C. "High-Flying Productivity, Material Handling in America's Best Plants," March, 2003, www.mhmonline.com/nID/2921/MHM/viewStory.asp.

## Chapter 7

Ballou, R.H. *Business Logistics: Supply Chain Management,* 5th ed., Pearson Education, Upper Saddle River, NJ, 2004.

Blanchard, K. *Supply Chain Management Best Practices,* John Wiley & Sons, Hoboken, NJ, 2007.

Bohman, R. "Take advantage of LTL Weight Breaks," *Logistics Management,* August 1, 2006, www.logisticsmgmt.com/.

Cavinato, J. *An Analysis of the Expansion of the Purchasing Field Into New Value-Added Roles in Organizations,* Institute for Supply Management, Tempe, AZ, 2001.

Christopher, M. *Logistics and Supply Chain Management: Creating Value-Adding Networks,* 3rd ed., FT Press, Upper Saddle River, NJ, 2005.

Duffy, R. "Global Sourcing on the Rise," *Inside Supply Management,* September, 2006.

Economic Policy Institute. "Rising U.S.–China Trade Imbalance Brings Labor Market Pain to All 50 States." Press release, January 12, 2005, EPI, Washington, DC, www.epinet.org/.

Ellram, L.M., and T.Y. Choi. *Supply Management for Value Enhancement,* National Association of Purchasing Management, Tempe, AZ, 2000.

Flynn, A., M.L. Harding, C.S. Lallatin, H.M. Pohlig and S.R. Sturzl, (Eds.). *ISM Glossary of Key Supply Management Terms,* 4th ed., Institute for Supply Management, Tempe, AZ, 2006.

Hines, T. *Supply Chain Strategies, Customer-Driven and Customer-Focused,* Butterworth-Heinemann, London, 2003.

Hinkelman, E.G. *Dictionary of International Trade,* 6th ed., World Trade Press, Novato, CA, 2005.

Leenders, M.R., H.E. Fearon, A.E. Flynn and P.F. Johnson. *Purchasing and Supply Management,* 12th ed., McGraw-Hill, New York, 2002.

Leenders, M. and A. Flynn. *Value-Driven Purchasing: Managing the Key Steps in the Acquisition Process,* McGraw-Hill, New York, 1995.

Lewicki, R., D. Saunders, J. Minon and B. Barry. *Negotiation,* 4th ed., McGraw-Hill, New York, 2003.

*Railroad Transportation Industry Yearbook.* Business Source Premier Database, New York, 2002.

Stanley, L. and D. Matthews. *Logistics and Transportation,* National Institute of Governmental Purchasing, Herndon, VA, 2007.

Stanley, L. and D. Matthews. "Logistics, Transportation." In *Encyclopedia of Public Administration and Public Policy,* Jack Rabin (Ed.), Marcel Dekker, New York, 2003.

Tzu, S., and G. Gagliardi. *The Art of War: In Sun Tzu's Own Words,* Clearbridge Publishing, Seattle, WA, 1999.

Van Weele, A.J. *Purchasing & Supply Chain Management,* 4th ed., Thomson Learning, London, 2005.

## Chapter 8

Blanchard, K., *Supply Chain Management Best Practices,* John Wiley & Sons, Hoboken, NJ, 2007.

Brady, W. *Managing Fixed Assets in the Public Sector: Managing for Service Excellence,* Universal Publishers, Boca Raton, FL, 2001.

Broecklemann, R. *Inventory Classification Innovation: Paving the Way for Electronic Commerce and Vendor Managed Inventory,* CRC Press, Boca Raton, FL, 1998.

Buddress, L. "Getting the Most From Your Indirect Purchasing Dollar," *ISM Annual Conference Proceedings,* Institute for Supply Management, Tempe, AZ, 2006.

Carter, P., J. Carter, R. Monczka, J. Blascovich, T. Slaight and W. Markham. *Succeeding in a Dynamic World: Supply Management in the Decade Ahead,* CAPS Research, Institute for Supply Management and A.T. Kearney, Tempe, AZ, 2007.

Cavinato, J., A. Flynn and R. Kauffman. *Supply Management Handbook,* 7th ed., Institute for Supply Management, Tempe, AZ, 2006.

Christopher, M. *Logistics and Supply Chain Management: Creating Value-Adding Networks,* 3rd ed., FT Press, Upper Saddle River, NJ, 2005.

Evers, P.T., and F.J. Beier. "Operational Aspects of Inventory Consolidation Decision Making," *Journal of Business Logistics,* (19:1), 1998, pp. 173–189.

Flynn, A., M.L. Harding, C.S. Lallatin, H.M. Pohlig and S.R. Sturzl, (Eds.). *ISM Glossary of Key Supply Management Terms,* 4th ed., Institute for Supply Management, Tempe, AZ, 2006.

Gianakis, G., and D. Matthews. *Warehousing and Inventory Control,* National Institute of Governmental Purchasing, Herndon, VA, 2008.

Hardcat Ltd., *Case Study: ANZ Bank,* www.hardcat.co.uk/casestudyanz.html.

Hines, T. *Supply Chain Strategies, Customer-Driven and Customer-Focused,* Butterworth-Heinemann, London, 2003.

Hurlbut, T. "Cycle Counting," *Inc.com,* www.inc.com/resources/retail/articles/200506/counting.html.

Kieso, D., J. Weygandt and T. Warfield. *Fundamentals of Intermediate Accounting,* John Wiley & Sons, Hoboken, NJ, 2005.

Manos, T. "Value Stream Mapping — an Introduction," *Quality Progress,* (39:6), June, 2006, pp. 64–69.

Micheau, V.A. "How Boeing and Alcoa Implemented a Successful Vendor Managed Inventory Program," *Journal of Business Forecasting,* (24:1), Spring 2005, pp. 17–19.

National Institute of Governmental Purchasing. *Dictionary of Purchasing Terms,* 5th ed., Herndon, VA, 2004.

Piasecki, D. "Optimizing Economic Order Quantity," *Solutions,* January, 2001, www .inventoryops.com/economic_order_quantity.

Rudski, R., D. Smock, M. Katzorke and S. Stewart. *Straight to the Bottom Line: An Executive's Roadmap to World Class Supply Management,* J. Ross Publishing, Fort Lauderdale, FL, 2006.

Stanley, L. and D. Matthews. *Logistics and Transportation,* National Institute of Governmental Purchasing, Herndon, VA, 2007.

Stock, J.R. "Reverse Logistics in the Supply Chain." In *Business Briefing: Global Purchasing and Supply Chain Strategies,* World Market Research Centres, Bristol, UK, 2001.

Womack, J., and D. Jones. *Lean Thinking,* The Free Press, New York, 2003.

## Chapter 9

Aguayo, R. *The American Who Taught the Japanese About Quality,* Simon & Schuster, New York, 1991.

Babich, K., and C. Pettijohn. *Sourcing in the Public Sector,* National Institute of Government Purchasing, Herndon, VA, 2004.

Blakeman, J. "Benchmarking: Definitions and Overview," Center for Urban Transportation Studies, University of Wisconsin-Milwaukee, June, 2002, www.uwm.edu/Dept/ cuts/bench/bm-desc.htm.

Blanchard, K. *Supply Chain Management Best Practices,* John Wiley & Sons, Hoboken, NJ, 2007.

Deming, W.E. *Out of Crisis,* Massachusetts Institute of Technology Center for Advanced Engineering, Cambridge, MA, 1986.

Dodson, K.M., H.F. Hofman, G.S. Ramani and D.K. Yedlin. "Adapting CMMI for Acquisition Organizations: A Preliminary Report." In *Special Report CMU/SEI-2006-SR-005,* D. Fisher and K. Kost (Eds.), Carnegie Mellon and Software Engineering Institute, Pittsburgh PA, 2006.

Ellram, L. *Strategic Cost Management in the Supply Chain: A Purchasing and Supply Management Perspective,* CAPS Research, Tempe, AZ, 2002.

Ellram, L.M., and T.Y. Choi. *Supply Management for Value Enhancement,* National Association of Purchasing Management, Tempe, AZ, 2000.

Ellram, L., and W. Tate. "Bank of America: Services Purchasing and Outsourcing," *PRACTIX,* CAPS Research (9), May, 2006.

Flynn, A., M.L. Harding, C.S. Lallatin, H.M. Pohlig and S.R. Sturzl, (Eds.). *ISM Glossary of Key Supply Management Terms,* 4th ed., Institute for Supply Management, Tempe, AZ, 2006.

Garrett, G.A., and R.G. Rendon. *Contract Management: Organizational Assessment Tools,* National Contract Management Association, Asburn, VA, 2005.

Hines, T. *Supply Chain Strategies, Customer-Driven and Customer-Focused,* Butterworth-Heinemann, London, 2003.

Hutchins, G. *Purchasing Strategies for Total Quality,* Business One Irwin, Homewood, IL, 1992.

Ishikawa, K. (D.J. Lu., Trans.). *What Is Total Quality Control,* Prentice Hall, Englewood, CA, 1985.

Karten, N. "Key Steps in Establishing a Service Level Agreement," 2003, www.nkarten.com/slaservices.html.

Kivisto, T., and V. Vivolainen. *Benchmarking Municipal Public Procurement Activities in Finland, Challenges in Public Procurement: An International Perspective,* PrAcademics Press, Boca Raton, FL, 2005.

Kuglin, F.A. *Customer-Centered Supply Chain Management,* AMACOM, New York, 1998.

Nelson, R.D. "John Deere Optimizes Operations With Supply Management Efforts," *Journal of Organizational Excellence,* (21:2), February, 2002.

Reese, A.K. "An Interview With Manufacturing's Number One Purchasing Professional," *Fabricating and Metalworking,* April 9, 2001, www.fandmmag.com/.

Stundza, T. "Assured Quality Critical in Global Sourcing," *Purchasing,* (136:11), August 16, 2007.

Tague, N. *The Quality Toolbox,* 2nd ed., ASQ Quality Press, Milwaukee, WI, 2004.

Van Weele, A.J. *Purchasing and Supply Chain Management,* 4th ed., Thomson Learning, London, 2005.

## Chapter 10

Flynn, A., M.L. Harding, C.S. Lallatin, H.M. Pohlig and S.R. Sturzl, (Eds.). *ISM Glossary of Key Supply Management Terms,* 4th ed., Institute for Supply Management, Tempe, AZ, 2006.

Hines, T. *Supply Chain Strategies, Customer-Driven and Customer-Focused,* Butterworth-Heinemann, London, 2003.

Hutchins, G. *Supply Management Strategies,* Working It, Portland, OR, 2002.

Mosconi, T. and P. Carter. "Strategic Measures and Measurement Systems for Purchasing and Supply," *Presentation at ISM's 89th Annual International Supply Management Conference,* April, 2004.

Rudski, R., D. Smock, M. Katzorke and S. Stewart. *Straight to the Bottom Line: An Executive's Roadmap to World Class Supply Management,* J. Ross Publishing, Fort Lauderdale, FL, 2006.

## Chapter 11

*American Heritage Dictionary,* 4th ed., Houghton Mifflin Company, Boston, 2006.

Blanchard, K. *Supply Chain Management Best Practices,* John Wiley & Sons, Hoboken, NJ, 2007.

Christopher, M. *Logistics and Supply Chain Management: Creating Value-Adding Networks,* 3rd ed., FT Press, Upper Saddle River, NJ, 2005.

Nagel, J., (Ed.). *Supply Chain Management: A Procurement Perspective,* Hargreen Publishing, Melbourne, 2003.

# Index